THE COUNTRY HOUSE GUIDE

THE COUNTRY HOUSE GUIDE

FAMILY HOMES IN THE HISTORIC HOUSES ASSOCIATION

Anna Sproule and Michael Pollard

CENTURY
London · Melbourne · Auckland · Johannesburg

Designed by Cherriwyn Magill

First published in 1988 by Century Hutchinson Ltd,
Brookmount House, 62–65 Chandos Place, Covent Garden,
London WC2N 4NW

Century Hutchinson Australia Pty Ltd
PO Box 496, 16–22 Church Street, Hawthorn, Victoria 3122,
Australia

Century Hutchinson New Zealand Limited
PO Box 40-086, Glenfield, Auckland 10,
New Zealand

Century Hutchinson South Africa (Pty) Ltd
PO Box 337, Bergvlei, 2012 South Africa

Set in Garamond 3 by Tradespools Ltd, Frome

Printed and bound in The Netherlands by
Royal Smeets Offset bv Weert

British Library Cataloguing in Publication Data
Sproule, Anna
The country house guide: family homes in
the Historic Houses Association.
1. Country homes——Great Britain
2. Great Britain——Gazetteers
I. 1. Title.   II. Pollard, Michael, *1931–*
914.1′003′21   DA660

ISBN 0-7126-1844-9

CONTENTS

FOREWORD

This book is different from other books about country houses in that it concentrates on those which are still in private hands. All belong to members of the Historic Houses Association, many of whose families have lived in them for several centuries and who now open them to visitors. Each, in its own way, exhibits that sense of continuity, individual taste and eccentricity that successive owners inevitably impose upon their homes and which is difficult to create artificially. It is this human element so clearly evident in a private house which brings the building to life.

Country houses are all about people. Whether they be magnificent palaces full of fine furniture and works of art, or manor houses with contents to match, their particular interest is not just in the architecture and the artefacts but in the story they tell of the people that lived there, upstairs and downstairs; how they lived over the centuries, and how they live today. Often the story extends to include an agricultural estate which, together with the house, forms an integrated socio-economic unit with as important a role to play in the local rural community today as ever in the past.

In common with other historic house owners I am frequently asked what it is like to open one's house to the public. Many people simply cannot contemplate the idea of sharing the privacy of their homes with strangers, particularly strangers who have paid to come in. In fact, of course, nearly all our great houses have been available, if not actually open, to the public since the day they were built. Indeed, in many cases they were designed precisely for the purpose of showing off the wealth, power and taste of their owners. To this end, the grand public rooms were often in a part of the house separate from that lived in by the family when they were not entertaining. In this situation, it is not too difficult to arrange things today so that the twentieth-century visitor can be accommodated without too much disruption to family life. In less grand houses, however, this is more of a problem and the competing demands of visitors and domestic privacy have to be reconciled.

When my wife and I came to Rockingham Castle in 1971, we knew we would have to open the house to the public. There were then, and remain today, three reasons: firstly, we need the money to help us maintain the castle; secondly, we should not feel content living in a place like Rockingham and its grounds, which is so much part of everyone's heritage, without enabling others to enjoy it as well; and thirdly, if we didn't open, people would come anyway! Our feelings towards opening are as much social as financial though the latter must come first as it is, of course, the key to the castle's survival. I am sure that this attitude is shared by many owners who, like us, see themselves as stewards of the house for one generation.

In our case, Rockingham was already open on a relatively small scale. My grandmother lived there before and during the last war and thoroughly enjoyed showing people round. She had a lively imagination, and a great fund of stories about the place, which were not always historically accurate. When my uncle left the Navy after the war, she handed him a little bag of money that she had collected from opening which formed the basis of a restoration fund for the house. My uncle did likewise for me, and it was with the proceeds of his opening that we were able to update the way the house was shown and provide the shop, tea-rooms and toilets required for the higher level of opening we needed to adopt.

Every historic house owner who opens his house to the public has to choose one of two distinct approaches. Sometimes, the answer is dictated by the size and geographical position of the house. In a large house with good

BURTON-CONSTABLE,

MR. CONSTABLE's HOUSE at BURTON-CONSTABLE for the future, will be fhewn upon MONDAY's *only*; (when MR. CONSTABLE is from Home).

A SERVANT will attend from Ten in the MORNING to Four in the AFTERNOON every MONDAY, for the above Purpofe.

BURTON-CONSTABLE,
December 8. 1778.

Historic houses have always been open to the public, as this notice shows

access to population centres, he may decide to run the opening on proper commercial lines with full-time professional staff and probably other attractions as well. Beaulieu, Woburn and Castle Howard are examples of this approach where the houses form part of a sophisticated leisure operation. They are run as a major business involving considerable capital investment and dependent on a flow of satisfied customers. Even then, however, few cover their running costs from the house opening alone.

The alternative is for the public opening to be run by the owner and his wife in order to keep overheads as low as possible and maximise funds available for repair and maintenance. These properties may be open on a more limited basis, but while their display and interpretative techniques might be less sophisticated than their larger brethren, visitors cannot fail to be aware that they are visiting a private house and seeing rooms in use today as they have been for centuries.

ROCKINGHAM CASTLE The home of Michael Saunders Watson.

The Historic Houses Association was formed in 1973 as the representative body for owners of historic houses, gardens and parks. The association's principal objective, stated in its Constitution, is to help them maintain their properties in the interests of the Nation. It achieves this by acting as a political pressure group on the one hand, and as a sort of trade association on the other.

Through the activities of the HHA, succeeding governments have recognized the good sense of encouraging and helping families to maintain historic houses and gardens at their own expense. Legislation has been introduced to protect these properties from the effects of capital tax where their owners maintain them and provide reasonable public access. There is still more to be done in this field, but the basis of preserving continuity of ownership from generation to generation now exists and this is a great step forward. Furthermore, with the setting up of the National Heritage Memorial Fund and other legislation for accepting property in lieu of tax, there is a safety net to catch the more important elements of the heritage when private ownership fails. If private ownership were to cease, however, the safety net could not possibly handle the situation. The private owner, therefore, has an essential part to play if we are to preserve the integrity of our heritage.

In its other role the HHA aims to help its members to maintain their houses, gardens and landscaped parks, by issuing advisory material, by holding seminars, and above all by providing a forum in which those with similar problems can meet and 'look over each other's fences'. We work closely with the National Trusts, English Heritage and other national organizations connected with heritage and tourism. We do, however, differ from the Trusts in that while they are corporate bodies, centrally funded, we are simply an association of individuals trying to run our own properties.

Anyone may join as a 'Friend of the HHA' for an annual subscription, similar to that of the National Trusts, which allows free entry to a large range of our members' properties.

As President of the HHA I am proud to commend this guide. I hope it will tempt you to visit houses you do not know and that it will present a new, lively perspective on those already familiar. By visiting them, you will not only be assured of a warm welcome, but you will be contributing to the active partnership between state, visitor and private owner which is a key factor in keeping our heritage alive.

Rockingham Castle
August 1987

President
Historic Houses Association

INTRODUCTION

Over a fireplace in Dalmeny House, near Edinburgh, hangs a painting of the third Earl of Rosebery and his family. Daughters Mary and Dorothea gather flowers, aided by the baby Francis. Hand-in-hand with his father at the centre of the canvas, the heir to the Earldom stands equipped with a miniature rake and wheelbarrow, prepared to tend some patch of childhood garden. In the gesture beloved of eighteenth-century portraitists, the Earl himself uses his free hand to point out features of his domain to his wife and eldest girl.

The portraitist responsible here, Alexander Naismith, took an interesting approach to the problem of giving impact to his formal portrait. He posed his group in a Forth-side landscape full of dramatic lights and shadows. Under a sky piled high with clouds, its members stand out with a clarity that is almost supernatural; despite their stiff gestures and their formality, they have an odd, arresting look of waiting for something.

At the other end of Britain, something of the same stiffly expectant quality shows itself in a painting of the Warde family, owners of Squerryes Court in Kent (see page 244). Here, at the command of painter John Wootton, the Wardes obediently disport themselves in the grounds of their new home. Just as in the Dalmeny picture, the head of the house proudly gestures towards his property, while his heir—a spruce young man on a dark horse—again occupies the centre of the stage. To the far left stands the figure of George Warde, friend and playmate of future hero James Wolfe.

As at Dalmeny and Squerryes, so in dozens of other historic family homes all over the country. Where there is—or was—a family, so there is often a large family picture, a group portrait or a 'conversation piece', demonstrating the family's size, membership, wealth and status in society.

In Loseley Park's Great Hall, for example, Sir More Molyneux and his family gravely contemplate their surroundings from within a giant frame. In the Drawing Room at Blair Castle hangs a delightful group portrait by Johann Zoffany, showing the third Duke of Atholl, his wife and their seven children in a lakeside setting: the Duke and his eldest son have just caught a fish. At Pencarrow, there are the four Misses St Aubyn, poised for ever in mysterious calm; at Fonmon Castle, there are the Joneses, portrayed with insight and elegance by William Hogarth.

Although there are exceptions, of which Blair's Zoffany is one, most of these family records in paint share to some extent the frozen, expectant quality that is so marked in the group at Dalmeny. Some of this, of course, is a by-product of the conventions and limits within which the artists were working. But it arguably has its true source in the very nature of what the artist was trying to show.

Whilst their clothes are often drawn with more skill than their characters, all these figures in a landscape still come across as real people, caught for a specific moment in their separate but intertwined lives. The artist's vision is a pre-photography version of the freeze-frame technique: let the film run on again, and they will all get on with their lives, in the surroundings they have made for themselves.

What were these surroundings like? Frequently, the portraitist includes these too. There, at some focal point in the painting, stands the family home; at Loseley, the family group is actually painted within it. Seen from inside or out, panelled or plastered, fronted with pillars or topped with spires and pinnacles, the building is included with the family because they were proud of its crusty antiquity, its chic elegance or its flamboyant grandeur. If they found it uncomfortable or ugly, they altered, embellished or rebuilt it.

Barnbougle Castle, the Rosebery home shown in the Naismith painting, was cold, pokey and damp. No effort is needed to see why the fourth Earl of Rosebery, when he grew up, should build and move into Dalmeny House.

Building anew has not always been the answer, or even possible. Some owners as long ago as three hundred years had to restore:

another Scottish noble—the Earl of Strathmore and Kinghorne, ancestor of the Queen Mother—laboured for forty years at the dreadful task of reclaiming Glamis from the ruin into which family debts had plunged it. (When he brought his new countess there in 1670, he was lucky to find any windows that had glass in them at all.) Many other home-owners, before and since, have been saddled with costs that initially seemed impossible to meet.

What, on behalf of their owners, do these buildings tell us? Although their messages take a variety of forms, the underlying theme is almost always the same: basic human need, unchanged in its essentials, over the centuries.

Rich and happy obsessives like the first Duke of Devonshire—who, once he had started to remodel Chatsworth, found that he

SLEDMERE HOUSE A well-stocked library was an essential component of a gentleman's house; this one was created by Joseph Rose for a redesigned Sledmere.

DALMENY HOUSE The third Earl of Rosebery and his family, painted by Naismith; the building behind them was another family home, the thirteenth-century Barnbougle Castle.

simply could not stop—are comparatively rare. The majority of builders and remodellers are driven by needs that are firmly rooted in the practicalities of living.

Not surprisingly, physical fear has in earlier times played a large part in deciding a home's appearance (just as it does in those gardens which still contain overgrown Anderson shelters). The battlements and slit windows of medieval castles are proof of the violence that the inmates could expect to receive and mete out, and so is the front door of Rousham Park: Sir Robert Dormer, Rousham's owner in the Civil War, bored holes in it through which he could fire at Cromwell's troops. As the likelihood of civil war or violent conflict receded, the need for fortification, or for burying a house in a secluded position, diminished. The country house became a means of proclaiming wealth, status and power, and this purpose persisted into the late nineteenth century.

However, there are fears other than that of

death. One of the greatest motivating forces, where building is concerned, is the fear of being outdone, outshone, and generally seen as socially, financially and even morally unworthy. Britain is full of homes that have been built, rebuilt, enlarged and modernized for this reason, often several times. New fortunes bring improvements with them just as surely as new poverty brings decay; the old-fashioned Tudor bricks are swallowed up in a coolly refined Georgian exterior, while this in turn is camouflaged by the exuberance of High Victorian Gothic.

A more positive side of the urge to show off surfaces in those homes that genuinely sheltered a living national treasure. But, as the Duchess of Marlborough found to her cost, living in the style the nation expects has a high price tag. Wellington, who made the same discovery, finally rejected the idea of building himself a palace, and opted for comfort rather than costly ostentation at Stratfield Saye—a decision that links him forever with the vast majority of those who express themselves through their homes.

Then as now, what the average home-owner wanted was a structure in which life could proceed as conveniently, comfortably and pleasantly as circumstances would allow. To this end, they spent huge amounts of time, money or both: covering up the bare structure with hangings and carpets; embroidering bed-curtains to keep out draughts; hiring a Robert Adam or a Joseph Rose to beautify the ceilings; or, like Wellington and other gadget-lovers, experimenting with central heating, double-glazing, or a Howden's Patent Atmospheric Air Dispenser.

And that was only the start. There then came the inevitable (and sometimes delightful) process of filling the house with the ordinary impedimenta of living: the pots and pans, the china and linen, the books for pleasure and study (or the pretence of it), the furniture that the occupants needed for their daily business of sleeping, eating, working, amusing themselves. The rich and cosmopolitan furnished their grand gilded rooms with gifts and perquisites from the royal courts of Europe. Country gentlemen might content themselves

with asking their estate carpenter to run up something in the modern style, but they were generally the pivot of fashion, establishing styles at home as well as importing them from abroad. Either way, these landowners sealed an impression of their personality on their sur-roundings that, as long as their possessions are kept together, remains as permanent as the building itself.

In many cases, of course, they were merely contributing to a gallery of tastes and aspir-ations that was already well stocked. It is a rare house that expresses the tastes of only one owner, and it is partly this crowded quality— this feeling that one is in the presence of several generations at once—that gives Bri-tain's historic homes and their contents part of their special appeal. And it still continues: as David Guthrie-James, a former owner of To-rosay Castle, commented shortly before his death, 'the "personality" of a house lies in what successive generations have put into it.'

The context in which he was speaking had a personal relevance: it arose from the journey he made round the Horn, as a deckhand on the windjammer *Viking*, shortly before the Second World War. The voyage, which also took him

LAVENHAM PRIORY A view of the house as it was in 1979, when it was bought by the present owners. It had been unoccupied for over a decade and was much the worse for wear.

LAVENHAM PRIORY The house and gardens, now restored. The structure is much as it was 400 years ago, but modern furnishings and paintings provide a comfortable family home.

to the Cape of Good Hope and South Australia, is now commemorated in photographs and other exhibits shown in Torosay's 'Viking Room'. In the centre of the room stands a large model of the ship itself, made during the journey by the *Viking* donkeyman. 'This involved him,' Guthrie-James recalled, 'in 676 hours of work—a labour of love indeed—and I invested my life savings acquiring it for the £13 I had in the PO Savings Bank.' He did not, he added, regret it.

At the other end of the scale is an object like the late seventeenth-century Flemish cabinet at Glamis. Finished in red tortoiseshell with ebonized mouldings, it was a wedding present from the 3rd Earl of Strathmore and Kinghorne to his wife Helen in 1662. It cost £60 and the receipt is still at Glamis. In his diary, the Earl wrote: 'At that time I caused bring home a verie fin cabinet, the better was not in the Kingdome in these days, which I never told my wife of till her coming home, and upone her first comeing in her owne chamber I presented her with the Keyes of the Cabinet'.

It is in experiences and objects like these that the true source of the historic house's importance can best be understood. Seen in a museum, the miniature windjammer would be, at best, an interesting object. Watched by the young deckie as it was made, then breathlessly acquired and brought home, along with an account of how it came there, it is very much more. It evokes a time, a place, the skills of one human being and the dreams of another. It is both a passport to the foreign country of the past, and a key to the feelings of those who lived there. So are all the other objects, from the exquisite to the mundane, that fill a house with a history: so, indeed, is the house itself. Each and every one is a conversation piece, alive with information about those who made them, chose them, used them. Although their messages often need translating, their present owners can—unlike a museum curator—often act as the most expert and subtle of interpreters: what they are interpreting is the past history of themselves and their families.

It is not mere age that makes a house historic; it is, rather, knowing what happened there, understanding those who made it and lived in it, and being able to reach out to them across the intervening years.

THE HOUSES

ADLINGTON HALL
CHESHIRE

Few of Britain's regional styles of architecture are as instantly recognizable as the black-and-white timbering of Cheshire. However, spectacular though Adlington Hall appears in its part-Elizabethan dress, its roots lie even deeper in its environment than this. Quite literally so: at the heart of the house stand two ancient oak trees, transformed by the craftsman's adze into carved pillars, but with their roots still in the ground. They are all that survive of the original hunting lodge from which the Hall grew—and of the forest that was cleared to make room for the hunting lodge.

This first Adlington, with its living oaken supports, was given to a medieval noblewoman called Ellen de Legh in 1315. There have been Leghs at Adlington ever since: courtiers, soldiers, judges and administrators, occasional rebels, and builders. It was a local law-giver, Thomas Legh, who at the end of the Middle Ages built a superb Great Hall round the oak-tree pillars, and gave it a hammer-beam roof. It was another Thomas—suspected of being a rebel papist, but still appointed Cheshire's High Sheriff—who gave Adlington its black-and-white dress.

Charles Legh, who built the Hall's contrasting Georgian sections, was also a High Sheriff but his enduring fame lies, not in his county or building activities, but in one of his friendships. The present-day Leghs possess a manuscript tune for a hunting song, dated 1751 and presented to Charles by its composer, Handel. Handel is also the most famous organist to have sat at the magnificent instrument sited between the Great Hall's two oaken pillars: the largest seventeenth-century organ in the country.

A LA RONDE
DEVON

Designed by women, inherited by women and bearing witness in extraordinary detail to what could be achieved by women of sensibility and stamina, A la Ronde is unique. The name can be translated 'All around', and round it almost is, but round buildings exist in plenty, and round houses are not unknown; it is female creativity that has given the house its unique quality—and the creativity of one female in particular, Jane Parminter.

Jane was born in 1747, the daughter of a prosperous Devon wine merchant. The culture in which this active, cultivated girl grew up was at a crossroads. The rationality of the eighteenth century was being troubled by the first stirrings of the Romantic urge, which would take delight in strong emotions, wild landscapes, the penumbra of the supernatural, 'Gothic' ruins, grottoes and hermitages. The mixture was to suit Jane's roving, enthusiastic spirit perfectly.

It was in middle age that she came into her own. Still—and always to be—unmarried, she took charge of a young orphaned cousin, Mary, an equally unmarried sister, Elizabeth, and

ADLINGTON HALL Built in about 1670 by 'Father' Bernard Smith, the organ in the Great Hall was played by Handel on his two visits to Adlington in the following century.

A LA RONDE The Parminter family, outlined by the scissors of silhouettist Torond in 1783. Jane Parminter is at the far left.

another unknown companion, and set off with them on the path beaten by so many members of the aristocracy: the Grand Tour.

A good Tour was a lengthy business, and Jane's lasted ten years. On their return, the delicate and weary Elizabeth speedily died. But, just as speedily, Jane started to translate what she had seen in Italy into a new house for herself and Mary. The result was A la Ronde: a fantastic mixture of Byzantine basilica and 'rustick cottage', containing eight interconnected rooms on its main floor. All give on to a central octagonal hall that extends upwards to an octagonal gallery—a vantage point from which, thanks to a trick of perspective, the floor seems quite dizzyingly distant.

Endearingly odd though Jane's design is, it also contains many practical features: folding seats to save space, triangular cupboards fitted in between the rooms, sliding doors. Nor does her inspiration stop there. The greatest glory of A la Ronde consists of the spectacular decorations she gave it. An expert in such contemporary drawing-room skills as shell-work and feather collage, she turned the gallery into an imitation of the Byzantine mosaic work she had admired in Italian churches; here, however, the mosaics were all made of feathers and shells. The sitting room, too, was decorated with a frieze made from exotic feathers, and the house is full of delicate pictures executed in the media of feathers, sand and seaweed.

Jane died in 1811, when she was sixty-four,

and is buried below the nearby 'Point of View' chapel, which she also designed. Mary outlived her by thirty-eight years, continuing mistress of A la Ronde and loving custodian of its garden of exotic plants. After her own death, the house stayed in the family and, indeed, maintained its strongly feminine tradition. It was the family women who inherited it, and it is the home of a woman today.

ALNWICK CASTLE
NORTHUMBERLAND

For well over 650 years, Alnwick Castle has been the home of the Percy family, Dukes of Northumberland. But it has been more than that. Standing about thirty miles (fifty kilometres) from the Scottish border, Alnwick guards the east-coast route from north to south, and no visitor can overlook its serious defensive purpose. In Victorian times, when the threat of Anglo-Scottish border skirmishes had vanished, the Castle became the scene of an ambitious building programme of which the pride and centrepiece is the suite of State Rooms approached by the marble Grand Staircase. This virtually complete interior redecoration was begun in the 1850s.

The Percy family came to England with William the Conqueror, and thereafter its members were never far from the centre of the historical stage. In 1309 Henry Percy acquired Alnwick and later fought with the English army against Robert the Bruce at Bannockburn. He identified Alnwick as a key site from which to pursue the continuing wars with the Scots, and began the remodelling of the Castle. He did not live to see its completion, dying in 1315, the year after Bannockburn.

From this time on, the Percys were embroiled in the Scottish and French wars of the fourteenth and fifteenth centuries, many members of the family dying in battle. They included the famous Hotspur, immortalized by Shakespeare. Hotspur's military career began at the battle of Berwick Castle, when he was only twelve, and ended with his death at the battle of Shrewsbury in 1403 at the age of thirty-seven. By this time the Percy family had been granted the Earldom of Northumberland, which became a Dukedom in 1766.

Other family members distinguished themselves in different ways, such as Bishop Percy of Dromore in Ireland, who rescued a collection of old ballads from a housemaid who was about to use it to light a fire. He published the collection as Percy's 'Reliques' of Ancient English Poetry in 1765. Scenes from one of the ballads, 'The Battle of Chevy Chase', are incorporated in the frieze of the Guard Chamber at the top of Alnwick's Grand Staircase.

Earlier, an errant Percy, Thomas, was misguidedly appointed by his cousin, the ninth Earl of Northumberland, to the post of resident Constable of Alnwick Castle and administrator of the estate. Thomas was a poor choice. Apart from terrorizing the tenantry, he became involved, as a Catholic, in the Gunpowder Plot of 1605. After the plot was discovered, he was hunted down and killed together with most of his fellow-conspirators, but the ninth Earl had to pay a price for his family connection: fifteen years in the Tower of London, and several unsuccessful attempts to implicate him in the plot. Eventually he bought his release.

The Percy family acquired immense wealth—its other houses included Syon House on the Thames and, until it was demolished in 1874, Northumberland House in London's Strand—and no expense was spared in the successive restorations and improvements of Alnwick Castle. It was the first Duke of Northumberland, who had come into the Percy estates by marriage, who commissioned Robert Adam to refashion Alnwick to the ideas of the mid-eighteenth century. Items of furniture designed by Robert Adam—for example, the miniature billiard-table and two writing tables in the Ante-Room of the State Apartments—are still to be seen at Alnwick, but his work was swept away in a further restoration in the middle of the nineteenth century.

Today's visitor can only marvel at the opulence of the settings of the Italianate style State Rooms, created under the guidance of fourth Duke of Northumberland. The marble for the walls of the Grand Staircase was brought from Carrara in Tuscany. Each step, 12 feet wide, is a single piece of stone. A sculptor was brought from Italy to create the ornamented ceiling. The mosaic floor of the Guard Chamber was made in Rome.

For all this splendour, Alnwick Castle remains, as it has been for generations, the heart of a vast estate—there are over 160 tenanted farms, some 7,000 acres of woodland and 13 villages—and an economic as well as a social focus for the northernmost reaches of England.

ALRESFORD HOUSE

HAMPSHIRE

Rodney is one of the great names in British naval history. He obtained his first command when he was still in his mid-twenties, and his career, in three phases, culminated in the so-called Battle of the Saints in April 1782, which safeguarded Britain's West India trade from the French.

Alresford House, however, belongs to the

ALRESFORD HOUSE The ornate panelling in the Dining Room, in the French style, was introduced in the 1920s.

*ALNWICK CASTLE Canaletto's **painting**, to be seen in the Music Room, shows the Castle as it was before the first Duke of Northumberland's restoration.*

first phase of Rodney's career. He was an ambitious man, and with good cause. His father had been ruined in the great financial scandal of the South Sea Bubble, and Rodney was brought up by his godfather. Consequently, he had no home of his own. He spent a large part of the 1740s chasing and capturing privateers in the Atlantic, from which he acquired over £10,000 in prize money. With this, he bought an estate at Alresford, conveniently near to his Portsmouth naval base, and in 1749 began the building of Alresford House.

It was usual in the eighteenth century for naval officers to spend long periods ashore between engagements, and Rodney used the first such gap in his service career to establish himself as a gentleman with substantial town and country interests. Patronage brought him the governorship of Newfoundland, an undemanding post, and meanwhile he became MP for Saltash and married his first wife, twenty-

three-year-old Jenny Compton. It was to Alresford that Jenny came as a bride, to build a happy domestic life for Rodney and later for their two children. But, sadly, it was not to last. Jenny died in childbirth within a few days of their fourth wedding anniversary.

The exterior of Alresford House has altered little since Rodney's time, though much has changed inside. The most notable original feature is the rococo plaster ceiling in the morning room, which features an eagle commemorating the name of the ship which was Rodney's first command and the device which he subsequently adopted for the Rodney arms and crest.

Alresford remained in the Rodney family until the late nineteenth century, but the next phase of development came in the 1920s when the house was owned by Dr Schwert, an Anglo-German art collector. The panelled dining room in the French style dates from this period, as does the Italian marble chimney-piece in the drawing room. The private Catholic chapel off the sitting room was added by Mrs Constable-Maxwell, the mother of the present owner, as a memorial to her husband and eldest son.

ARBURY HALL

WARWICKSHIRE

The gentry of the late eighteenth century were great 'improvers'. If they had land, they set about farming it more efficiently. They landscaped their parkland. At home, they began to react against what they saw as the barren Classical style of architecture and created the Gothic Revival. The more energetic landowners did all these things.

'Improvement' is what happened at Arbury Hall, which is a rare example of the Gothic Revival in its first flush. In 1734, Arbury Hall was inherited by Sir Roger Newdigate, who was then only fourteen. After a conventional youth for a young English gentleman of the time, education at Oxford followed by the Grand Tour, Sir Roger married Sophia Conyers,

ALNWICK CASTLE This Triple Portrait by Titian is one of a collection of fine pictures in the Ante-Room.

ARBURY HALL The elaborate fan-vaulting in the Saloon is a copy of the ceiling of the Henry VII Chapel in Westminster Abbey.

daughter of an Essex county family, and settled at Arbury Hall. Round about the late 1740s he began to plan the rebuilding of Arbury in the Gothic style. He left intact the Elizabethan exterior he had inherited, but the interior was completely transformed. Sir Roger's work ran in parallel with Horace Walpole's similar, but more ambitious, scheme for Strawberry Hill near Twickenham, so he could claim to be one of the pioneers of the Gothic Revival.

Like Walpole, Sir Roger based many of his newly created rooms on true Gothic originals. The fan-vaulted ceiling of the Saloon on the east front, for example, is modelled exactly on that of Henry VII's chapel in Westminster Abbey. Sir Roger worked his way steadily from room to room, and as he lived to the age of eighty-seven he had the pleasure of seeing his vision brought to completion before he died.

Neither of Sir Roger Newdigate's marriages—Sophia Conyers died in 1774, and Sir Roger later married Hester Mundy, who also pre-deceased him—brought him an heir, and the Newdigate baronetcy died with him in 1806. Ownership of Arbury passed to a succession of cousins and nephews until 1902, when

Sir Francis Newdigate Newdegate, former Governor of Western Australia, began the present line.

In this intervening period, impressions of life on the Arbury estate and of Arbury Hall itself found their way into literature through the works of George Eliot, who was born, as Mary Ann Evans, at South Farm on the estate in 1819. She spent the first twenty-one years of her life at Arbury, and when, in the 1850s, she came to write her novels, she drew freely on her early memories. In *Scenes of Clerical Life*, her first published fiction, Arbury Hall is thinly disguised as Cheverel Manor, and Sir Roger Newdigate as Sir Christopher Cheverel. The publication of *Scenes* caused considerable offence locally but, undeterred, George Eliot drew heavily on her Warwickshire roots for her later novels such as *Adam Bede* and *The Mill on the Floss*.

An elaborate and self-inflicted family joke lies behind the collection of embroidered stools to be found in the schoolroom adjoining the Chapel. These embroideries are the work of

ARBURY HALL Sir Roger Newdigate, fifth baronet, in his new Gothic Library, painted by Arthur Devis.

Sophia Conyers, whose failing was, it seems, untidiness. Her designs show playing cards left negligently on one stool while a fan lies forgotten on another. Sir Roger and his first wife may have left no children, but Sophia left behind a charming vignette of her personality.

ARLEY HALL
CHESHIRE

Elizabethan, or 'Queen Elizabethan'? The two men responsible for the patterned brickwork, mullioned windows and extravagant chimneys of Arley Hall—Rowland Egerton-Warburton and his architect, George Latham—were never in any doubt about the answer. 'Queen Elizabethan' was the phrase they coined: Elizabethan in every last detail of decoration, but equipped with the plumbing, kitchens and other amenities suited to the age of the Industrial Revolution.

The businesslike approach Arley's creators took to comfort was sorely needed, for the building that their Elizabethan fantasy replaced was, by the 1830s, lacking in any pretence of it. The ancestral home of the Warburtons, dating from the fifteenth century, had been patched up, altered and pulled about to the point where it had ceased to be viable. The drains stank, and the rats were appalling. Rowland's young wife, Mary, took a robust view of rats: 'as a girl,' her son later recalled, 'she and her sister would lie in wait with tongs to seize them leaving their holes at night.' But the Arley rats rampaged in troops down the corridors, and Mary and her husband soon decided they had had enough.

It would have been easy for Rowland to build a house that looked as up-to-date as its plumbing. However, like many of his contemporaries, he lived in a state of happy split-mindedness: he believed in progress, but he was also totally in love with the past. The domestic part of Arley Hall, with every last detail checked for its truly Elizabethan character, was only one of the monuments he left to his passion. Another is the Arley Hall chapel, whose piously Gothic style expressed his growing interest in the Oxford Movement: a body that, in religious matters, was also seeking to recreate the style and inspiration of the past.

Rowland's enthusiastic approach to detail shows nowhere as clearly as in the chapel's windows. Faced with the task of choosing amongst the medieval patterns he was offered, he opted for them all. As a result, each window is subtly different in its tracery. When Arley's private place of worship was finished, he attended every day—even, dressed in his scarlet, on mornings when he went hunting.

In an Elizabethan barn—a genuine one—in the grounds hang two coats of arms, belonging to the two sides of Rowland's family. Under them hang lines from Rowland's pen:

> If proud thou be of ancestors for worth or wisdom famed
> So live that they if now alive would not of thee be shamed.

His own code, to which Arley itself is proof.

ARLEY HALL *Edwardian summer in Arley Hall's walled garden, painted in watercolour by Piers Egerton-Warburton.*

ARUNDEL CASTLE

WEST SUSSEX

The Duke of Norfolk is no ordinary Duke. For the past 500 years the title has carried with it the honour of Premier Duke and the offices of Earl Marshal and Chief Butler of England. Confusingly, the Dukedom of Norfolk has no connection with the county, and for over 700 years the Dukes of Norfolk have lived at Arundel Castle.

Although, at first sight, the Castle looks to the visitor like a piece of medieval history transported unaltered to the present day, it is in fact an example of careful restoration and reconstruction. Much of the original castle was destroyed when Arundel was besieged by the Parliamentary army in 1643, during the Civil War, and from about 1780 until the beginning of the present century the work of putting the Castle together again proceeded. The result is not an accurate model of a Norman castle, but a romantic dream. This is how castles *should* have looked rather than how they actually *did* look.

The Fitzalan-Howard family has held the Dukedom of Norfolk since it was created in 1385, by which time the family had been established at Arundel for almost a century and a half. It has proved a remarkably durable dynasty, having survived martyrdom, execution for treason, banishment to prison for six years, death in battle—and, for most of three centuries, remaining true to Catholicism despite official penalties and popular suspicion. The parish church at Arundel, just outside the Castle grounds, is a reminder of that religious steadfastness. The west end is an Anglican church. The east, which can be approached only from the Castle grounds, is Catholic. Ruined in the siege of 1643, it was restored in 1886 as the Fitzalan-Howards' private chapel.

One figure stands out from this record of piety, and it is that of Charles, the eleventh Duke. Before he inherited in 1786, he had renounced the Catholic faith, and he threw himself with enthusiasm into politics—he was

ARUNDEL CASTLE The gilded state bed made specially for the visit of Queen Victoria to the Castle in 1846.

a Whig with republican tendencies—and into the pleasure-seeking company surrounding the Prince of Wales, later to become Prince Regent and ultimately George IV. When the Prince built the Pavilion at Brighton—a convenient twenty miles from Arundel—the eleventh Duke was a regular visitor, and the Prince and his guests would vie with each other to drink themselves under the table. Eccentric in behaviour and dress—he was once mistaken in the street for a butcher—the eleventh Duke had a dislike of soap and water, and he could be washed by his servants only when he was dead drunk. Seen in the afterglow of history, he makes a picturesque figure, but when he died in 1815 those who wrote obituaries of him did not mince their words. For all that, he had an immense pride in the family tradition, and it was he who replanned the park at Arundel, began the reconstruction

of the Castle, and left behind the plans for further improvements which were carried out by his successors.

The only parts of the original post-Conquest Castle still standing are the Keep—which would once have contained the best domestic rooms—together with the Barbican, whose arch still shows the marks of cannonballs from the siege of 1643, and the inner gateway. The remainder of the Castle is largely a feast of Neo-Gothic, inspired by the plans of the eleventh Duke. Among the first works he carried through personally was the conversion of the former private chapel into what is now the Dining Room. Unfortunately one of the prominent features of the conversion, a huge stained-glass window showing Solomon entertaining the Queen of Sheba, was removed in 1846 in order not to offend Queen Victoria, who was due to visit. The final stage in the reconstruction of the Castle as it is seen today was carried out by the fifteenth Duke from about 1875, and it is a celebration in stone of the Catholic Revival in England, particularly the Gothic effects in, for example, the picture gallery and the drawing room.

One of the undoubted triumphs of the eleventh Duke's restoration, round about 1800, was the Library, with its vaulted ceiling and its fittings in carved Honduras mahogany. Among the 8,500 books are many unique manuscript and printed volumes of Catholic history.

Heraldic decorations are a feature of many rooms in the Castle, notably in the Barons' Hall, where armorial symbols in the stained glass of the east windows represent the history of the Fitzalan-Howard family from the twelfth century almost to the present day. This emphasis on heraldry reflects the major function of the hereditary office of Earl Marshal as head of the College of Arms. The Earl Marshal's other duties include attendance on the sovereign on state occasions—a duty which, in the past, some Dukes of Norfolk had to delegate to deputies since, as Catholics, they were disbarred. More recently, however, Dukes of Norfolk have resumed this role personally, and the sixteenth Duke in particular, between 1917 and 1975, became well-known to the public as 'master of ceremonies' at a large number of state occasions. The Earl Marshal's State uniform and other robes and mantles associated with these great occasions of state are in the East Drawing Room.

ATHELHAMPTON

DORSET

The windows of Athelhampton are a family tree in glass. Brune and Faringdon, de Mohun and de Clevedon, Long, Wadham and Kelway . . . framed in stonework and sky, the arms of all those who allied themselves to the makers of the house glow in their heraldic colours. So do the arms of Athelhampton's creators themselves: the Martyns, with their crest of a chained ape, or martin, inspecting itself in a mirror. 'He who looks at Martyn's ape, Martyn's ape shall look at him', ran the mocking family motto.

The Martyns had been Lords of Athelhampton since the time of Richard II. By the fifteenth century, at the very close of the Middle Ages, the Martyn of the day—Sir William—was a man of considerable importance and wealth. He held the highly lucrative right to collect all duty payable on wine in the south of England. In 1493, he would be elected Lord Mayor of London; before that, however, he set his seal on his local power by building a battlemented (and therefore defensible) mansion, with a wine cellar below.

Some of Martyn's battlements can still be seen today, surmounting Athelhampton's porch and its Great Hall. It is here that the house's stately sequence of glazed heraldry begins. In the wing that William's son, Christopher, added at right angles to his father's house, there is more, decorating the windows of Athelhampton's drawing room, or Great Chamber. There is more still in the State Bedroom, where the arms of the Martyns and the later owners, the Brunes, are joined by those of the Cookes, whose home Athelhampton now is. They, too, have Martyns in their ancestry—and an ape is still the family badge.

ATHELHAMPTON
Intricate carving decorates the massive posts of the bed in the State Bedroom, where the Martyn crest reappears on the stone fireplace.

AVINGTON PARK

HAMPSHIRE

Avington Park, once the lodging of royalty, rose to greatness because local clergy refused to give house-room to a royal mistress. In the seventeenth century, the nearby city of Winchester became a favourite haunt of King Charles II. On one visit, he was put up at the Deanery; however, the cathedral hierarchy totally refused to extend a similar welcome to his companion—'poor Nelly', as the king called her, or Nell Gwynne.

After being accommodated elsewhere, poor Nelly fades out of the Avington story. But another member of Charles's retinue, Groom of the Bedchamber George Brydges, was inspired by her problem to enlarge his ancient house and turn it into something that could be offered as lodgings to his royal master. So Avington was launched on a career of rich man's playground.

It was also the playground of at least one rich woman: George's wife, Anna Maria, former Countess of Shrewsbury and a noted female rakehell. Rumour had it that she had watched the murder of her first husband by her lover in a duel—while, dressed as a groom, she held the lover's horse. Her second husband also came to an untimely end: he drowned in Avington's lake while trying to rescue his pet dog. Anna Maria brought a huge fortune to Avington and spent some of it on the delicate painted decoration that still adorns the ceiling of the house's Great Saloon.

In the middle of the eighteenth century, the house passed to the third Duke of Chandos. The Duke already had a country house, the ostentatious Canons, but it was Avington that he and his Duchess preferred. Like their predecessors, they enlarged and altered the house, giving it its great staircase with the Greek honeysuckle motif, and incorporating Mrs Brydges' pictures into the newly gilded Saloon ceiling.

The association of Avington with high living continued into the nineteenth century.

George IV and his secretly wed wife, Mrs Fitzherbert, were regular visitors, especially during the Hampshire May Day celebrations, or Mayings.

Avington's own permanent springtime looked set to go on past the era of the Hanoverians and into that of Queen Victoria. By mid-century, however, unlucky speculations had forced a ruined Duke of Buckingham and Chandos to sell up. Avington lost its royal connections (in fact, it was bought by the younger brother of the poet Percy Bysshe Shelley) and recommenced a sober existence as a family house, but the state rooms, the great staircase and the majestic entrance front still recall the days of royal favour.

AVINGTON PARK The tables in the Main Hall, which date from 1700, are of painted slate, and once stood in the Dairy.

AYTON CASTLE

BORDERS

When Samuel Langhorne Clemens—alias Mark Twain—visited Scotland in 1873, one of the homes that caught his attention was Ayton Castle, on the main

Edinburgh road just north of Berwick. One of its contents in particular seized his fancy; so much so that he took direct steps, and opened negotiations with Ayton's owners. His purchase now reposes in the Mark Twain Museum in Connecticut: the fireplace from Ayton's dining room.

Although this part of Ayton's original decor is now missing (though replaced), the rest remains: the plasterwork, woodwork, fittings and painted walls that were all part and parcel of a Scottish Baronial establishment in the 1840s. The entrance hall is particularly impressive, with its hand-painted walls and ceiling. Also on the ceiling are the signatures of the Edinburgh craftsmen who did the work.

The coats of arms that are proudly displayed are those of the Castle's builders, the Mitchell-Innes family. Unfortunately, misfortunes overtook the Mitchell-Inneses soon after their home's completion and, only twenty years after it had been built, it risked becoming a ruin. If a buyer had not stepped in with an offer, Mark Twain would not have been the only person to cannibalize the building. In 1880, however, it was bought by the Liddell-Graingers, who recently celebrated a century—broken only by the Second World War—of family occupation.

AYTON CASTLE The Dining Room in which the ceiling and woodwork, though not the fireplace, date back to the 1840s.

BAMBURGH CASTLE

NORTHUMBERLAND

Sea and land; Saxon piety and Norman might; Lindisfarne of the Gospels, and Bamburgh Castle. . . . On the coast of Northumberland, the forces that shaped Britain's early history meet with elemental vigour. Crouched on its basalt rock, Bamburgh still indeed has the power to inspire awe. Although its great days as a fortress ended with the advent of medieval artillery, its natural position and its centuries as a centre of power have combined to give it an aura of indestructible strength.

The ease with which Bamburgh's rock can be defended against attackers made it a natural place for a local chieftain to live—and the oldest traces of habitation found on the Bamburgh citadel are locally made cooking pots dating from 2,000 years ago.

Roman Bamburgh has made its presence felt through the discovery of long-discarded kitchenware. However, the Romans' main concern is indicated by discoveries of another type: Bamburgh was probably the site for a beacon to warn against invaders from the other side of the North Sea. In the fifth century, however, the Romans left. The resulting power vacuum was filled by the Anglo-Saxons, and it was the Saxon rulers of Northumbria who in the seventh century brought Bamburgh into its brief but dazzling 'Golden Age'. By the time they were overwhelmed in turn by the Vikings, they had established a powerhouse of thought and art at nearby Lindisfarne that would spread its influence across Europe. And, with a more prosaic aim, they had constructed a 70-foot-deep (21 metres) well on the Bamburgh citadel that was renowned for the purity of its water.

Capped by its modern head, the Saxon well

can still be seen today, in the hall of Bamburgh's Keep. Together with the rock into which it was quarried, it is in fact the Castle's reason for existence. The Castle the Normans built round it fully justified its design by thwarting attackers during four centuries of unrest, revolt and full-scale war. It saw the arrival of kings and the imprisonment of princely rebels from Wales and Scotland. In all likelihood, it briefly sheltered the Stone of Destiny, wrested by Edward I from its resting-place at Scone and transported to the English Abbey of Westminster.

Bamburgh was finally overcome by Yorkist artillery in the Wars of the Roses, after which its fortunes fell into a decline which threatened to overwhelm it completely; only the great Norman Keep, with its well, seemed immune. Finally, however, the formerly great fortress was rescued through the unlikely agency of two eighteenth-century churchmen.

Repaired and restored, Bamburgh became a local centre for medical care, education and poverty relief. Restoration continued after it was bought in 1894 by the first Lord Armstrong, and some sections have been turned into apartments. Today, as the present Lord Armstrong points out, it is probably home to more people than it has been for 500 years.

BARFORD PARK
SOMERSET

Like some houses that are much bigger, Barford Park is a master of surprise. To those who come on it unawares, the building reveals itself with dramatic suddenness: a vision in rosy brickwork, with a three-storey main block and elegantly curving wings. But Barford is a country house in miniature. Proportions, decorations, appointments: everything is there, but drawn to a greatly reduced scale. And, as with a miniature portrait on ivory, much work went into producing such pocket-sized perfection.

Initially a farmhouse, it probably received its brick-and-stone dress somewhere around

BARFORD PARK 'A vision in rosy brickwork': originally a farmhouse, Barford Park was transformed into a miniature country house with curving wings in the early eighteenth century.

BAMBURGH CASTLE Crouched on its basalt rock, the fortress built by the Normans has dominated this stretch of the Northumbrian coastline for almost 900 years.

1710. The wings, and the distinction they bring to the building, went on slightly later. One contained the stables and the other the kitchen. And then, when funds allowed, a final touch was given by the addition of the central-block's attic floor.

No one knows who should take the credit for this clever remodelling. It is known, however, that the family who picked up the bill was initially called Jeanes and then, after some shifting around in the family tree, Guy or Everard. It was probably Andrew Guy, High Sheriff of the county, who combined style with usefulness by adding the wings. And it was certainly his great-grandson, Captain John Everard, who occupied the building longest. He died in 1937, aged a hundred, having owed his longevity—or so he swore—to drinking water rising from the spring in Barford's garden.

BEAULIEU PALACE HOUSE AND ABBEY

HAMPSHIRE

On a summer's day in 1204, a party of thirty monks arrived from France at a wooded site near the Solent, in Hampshire. They were Cistercians, wearing the distinctive natural-wool-coloured habits of their order. The site, next to King John's hunting lodge in the New Forest, had been given the name Beau Lieu, the 'beautiful place'. The foundation of Beaulieu Abbey had begun, under the patronage of King John himself. It was his only religious foundation—the consequence, it is said, of a nightmare in which he saw himself being beaten by a group of Cistercian monks as they took their revenge for his persecution of their order.

Like other Cistercian foundations, Beaulieu was intended from the start to be a self-sufficient estate. The monks recruited lay brothers, craftsmen with building or agricultural skills, to help them, and also made use of local hired labour. The need to provide food and an income meant that agricultural and building work had to proceed side by side, and consequently the Abbey rose slowly. Not until 1246 was the Abbey church—which had first priority—finished, and building of the remaining parts of the complex extended for some thirty years after that.

As an abbey, Beaulieu prospered for nearly three centuries. Then, in 1538, Henry VIII proclaimed the Dissolution of the Monasteries, and on 2 April the King's representative, William Petre, arrived to take over the Abbey.

For some reason the scale of destruction at Beaulieu at the Dissolution was smaller than at most other monasteries. The Abbey church was destroyed together with the Chapter House and part of the Cloisters, but the Gatehouse, the lay-brothers' quarters and the monks' refectory were spared. When, in July 1538, the manor of Beaulieu came to be sold for £1,340, the buyer acquired 8,000 acres (3,238 hectares) and a property which was not a mere heap of ruins but one, in today's estate-agents' jargon, 'ripe for development'. He was Sir Thomas Wriothesley, later Earl of Southampton and the direct ancestor of Beaulieu's present owner. He converted the Great Gatehouse into a manor house and seems to have used it as a hunting lodge rather than as a permanent home.

A succession of marriages brought the estate to the Montagus, a family of notable eccentrics. The widowed first Duke of Montagu, having acquired Beaulieu through his first marriage to a Wriothesley, sought the hand of the wealthy Duchess of Albemarle. She declared, however, that she would not marry again except to royalty; whereupon, the story goes, the first Duke announced that he was the Emperor of China and the marriage went ahead. The first Duke's son, John, inherited his father's eccentricity and had a great liking

for practical jokes. However, there was also a serious side to his character, and he put great effort into establishing the village of Buckler's Hard – just six miles (ten kilometres) away – as a port for the sugar trade. The plan failed, but Buckler's Hard became a naval- and merchant-shipbuilding centre.

After John's death, Beaulieu passed through the female line to the Buccleuch family. In 1867, the Duke of Buccleuch gave Beaulieu to his younger son Henry, created Lord Montagu of Beaulieu in 1885.

The first Lord Montagu set about turning Palace House into a family home. Some of the piecemeal additions of previous owners and tenants were removed, new rooms were created, and where possible the remains of the original buildings were incorporated in the new work. The original narrow stone staircase was replaced with a wide Victorian sweep. The porch of the Great Gatehouse became the present Lower Drawing Room. The Private Dining Room and the Upper Drawing Room were fashioned out of the original Cistercian chapels. The fan vaulting of the Dining Hall was restored and picked out by additional light.

The present Lord Montagu, inheriting Beaulieu on his twenty-fifth birthday in 1951, found himself the owner of a splendid house whose running costs were, however, frightening. He decided to open Palace House to the public, as the Abbey ruins had been for some years, and became one of the first owners of an historic house to make a positive effort to attract visitors. From there, the project grew until it now includes the National Motor Museum in the Abbey grounds and the Maritime Museum at Buckler's Hard.

The National Motor Museum, incidentally, is no arbitrary addition to Beaulieu. The present Lord Montagu's father was one of the pioneers of motoring in the greatcoat-and-goggles days. His contributions to the early days of motoring and aeronautics are recorded in photographs which are on display in the Corridor Gallery at Palace House, where many Montagu family mementoes have been collected.

BEESTON HALL Built in 1786 in the fashionable Gothic style, the Hall has a distinctive Norfolk touch—a facing of knapped flint.

BEESTON HALL

NORFOLK

It was on 15 April 1918 that **Tsar Nicholas II** of Russia, his Tsaritsa and their five children were brought by revolutionary soldiers to the town of Ekaterinburg, now renamed Sverdlovsk, on the eastern slopes of the Ural Mountains. Here, they were to spend the last two months of their lives, the adults reading, the girls knitting and doing embroidery, and the sick only son Alexis playing with toys. They were already under sentence of death, the only obstacle being the impenetrable bureaucracy which was to prove as much a feature of the revolutionary regime as it had been of the Tsar's. But Ekaterinburg was alive with rumours of rescue plans, escape attempts, and appeals to the Bolsheviks for clemency.

The British Consul in Ekaterinburg at that time was Thomas Preston, a young diplomat who had joined the service after an adventurous youth prospecting for gold in Siberia. Given that the Tsar and King George V were cousins, it was natural that much of the activity aimed at saving the life of the Tsar should centre round the British Consulate. The Consul spent long hours discussing ways of escape, but no solution presented itself. There were 10,000 Red Army soldiers in the town, and all too few of the civilian population could be trusted. Spies were everywhere. At least one serious plan for rescue was put together, but it foundered. At last, the end came. On the night of 16–17 July the Imperial family was taken down to the cellar of the house where they were imprisoned, and shot.

Thomas Preston was implicated in the rescue plans and was sentenced to death, but the timely capture of Ekaterinburg by the White army prevented the sentence from being carried out. The Consul lived to tell the tale to, among others, George V, on his return to England.

There are many souvenirs at Beeston, his family home, of the time he spent in Russia, such as the painting in the Staircase Hall of the Tsar's Cossack escort in 1914 and the candelabra, samovar and firescreen in the Dining Room, all acquired during his period as Consul.

As Sir Thomas Preston, he succeeded to the baronetcy late in life on the death of his cousin, and lived on until 1976. His part in the historic events of 1918 was in line with the tradition of service to the country which has been the hallmark of the Preston family of Beeston Hall. An earlier Preston was a herald at the court of Charles I; another, an active supporter of William of Orange; yet another, a distinguished soldier in the First World War. But it was Jacob Preston, who preferred his own garden to the wider world of politics and court life, who created Beeston Hall. He was very much a man of the eighteenth century. He had acquired his tastes on the Grand Tour, and became a Fellow of the Society of Antiquaries. In the 1780s he conceived the idea of demolishing the old Hall and rebuilding in Gothic style with a local vernacular touch—square-knapped flint facing—which makes the new Hall architecturally interesting. Unfortunately, he did not survive to enjoy the result; in November 1787, with work almost finished, he was setting out to visit another of his works, the local 'house of industry' for the poor, when he had a heart attack and fell dead from his horse.

BELVOIR CASTLE Hand-painted silk woven in the eighteenth century adorns the walls of the Chinese Bedroom, complemented by a bedspread of Chinese embroidered silk.

BELVOIR CASTLE

LINCOLNSHIRE

There have been three Belvoirs. The first, called Belvedere by the Normans, was in traditional motte-and-bailey style. Demolished after the Civil War, it was replaced by a new structure. By the end of the eighteenth century, conditions at Belvoir were, to put it mildly, rough. Visiting in 1789, two years after the death of the fourth Duke, the Honourable John Byng reported that it contained 'not a habitable room or a bed fit to sleep in'. He put this down to the late Duke's gambling, combined with the attentions of a 'very drunken, dawdling housekeeper'. As the nineteenth century dawned, Belvoir was in a bad state, and it was fortunate that the fifth Duke, determined to bring about improvements, had a Duchess who was equally keen to put her mark on the Castle.

The Duchess had some architectural flair. She also had enthusiasm, and she and the Duke together embarked on a virtually complete rebuilding of Belvoir, aiming to reflect the improved social position of the Manners family—the family name of the Dukes of Rutland—and to recall the Castle's origins. They chose as their architect James Wyatt.

It was a mammoth work of reconstruction which began in 1801. After fifteen years, the south-west and south-east fronts were completed and the finishing touches were being put to the grand staircase and picture gallery in the north-west front. But early in the morning of 16 October 1816 fire broke out. Spreading rapidly despite the efforts of Belvoir's large staff, it destroyed the north-east and north-west fronts, ruined the grand staircase and—perhaps worst of all—consumed about thirty pictures by Reynolds, Titian, Van Dyck and others from the collection of the fourth Duke, a discerning patron of the arts.

It was a bitter blow, but the family—in particular the Duchess—was not daunted. Wyatt was dead by this time, and the Duchess enlisted the aid of the domestic chaplain, the

BEAULIEU PALACE HOUSE AND ABBEY Sir Thomas Wriothesley, who bought the manor of Beaulieu after the Dissolution for £1,340.

Reverend Sir John Thoroton, as her architectural mentor. Opinions of the resulting reconstruction varied, the diarist Charles Greville describing the new Belvoir as a 'sad mess'.

Elizabeth, fifth Duchess of Rutland, died in 1825, but, in sculpture and painting, her image still presides over Belvoir. The Elizabeth Saloon is devoted largely to her memory. A statue of her by Matthew Wyatt stands beneath a ceiling which portrays the Duke and Duchess and their four children, together with deeply symbolical representations of, among others, Mercury, Venus and Cupid. Jupiter also appears, with the head of the Duke of York, son of George III and one of Elizabeth's ardent admirers. Elizabeth is there again in the Regent's Gallery, over the fireplace, in a portrait by Hoppner.

Charles Greville's strictures on the rebuilding of Belvoir did not deter visitors—including Greville himself—from taking advantage of the fifth Duke's continuing hospitality, and the entertaining at Belvoir became legendary.

Household accounts show that, for example, in a period of less than four months in the winter of 1839–40 some 2,000 people dined at the Duke's table and about 13,500 in the steward's and servants' quarters and in the nursery. Provisions for this multitude included over 10 tons of meat (not counting 2,600 head of game), 3,500 gallons (15,900 litres) of ale (brewed in the village and stored in the Castle cellars) and 200 dozen bottles of wine.

Frequent among the guests who took part in these feasts was the statesman and novelist Disraeli, a political associate of the fifth Duke's younger son. Disraeli sang for his many suppers when he came to write his novel *Coningsby*, published in 1844. In it, Belvoir appears in the disguise of 'Beaumanoir', a delightful house with flowers everywhere and easy chairs of the utmost comfort. 'The Duke' in *Coningsby* is indeed the fifth Duke of Rutland, and his two sons are, respectively, the 'Marquis of Beaumanoir' and 'Lord Henry Sidney'. Another picture of Belvoir's baronial lifestyle appears in Greville's diary, in which he describes his attendance at the Duke of Rutland's birthday party in 1834. The church bells rang, there was free meat and ale for the villagers, a military band played each morning on the terrace of the Castle and no dinner service was used twice.

This display of wealth, however, concealed another side of the fifth Duke's character. The Manners family had embraced Disraeli's 'Young England' movement, one of whose principles was the responsibility of the aristocracy for the well-being of the less-privileged classes. The fifth Duke carried this into his everyday dealings with the villagers of Belvoir. He took seriously his duties as a Poor Law Guardian, regularly visiting the poor of the area and urging them to complain to him if they were not properly fed and looked after. If this sounds unacceptably paternalistic to twentieth-century ears, it must be remembered that the attitude of most of the upper classes to the plight of the poor was indifference: another noble Duke advised the peasantry to take curry powder to warm their bellies.

Belvoir Castle today echoes its Victorian era of opulence, and visitors can compare the architectural styles of James Wyatt, the first architect of the nineteenth-century rebuilding, and his successor Sir John Thoroton. The Porch, Pre-Guardroom, Guardroom and Grand Staircase are all Sir John's work; the Regent's Gallery—at 131 feet (40 metres) the longest room at Belvoir—was spared from the fire of 1816 and is as James Wyatt visualized it. Taking pride of place in the Regent's Gallery—for both artistic importance and association—is the series of Gobelin tapestries on 'The Adventures of Don Quixote'. A present to Louis XVI of France in 1770, they were bought in Paris by the fifth Duke of Rutland in 1814 and speak of the standard that the fifth Duke and Duchess were aiming for in their refurbishment of Belvoir.

BERKELEY CASTLE

GLOUCESTERSHIRE

'Savage, and old, and unique' is the present owner's verdict on Berkeley Castle. The earliest surviving part of the present Castle is the twelfth-century Keep. It was in the Keep that the most celebrated event in Berkeley's long history took place.

On 24 January 1327, Parliament proclaimed Edward III king, deposing his father, who was imprisoned in Kenilworth Castle. There remained, however, the problem of what to do with the deposed monarch, who was likely to be the focus of dissent while he lived. It was decided to hand him into the care of Thomas, Lord Berkeley, and Sir John Mautravers, Thomas's brother-in-law, and to take Edward II in supposed secrecy to Berkeley Castle. But there was evidently a spy in the camp, for the ex-king was followed from Warwickshire by a small army led by a Dominican father, Thomas Dunhead, who mounted an attack on the Castle. They succeeded in rescuing Edward but he was recaptured at Corfe Castle in Dorset and returned to Berkeley. From this point on, history is vague,

BERKELEY CASTLE The legendary Berkeley Hounds, whose territory covered 100 miles, from a watercolour by Lionel Edwards.

but the supposition is that Edward had become too much of a danger and embarrassment to be allowed to live.

It is not easy to piece together the truth about an event that happened over 650 years ago, especially when the few accounts of it are clearly biased. Some concur with the family tradition that Thomas of Berkeley, having treated Edward too kindly, was ordered away on royal business and left the prisoner to Sir John Mautravers, but this theory is confounded by the Castle account books (still preserved) which show Thomas as being in residence. What is certain is that an official announcement was made that Edward had died a natural death at Berkeley on 21 September 1327. It is equally certain that his death was not a natural one. There, certainty ends. It is said that an attempt to kill the former king was made by subjecting him to starvation, the stench of rotting corpses in the dungeon below his room (now part of the much-enlarged King's Gallery), and general neglect. His strong constitution resisted this, the story goes, and he was finally despatched with a red-hot spike. We shall never know the truth; but the visitor to the King's Gallery, and its adjoining cell and 28-foot dungeon beneath, is free to construct his own scenario.

Over the next two centuries, the Berkeley family and its Castle had chequered histories, partly through the lack of heirs, partly through family squabbles, and partly through the profligacy of William, a fifteenth-century Berkeley known as 'William the Waste-all'. He traded in Berkeley and its estates in exchange for various titles granted by Henry VII, one of many deals by which Henry became 'the richest prince in Christendom'. Castle and estates were restored to the family in 1553 when Edward VI came to the throne, and the new owner was nineteen-year-old Henry Berkeley.

There are many pleasing vignettes of Henry, who lived to the age of eighty, enjoying his restored estate. An enthusiastic breeder of hounds, keen falconer, skilful bowls-player, and fond of company, he was noted for his lack of 'side'. He would invite his servants to join him in the Castle for backgammon, chess or cards, taking care to keep the stakes small so that they were neither excluded from playing nor ruined by it. His wife Katharine may not have approved of this practice, for in 1601 she issued instructions that gentlemen servants who came 'to sit at play with my Lord and me' must wear their livery and not turn up in their ordinary clothes.

Such peaceful scenes were interrupted briefly during the Civil War. Parliamentary troops put the Castle under siege for three days, at the end of which they captured it. It was during this incident that the breach which still exists in the wall of the Keep was made. By some anomaly, the family is forbidden by Act of Parliament from repairing it. The Berkeleys were awarded an Earldom by Charles II in 1679 and evidently sank back into the seclusion of Gloucestershire life, with the exception of the branch of the family that lent its name to Berkeley, Virginia.

It was the fifth Earl who had made the Berkeley name famous in the annals of hunting. Hunting in those days was a hard season's work. The Berkeley Hunt could progress in stages from the Castle to London and back again without leaving Berkeley land. It began the season on its home coverts, moved on to Nettlebed in Oxfordshire, then on to Gerrards

Cross in Buckinghamshire, and so home again. When the amount of travelling began to pall, the Hunt even formed a subsidiary, the Old Berkeley Hunt, based in the Home Counties and the subject of a painting by Benjamin Marshall which can be seen in the picture gallery. This Hunt still survives, known since 1970 as the Vale of Aylesbury but still indulging the Berkeley eccentricity of dressing in yellow rather than hunting pink.

BICKLEIGH CASTLE

DEVON

Bickleigh Castle, on the bank of the River Exe, is more than its name implies. Of the original castle, only the red stone Gatehouse remains. But it is surrounded by what amounts to a whole tiny village, with barns, thatched cottages, a farmhouse, and a chapel—also thatched and, dating from shortly after the Norman Conquest, probably the oldest complete building in Devon.

People have been living at Bickleigh since the Conquest and earlier, the first recorded owner being one Alward the Englishman: so called, presumably, to distinguish him from the Normans who were compiling the Domesday Book. The Gatehouse itself dates from the final years of the fourteenth century, when Bickleigh came into the possession of the Courtenays, Earls of Devon. They rebuilt the existing Norman castle, and set it aside for their younger sons. A problem arose, however, when one of these died, leaving an even younger daughter.

Her name was Elizabeth, and she was an heiress. A related family, the Carews, agreed to move into Bickleigh to act as guardians for her, but this did not solve the Courtenays' difficulties. Indeed, these soon became much worse, for Elizabeth fell in love with a young Carew called Thomas and ran away with him.

Thomas is described as 'young and lusty, of an active body, and a courageous mind'. At that time—the early Tudor period—England was at war with Scotland. To Thomas, taking

BICKLEIGH CASTLE *The Norman interior of Bickleigh's tiny chapel, believed to be the oldest complete building in Devon.*

arms against the northern foe seemed an easier option than facing Courtenay anger; he covered himself in glory at the Battle of Flodden, returned to Bickleigh a hero, and succeeded in getting his runaway match accepted. Bickleigh, indeed, became Elizabeth's dowry, and it remained a home to the Carews until, wrecked by Cromwell's troops, it dwindled into a collection of farm buildings.

When its complex of buildings were restored this century, two skeletons were found in the floor of the tiny chapel. It is believed they were those of Thomas and Elizabeth.

BLAIR CASTLE

TAYSIDE

With its turrets, stepped gables, battlements and white harled walls, Blair Castle—home of the Dukes of Atholl since the Duchy's creation—is everyone's idea of what a

Scottish castle should look like. It owes some of its outlines, in fact, to the Victorian reconstruction of a much-altered original building. But, behind both the Victorian exterior and the Georgian interiors that were created in the previous century, the remains of the original Blair still exist: a fortified tower built in 1269 by a local warlord called Comyn, or Cumming. The building's long history bears witness to Scottish culture just as strongly as does its appearance.

Sited on the main route through the central Highlands, and owned by one of Scotland's great nobles, Blair inevitably attracted both military and royal visitors. On occasion they were one and the same. The most notable soldier-visitor was Prince Charles Edward Stuart: Bonnie Prince Charlie, the 'Young Pretender', leader of the Jacobite rebellion of 1745. The Young Pretender's entrée to Blair was provided by one of its former residents, the

continued on the road that would end at Culloden and disaster. The second Duke held on to his possessions and, firmly rejecting the political and architectural claims of the past, did the right thing by remodelling his home in Georgian (and therefore Hanoverian) style. While he robbed the exterior of its characteristically Scottish character, his superb interiors —especially the Dining Room—more than make up for it.

Royalty who visited Blair in peace included both of Scotland's most famous female rulers, Mary Queen of Scots and Queen Victoria. To entertain Mary, a hunt was staged at which 360 deer were killed, along with 5 wolves. No wolves were available for Prince Albert during Victoria's visit (the last in Scotland was killed in 1743). However, the royal couple's stay doubtless helped to increase their shared passion for the Highlands: a passion that, combining tartans, deer-shooting and the 'baronial'

BLAIR CASTLE Highland parade in the high Victorian era. The castle was, and still is, the home of the Atholl Highlanders, the only private army in Europe.

Marquis of Tullibardine, who was the eldest surviving son of the first Duke of Atholl and in exile for taking the Jacobite side in the earlier revolt in 1715. But Tullibardine—perhaps hoping to regain the ducal inheritance that had passed to his younger brother James—had again backed the wrong horse.

After a few days' stay, Bonnie Prince Charlie

style of architecture, would soon claim huge numbers of adherents. As a result, Blair and many of its fellows were later reinvested with memories of a period its owners had once rejected.

Stuart, Hanoverian, Victorian: the Blair Castle of today shows how it felt to live through all three eras and—indeed—how it

SARAH DAUGHTER AND HEIRESS
OF RICHARD JENNINGS OF SANDRIDGE
IN THE COUNTY OF HERTFORD ESQ.
WIFE OF JOHN CHURCHILL
DUKE OF MARLBOROUGH

BLENHEIM PALACE *Sarah, first Duchess of Marlborough. After the Duke's death, she worked on tirelessly to complete Blenheim as a fitting monument to the man she loved.*

felt to die in them. In the course of the nineteenth-century reconstruction work, Blair provided a grim reminder of its prime function as a military stronghold. During the Commonwealth of the 1650s, a valiant young Atholl tried to retake the building for the Stuarts: three skeletons, hidden under a floor near the former prison, indicated the price of failure.

BLAIRQUHAN CASTLE
STRATHCLYDE

It is five or six miles from Maybole to Blairquhan, and on a day in November 1854 a packman from Maybole travelled the road with a heavy heart. He had news for the laird of Blairquhan, which he left at the keeper's lodge: the laird's eldest and favourite son James had died of wounds in the Crimea.

It was a bitter blow to the laird, Sir David Hunter Blair, who had been looking forward to handing over the estate to James, MP for Ayrshire and a lieutenant-colonel in the Scots Fusilier Guards. Blairquhan was the house that Sir David had created thirty years before for his second wife—his first wife having died in 1820—and their eight children. The carefully planned scheme of succession had gone awry. Sir David was seventy-six when the news came. It was too much for an an old man to take in his stride, and he died, still mourning, three years later. Before his death he saw erected the monument to James which stands on the summit of Craigengower, on the opposite side of the Water of Girvan.

When Sir David inherited the Blairquhan estate in 1800 its seat was a barely habitable castle which for about fifty years had been let to tenants; there was also a smaller, newer house, Milton, where Sir David lived. Although the new young laird had ambitions to build a larger house to replace the castle, he seems to have been in no great hurry; various plans were prepared, but came to nothing. It was not until after the death of his first wife that he eventually commissioned the present house. In 1821, work began, on the site of the old castle, to designs by William Burn. The bridge and lodge were built at the same time. By 1825 Sir David was able to settle at Blairquhan with his second wife and, on the profits from a royal patent for printing Bibles, psalms and catechisms in Scotland and a contract for government printing, to raise their family of six sons and two daughters there.

The impression of the house today is enhanced by the fact that the furniture originally ordered by Sir David from Thomas Dowbiggin of London and James and Matthew Morrison of Ayr is still in place throughout, together with the various objects—such as the busts of Wellington, Apollo, Napoleon and Sir Walter Scott—which were added as grace notes. Together, they make up a picture of nineteenth-century family life which was, at the end, marred all too cruelly by the news brought by the packman from Maybole.

BLENHEIM PALACE
OXFORDSHIRE

Built in celebration of a famous victory, a centre of society and politics for nearly 300 years and the birthplace of Sir Winston Churchill, Blenheim stands close to the heart of England in physical and historical splendour. Queen Anne gave the manor of Woodstock, formerly the site of a royal hunting lodge, to the first Duke of Marlborough, in honour of his victory over the French and Bavarian armies at Blenheim in Bavaria in 1704. The additional promise of a house to be built on the site at royal expense was a grand gesture. Yet there was a time during the building of Blenheim when the gesture looked an empty one and the project seemed likely to end in tears.

As a young courtier, John Churchill had married a lady-in-waiting, Sarah Jennings. They became Duke and Duchess of Marlborough in 1702, when John was fifty-two and his Duchess ten years younger, following his string of early victories in the War of the Spanish Succession. The Churchills were true favourites at court. As well as the £5,000 a year pension that came with the Dukedom, their various emoluments from the Crown, for a variety of duties ranging from the Duke's command of the English forces to the Duchess's appointment as Groom of the Stole, came to well over £50,000 a year—say, £1 million at today's value. They could, it seemed for a time, do no wrong.

However, the inscription on the East Gate at Blenheim recording the gift of a 'munificent sovereign' tells only half the story, although, curiously, as late as 1914 the ninth Duke of Marlborough made a 'tribute of gratitude to the memory of the Queen by whose hand [Blenheim] was bestowed.'

The Duke and Duchess unfortunately failed to get anything in writing about the Queen's gift. This was all very well while the Duchess retained her position at Court and, even more

BLENHEIM PALACE The 180-foot Long Library was designed by Vanbrugh as a picture gallery. Today, it combines both uses.

important, her appointment as Keeper of the Privy Purse. In 1710, however, the Duchess was out of favour. By that time Queen Anne had paid out £220,000 for the building of Blenheim, but there was another £45,000 outstanding and work was not yet complete. Treasury payments ceased, leaving the Marlboroughs to finish the building themselves. Their position was not made any easier by the fact that the extravagant and theatrical Vanbrugh had been employed as architect. When friends fall apart, they often fall apart noisily, and this was so in the case of the Queen and the Duchess. Whose fault was it that Vanbrugh had been commissioned for Blenheim? The Duchess, claimed the architect, producing written evidence. The Queen, said the Duchess, adding that she had never liked Vanbrugh's designs anyway. The luck of the Marlboroughs was at a low ebb. The Duke, his famous victories now forgotten, was accused of corruption and even of letting his officers die so that he could sell their commissions. He was sacked as Army commander. In 1712 all building work at Blenheim ceased and the Duke and Duchess left for self-imposed exile on the Continent. They did not return until Queen Anne's death two years later.

Work on Blenheim was now resumed, and so were hostilities between the Duchess and Vanbrugh. He had taken advantage of the Marlboroughs' absence to set himself up in the now-vanished Woodstock Manor, which he had restored for his own occupation. There were further quarrels about fees. 'I have made Mr Vanbrugh my enemy', the Duchess reported, 'by the constant disputes I had with him to prevent his extravagance.' Vanbrugh, however, seems to have been beyond restraint—though it must be added that the flourishes and extravagances that brought the Duchess so much anguish make up much of the magnificence that the visitor admires today. Finally, with the Palace still unfinished, Vanbrugh stormed off in a huff in the autumn of 1716. The first Duke died in 1722, leaving the Duchess working, as she remarked, 'like a packhorse' to complete Blenheim over the

BLAIRQUHAN CASTLE The mid-eighteenth-century laird of Blairquhan, James Hunter Blair, with his family, painted by David Allan at his wife's home, Dunskey.

remaining twenty-two years of her life. She never forgave Vanbrugh, and when he came to Blenheim in 1725 as one of a visiting party he was refused admittance even to the park.

Cantankerous and spiteful though she was, Sarah Churchill must be given credit for one quality: her enduring love for her husband. Her completion of Blenheim was a debt of honour to him. In her widowhood she refused several offers of marriage, one, from the Duke of Somerset, with the words: 'If you could lay the empire of the world at my feet, you should never share the heart and hand that once belonged to John, Duke of Marlborough.'

If Blenheim is less a home than a series of theatrical settings, that was Vanbrugh's style. On the ceiling of the Great Hall, Marlborough is seen demonstrating the plan of battle at Blenheim. Blenheim is featured again in the Green Writing Room, in a tapestry showing the Duke receiving the French surrender. Vanbrugh's exuberance is seen at its greatest in the Long Library, which he designed as a picture gallery. As for Sarah, she is seen in the Green Drawing Room in two celebrated portraits by Kneller, showing the aspect of her that must have won John Churchill's heart. Duke and Duchess both appear, with five of their children, in Closterman's large painting which hangs in the corridor to the west of the Great Hall, and in Rysbrack's monument, with their two sons, in the Chapel.

Blenheim's place in more recent British history is assured by its having been the birthplace of Sir Winston Churchill. The room where he was born is plainly furnished and contrasts sharply with the glitter of the grand rooms; it was once part of the domestic chaplain's apartments. It was only by chance that Sir Winston was born at Blenheim, though for a period before the birth of his cousin who became the tenth Duke he was heir to the Dukedom.

Blenheim, however, played an important part in Sir Winston's life, and he often returned there. It was in the Temple of Diana beside the lake that he proposed to Clementine Hozier. His love of Blenheim and his pride in what it stands for are reflected in his painting of the Great Hall, which hangs in the Churchill Exhibition room. And from the portico of the Saloon, the state dining room, can be seen the tower of Bladon church beside which Sir Winston was buried in 1965.

BODRHYDDAN HALL

CLWYD

Behind the late-Victorian front of Bodrhyddan Hall, in early Queen Anne revival style and with a distinctly Dutch appearance, lies a house whose origins go back to early Tudor times. The Victorian refashioning was undertaken in response to the demands of a large nineteenth-century family, and at the same time it turned the formerly south-facing house to face west.

The alterations did not meet with the approval of the traveller Augustus Hare, a cousin of the owner. 'The fine old house has been altered by Nesfield—"restored" they call it—but, though well done in its way, the quaint old peculiar character has gone,' Hare wrote in his diary. William Nesfield had by that time established his reputation with such work as the Lodges in Regent's Park, London, and at Kew Gardens, and Kinmel Hall, five miles (eight kilometres) from Bodrhyddan.

There are traces of the house's Tudor origins, including the inner walls of the Great Hall, and it seems likely that Bodrhyddan Hall was originally built to provide a more comfortable second home for the owners of Rhuddlan Castle, two miles (3·2 kilometres) away. The family name of Lord Langford, who lives here today, is Rowley-Conwy, and Conwys have owned Rhuddlan Castle since the thirteenth century. They are still hereditary Constables— that is, keyholders—of the Castle, and the family has owned Bodrhyddan Hall since its first version was built. The Charter of Rhuddlan granted in 1284 by Edward I is in the Front Hall, together with armour from Rhuddlan Castle.

The Conwys were prominent in the

BODRHYDDAN HALL The oldest of the collection of armour was made at Augsburg in 1485 and saw action at Bosworth that year.

Crusades, and this accounts for the number of Crusading symbols—such as Saracen's Head motifs on the gateposts at the head of the old drive—in and around the house. In 1696, having survived the Civil War, the Conwy family consolidated and began to rebuild its home, and apart from Nesfield's west front the present house dates largely from that period. About a century later the Big Dining Room— now the family's picture gallery—was added.

Bodrhyddan's contents are an interesting and eclectic collection of objects such as might come into the possession of a family over hundreds of years. They range from medieval armour to two mummy cases and other Egyptian items which came to the house with a returning honeymoon couple in 1836.

BOUGHTON HOUSE

NORTHAMPTONSHIRE

In the story of Boughton House, contradictions fall thick and fast. In its original form, it was an English monastery. However, both the hall where the monks once congregated, and the pond where they bred fish for fast-days, have been swallowed up by one of the most worldly, consciously elegant country houses in England.

Boughton's setting is rural Northamptonshire. Its true home, however, is France: the France of the Sun King and his great palace of Versailles. And, worldly though its appearance is, it also has an element of fairy-tale about it. It is an acknowledged 'Sleeping Beauty' among houses, preserved undisturbed and magically unchanged over the years through a freak of chance. No lover of the Picturesque or the neo-Gothic ever got near it, and Boughton's arcaded main front remains as immaculately French in its inspiration as on the day its owner first saw it in its entirety.

The whole building proves him to have been a man of taste, backed by wealth. What it fails to show is the source of that wealth. Virginal-looking Boughton is, in fact, the creation and masterpiece of the restorer of Beaulieu: Ralph Montagu, courtier to the later Stuarts and their successors, sometime ambassador to the Court of Louis XIV and collector of fabulously wealthy widows. His Northamptonshire building operations started shortly before his successful wooing of the Duchess of Albemarle; presumably, her fortune helped finance the work through the 1690s.

Created an Earl as the rebuilding of Boughton started, Ralph Montagu went on to fill his new home with treasures worthy of his advancing career: a pair of magnificent mirrors, a writing table from Versailles; a set of Van

Dyck oil sketches; tapestries from the famous Mortlake factory outside London, which Ralph now owned. Everywhere, the Earl and future Duke had the satisfaction of seeing his riches and power reflected. Everywhere, too, the heraldry of the Montagu family was displayed: on a Mortlake table cover, on a looking glass, on a pink carpet in Persian style, dating from the 1580s and possibly one of the first ever to have been made in Britain.

BOUGHTON HOUSE A ring of miniature dolphins forms the feet of this rare pot-pourri *pot, dating from 1759.*

His advantageous marriages bought Ralph more than wealth; they brought him an heir as well. Indeed, it was thanks to his son John that he came by the Montagu dukedom; he pleased Queen Anne by marrying the young John Montagu to the daughter of her bosom friend, the Duchess of Marlborough. But, in spite of the splendour with which it had surrounded itself, the Montagu dynasty was not to last. Boughton soon ran short of male heirs and, as the eighteenth century came to its close, it passed via marriage into another ducal family, the Buccleuchs. They had other homes and other estates besides their recent acquisition, and Boughton entered the enchanted sleep that preserved the taste of Ralph Montagu intact.

BOUGHTON MONCHELSEA PLACE

KENT

Dick Whittington was not the only lad from the provinces to come to London to seek his fortune and end up as Lord Mayor. About a century after Whittington, a young man from Yorkshire followed the same path. His name was Robert Rudston, a draper by trade. He had amassed a considerable fortune by 1551, with land in Northamptonshire and

Middlesex, and in that year he bought the manor of Boughton near Maidstone.

Shortly after buying Boughton, Robert Rudston became involved in the revolt of the Men of Kent, led by Thomas Wyatt, the poet's son, from whom Rudston had bought the manor. The aim of the rising was to prevent the marriage of Queen Mary to Prince Philip of Spain. It was planned at Wyatt's home Allington Castle, not far from Boughton Monchelsea. The short-lived revolt was all over inside a fortnight, and the conspirators brought to justice. Rudston spent about a year in the Tower of London and all his property was confiscated, but he was more fortunate than Wyatt, who was beheaded. Rudston bought his release by repurchasing his manor for

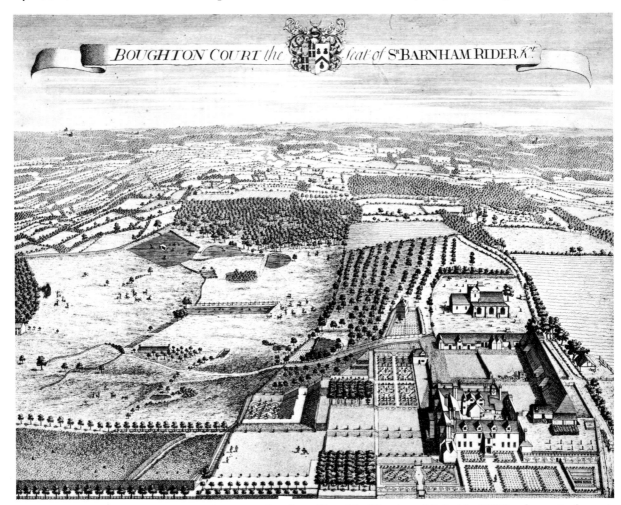

BOUGHTON MONCHELSEA PLACE An engraving from Harris's 'Kent', published in 1720, shows the house in its finest hour. Later, the north and west wings were removed.

£1,000, and was soon back at Boughton planning the rebuilding of the house.

It was an ambitious project. Rudston began with the present east wing and then added wings on the north and west. When he died in 1590 he left behind him a very substantial country house, faced with locally quarried ragstone. Further work in the late eighteenth century added the battlements and other Gothic touches. By this time the house had passed by inheritance into the Rider family, who kept it until the mid-nineteenth century.

Many houses pass out of their founding families because of failing fortunes, but what seems to have happened at Boughton Monchelsea is that those who inherited the house simply lost interest in it. It passed to a succession of bachelors and childless couples, and, being too large for their purposes, it was pruned to more manageable proportions. Robert Rudston's north and west wings disappeared some time in the eighteenth century and were replaced by domestic offices. A century later, the then owner deserted Boughton to live in Wales, and when he died in 1887 the last of the Riders declined to settle there. In 1888 the connection with the Rudston family ceased, and fifteen years later the house was bought by Colonel G. B. Winch, chairman of the Kent brewers Style & Winch. The house retained the tapestries and furniture in the Four-Poster Bedroom and the library of a nineteenth-century Rider, Thomas, thus still providing a link with Boughton's more substantial past.

···

BOWDEN HOUSE
DEVON

···

During the wholesale massacre of British country houses that took place after the Second World War, Bowden House was one of the fortunates that got away. A Tudor mansion full of secrets, it has strong historical links both with its local centre of Totnes and with Revolutionary America. Links with America were resumed in the war when the building

BOWDEN HOUSE The spectacular plasterwork that decorates the front hall dates from the early nineteenth century.

was used as a base for GIs preparing themselves for the D-Day landings. After the GIs went, the house became a school; however, it then fell into disrepair, and permission was sought to demolish it.

At this point, Bowden's fortunes changed. The county council ruled that the house should stand. It was later sold, and its present owners embarked on a massive restoration programme that brought surprise after surprise into the light of day. One of Bowden's revelations was a row of twenty bread ovens; a Tudor owner, it seems, used to feed 200 of the local poor from his kitchens every day. Another one was a mysterious wall painting, showing the traditional Tudor rose with its pointed sepals, and dating from the reign of the first Tudor, Henry VII. Evidence, perhaps, that an early owner was making clear his allegiance to the rising star of the newly arrived dynasty?

Further discoveries include a sealed room below cellar level, mantraps, cannonballs and a magnificent overmantel in carved oak, showing the crest of the Dukes of Bedford. It had been covered in *nine* coats of paint.

BOWHILL

BORDERS

In 1878 the Duke of Buccleuch was the second-largest landowner in Britain, with nearly half a million acres (over 200,000 hectares) spread over thirteen counties in Scotland and England. There were five houses in Scotland and two more in England. One of the Scottish houses—essentially a hunting lodge transformed by successive extensions into something approaching a palace—was Bowhill, which is still owned by the Buccleuch family.

'Sweet Bowhill', it was called by Sir Walter Scott, who, as a member of the family and a friend of the fourth Duke, knew it well. The relationship between writer and Duke is commemorated in the Study at Bowhill, where one of Sir Henry Raeburn's portraits of Scott dominates a collection of Scott mementoes.

The art collection of the Buccleuch family at Bowhill is in a class of its own, benefiting from many items transferred there from Dalkeith Palace and from Montagu House, the family's former London home.

The Monmouth Room contains relics of the ill-fated Duke of Monmouth, the son of Charles II and his mistress Lucy Walter. The Duke married Anne, Countess of Buccleuch in her own right, who was created Duchess of Buccleuch in 1663. It was in the spring of 1685 that Monmouth embarked on the final chapter of his life, so much of which he had devoted to his claim to be Charles II's rightful heir. His last attempt to gather an army behind him ended in the New Forest two months later, and he was executed on 15 July 1685. Together with full-length portraits of Monmouth and his wife Anne, the Monmouth Room includes his cradle, seal, sword, saddle and harness as Charles II's Master of the Horse, and, in macabre contrast to these emblems of success, the white linen shirt in which he was executed. As she was Duchess in her own right, Anne retained her estates, and lived on at Dalkeith Palace until 1732.

The present Bowhill, however, postdates these events. There was an earlier house, built in 1708, but if any of it remains it is within the walls of the later 1812 building. During the nineteenth century a succession of architects slowly extended the house, and it became the favoured home of the Dukes of Buccleuch. The fourth Duke—Sir Walter Scott's friend and kinsman—began a programme of agricultural improvement on the estate, which was carried on by his son. The fourth Duke as a child is the subject of Reynolds's celebrated 'Pink Boy', which hangs in the Dining Room at Bowhill.

BOWOOD The Picture Gallery: formerly the Orangery that Robert Adam designed for the first Marquess of Lansdowne in the 1760s.

BOWOOD

WILTSHIRE

Spreading at ease on its sunlit terraces, Bowood is nonetheless a haunted house. Its ghost is no headless horseman or black dog, but another building: the building that was once known as the 'Big House' and that, in turn, incorporated an earlier house still. Although they are no longer there, these two earlier Bowoods still make their presence felt through their successor. So, indeed, does another great house that did not even stand on the Bowood site: Lansdowne House in London's Berkeley Square. However, the influence all three shed is benevolent.

It is to Lansdowne House, for example, that the current Bowood owes its collection of pictures and statuary. And it was the Big House that endowed it with the gallery where the collection is housed, and with the gallery's surroundings: the Italian garden on the terraces and the park behind, with its lake by Capability Brown and the enormous Cedar of Lebanon that he probably planted. (It is said to be the biggest in Britain.)

Today's Bowood started as a mere extension of the Big House, which had been built up round its predecessor by John Petty, first Earl of Shelburne. The new additions included a stable and kitchen block at one corner of the emerging building. Though handy, the service block had one glaring defect: it was designed in the form of a double, open-fronted courtyard, like a huge letter E, and the yard gave straight on to the area overlooked by the Big House itself. The Earl's son William, first Marquess of Lansdowne, decided to alter this state of affairs—and, both at his London home and at Bowood itself, he had already employed just the man to do it. The leading Scottish architect, Robert Adam, was called in to screen the front of the service block with the

long greenhouse, or Orangery, that is now Bowood's picture gallery.

Around the same time, the arrival of the Marquess's baby son made other domestic alterations necessary. The part of the Big House nearest the service wing was fitted up as a nursery: a cosy arrangement that in later years frequently drew the Pettys to treat it as their main quarters. They now had a 'Little House' as well as a big one—and it is this, complete with the service courts and the Orangery, that has survived.

To today's visitor, the Little House at Bowood seems built on a large, and even majestic, scale. Only the grassy outline of its defunct parent shows to what extent its name is justified.

BRAEMAR CASTLE
GRAMPIAN

The junction of the waters of the Clunie and the Dee, commanding the way to east, west and south, has an obvious strategic importance in a country of rival clans and government oppression. Braemar saw the great

*BRAEMAR CASTLE **Putting Braemar on the map.** The Braemar Gathering, originally a clan meeting, became under Queen Victoria's patronage a major Highland social occasion.*

gathering of the clans which signalled the start of the 1715 Jacobite rising, and the Earl of Mar, who was host on this occasion, paid the price, when the rising was crushed, by forfeiting his estates. The original Braemar, built in 1628, was largely destroyed. In 1746, after Culloden, Bonnie Prince Charlie slipped away to France after delivering his infamous exit line, 'Let every man seek his own safety as best he can', leaving his followers to be hunted down by Hanoverian troops and his country to English occupation.

The instruments of the English occupation of Scotland after the '45 were a network of military roads and a series of forts built at key points along them. One of these was at Braemar. Restoration of the castle was begun in 1748 under the guidance of John Adam, brother of the celebrated Edinburgh architect Robert Adam, whose work included the curtain walling and the heightened tower enclosing the granite staircase. The function of Braemar as reconstructed, and of the other castles strung along the military roads, was to act as a watch-tower to guard against rebel activity and staging-posts for the parties of troops moving between the major barracks.

By the end of the eighteenth century, the fear of Scottish rebellion had receded, the cost of maintaining the military road network had become unmanageable, and in any case the new threat to England was from France. Returned to the Farquharson family, the castle's military role was over, and it was time for it to play a new part as a family home. Braemar's military past is, however, never far from view. Apart from the basic plan of the house, which remains that of a highland garrison, there is less formal evidence such as the name 'John Chestnut, sergeant', roughly carved, with others, on the shutters of the Drawing Room in 1797.

The ease of communication that had in the past given Braemar its strategic importance now facilitated a new role as the setting for the Braemar Gathering. Spending what became her traditional late summer holiday at Balmoral, a few miles away, Queen Victoria was a frequent visitor to the Gathering and the Castle, although, as she confessed to her diary, she considered the Gathering 'a poor affair' and 'a thing we always disliked'. Nevertheless, the Queen's patronage put Braemar firmly on the nineteenth-century social map of Scotland.

BRAMHAM PARK Portraits in the Hall include those of the Duke of Cumberland and of former guest Queen Anne.

BRAMHAM PARK

YORKSHIRE

French formality and memories of the hunting field; Versailles and hound breeding; the Sun King and Jorrocks. . . . In unique fashion, Bramham Park combines two influences that ordinarily have little in common. It owes the walks, vistas and ornamental cascades in its grounds to its builder, who worshipped at the shrine of the great French landscape gardener, André le Nôtre. The double stairway curving down from the garden front was copied from a French model by an owner who, in the early 1900s, rescued Bramham from the decay that had overtaken it. But, in between them, came a pair of ebullient characters who raised the house to be a sportsman's paradise—and, in doing so, nearly ruined it.

Anne Dutchess of Monmouth and Buccleugh.

BOWHILL *Anne, Duchess of Monmouth and Buccleuch, whose portrait hangs above the Library fireplace.*

In its early days, Bramham was not so much racy as semi-regal. Its builder, Robert Benson, first Lord Bingley, was a talented financier and man of affairs who would become Chancellor of the Exchequer under Queen Anne, and Treasurer of the Household under George II. Anne, indeed, was to be numbered among the visitors to her chancellor's new mansion in Yorkshire and, in token of her gratitude, she presented Bingley with the Kneller portrait of herself that now hangs in Bramham's Hall.

Bramham was in fact to be owned by only two Bensons, for Robert was succeeded by his daughter, Harriet. The next Lord Bingley was Harriet's husband, George Fox—but he was also the last, for their son died before his parents and Bramham passed to a nephew, James Fox. The new owner, who was known by the affectionate nickname of 'Jemmy', was a delightful person: highly cultivated, a man of affairs, generous with his enthusiasms, and not immune from private fears about his image. A friend of William Pitt, he was MP for Horsham.

On moving to Bramham, he gave full rein to joint passions for estate management and hunting. The organizer of the Bramham Moor Hunt, he posed for the inevitable family portrait in his hunting pink. Then it occurred to him that this might not go down well with his neglected constituents in Horsham, whose interests he was meant to be devotedly representing in Westminster. The artist, Benjamin West, was told to repaint the coat in black.

Generous to the last, Jemmy left his wife and his younger children well provided-for when he died. But this generosity would serve Bramham ill, for it coincided with that scourge of great estates, a reckless heir. George Fox—'the Gambler'—took sport even more seriously than his father did. His social circle was that of the Regency bucks; a friend of the Prince Regent himself, he ran up debts that placed a huge burden on the estate. An expensively failed marriage did not help matters, and a major fire destroyed many Fox possessions on which funds could have been raised. All that Gambler George really gave his home were the gilt cups that now stand on the sideboard in the East Room: he won them with greyhounds he had bred.

Although his successors tried mightily, there was no repairing all the damage done by George during the nineteenth century. The debts were paid off, but the house stood empty. The superb gardens were maintained, but an elm tree managed to seed itself on the front steps up which Queen Anne had once walked. By the turn of the century, this tree stood considerably taller than the building. Six years later, however, and in the very nick of time, the Gambler's great-grandson came to the rescue, started restoration work, and reaffirmed Bramham's connection with French tastes in building.

However, Bramham's contents—and particularly its pictures—continue to reinforce the influence of the sportsman and the hunting field. And the splendid ghost story that Bramham can boast also falls into a sporting category. The park is said to be haunted by warhorses fleeing riderless from a local medieval battle. In the 1930s, the present owner's father was riding in the park when he heard the sound of hooves. Assuming that it was the staff of the Bramham Moor Hunt coming towards him, he opened a gate for them and waited by it. Nothing came.

BREAMORE HOUSE

HAMPSHIRE

There is something different—at first glance, indefinably—about Breamore House. Tricks of light, a precise and neat touch in the decoration and furnishing, a kind of reticence which contrasts with the studied opulence of so many English country houses?

Perhaps, for this apparently very English setting has been subjected to the strong Dutch influence of the Hulse family, who have owned Breamore since 1748 and who still live there today. The family had arrived from Holland with William and Mary in 1688, Dr Edward

Hulse being physician to William of Orange and going on to serve him in England. The purchaser of Breamore in 1748 was his son, Sir Edward Hulse, first baronet, also a doctor, and physician to Queen Anne, George I and George II. He presented the house to his son, also eventually Sir Edward; and it was this Sir Edward Hulse who established Breamore as a country seat and created the estate around it.

In 1741, when he was twenty-six, the second baronet married a pretty sixteen-year-old, Hannah Vanderplank. Although clearly of Dutch origin, her parents lived in London. The marriage was evidently a happy one, and Hannah bore Sir Edward three sons and five daughters. The portraits of these three generations of the Hulse family are to be seen in the Blue Drawing Room at Breamore, together with the set of decorated Dutch marquetry furniture which was Hannah's wedding present from her father.

The early years of Hulse ownership brought lighter times to a house that had earlier accumulated, in little more than fifty years, some grisly history and associations. It was built in the early 1580s by a rich merchant, William Dodington, who in 1600 scandalized Elizabethan London by committing suicide in advance of an impending lawsuit. He chose a spectacular way to die: in broad daylight, he climbed up the steeple of St Sepulchre's Church in Holborn and threw himself off, breaking his neck.

It is the serenity of the Hulse family, however, that makes its presence felt in the house today; though this serenity was interrupted in 1856 when fire swept through the house. Its spread was not too fast, fortunately, to prevent most of the contents being saved. These include, hung in the Dining Room, a fine collection of paintings of the seventeenth- and eighteenth-century Dutch schools. By contrast, and very English, is Thomas Hudson's eighteenth-century 'The Boy with the Bat', believed to be one of the two oldest paintings of cricketers. On a more domestic scale, the kitchen is displayed as it would have been in use in the nineteenth century.

BRETFORTON MANOR
HEREFORD & WORCESTER

In November 1907, a country-house party took place at Bretforton Manor that, even by the opulent standards of the time, was particularly diamond-studded. Its focus was the nearby Wood Norton Manor, home of the exiled King of France, now called the Duc d'Orleans. His sister, Princess Louise of France, was marrying the brother-in-law of the King of Spain—and so many princes, ambassadors and members of Europe's nobility were on the guest list that the Duke had to seek help from his friend and neighbour at Bretforton, Henry Ashwin. So the Ashwins' guest list for

BRETFORTON MANOR The manor's large collection of ancillary buildings includes this timbered thatched barn.

November bore some exotic names: the Duc d'Alençon, the Duchesse de Vendôme, the Grand Duke Vladimir of Russia and his wife.

After a week they had gone; but the Bretforton Manor they knew—home of the Ashwins for over 400 years—is the same. Indoors, there is still the oak panelling from 1871, the overmantel (again in oak) from the seventeenth century, the priest's hole from the same period. Outside in the grounds, the evidence of earlier life at Bretforton goes back considerably further, and includes a dovecot with 280 pigeon holes, the ruins of a Saxon

BREAMORE HOUSE An eighteenth-century view of Breamore after the estate had been bought by the royal physician, Sir Edward Hulse, and given as a wedding present to his son.

church, and the original village stocks.

The Ashwins have now gone too, but one resident from their period is more persistent. What, one wonders, would the Grand Duke and his fellow guests have made of Bretforton's ghost: the butler who died in 1945 and still has a penchant for opening doors?

BROADLANDS

HAMPSHIRE

'This place,' a Hampshire landowner wrote to his son in 1736, 'all together pleases me above any place I know . . . I have two salmons caught out of the River by me.' The river was the Test, Mecca of fly fishers; the angler was Henry Temple, first Viscount Palmerston and future grandfather of the great Victorian statesman, 'Pam'. And the place was Broadlands: not then the beloved home of Lord Mountbatten, where both the Queen and the Prince of Wales began their honeymoons, but a Tudor manor house of formal and somewhat old-fashioned appearance.

Its main claim to fame lay not in the house at all but in the grounds: the mulberry trees planted by King James I, who had visited Broadlands three times. The occasion was the granting of Romsey's Royal Charter, but the mulberry was a favourite with James for a different reason: at his own favourite residence of Theobalds in Hertfordshire, he was trying to rear silkworms, and he had a natural interest in promoting the culture of his fledgling industry's raw material.

By the time Viscount Palmerston moved in, the royal trees were well over a hundred years old, and he exempted them from his plans to bring his new purchase up-to-date. Elsewhere, however, he threw himself into remodelling work with energy. As he told his son:

'I have many men at work here of all kinds, doing the necessary things to make this a convenient, comfortable habitation, and making the river the main object of pleasure. . . So I propose a very large, fine stable yard for myself enclosed within itself, and all offices as brew house, laundry, coach houses, wood houses, etc. . .

The young Henry Temple, who became the second Viscount Palmerston when he was only

BROADLANDS Lord Louis Mountbatten and his wife—née Edwina Ashley—on their wedding day in 1922. Broadlands, where they began their honeymoon, belonged to her father.

seventeen, carried on the improvements, with Capability Brown directing operations. Slowly a new Broadlands emerged: a Palladian Broadlands, with a pillared entrance and exquisite plasterwork, surrounded by a park of superbly contrived naturalness. In this setting, the second Viscount entertained some of the leading literary and artistic figures of the day, including Joshua Reynolds, Garrick and Sheridan. It was Sir Joshua who gave his Hampshire host the charming portrait—now hanging in the Broadlands Dining Room—of yet another visitor: Emma, Lady Hamilton.

The third Viscount, Henry John Temple (1784–1865) also succeeded to the title at seventeen. He lifted the already distinguished reputation of Broadlands to new heights. One of the architects of British world dominance in the Victorian period and twice Prime Minister (1855–8; 1859–65), he was also extremely popular with the electorate, who delighted in his image of a bluff, 'up-and-at-'em' country squire. In his personal life, Pam was just that: he loved his Hampshire home, and would regularly ride or coach the 160-mile (260 kilometres) round journey from Westminster and back to spend his weekends at Broadlands.

Pam left Broadlands to his stepson, Lord Mount Temple, and it was through the Mount Temples that it eventually passed to the Mountbattens. In 1922, when Lord Louis Mountbatten married Edwina Ashley, the house belonged to her father; she inherited it just before the Second World War.

At Broadlands, memories of Lord Mountbatten are most densely concentrated in the former stable block, which houses the Mountbatten Exhibition opened by the Prince of Wales shortly before his own wedding in 1981. But the whole house is today permeated with his personality and family connections. The Gun Room contains both Lady Romsey's fishing tackle and the Earl's collection of walking sticks; pictures in the library (now Lord Romsey's study) include an immensely long painting of George VI's coronation procession, with Lord Mountbatten riding behind the coronation coach. Commemorative books displayed in the Oak Room recall other times and other coronations: those of his great-uncle and uncle, both Tsars of Russia. The North Staircase gives the Earl's family tree in portraiture, starting with the sixteenth-century Philip the Magnanimous of Hesse, who rallied to the support of Martin Luther.

It was the Prince of Wales who also opened Broadlands itself to the public. 'It was a beautiful sunny day,' Lord Romsey recalls, 'and my grandfather was on top form as he showed Prince Charles around. He greeted the first paying guests, an American family, with a smile and a joke as he refunded their money. One thing soon became clear, my grandfather loved being a stately home owner.'

The year, however, was 1979 and the Earl's delight was cut grievously short. Lord Romsey continues: 'I was married not long after my grandfather's tragic assassination in August 1979 and my wife and I decided that the best memorial we could offer to him was to continue the opening of the house and to create the Mountbatten Exhibition as he had always envisaged.'

BROUGHTON CASTLE

OXFORDSHIRE

Broughton Castle is a house that almost died. But, unlike so many country houses which were brought close to destruction by civil war or local rebellion, Broughton's brush with extinction came about through the flirtation of one of its owners with the temptations of Regency decadence.

Broughton came to the Fiennes family by marriage in 1451, four years after the family had acquired the barony of Saye and Sele. They have treated the house—it is really a castle only in name—with respect, later clothing the original moated, medieval manor in Elizabethan garb and making of it a fine mansion yet with most of its original features preserved.

The Fiennes family was active in court circles, and in 1604 James I and his Queen

BROUGHTON CASTLE The unusual carved interior porch of the Oak Room, once Broughton's dining room.

stayed at Broughton; a bedroom is still known as Queen Anne's Room. In 1624, the year before the King's death, the seventh Baron Saye and Sele was created the first Viscount. In the years leading up to the Civil War he helped to organize opposition to Charles I, and was host at Broughton to secret meetings which were held in the present Council Chamber.

Meanwhile, he interested himself in the colonization of America, and was a leading member of a company that organized an early settlement in Connecticut; the town of Saybrook, Connecticut, is named after him. Despite his political activities, however, the hazards of the Civil War left Broughton virtually untouched. There was a brief Royalist siege and occupation, but little damage was done.

It was William Thomas, the fifteenth Baron, who interrupted the calm of this evidently happy and well-cared-for house. He left the Oxfordshire countryside for the headier pleasures of Belvedere in Kent, and the company of Oxfordshire gentry for the competitive glitter and extravagance of the Prince Regent, the future George IV. Broughton was neglected to the point where it was covered with ivy and, according to a report in 1819, 'daily dilapidating in use'. So low did William Thomas bring the family fortunes that in 1837 an eight-day sale was held to dispose of the contents of Broughton, even down to the swans on the moat.

The resurrection of Broughton was the work of the sixteenth Baron, Frederick. Frederick was archdeacon of Hereford, and this ecclesiastical connection brought him into contact with the work of George Gilbert Scott, the church architect whose work also included London's Albert Memorial. From 1865 to 1880 a programme of restoration was carried out at Broughton under Scott's direction. His innovations were modest, substantially restoring the house to its pre-Regency heyday.

BROWSHOLME HALL
LANCASHIRE

In the closing years of the eighteenth century, one of Britain's greatest artists, J.M.W. Turner, produced a sequence of watercolours that depicted the country houses of Lancashire. Among them was a painting of a massive, honey-coloured building, almost symmetrical in outline, and boasting a pillared portico three storeys high. The house the picture shows—and where, indeed, it now hangs—is Browsholme Hall, home of the Parker family since 1507, and the same in many essentials as when Turner painted it.

Some of the windows, however, are rather different; there is also now a small bell-tower and a 'new' dining room, inserted by the same Parker who brought Turner to Browsholme in the first place. The drawing room, too, dates from just after Turner's visit and owes its existence to the same man: Thomas Lister Parker, antiquarian, patron of the arts, landscape gardener and—ultimately—an exile from the house he loved.

Thomas Lister was one of those people who have a gift for friendship. He was popular with everyone, from the Prince Regent to the headmaster of his old school in nearby Clitheroe. Since he also enjoyed aesthetic gifts of the highest order, the circle of his acquaintance included collectors, antiquaries, connoisseurs of the arts, and artists themselves—including Turner. It seems likely that he introduced the painter to the men who would be amongst his most important patrons, Sir John Leicester and Walter Fawkes; Leicester was in fact a cousin of the Parkers.

As a cultivated man, Thomas Lister naturally did the Grand Tour (including a visit to Russia). Naturally, too, he divided his time between his country estate—which he improved with extensive tree plantings—and London. But, for all that it gave his gifts their highest outlet, London was to be his undoing. He overspent; he so admired a young actor that he trailed him from city to city and lavished presents on him; he overspent again. At last, he was so down on his luck that he had to sell up his Lancashire home lock, stock and barrel, thereafter entering a curious existence of genteel homelessness.

It could have been worse. The purchaser of Browsholme was also Thomas Lister's heir, another Thomas Parker, so the connection with Browsholme did not have to be completely severed. In 1827, the former Prince Regent—now King—gave his old acquaintance the sinecure of royal Sergeant

BRYMPTON D'EVERCY *A lady keeps wicket. A charming vignette from the I Zingari Cricket Collection.*

Trumpeter; the money attached was minimal, but it did at least uphold Thomas Lister's dignity. His friends were happy to give him living space in their homes, while artists and antiquarians accorded him the utmost respect. And, at Browsholme itself, the whole house ensures that his gifts should have the sort of memorial he would have most wanted.

BRYMPTON d'EVERCY

SOMERSET

On the admission of the present owner, the quirky South Front of Brympton d'Evercy is an architectural disaster. The row of first-floor windows has pointed lintels—except for the final one on the right, which is rounded. The central feature of this elevation is—the drain pipe. As an attempt at grandeur in the Inigo Jones manner, it doesn't quite come off. The name of the architect is unknown, but building of the South Front was begun twenty-six years after Inigo Jones's death. If he had a hand in the original design, it must have been a very sketchy one.

In 1697, some forty years after the South Front was added for the Sydenham family which had owned the house for two centuries, Brympton d'Evercy went on the market. Its next owner had to sell to pay his debts, and the new buyer, in 1731, was Francis Fane, barrister and MP. At this stage the house looked substantially as it does today. Until then, it had had an uneventful history, but the Fanes were soon to bring it a dash of colour. Francis Fane's brother Thomas, to whom Francis left Brympton d'Evercy, inherited the title of the Earl of Westmorland. The tenth Earl, John, scandalized society by eloping to Gretna Green with a rich heiress, Sarah Child, with her father in hot pursuit. The marriage took place, however, and produced two children. The youthful escapade evidently did not blight the tenth Earl's career, and he went on to hold a number of government posts including Post-master General, Lord Privy Seal and Viceroy of Ireland. He married a second time and there was one child, Lady Georgiana Fane. Mother and daughter decided to rehabilitate Brympton d'Evercy as their permanent home, and the present contents of the house date mainly from their occupation.

Lady Georgiana never married. There is a family story that, as a girl, she fell in love with her father's aide-de-camp, a young and, at that time, impoverished officer named Arthur Wellesley. Wellesley, it is said, sought the tenth Earl's permission for the marriage, but was told that he was quite unsuitable as the husband of the daughter of an Earl and Viceroy. Though they corresponded for the rest of the officer's life, the couple went their separate ways—Georgiana to settle at Brympton d'Evercy and Wellesley to become the Duke of Wellington, hero of Waterloo and Prime Minister. Georgiana lived on until 1875, outliving the Duke by twenty-three years.

Georgiana was succeeded at Brympton

BROWSHOLME HALL The Hall's exterior, as painted by J. M. W. Turner at the end of the 1790s. Its appearance—except for the bell tower—has not altered significantly.

d'Evercy by her nephew, **Sir Spenser Ponsonby**, who assumed the name Fane on his inheritance. Sir Spenser had had a distinguished court and diplomatic career which had included the duty of bringing back the Peace Treaty with Russia that ended the Crimean War. When he arrived with it at the Foreign Office in the early morning, he found the place deserted except for a cleaning lady washing the steps. He left the Treaty in her charge while he went to his club for breakfast.

Sir Spenser was also a famous cricketer. As treasurer of the MCC, he laid the foundation stone at Lord's. He was also co-founder of two notable amateur teams, the Old Stagers at Canterbury and the I Zingari. Among the present contents of Brympton d'Evercy is the I Zingari Cricket Club Collection which has been assembled by the present owner, Charles Clive-Ponsonby-Fane.

BRYN BRAS CASTLE

GWYNEDD

The casual passer-by might take Bryn Bras for an ancient castle, as likely as not to have been in the same ownership for centuries. He would be wrong on both counts. The Castle is little more than 150 years old, and in that short time it has had no less than fifteen owners.

A romantic fantasy castle on which work began in 1830, Bryn Bras was built for Thomas Williams, a newly married Bangor attorney. Williams, whose family had owned the land round about for generations, had made a good marriage to the daughter of the High Sheriff of Anglesey, and no doubt the Castle reflected his social aspirations. A succession of short periods of ownership followed Thomas Williams's death in 1874, until in 1897 the Castle was bought by Frank Barnard, who ran it as a shooting estate with a stud farm in the grounds. After his death in 1918, some handsome profits were made by three speculators who owned Bryn Bras in succession, almost doubling its price (to £7,250) in little more than a year. With the purchase of the Castle by Duncan Alves, an oil tycoon, in 1920, Bryn Bras entered a period of social prominence.

Alves was active politically, and Lloyd George was a frequent visitor. It has been suggested, perhaps unkindly, that Alves hoped for one of the knighthoods, peerages or other honours that Lloyd George dispensed so lavishly. Certainly he resurrected his family crest—a wheatsheaf with the legend *Deo Favente* (by God's favour)—and liberally displayed it at various points in the house. He did not receive his honour.

He spent a considerable amount on alterations at Bryn Bras in the 1920s, including the conversion of the stables into a ballroom with stained-glass windows and the addition of various castellated buildings to the garden. (Under a later owner the ballroom became a poultry-house, surely one of the few to have such glorious fenestration.)

BRYN BLAS CASTLE A case of deception. Confounding first impressions, the Castle dates from only 1829.

Alves moved to London in 1939 and planned to sell Bryn Bras the following year, but war intervened and the Castle was occupied by an evacuated school. After the war there was another period of short ownerships until the present owners took over in 1965.

BURGHLEY HOUSE

LINCOLNSHIRE

A house fit for royalty: this is how Burghley was first envisaged, then built, then added to in nobler style still. Though never owned by any of Britain's ruling dynasties, it was from the first accepted by their members as a suitable setting for themselves. One of the greatest of Britain's non-royal palaces, it remains a prodigy of grandeur to this day. Its airy domes and turrets, its huge art collection, the crowding gods and nymphs who tumble off its painted ceilings: all add up to a vision of supreme profusion, dizzying in its extent.

Its creator was one of Queen Elizabeth I's most valued statesmen: her Lord High Treasurer and Chief Minister, Lord Burghley. In the hazardous days of Mary Tudor's reign, William Cecil—as he then was—linked his fortunes to that of the threatened younger daughter of Henry VIII. In 1558, following Mary Tudor's death and the firm re-establishment of Protestantism, Elizabeth finally emerged into the light; Cecil emerged with her and his career followed hers to the peaks.

In fact, he started constructing his new house just before his patroness succeeded to the throne, but his own speedy progression through the ranks of the state administration and entrance into the nobility meant that he had no need to stint himself on his building plans. Indeed, the reverse was true: he aimed to create a house that the Queen would wish to visit, and he succeeded. The amazing thing was that—responsible though he was for running a kingdom—he designed most of the new building himself.

Inside Burghley, the main witnesses to its designer's plans are the Great Hall with its hammer-beam roof, and the vaulted Old Kitchen, now dominated by shining rows of copperware, its gigantic painting of an ox carcass, and the display of turtle skulls (whose owners long ago became soup.) Elsewhere, the work of other Cecil minds is evident. In 1605, Elizabeth's successor, James I, made Burghley's elder son Earl of Exeter and, in the hands of the new earl's line, the house inevitably began to evolve from its Elizabethan original into something that kept pace with the owners' status and wealth.

After the Lord Treasurer himself, the main creators of Burghley are the fifth Earl, John, and the ninth, Brownlow. John, who ruled over the house in the last quarter of the seventeenth century, was a connoisseur of the arts who combed Europe for pictures, tapestries and furniture that pleased him. Both Florence and Venice yielded up their treasures to him; so did France. He also combed Europe's workshops for artists to help him change Burghley into a celebration of the baroque. One such was the wood-carver Grinling Gibbons; another was the iron-smith Jean Tijou; a third, the fresco painter Louis Laguerre, was Tijou's son-in-law, and godson of Louis XIV himself.

A fourth was Antonio Verrio, also a painter, and it is to Verrio that Burghley owes one of its greatest triumphs: its sequence of state apartments, later called the 'George Rooms' to commemorate a visit projected but never made by the Prince Regent. Prinny may never have graced them with his presence, but plenty of other beings do. Even when empty, the George Rooms—dressing room, bedroom, drawing rooms—give the impression of being full of people. The painted and woven canvases that cover the walls are partly responsible for this crowded effect, but it is Verrio's ceilings that are its main creators. Products of the baroque at its most joyously extravagant, they teem with energy.

The climax to the sequence of classical imagery comes in the last room of all, where Verrio achieves his masterpiece. Here, in the 'Heaven Room', his imagination explodes off

BURGHLEY HOUSE The tenth Earl of Exeter and his wife: born a farmer's daughter, she was nicknamed the 'cottage countess'.

the ceiling, invests the walls with an entire mythological universe and, thanks to his *trompe-l'oeil* technique, reaches uncannily out to the dazzled onlooker. 'Heaven's' creator has, incidentally, included himself among his cast of thousands: he is the scribbler with the brown cloak, crouched by the Cyclops' forge.

Brilliantly decorated as they were, the state rooms were left for Burghley's other great modernizer, the ninth Earl, to complete. Brownlow, like many other eighteenth-century owners of great houses, enlisted the aid of Capability Brown, who redesigned the grounds and made changes to the buildings. However, the ninth Earl took care to work round and with the fifth Earl's improvements, with the result that Burghley carries the stamp of both John's opulence and Brownlow's neo-classicism. But, although these two were the main architects of post-Elizabethan Burghley,

they are joined by others whose existence and tastes are made visible throughout the house and grounds. There is, for example, Brownlow's successor Henry: tenth Earl and first Marquess of Exeter, and builder of the gates of the house's main entrance, called the Bottle Lodges. There was another Brownlow, who played host twice to Queen Victoria and, on the second occasion, installed in the second 'George Room' the magnificent crimson-hung bed in which Victoria and Albert slept during their stay. In the present century, there is the sixth Marquess: the champion hurdler of Olympic status, and organizer of the 1948 Olympic Games in London.

It is the legacy of these and all the other figures who have lived in Burghley over the past 400 years that ultimately makes the house's profusion of impressions so powerful.

BURTON CONSTABLE HALL

NORTH HUMBERSIDE

In 1767, a craftsman living near Hull delivered to his employer a handsome set of dining-room furniture: a seven-leaved dining table and eight chairs, with wheatsheaf backs and horsehair seats. John Lowry, estate carpenter to William Constable, Lord Paramount of the Seigniory of Holderness, was fitting out the new dining room at Burton Constable Hall in the style of Hepplewhite.

In fact, Constable—though a good judge of distinguished craftsmanship—was here getting a better bargain than even he knew. George Hepplewhite's widow Alice was not to publish her husband's furniture designs until 1788, over twenty years after the ruling genius of Burton Constable's workshops had produced his own 'pre-Hepplewhites'.

Lowry, however, was not the only outstanding craftsman to work for Burton Constable's owner. Thomas Chippendale designed the furniture in the house's Great Drawing Room and charged the extremely high fee of £1,000 for it. Capability Brown drew up plans for landscaping the park. Indeed, he also submitted a design for remodelling the ceiling of the house's Great Hall, but had it turned down; this job—like much else at Burton—went to a local man, James Henderson of York. (Henderson's fee, in contrast to Chippendale's, was a halfpenny over £52 17s.)

The Constables of Burton Constable were Roman Catholics and, in spite of the august family title inherited from a sixteenth-century ancestress, William was barred by his faith from entering public life.

He went on the Grand Tour; he married (his first choice turned him down because he wasn't pious enough); he remodelled his Elizabethan family home in the style of the eighteenth century. But his real interest was science, in most of its then known branches. A Fellow of the Royal Society, he interested himself in botany, geology, physics and zoology. For his scientific work, he appropriated the Long Gallery designed by his father; he called it his 'philosophical room', and it was here that he experimented with gases, vacuums and static electricity.

The equipment he used is today in the house's Museum Rooms. But his influence is felt throughout the building he remodelled, from the choice of a ceiling down to that of a table-top in the ballroom. The frame is, yet again, by Chippendale, but the top itself is a tiny museum in its own right: its inlay consists of 165 marbles and other geological specimens.

William's influence is felt in another way in the hall's Gold Bedroom. His amiable ghost was last seen there by the grandmother of the present owner—the forty-sixth Lord Paramount of the Seigniory of Holderness.

BURGHLEY HOUSE The last in Burghley's progression of Great State Rooms on the south front, the Heaven Room is also the ultimate masterpiece of painter Antonio Verrio.

BURTON COURT

HEREFORD & WORCESTER

The squire was coming home from the war. The carriage brought him, along with his wife and three-year-old son, from Leominster station to Eardisland. There, the horses were taken out of the shafts and the villagers themselves drew the squire in his carriage to his new home.

The war in question was the Boer War. The squire was Colonel Peter Legh Clowes. His new home was Burton Court, made over to him six years before but awaiting the Colonel's retirement before he could move in.

The Edwardian period saw sharp divisions beginning to appear among the owners of country houses. Those whose money was in

BURTON COURT *The entrance front, added in 1912, is an early work of the distinguished architect Clough Williams-Ellis.*

land had been hard hit by agricultural depression and were tightening their belts. By contrast, there was a new breed of country-house owners whose wealth came from commerce and industry. The Clowes were in the second category: Mrs Clowes was the heiress to the owner of a Liverpool shipping line. Accordingly, the years leading up to the First World War were Burton Court's heyday.

Twenty-three staff were kept in the house alone, with more, of course, in the coachhouse and grounds. Two by two, crocodile-fashion, they were required to walk to the village church on Sunday mornings along the now-overgrown Church Walk.

All this came to an end in 1914 with the outbreak of war. It came to an end in a very personal sense for the Clowes family, since their only child Warren, the boy who had been brought to Burton Court after the Boer War, was killed in action just a few months before the Armistice. His father died in 1925, and although Mrs Clowes lived on until 1949 the end of the estate was in sight. In 1950 it was broken up, leaving Burton Court itself to be bought by the present owners ten years later.

The owners of Burton Court seem to have lived quiet country lives. They were modestly, but not ostentatiously, prosperous. The house reflects this: there are no Adam fireplaces or interiors by Kent. The rebuilding of the original house—of which the Great Hall, dating from the fourteenth century, is all that remains—was begun in the Regency period, presumably by local craftsmen. It was a Hereford architect, Frederick Kempson, who undertook 'Victorianization' about 1860. Architecturally, the most distinguished work is the entrance front, designed by Clough Williams-Ellis in 1911, at the start of his career.

The former spirit of a country-gentleman's house is today ingeniously recaptured with an exhibition of period costumes. The results add a freshness to the restored rooms.

CADHAY

DEVON

Tales of a lost fortune and a great naval victory lie behind the mullioned windows of Cadhay. The present house originated in Henry VIII's reign, when the estate came by marriage to the Haydon family. John Haydon was a prosperous lawyer with a practice in Lincoln's Inn and another in Exeter. The Hall and two sides of the courtyard were completed in his lifetime, and the remaining side, faced in chequered sandstone and flint, was added by his son Robert.

The Haydons were passionate Royalists, and signalled their allegiance by placing statues of Tudor monarchs over the courtyard's four doors. The so-called 'Court of Sovereigns' is a distinctive feature of the house. The four monarchs featured are Henry VIII, Edward VI, Mary and Elizabeth, and a date inscribed under Elizabeth places these additions in 1617.

It seems, however, that the enthusiasm of the Haydons for the monarchy led them into extravagant ways. At any rate, by 1683 Cadhay was £17,000 in debt and heavily mortgaged. The Haydons' other estates were sold off one by one, and finally, in 1736, Cadhay followed.

The new owner was another Lincoln's Inn

CADHAY The curved beams of the Roof Chamber once formed the roof of Cadhay's Great Hall, built in the Tudor period.

lawyer, William Peere Williams, who restored the house and made some eighteenth-century 'improvements'. These included putting an extra floor in the Great Hall to make the dining room, and replacing the mullioned windows on the entrance front and on three sides of the courtyard with sashes.

When William's widow died in 1792, the ownership of Cadhay passed to Admiral Graves. Two years later the Admiral distinguished himself as Lord Howe's second-in-command in the battle of the 'Glorious First of

June' between the British and the French Revolutionary navies. Badly wounded, he fought on gallantly and was rewarded with an Irish peerage. He died at Cadhay in 1802. Shortly afterwards the furniture was sold and the house was divided in two, the dining room ignominiously becoming a farmhouse kitchen with the original fireplace—now restored—accommodating a kitchen range. Cadhay's fortunes were revived in 1910 when it was bought and restored by a Cambridge don, Dampier Whetham, who sold the house twenty-five years later to the family who now live there.

CAPESTHORNE HALL
CHESHIRE

On the main stairs at Capesthorne Hall is a portrait of William Gladstone that could scarcely—if he had heard about it—have pleased the Grand Old Man. A roundel set into the wrought-iron balustrade, it shows the Liberal Prime Minister wearing, not just the famous Gladstone collar, but also a felon's noose round his neck. The picture has some of its origins in plain political rivalry, for the man responsible, William Bromley-Davenport MP, was a fanatical Tory. But the main reference behind this political jest was an older and much grimmer one. The felon with the rope, crest of the Davenports, recalled the family's original power of summary life and death over the Cheshire forests they once ruled in the name of the king.

Both funny and frightening, the Gladstone roundel is an apt symbol of Capesthorne itself. Originally a Georgian replacement of a much earlier building, it was remodelled by the prominent nineteenth-century architect Edward Blore to meet the wishes of a romantically minded Davenport, and the result was amazing. Some of Blore's work was undone by a catastrophic fire in 1861, but fellow-architect Anthony Salvin made good much of the damage in Blore's Jacobean style. With its blackened towers and turrets, Capesthorne today may strike the visitor as splendid, weird,

CAPESTHORNE HALL The portraits on the Main Stairs include the Gladstone roundel and this Luca Giordano self-portrait.

fearsome or possibly wildly comic. What it will not do is leave him or her unmoved.

At the same time, however, it has a pronounced gentler side. There is, for example, the little theatre, built for family theatricals in 1890, and still used for productions. There is, too, the Georgian chapel, a relic of the earlier Capesthorne and, again, still in use. Inside the house, a four-poster bed is hung with the tapestries that Dame Dorothy Davenport spent twenty-six years producing at the start of the Jacobean period; every so often, she would embroider in her initials and the date.

The great glory of Capesthorne, however, is probably the portraits, especially the female ones: Lady Margaret Beaufort in her gable headdress; Augusta Bromley-Davenport in a strawberry-pink robe; Jane Lane who, after the Battle of Worcester, helped Charles II escape. But the most appealing of all is neither a Capesthorne chatelaine nor a royal rescuer, but a young girl: Caroline Davenport-Bromley, dressed in splendour for a Victorian ball.

CARLTON TOWERS
NORTH HUMBERSIDE

Carlton Towers is a manor house with Jacobean origins concealed within a casing of Victorian Gothic extravagance. The manor of Carlton has been in the possession of the steadfastly Catholic Stapleton family since Norman times. The three-storeyed house built early in the seventeenth century is the core of the present building, together with the stables and chapel added a century later. In the nineteenth century the Stapletons successfully laid claim to the barony of Beaumont, which had been dormant since 1507. It was the ninth Baron, the second of the revival, whose building mania and eccentricity are reflected in the exuberant exterior of today's Carlton Towers.

The eccentric Lord Beaumont chose as his architect Edward Pugin, son of the more famous Augustus, and the two men were well matched. Pugin was an argumentative man and though work began in 1873, it was not long before Pugin and Lord Beaumont quarrelled. Pugin left, and was replaced by John Francis Bentley, the ecclesiastical architect who was later to be commissioned to design Westminster Cathedral. It must by now have been clear that the rebuilding at Carlton was running into trouble, but Lord Beaumont soldiered on, running deeper and deeper into debt. Finally even he had to call a halt. The original plan was for a great sweep of state rooms 400-feet (122 metres) long, opened up by a succession of double doors. The effect is impressive enough, even though only half the length was built—but the double doors at the far end of the Picture Gallery are bogus. On the other side of them is a brick wall, marking the point at which the ninth Lord Beaumont had to stop. He died in 1892 from pneumonia, still only in his forties, leaving a heavy burden

BURTON CONSTABLE Scientific instruments and specimens recall the spirit of enquiry developing in the eighteenth century.

of debt behind him which could be relieved only by selling off most of the estate.

What was left was saved by the fortunate marriage of Miles, Henry's brother and the tenth Lord Beaumont, to a rich heiress, Ethel Tempest. She was the daughter of Sir Charles Tempest of Broughton Hall in Yorkshire. Many of the treasures of Carlton Towers—for example, the contents of the Picture Gallery— were brought there by Ethel Tempest. Miles was killed in a shooting accident two years after their marriage. It was their daughter Mona's marriage to Lord Howard of Glossop— their eldest son Miles became the seventeenth Duke of Norfolk—that united two of England's leading Catholic families, the Fitzalan-Howards and the Stapletons, and brought Carlton Towers to the Norfolk family.

One of the relics of the Catholic traditions of the house is the priest's hiding-hole, which formed part of the seventeenth-century structure. These were common in Catholic households, where a priest might need to be concealed in a hurry. The hiding-hole at Carlton Towers is exceptionally large, and cleverly disguised between two floors, the entrance being through a trap-door in the false floor of a cupboard beside the fireplace of one of the bedrooms.

CASTLE HOWARD

NORTH YORKSHIRE

In 1693, catastrophe gave Charles Howard, third Earl of Carlisle, the greatest chance of his life. Newly succeeded to the earldom—his father had died only the year before—he had been made Lord Lieutenant of Cumberland and Westmorland at the same time, and was acting Earl Marshal of England. As a leading public figure, he now needed a domestic setting that matched his achievements and aspirations. And, at just this point, fire completely gutted his Yorkshire possession of Henderskelfe Castle. The building with which he replaced it was Castle Howard: one of the greatest houses in Britain, itself housing one of the country's

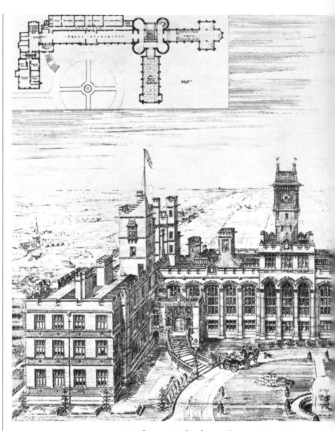

CARLTON TOWERS *What might have been: Pugin's scheme for Carlton Towers. Argument and debt cut it short.*

great private art collections and now, as the main setting for television's *Brideshead Revisited*, celebrated throughout the world.

Awe-inspiring as it appears today, Castle Howard reduced those who saw it while it was new to something like stupefaction. 'Nobody had informed me', wrote eighteenth-century politician and author Horace Walpole, 'that at one view I should see a palace, a town, a fortified city, temples on high places, woods worthy of being each a metropolis of the Druids, the noblest lawn in the world fenced by half the horizon, and a mausoleum that would tempt one to be buried alive.' While this was an age that favoured elaborate compliments, Walpole summed up in a phrase that cannot be bettered for simplicity: 'I have seen gigantic palaces before, but never a sublime one.'

At first, Lord Carlisle's glorious creation

looks symmetrical: a central block, topped by the dome that is the building's most famous feature, and flanked on each side by a projecting wing. The impression, however, is deceptive: the two wings are in fact strikingly different in size and design. Castle Howard as it appears today is the work of more than one generation of earls, and it was the fourth of the line who, in the 1750s, added the west wing to the still unfinished building. It was also the fourth Earl who, with a collection of ancient Egyptian and Roman statuary, laid the foundations of Castle Howard's art treasury. But he was soon outdone by his son Frederick, who succeeded to the earldom at the age of ten and held it until his death 67 years later.

In early life, Frederick was a man of fashion and a gambler (frequently a reckless one); later, he became a statesman of vision and skill. He went everywhere, knew everyone; he was also an impassioned devotee of the beautiful, the noteworthy and the curious. Castle Howard consequently contains—for example—the fifth Earl's portrait by Reynolds; the 'Salome' by Rubens, which had been in Reynolds' own collection; a plaster cast of the Dying Gaul, picked up by the Earl for £25; and—perhaps the most extraordinary item of all—the Greek altar from behind which the Delphi Oracle had given her cryptic pronouncements. This was given to Frederick by fellow-collector Sir William Hamilton, husband of Emma. Earlier, it had been snatched from the clutches of the French at Naples by Emma's lover, the illustrious Lord Nelson.

All through the house, Howard possessions bear eloquent witness to centuries of family activities and tastes. The contents range from portraits by Holbein and Gainsborough to a child's high chair by Chippendale; from the silver-gilt tankard of the first Earl, presented to him by the king of Sweden, to the wheelbarrows used by the seventh—then Lord Lieutenant of Ireland—for cutting the first sods for new Irish railway ventures. In the Antique Passage, the black basalt figure of an Egyptian king kneels in stately homage; in the Stable Block beyond the west wing, thousands of historical costumes are displayed, in settings of the periods they first graced. The costume collection is, in fact, the largest British one in private hands, and is constantly being enlarged; the traditions started by Frederick and his father are therefore set to continue into the twenty-first century.

CASTLE HOWARD The picture-collecting fifth Earl, arranging the Long Gallery with his son, by Yorkshire artist John Jackson.

CAWDOR CASTLE Lady Caroline Howard, of Castle Howard. She became the wife of John, the first Baron Cawdor and nineteenth holder of the ancient Thanedom of Cawdor.

CAWDOR CASTLE

HIGHLAND

At the heart of Cawdor Castle, in what was once the dungeon, stands a bare, gnarled stake. It appears to grow out of the floor itself and, indeed, once did. It is the Cawdor Thorn Tree. In other cultures, this venerable object might well have become the house's totem; here, however, it performs a more important function still.

Thanks to Shakespeare, the ancient title of Thane—or baron—of Cawdor has won international renown, and it was one of the earliest Cawdor thanes that laid Cawdor Castle's foundations. According to legend, directions for choosing the site came to him in a dream. He should, the dream instructed him, load a donkey with gold and let it wander in the area of his choice; where it lay down to rest in the evening, there should he build his house. After browsing its way through the day, the laden animal finally settled for the night by the trunk of a scrubby thorn. The thane—possibly cursing his luck—refused to cut the tree down, but instead constructed the ground floor of his new dwelling round it.

At this point, the story used to end; however, a sequel has now been added. Using modern scientific techniques, the wood of the Cawdor Thorn has been dated to 1372; a result that accords with the long-held theory that Cawdor's oldest portion dates from around the 1370s. As so often happens, at the centre of a myth lies a grain of truth.

It was the third Thane of Cawdor—William—who started the construction of the central tower house. The Macbeth of both Shakespeare and history lived during the eleventh century rather than the fourteenth, so the link between Cawdor and King Duncan's death also belongs in the realm of myth. But Shakespeare, when he chose a medieval castle as the setting for his drama of regicide and guilt, was choosing surroundings of a type that would be familiar to audiences of his own period. In the world's imagination, therefore,

Cawdor, quintessence of a Scottish fortress home, is forever the scene where Macbeth slays his lord.

Shadowed by the dizzying walls, or descending the tight spiral of the stairway to the dungeon, the visitor has indeed no difficulty in sensing the violence that once surrounded the family. The fourth Thane of Cawdor, for instance, was murdered. So with the eleventh. The ninth—a little girl called Muriel—was branded by her nurse on the hip with a red-hot key; if she were to be kidnapped, the nurse hoped, the mark would aid recognition.

However, Cawdor is a home as well as a fortress and, interwoven with memories of distant feuding, it displays many of the elements of ordinary domestic life. Cawdor's amenities include both a small 'bottle dungeon' (possibly a concealed room for hiding ransomed prisoners) and a grand bedroom with Venetian bed and velvet hangings. The building that boasts battlements and murder holes is hung inside with family portraits: among them is a picture of Emma Hamilton, a friend of the nineteenth Thane and his wife.

Most evocative of all, perhaps, is Cawdor's 'old kitchen', first used in the seventeenth century. Then, as now, people had to eat; they wanted their beds warmed and their clothes pressed. The old kitchen's contents include flat irons and a warming pan, pots and pans and earthenware dishes, a churn for making butter, and a bucket yoke for carrying the milk for it. Technology may change; but the needs of a family, never.

CHALCOT HOUSE

WILTSHIRE

The heads of noble families in the past had three main objectives in building their country seats: they needed more room for their increasingly large families, the result of medical advances which meant a bigger survival factor for mothers and young children; they wanted to make a mark of their prosperity on their estates; and they wanted to leave

CHALCOT HOUSE A late eighteenth-century Bavarian painted bed, its headboard richly decorated with sacred and profane images.

something of significance behind them. Many would no doubt have been appalled to know that, so far from being a blessing, many of those large houses were to become an embarrassment to their descendants. What do you do with quarters built for a dozen living-in servants when you're lucky if you can persuade a cleaner to come in twice a week? And what about the damp, the dry rot, the vast expanse of roof needing regular upkeep?

Chalcot House near Westbury is a case in point. Its history reflects perfectly the temptations of fashion over the centuries, and, ultimately, the twentieth-century impracticality of a great house of the past. It began life as a medieval manor, of which a few beams still survive in the roof. Around 1680 it was given a Palladian front. Two centuries later there was a vast enlargement to suit the large staffs kept in Victorian times, the scale of entertaining indulged in by country-house owners, and the necessary accoutrements of shooting. Within a hundred years all this had become not only obsolete but also impossible to maintain, and when the present owners moved in to Chalcot in 1971 they had to decide how much of the house should be saved.

What went was a large proportion of the Victorian additions, but not the earlier gold-and-white ballroom. The result is a house with its essential qualities retained and yet adapted to the needs of the present day. Chalcot was deservedly given a European Architectural Heritage Year award in 1975 for this successful solution to an all-too-common problem.

CHAMBERCOMBE MANOR

DEVON

Concealed in its deep, wooded valley, Chambercombe Manor is itself a house of concealments. It contains no less than three hiding places of the type that, even singly, have made many larger houses famous. Smugglers' passage, priest's hole, hidden chamber: Chambercombe has them all, with overtones of a crime worse than smuggling.

The mysteries cling closest to the hidden room—discovered, it appears, in the early nineteenth century when an occupier was mending the old manor-house's roof. Noticing the outline of a blocked-in window, he discovered that there was no room indoors which this could once have lit. Further detective work brought another, much more gruesome, discovery. Between two of the manor's bedrooms there was another, now sealed up. In it stood the remains of a bed, once a good one. And on the bed lay a woman's skeleton.

Who was she? In October 1865, the weekly magazine *Leisure Hour* published a story which purported to reveal that she had been a lady of quality who, on her way to visit relatives at Chambercombe, was wrecked on the Hele rocks nearby. She was rescued, brought to the manor . . . and murdered? However she met her end, the corpse lying on its fair bed was stripped of all its jewels, and the room where it lay was walled up. Not surprisingly, Chambercombe has a reputation for being haunted.

The room next to the secret chamber also has a ghost, but one that haunts the memory rather than the living present. It was once the bedroom of Lady Jane Grey, the sixteen-year-old who, as a remote connection of the royal house of Tudor, was put on the throne of England by her scheming family in 1553. She reigned for only nine days, and was later executed.

Her father was Marquess of Dorset, and Chambercombe had come to him from his mother. The earliest recorded owners of the manor itself were the Champernons of Ilfracombe, who were in possession shortly after the Norman Conquest. In the fifteenth century, Champernon descendants built the oldest part of today's manor and worshipped in its tiny private chapel, 10 feet by 6 feet (3 metres by 1·8 metres).

CHAMBERCOMBE MANOR Lady Jane Grey's room, now called the Elizabethan Room after the magnificent oak bed that dominates it.

The Greys would have worshipped there, too, but they did not remain in possession long. Although Lady Jane's father—by then Duke of Suffolk—was pardoned for his role in the Lady Jane plot, he speedily became involved in a further attempted coup against Mary Tudor, and was beheaded in the same month as his daughter.

Today, the Grey family's arms still ornament the chimneypiece of Lady Jane's former room: a memory of a life tragically destroyed by the politics of her elders.

CHATSWORTH
DERBYSHIRE

At Chatsworth, 'Palace of the Peak', there lies in the Chapel Passage a fragment of classical art that arrests attention through its simplicity. It is half of a gigantic stone foot, the left one. Six times life size and shod in a delicately wrought sandal, it comes from a statue created by a Greek sculptor around the beginning of the Christian era. Its right-hand twin now lies in a museum in East Berlin.

Elsewhere in the corridor, the scale of the exhibits is reversed, from mammoth to miniature. At child's-eye level in a show cabinet stands a collection of tiny furniture: mirrors, a spinning wheel, chairs, a harpsichord, even a minute coach. They are all made in filigree silver.

Micro-carriage and giant's foot, Lilliput and Brobdingnag: contrasts of this sort appear time and time again at Chatsworth and contain at least part of the key to the depth of the impression made by the Derbyshire home of the Dukes of Devonshire. The house is so huge, so magnificent; its details are so neat, so beguiling, so finely worked.

Up, for example, from the first floor to the second climbs the Great Stair with its gilded balustrade by Jean Tijou; underneath it is tucked a child's small goat-cart, decorated with wriggling snakes like the one in the Devonshire family crest, and dating from only a little later. Again, Chatsworth's suite for grand visitors, the State Apartments, is riotously decorated by Verrio and Laguerre, the same artists who were responsible for the wall-paintings at Burghley. But a door of the State Music Room, though it also employs the *trompe-l'oeil* technique they favoured, uses it to a different end. It shows, not some scene of mythological tumult, but a violin: a violin with its bow, hanging quietly from a knob on the woodwork until its owner retrieves it. The deception of the eye is total. As today's Duchess of Devonshire comments, it is hard not to reach out to see whether or not it's real.

The 'violin door' is, in fact, an import from the Devonshire's London home on Piccadilly (now demolished). But Chatsworth's baroque muralists were not without a sense of humour of their own. In the State Dining Room, Verrio's ceiling displays—among others—the figure of Atropos, the Fate who cuts the thread of life with her shears. The artist has given her the face of his patron's housekeeper, with whom he did not get on. The lady's name was Mrs Hacket and she, like Verrio himself, was employed by the first Duke of Devonshire: William Cavendish, Chatsworth's main creator. He was not, however, the only one, nor indeed the first. That distinction goes to Britain's Grand Old Lady of mansion building, Bess of Hardwick. The first house on the Chatsworth site was constructed in the middle of the sixteenth century by Bess and the second of her four husbands, Sir William Cavendish.

CHATSWORTH Designed by William Kent, this baby-carriage is decorated with snakes inspired by the Devonshire family crest.

An embroidered portrait of her creation shows a three-storey, battlemented building with square towers at the corners and curious triangular ones either side of the main entrance. As well as being a home to the Cavendishes, it featured on the dismal list of houses that served as prisons to Mary Queen of Scots: the fourth of Bess's husbands, the Earl of Shrewsbury, was appointed the Scottish Queen's official gaoler.

Mary's prison has been totally swallowed up by the building operations of Bess's great-great-grandson, the first Duke. Succeeding in the 1680s to what was then only an Earldom, this William started almost at once to update his country home. He also turned it into a prison on his own account. Fined £30,000 for brawling, he refused to pay and, when King James II sent a company of soldiers to arrest him, he promptly rounded them up and clapped them under lock and key.

James—who, as a Catholic, took a suspicious view of the firmly Protestant Earl—summoned William to London; pleading his building works, William politely refused. And, indeed, the work went ahead: down came the Elizabethan south front, and up went the palatial new one with its roofline of urns and balustrades. But the Earl was not so busy that he could not find time in 1688 to help hatch the plot to oust James and bring the Protestant William of Orange to Britain.

The plot succeeded; Earl William was rewarded by a Dukedom; and the building operations went on . . . and on . . . and on. By the time he died in 1707, the Duke had rebuilt the entire house, turned a hill into a large rectangular pond, and tamed the surrounding Derbyshire wilderness into an imposing sequence of walks, avenues, parterres, and mazes large and small.

William's garden was not to last. But, rather than scaling down their predecessor's efforts, two future dukes responded to the challenge. In the mid-eighteenth century, the fourth Duke tackled the grounds' now out-dated formality. With the help of Capability Brown, he abolished the parterres, planned the

CHATSWORTH The Painted Hall. The fireplace inscription describes (in Latin) how the sixth Duke of Devonshire inherited 'this most beautiful house' in 1811.

park, altered the course of the River Derwent, and pulled down part of the nearby village of Edensor which got in the way.

In the nineteenth century, the sixth Duke surpassed him: with the help of Joseph Paxton, the Chatsworth grounds became one of the great botanic gardens of the day. Paxton's Great Conservatory, dry run for his later Crystal Palace, has, alas, been a victim of time. However, another achievement of the Devonshire–Paxton partnership is still going strong: the Emperor Fountain, with its jet of over 280 feet. In true Chatsworth style, it was made by draining a whole moorland area into a special reservoir. Also in Chatsworth style, its plume of water is one of the highest in Europe.

CHAVENAGE
GLOUCESTERSHIRE

Everyone who becomes Lord of Chavenage has a dramatic experience in store, though he does not live to tell the tale. The story goes that every Lord of Chavenage who dies in the house is carried away in a coach drawn by a black horse and driven by a headless man in the robes of the Order of the Garter. As the coach passes through the gateway it explodes in flames.

The story goes back over 300 years to the Civil War. At that time, Chavenage was owned by the staunchly Parliamentary

CHAVENAGE *The room occupied by General Sir Henry Ireton, Cromwell's second-in-command, on his visit in 1648.*

Stephens family, who were related by marriage to Oliver Cromwell. The house was used from time to time by Cromwell, and in the winter of 1648, with Charles I in captivity, Cromwell and his second-in-command, Henry Ireton, came to Chavenage to seek Stephens's support for the King's impeachment. They were apparently unsuccessful the first time, but returned later and obtained Stephens's agreement.

On hearing the news, his daughter Abigail was horrified and cried out that the house where such a deed had been planned would be cursed for ever. The black coach is the curse, and its headless driver is, of course, Charles I.

The rooms where Cromwell and Ireton are said to have stayed are preserved with their original early-seventeenth-century tapestries and a number of Civil War mementoes, including Charles I's death mask.

Chavenage has another, less gruesome, legend, also set in the Civil War. It seems that a young lady of the house—perhaps Abigail Stephens—was in love with a Royalist Berkeley of Beverston Castle, less than two miles (three kilometres) away. It was safe to meet

only when there were no Parliamentarians at Chavenage; and so the girl would place a candle in a window to indicate that it was safe for her lover to call. The window concerned in this tale is the small oblong one the right-hand side of the porch leading to the garden.

At the time of the Civil War, the present house was less than a century old. The Stephens family, prosperous wool-farmers, had bought it in 1564. Their prosperity began to run out with the decline of the West Country wool industry, and by the nineteenth century the house was empty and heavily mortgaged. Despite this, many of the features of its earlier history are intact, including the tapestries and some of the bedroom furniture. Chavenage was bought by the Lowsley Williams family in 1894, and the ballroom, with its sprung maple floor, is an Edwardian addition.

CHENIES MANOR HOUSE
BUCKINGHAMSHIRE

It was the sixteenth-century courtier John Russell who saw in Chenies Manor House the key to his own advancement. He came into ownership by marriage, and turned a semi-fortified manor house into a place fit for kings and queens, their families and their courts, to visit. It is a house designed for intrigue, whether political or amorous: there are numerous hidden passages, hidey-holes, chimney-rooms and escape tunnels.

John Russell devoted his life to the service of the court and was repaid for his dedication first with a peerage and later with higher honours, laying the foundation for the revival, a century later, of the Dukedom of Bedford. He joined the royal household in 1523, and three years later he married a widow who brought him Chenies as her dowry. (Later, she also saved his life: when he got malaria in 1538, she dosed him with what was probably quinine—the first time it was used in England.) Almost at once he set about restoring and converting the house for the use he had in mind for it. Three centuries before, in the reign of Edward I, the place had been a royal hunting lodge. Very well: Russell would make it fit for royalty again.

Henry VIII, Russell's patron, became a frequent visitor to the restored house, and was so impressed with the builders' work that he commissioned them to go on to Hampton Court. Perhaps the most significant of Henry's visits was in 1541, when his party included his fifth wife, Catherine Howard, and, among a retinue of courtiers, Catherine's cousin Thomas Culpeper. Culpeper had been Catherine's lover before her royal marriage, and they had kept up the relationship since. As it happened, the King was unwell; an ulcerated leg made it

CHENIES MANOR HOUSE Tudor exuberance expressed in the ornamental chimneys, rivalling those of Hampton Court.

difficult for him to move about.

By this time Henry was nearing the end of his life—he was fifty—and his more rumbustious days were over. Control of both his personal and political life was beginning to slip away. Catherine and Thomas Culpeper took

full advantge of the situation, and it is said that the halting footsteps of the lame Henry are sometimes heard on the stair and gallery leading to the room where Catherine was lodged. It may have been on this occasion that Archbishop Cranmer's informers gathered their evidence of Catherine's adultery. At any rate, it was only months later that Culpeper was executed, followed shortly by Catherine herself.

The royal quarters had further adventures in store. Elizabeth I was to become a frequent visitor, often accompanied by her chief minister William Cecil, Lord Burghley, the founding father of the Salisbury dynasty. The room in which Queen Elizabeth is thought to have held court is oak-floored, with contemporary tapestries and furniture. Her state bedroom is now a billiard room, where Russell family portraits look down on the green baize.

Shortly after Elizabeth's death, Chenies entered a period of decline. There were no more royal parties. The Long Gallery was used as a barrack for Parliamentary troops during the Civil War. Later, Francis Russell, the fourth Earl of Bedford, concentrated the family interests in Bedfordshire. There, he built a splendid new house on the former site of Woburn Abbey. Although Chenies remained the burial-place of the Russells, as it still is, the Manor House was let as a farmhouse and suffered neglect. Horace Walpole, visiting it round about 1750, described it as being 'in piteous fragments'. About the same time, a surveyor's report recommended demolition.

Fortunately, the surveyor's draconian solution was not followed, and although some of the more decayed parts, including most of the domestic offices, were taken down, the Gatehouse and Henry VIII wing were restored. In 1830 the sixth Duke of Bedford allowed the parish of Chenies to use the Long Room as a meeting-place, a function it continued to carry on regularly until the 1960s and which it still fulfils from time to time. It is pleasant to think of the villagers of Chenies meeting and dancing in the room where kings and queens of England were entertained.

CHICHELEY HALL

BUCKINGHAMSHIRE

Standing square at the end of its great sweep of lawn, Chicheley Hall is a house that teases the mind with a sense of the familiar. Red and white and approached by its ruler-straight path, it calls up images from a distant personal past. It is a house from a child's book; a house from a sampler.

On close acquaintance, its teasing quality deepens. Chicheley is also a house full of tricks. There's a staircase with alternating treads, and a library that masquerades as a plain panelled room (the clue is to look for the hinges on the panels). Outside, high up on the corners, there are four silent watchers, whose stone gaze meets yours with a shock when you finally spot them. Poised to leap outwards and downwards, they are four stone rams, emblems

of the Chester family, Chicheley's builders. And, indeed, the whole entrance front they help guard is something of a hoax: seen from the air, the house is not quite the shape its boldly-curving cornice implies.

So Chicheley, far from being familiar, is in fact highly unorthodox: horrendously so in the eyes of family friend Burrell Massingberd, who made a site visit in 1722, when the house was near completion. Its construction was mainly directed by Warwick architect Francis Smith, but Burrell, who admired the then developing Palladian style, was keen to offer advice. Chicheley's owner, sportsman and courtier Sir John Chester, appears to have gone along with his friend for a while. But then, in Burrell's absence, he rebelled. He liked his door-frames elaborate and ornate: flamboyant echoes of the baroque style used by the great secular and ecclesiastical princes of Italy. By the time his adviser realized this, it was too late. 'So when', as poor Burrell told his wife, 'I came to Chicheley I was so fretted to see such havoc made in the architecture, especially in the garden front, which was at first all laid out by my direction, that if Sir John had been home when I first saw it, I should not have foreborne the rudeness of exposing all the faults to the utmost.'

Happily, Sir John did not come back until his friend's hurt feelings had cooled. But, all the same, Burrell's ideas on style did not go unheeded. As a result, Chicheley springs another of its refined jokes as soon as the visitor walks through its Vatican-inspired front door. Instantly, the impression of doll's-house crossed with Italian palace is eclipsed; one is standing in the cool, calm elegance of a Palladian hall, adorned with marble columns and hung with family portraits.

One of these shows a young man in naval uniform—and it is here that Chicheley stages what is perhaps its biggest surprise of all. This British red-brick mansion, situated almost as far inland as you can go, is in fact filled with memories of one of the island's greatest naval heroes: the first Earl Beatty, a rear-admiral while still in his thirties and hero of the Battle of Jutland. In 1952, the house was bought by his son; today, one of its panelled rooms is given over to the first Earl's possessions (including the flag flown at Jutland by his ship, HMS *Lion*).

Even here, however, Chicheley's humorous and quirky builder manages to make his now remote presence felt. The walls are all panelled in oak—except one. This, of inferior wood, has been carefully painted and grained to look like its fellows. As the family who now live there ask: 'Was Sir John running out of money, or simply testing his powers of observation?'

....

CHIDDINGSTONE CASTLE

KENT

....

Arrows, spears, and the armour of Japanese warlords; samurai swords, and the clay guardians of ancient Japanese tombs; the largest collection of Japanese lacquer shown in the west. . . The repository of these triumphs of oriental art and technology is in Kent, close to Hever, and takes the unlikely form of a Gothic-revival castle, with turrets, towers, battlements and an imposing gatehouse.

Nor do the contents of Chiddingstone stop at memories of the shoguns. They also include a huge collection of Royal Stuart relics, and another of Egyptian antiquities that features—

CHIDDINGSTONE CASTLE Denys Bower found this extremely rare Italian jewel box in an antique shop in a Welsh seaside town.

among much else—a probable portrait bust of Queen Cleopatra. Chiddingstone is not one cornucopia of the past, but three. The astonishing thing is that one man alone was responsible for filling them.

Denys Bower was not a man of Kent, nor yet a country-house owner. He came from Derbyshire, where his family worked on the staff of the former London Midland & Scottish Railway. In his spare time, his father collected Chinese porcelain. On emerging from grammar school in 1922, Denys went to work as a bank clerk and remained behind his bank counter for the next twenty years. In his mind, however, he roved much further afield.

He had inherited both his father's passion for antiques and his interest in oriental art. He now spent every penny he could save on collecting objects that pleased him. He was anything but well-off; but fortune favoured him, especially as far as the Japanese collection was concerned. The great flood of *objets d'art* that came to the west after the Meiji Restoration of 1868 had lost its fashionable appeal, and prices were low.

Meanwhile, Denys also gave full rein to a long-felt passion for the Royal Stuarts, and a newer one—acquired in the wake of the Tutankhamun discoveries—for the artefacts of Ancient Egypt. He collected bronzes of Egyptian gods, and Lely's nude portrait of Nell Gwynne; stone vases 6,000 years old, and the drinking vessel used by Bonnie Prince Charlie when he met Flora MacDonald; the Cleopatra bust, and broadswords wielded in the '45.

In 1942 Denys left the bank to sink himself totally in his life's work. He came to London and set up as an antiques dealer. In the 1950s, the neo-Gothic castle at Chiddingstone came on the market, and he bought it. When he died in 1977, he left a unique personal museum, displayed in the domestic setting that suits such a collection best.

Today, Denys Bower's beloved possessions and the building that houses them are managed by a trust. Their late owner, the executors comment, was 'probably the most remarkable English eccentric since Beckford'. Without doubt, he was also the only one to achieve so much in circumstances that—on the face of it—were so discouraging.

CHILLINGHAM CASTLE

NORTHUMBERLAND

The heavily fortified appearance of Chillingham Castle is not make-believe. Several times in its 700-year history the owners of the Castle have had to defend themselves, and twice it has fallen to the besieging enemy.

There was already a tower house at Chillingham in the thirteenth century, and this was extended in the fourteenth to include the existing south-west tower and part of the curtain walling. It was necessary in those days to obtain a royal licence to add fortifications to a house, but the de Heton family, then owners of Chillingham Castle and veterans of the Crusades, had no difficulty in this respect. Chillingham was vulnerable enough to raids from across the nearby Scottish border to justify strong defences.

By 1348 Chillingham was a castle in the traditional form, with a tower at each corner, a central courtyard, and a Great Hall which occupied the east side. Two centuries later, it had an opportunity to prove its worth. Following the Dissolution of the Monasteries, the so-called Pilgrimage of Grace was organized in the north of England. The plan was to march on London with priests at the head of the column bearing crosses and holy pictures. The effective master of Chillingham Castle at this time was Sir Robert Ellerker, who was guardian to the young heir to the estate. He refused to join the rebels led by Robert Aske, and Chillingham was put under siege. There was some damage to the north curtain wall and towers before the rebels moved on to Doncaster, where they were met by the royal forces and their protest was defused.

The damage was quickly repaired, and then, in Elizabethan times, there was extensive reconstruction work, followed by more in the eighteenth and nineteenth centuries. However, for about fifty years after 1933 the Castle was unoccupied and lay neglected until it was bought, and is now being restored, by the present owner.

CHILLINGTON HALL

STAFFORDSHIRE

There are families whose names crop up time and again in footnotes to English history, and the Giffards, who have owned Chillington Hall for over 800 years, are among them. Three Giffard brothers, Walter, Osborne and Berenger, came from Normandy in 1066 with William the Conqueror, and it was not long before the family was established, with manors in Wiltshire, Warwickshire

CHILLINGTON HALL The Saloon, part of Sir John Soane's work when he was engaged to redesign the Hall in grander style.

(Chillington was at that time a Warwickshire manor) and elsewhere. It remained close to court life and political intrigue for 500 years.

At the Reformation, the Giffard family remained true to the Roman Catholic faith, and this led them into trouble with Queen Elizabeth. Staying at Chillington in August 1575 on her way to Stafford, she found that John Giffard, then head of the family, was not going to the parish church. He was summoned to explain himself to the Privy Council, and fines and a period of imprisonment followed.

The Giffards followed the Catholic custom of the time and sent a younger son, Gilbert, to France to be trained for the Jesuit priesthood. He returned in December 1585 with the intention of acting as go-between on behalf of Mary Queen of Scots and her supporters in France. However, Gilbert Giffard was arrested and 'turned', agreeing to work for Queen Elizabeth's private secretary, Sir Francis Walsingham. Walsingham sent Giffard to Staf-

fordshire; in her long progress round the country from one house to another, in the care of nobles loyal to Elizabeth, Mary was being moved from Tutbury to Chartley. There is not much to be said for the behaviour of any of the participants in this phase of English history, except for that of the wretched Mary herself, and Gilbert Giffard found himself intercepting Mary's correspondence. His discoveries, which included details of Spanish plans for the invasion of Britain and of Anthony Babington's plot to murder Elizabeth, provided part of the evidence when Mary came to trial in the autumn of 1586. As Swinburne wrote of this period: 'Traitor was played off against traitor, and spies were utilized against assassins, with as little scruple as could be required or expected in the diplomacy of the time.' On 7 February 1587 Mary went to the block at Fotheringhay Castle, but this did not make the world safe for Gilbert Giffard. He fled to France, and died sometime later in prison. Spies are rarely rewarded for their pains. Ironically, Chillington Hall had been considered, but rejected, as a possible house of confinement for Mary.

The Giffards played a significant part, too, in the Restoration, helping, with the Pendrell family, the escape and subsequent protection of Charles II in 1651. It was at Boscobel House, two miles away, that Charles found shelter in the 'Royal Oak'.

All these excitements were over before the building of the present Chillington Hall began. In 1724 Peter Giffard launched on the task of converting the Tudor mansion to a country house more in keeping with the status of a country-gentleman's family of the eighteenth century. The work was carried on by his grandson, Thomas, who commissioned Sir John Soane, architect of many country houses and of the Bank of England, to design what is now the main portion of the house, with its impressive portico. Soane's interior style is seen at its most typical in the clerestory-roofed Saloon. Chillington Hall, in architecture and furnishings, is unmistakably an eighteenth-century house, with only the stones within the walls to whisper of its more rackety earlier life.

CHILLINGHAM CASTLE *The two handsome marble chimney-pieces in the Great Hall were rescued from Wanstead House in Essex, which was demolished in 1822, and incorporated in the restoration.*

COMBE SYDENHAM HALL

SOMERSET

The exploits of Sir Francis Drake have exerted a powerful influence on the imagination of the West Country ever since his death off the West Indies in 1596. He was only about fifty years of age, and it is perhaps the sense of 'unfinished business', combined with the fact that he died far away from the area so closely associated with him, that accounts for the number of legends that have grown up around his name.

The best known of these stories is about 'Drake's Drum', which is said to be heard by the citizens of Plymouth whenever England is in mortal danger. Another concerns Combe Sydenham Hall and 'Drake's Cannonball', a meteorite weighing over 100 pounds (45 kilogrammes) which can be seen in the Great Hall. In 1583, after the death of his first wife, Drake came to Combe Sydenham to court Elizabeth Sydenham, a former maid-of-honour at Court. Sir George, however, rejected Sir Francis as a suitable match for his daughter.

Undeterred, Sir Francis persuaded Elizabeth to agree to wait for him, and returned to Plymouth and the sea.

He was away for more than a year, during which time Elizabeth agreed to marry someone else. On the day of the wedding, as the guests assembled, the story goes that there was a flash of lightning and 'Drake's Cannonball' hurtled from the sky to land at Elizabeth's feet. She declared it to be a warning shot fired by Drake, and refused to go ahead with the wedding. When Drake next came to Combe Sydenham, in 1585, it was to marry Elizabeth. In between Drake's adventures at sea, they had eleven years of happy marriage until Sir Francis died in the West Indies, in 1596.

The Hall today is a remnant, the west wing, of the house built by Sir George Sydenham, Elizabeth's father, in 1580 and substantially rebuilt in 1660 though with some parts, such as the porch and entrance hall, virtually unaltered. The estate passed out of the hands of the Sydenham family after the seventeenth century and went through a period of decline, including some years when it was used as a wool store. Its fortunes revived when it was bought by the present owners in 1964.

CORSHAM COURT

WILTSHIRE

The pride and glory of Corsham Court is its collection of fine art and furniture, carefully assembled in the eighteenth century by Sir Paul Methuen, extended by inheritance in the nineteenth century, and zealously preserved and guarded since by the Methuen family. The

CORSHAM COURT From the collection in the Cabinet room, Fra Filippo Lippi's Annunciation, *painted c.1463 for the Cathedral Church of Pistoia. On the left is the donor, Jacopo Bellucci.*

setting for these masterpieces is itself magnificent, thanks to the architects Capability Brown and Robert Adam. Further extensions by John Nash, begun in 1800, unfortunately had to be abandoned because of problems with damp, and some fifty years later the architect Thomas Bellamy completed the house as it is today. The eighteenth- and nineteenth-century additions were skilfully grafted on to the E-shaped Elizabethan house of Cotswold stone, built in the 1580s for Thomas Smythe, a London haberdasher and Collector of Customs.

The Methuens were of Scottish descent, and one branch of the family had a long history of service in the Diplomatic Corps. It was a member of this branch, Sir Paul Methuen, who built up a substantial collection of pictures and art objects over a lifetime in the diplomatic service. He did not marry, and on his death his collection was inherited by his cousin and godson, also christened Paul. This Paul's side of the family had made a fortune in the West Country wool industry and had strengthened

its position by marrying into another Wiltshire wool dynasty. In 1745, in anticipation of his inheritance, Paul Methuen bought Corsham Court and began to plan its reconstruction as a display gallery. He inherited the Methuen collection in 1757, and three years later Capability Brown began work. In 1844 a descendant of Paul Methuen married the only daughter of the Reverend John Sanford, another noted art connoisseur, and his bequest was in due course added to the Corsham collection.

The result is one of the most important collections in England still in private hands, and the fact that it has been preserved intact through the social, political and fiscal upheavals of this century is a tribute to the determination of the Methuen family. With its crimson silk hangings, its fine furniture, its marble fireplaces and mahogany doors and architraves, the suite of State Rooms is an incomparable setting for the art treasures.

DALEMAIN

CUMBRIA

At Dalemain in Cumbria, the Georgian period is represented, not by one house, but two. And, of the pair, it is the smaller that has the more impeccably eighteenth-century pedigree, for its larger fellow demonstrates a typical country-house mix of construction dates and styles: eighteenth-century façade, Elizabethan interiors, medieval great hall, Norman pele tower.

Dalemain's smaller Georgian structure is very much smaller indeed: a 'babyhouse', or dolls' house, it stands against the wall in the big house's nursery, in company with such other children's delights as a rocking horse and Dinky cars. Built at some point in the 1740s, it contains its original eighteenth-century fixtures and fittings: a four-poster bed with exquisitely turned posts, a dining table, and pewter pots and pans in the kitchen. Its first owners were the children of Dalemain's Georgian improver, Edward ('Blackcap') Hasell; its

COMBE SYDENHAM HALL 'Drake's cannonball': the meteorite on the table was said to have been a warning to Drake's future wife.

builder probably the estate carpenter.

Although Edward was chairman of the Carlisle Assize Court at the time of the Scottish rising in 1745, he actually got his grim nickname from a much jollier source. His

DALEMAIN A recruiting poster for the local militia, originally raised in 1819 by the fifth Edward Hasell.

habitual black cap was a landmark on the local hunting field. The house where his great-great-great-great-granddaughter still lives belies expectations in a similarly genial way. As a former defensive building, it has played its part in military and other emergencies: in 1172, for example, one of Thomas à Becket's murderers sheltered there, and the base of the old pele tower now houses a museum dedicated to the Westmorland and Cumberland Yeomanry. But, as tokened by the dolls' house, the true keynotes of Dalemain are tenderness and intimacy.

The nursery is not the only delight hidden behind its austere pink sandstone front. There are curious 'courting chairs', made in the plainest of plain woodwork, but wide enough for two. There is the former housekeeper's room, furnished with the fittings and equip-

ment of eighty years ago. Above all, there is the Chinese Drawing Room, whose bower-like wallpapering was bought by Blackcap and his mother on a visit to London around the time that the dolls' house was being made.

DALMENY HOUSE

LOTHIAN

In the narrow slice of land between the Firth of Forth and the main road from Edinburgh to the Forth Bridge stands one of the greatest treasure-houses in Scotland. Tapestries designed by Goya, portraits by Bronzino and Rembrandt, Captain Cook's sea-chest, Napoleon's desk from St Helena, Marie Antoinette's china model of her pet spaniel—these are only a tiny proportion of the contents of Dalmeny House, home of the Earl of Rosebery.

Given the historical connections between Scotland and France, it is no surprise that many of Dalmeny's treasures are French. But these intimations of the Auld Alliance are to

DALEMAIN Exotic birds perch amongst the flowering trees that decorate the Chinese Drawing Room's handpainted wallpaper.

some extent deceptive, for Dalmeny houses two distinct Aladdin's Caves, and one of these is English: the pick of the French contents of Mentmore: near-fabulous Mentmore, once the home of Baron Meyer de Rothschild and of his only child Hannah. It was Hannah who, on her marriage to the fifth Earl of Rosebery, brought Mentmore into the Earl's family and with it her father's dazzling collections.

Before the great Mentmore sale of 1977, the present Earl and his family reviewed the Baron's treasure chest, then selected the best of the eighteenth-century French collections. As displayed in the Drawing Room at Dalmeny, their choice embraced tapestries, furniture, porcelain and carpets—including a Savonnerie rug, initialled MTL, which may have been the royal throne rug of the *Roi Soleil* and of Maria Theresa, his wife.

Although so many of the French items at Dalmeny arrived there via the Rothschild connection, there is one important group that did not. Hannah's husband Archibald, the future Liberal Prime Minister (1894–5), combined political skills with outstanding scholarship and a passionate interest in Napoleon. In addition to writing a biography of the Emperor, he devoted much care and effort to collecting items connected with Napoleon's life. Dalmeny's Napoleon Room contains the results.

On the walls, paintings and prints celebrate the great commander's military engagements—Lodi, Marengo, the bombardment of Madrid—and the women in his life: Josephine, Marie Louise of Austria, and Madame Mère (his mother). In a corner there is the imperial shaving stand, with an ornate portrait of its owner in ormulu. Close by is a much plainer, but more august, piece of furniture: the straight-backed wooden chair that Napoleon used as his seat of state in his days as First Consul.

At the end of the room, the focus changes from glory to regrets. Here is Napoleon's desk from Longwood, his home-in-exile in St Helena, two of the Longwood chairs and a louvred screen. And, facing the First Consul's

seat is another whose presence symbolizes the very moments of Napoleon's ultimate downfall. A comfortable object in red leather, it is the campaign chair that the Duke of Wellington used at the Battle of Waterloo.

DEENE PARK

NORTHAMPTONSHIRE

Deene Park has been in the Brudenell family for over 400 years, but two figures stand out arrestingly in its history. In 1837—the same year that Queen Victoria came to the throne—the house was inherited by the seventh Earl of Cardigan. He was then forty and already had a tempestuous life behind him. He had risen rapidly in the army since he joined it in 1824, but although he evidently pleased those responsible for promotion he did not endear himself to his officers or his men. Within two years of his appointment as

DALMENY HOUSE The victor of Lodi: the young Napoleon Bonaparte, painted by Appiani, greets the Recording Angel.

DEENE PARK Lord Cardigan tells Prince Albert and the royal children about his Crimean exploits. It is said that Queen Victoria ordered that she should be painted out.

Colonel of Hussars he arrested over 700 men, 105 of whom were court-martialled. A man of choleric temper, he came close to ruin when he was tried by his peers for shooting a fellow officer in a duel. Surviving this, he went on to become in 1854 the hero of the Charge of the Light Brigade at Balaclava, and although history has delivered a sour verdict on this engagement there is no doubt of Cardigan's heroism, pig-headed though it may have been. There are many relics of Balaclava at Deene Park, including a painting by de Prades of the seventh Earl leading the Charge, a presentation sword to mark the occasion, and the stuffed head of his charger, Ronald.

The seventh Earl by no means faded from the public gaze after the Crimean War, though his reputation turned in a different direction. An inveterate womanizer, he turned from his failed marriage and openly lived with Adeline de Horsey, twenty-seven years younger than himself, eventually marrying her in 1858 when his first wife died. Cardigan's exploits with Adeline and others are said to have so distressed Queen Victoria that she ordered her royal figure to be removed from a painting by James Sant, now in the White Hall at Deene Park, showing Cardigan telling the royal family of his Crimean adventures.

Cardigan died in 1868, but Adeline de Horsey, amazingly, lived on at Deene Park until 1915, when she died aged ninety-one. No doubt in the earlier period of her widow-hood she made good use of the secluded octagonal summerhouse the seventh Earl had built in the gardens for his own amorous purposes; even during her ten-year marriage, she was never particularly faithful. Her

DITCHINGHAM HALL *The main staircase, guarded by a stuffed specimen of the famous Chartley herd, bred since the thirteenth century. The breed is descended from the wild cattle of Staffordshire.*

behaviour, together with her eccentricities of dress, her enthusiasm for the bicycle, and the blonde wig she adopted in her later years, kept her out of society circles, but this seems to have caused her no regrets. The pictures of her at Deene Park in her younger days, and the plaster head of her with Cardigan in the White Hall, show that, as far as beauty went, she had nothing to regret.

DETILLENS
SURREY

Detillens stands in the centre of Limpsfield village, apparently a Georgian house such as might have been owned by a prosperous professional man. This is a case where appearances are deceptive, however. Behind the Georgian front, dating from about 1725, is a hall house of the traditional Weald type, built in the fifteenth century and still with most of its original timbers.

Originally, the basis of this type of house was a great hall which extended from the ground floor to the roof. In the centre would be a hearth with holes in the roof above to carry away the smoke. A later style replaced the hearth fire with braziers or baskets of burning fuel, and at Detillens a hook for this purpose can still be seen in the roof timbers. The present central chimney dates from the early sixteenth century. Some time in the same century the hall was divided to make the principal bedroom above, where the tie beam and crown post can be seen. The survival of the original beams for over 550 years is attributed to the smoke from the central fire.

The unusual name of the house is derived from one of its owners, James Detillen, of French Huguenot descent, who bought it in 1773. By this time the present façade had been in place for some fifty years. Detillens has been fortunate in having had a succession of sympathetic owners, as a result of which details of the original construction can still be seen, down to the marks of fifteenth-century carpenters on some of the timbers.

DETILLENS The Georgian front, concealing behind its prim exterior a Wealden hall house dating from the fifteenth century.

The contents include two collections of particular interest. One is of paintings by the eccentric 'cat' artist Louis Wain, who was born in 1860. In 1884 the *Illustrated London News* published the first of the pictures that were to make him, as a *Punch* critic wrote, 'the Hogarth of cat life'. He went on to become famous through a series of illustrated annuals and the postcards he produced for Raphael Tuck.

The second collection is of British and foreign Orders and Decorations. This includes, in addition to examples of Orders which are still awarded, such as the Order of the British Empire and the Order of the Bath, such exotic decorations as the Order of the Golden Fleece of Austria and Spain and the Order of the Doranee Empire of Afghanistan. The latter is a great rarity, since only twenty-four were ever awarded.

DITCHINGHAM HALL
SUFFOLK

At the foot of the main staircase at Ditchingham Hall, an impressive and unusual host welcomes visitors. It is a stuffed Chartley bull which has found its resting-place far from its ancestral home in Staffordshire. In this respect, it echoes the experience of the Ferrers family, breeders of the Chartley herd since 1248 and now the owners of the Ditchingham estate. The Chartley herd was bred from the wild cattle of the Ferrers' Staffordshire domain, and remained with the family until 1905, when it was sold. In 1970, it was bought back by the present Earl Ferrers and now flourishes at Ditchingham. Similarly, the Ferrers family, who came to Britain with the Conqueror, have come at last, after many vicissitudes, to Suffolk. Along the way, they founded a Cluniac priory at Tutbury on the Staffordshire/Derbyshire border, saw their castles at Tutbury and Duffield razed to the ground in 1173 as a punishment for challenging the king, forfeited all their property to the Crown a century later, picked themselves up again and, on their Leicestershire estate, erected the only chapel built during the Commonwealth.

This chapel was in the park of the last of the Ferrers houses, at Staunton Harold near Ashby-de-la-Zouch. Staunton Harold Hall was sold in 1954, but its 'Golden Gates' now grace the grounds at Ditchingham. They are, like the Chartley bull, among many echoes of Ferrers family history to be seen here. The Queen Anne house also contains, for example, a huge parchment, 13 feet long by 6 feet wide, known as the 'Lesser Shirley Pedigree'. Emblazoned with 18 bust portraits and 374 heraldic shields, it was compiled in 1627 by the then Clarenceux King of Arms. The Shirleys had acquired the Ferrers estates by marriage, and it was Sir Robert Shirley, an ardent Royalist, who built Staunton Harold chapel. Challenging this heraldic record in scale is a Van der Vaart portrait over 10 feet square showing the first Earl Ferrers—today's Lord Ferrers is the thirteenth—and his family. (It was, in fact, the thirteenth Countess who introduced the Ferrers to Ditchingham. Built in 1711, it had been the home of her own family, the Carrs from Yorkshire, who bought the estate last century.) But nothing, surely, is so surprising, or in a strange way so evocative of the past of a great landed family, as the prize beast that stands sentinel at the foot of the Ditchingham stairs.

DODDINGTON HALL
LINCOLNSHIRE

Externally, Doddington Hall is an Elizabethan manor house straight from the history books, with its perfectly symmetrical front elevation of local brick and stone mullions crowned by three cupolas. It is the more remarkable for its location in the flat Lincolnshire countryside, which seems to accentuate its importance.

The Hall was built in the closing years of the sixteenth century for Thomas Tailor, who was Registrar to the Bishop of Lincoln. Its architect was the celebrated Robert Smythson, designer of the greatest Elizabethan prodigy houses, Longleat, Hardwick and Wollaton. Smythson's hallmark was the celebration of prosperity and internal security under Elizabeth I. Unlike country houses built in the defensive mood of earlier times, Doddington faces the outside world with confidence.

Passing by marriage to the Hussey family and eventually to the Northumberland-based Delavals, Doddington—which by all accounts was not as comfortable internally as its exterior suggested—went through a period of neglect from which it was rescued by Sir John Delaval in 1760. Among the features of Sir John's restoration work are the magnificent main staircase and, remarkably and two hundred years ahead of its time, a system of double-glazing to try to keep out Doddington's infamous draughts.

The Delavals were a picturesque family well suited to the extravagant lifestyle of the Georgian period. They ran their own London theatre and production company and went in for lavish parties where extravagant practical jokes were played. In the end, however, they were ruined by gambling and litigation, a typical example being the family feud over the inheritance of Doddington. This led to Sir John chopping down all the trees on the estate in revenge for having, as he thought, lost it to his younger brothers. In fact, the quarrel was patched up, and Sir John, later Lord Delaval,

DODDINGTON HALL Robert Smythson's east front faces the world in a celebration of Elizabethan prosperity. The graceful symmetry of the present Georgian rooms comes as something of a surprise.

spent the rest of his life at Doddington, no doubt regretting his haste with the axe.

Doddington left the ownership of the Delavals in 1825 with the death of Sarah, an only daughter. She had married a Dover man, James Gunman, but had an affair with the commandant of Dover Castle, George Jarvis. Sarah died young of consumption in 1825, leaving Doddington to George Jarvis, and he enjoyed the estate for a further twenty-five years. Perhaps unusually for a soldier, George Jarvis was an artist of merit, and his pictures and wood-carvings are in the Print Room on the ground floor of the north turret. It is not without irony that among the other paintings at Doddington Hall is a collection of naval scenes which came to the house from the other man in Sarah Delaval's life, James Gunman.

DORFOLD HALL

CHESHIRE

What draws visitors to Dorfold Hall is a ceiling—the ceiling of what was the Great Chamber. It dates from the original Jacobean house started by Ralph Wilbraham in 1616, and, apart from its beautiful execution and present condition, it is of interest as being precisely of its moment in history.

In March 1603, James VI of Scotland acceded to the throne of England as James I, and it seemed for a time as if the union of the two kingdoms could finally be achieved. As we now know, it was a false dawn, and it was to be another century before union was officially pronounced, with consequences that led to a further fifty years of conflict in Scotland. But the ceiling at Dorfold was created in the first flush of enthusiasm for James I, embodying as it does the emblems of the Tudor rose, the thistle and the fleur-de-lys. It is a truly amazing piece of work, one of the finest Jacobean ceilings in England.

The Wilbrahams were prominent Cheshire lawyers, and after five generations Dorfold Hall passed into the ownership of another lawyer, James Tomkinson. He employed Samuel Wyatt to make alterations to the ground floor and also to design new interiors for some of the rooms. The next stage in the development of the house came in the

DORFOLD HALL The barrel-vaulted ceiling of the Drawing Room, a fine example of exuberant Jacobean plasterwork.

nineteenth century, when an east wing (now largely demolished) was added to accommodate hunt servants and guests. About the same period, the gardens were laid out by William Nesfield, the royal adviser on landscaping.

DORNEY COURT

BERKSHIRE

Thanks to the dictates of status and fashion, many of Britain's historic homes look much newer than they really are. But, though both grand and fashionable, the Palmers of Dorney Court successfully resisted most urges to remodel their house and, as a result, Dorney looks just what it is: a rose-pink, timbered manor house, topped with a roofline full of quirks and surprises, and bathed in an atmosphere of antiquity. It was built, in fact, around 1440.

Inside, it's the same story. The date carved on Dorney's kingpin is 1510, and the plan of the rooms has scarcely changed since. At its heart is the Great Hall, where the Lord of Dorney Manor would eat his meals on the dais, and where manorial justice would be dispensed.

At one end of the Hall, in medieval fashion, arches lead through a wooden screen to the kitchen, cellars and pantry; at the other lies the Parlour with, above it, the Great Chamber (now the main bedroom). Even the earliest Palmer—Sir James, who came to Dorney during the reign of Elizabeth I—would still be able to find his way around the home of his descendants.

Although the historical interest of Dorney as a building is rooted in the early years of the Tudors, its interest as a home starts later, in the period of the Stuarts. After the Civil War, Roger Palmer risked his life in attempts to bring back Charles II from exile; with the Restoration, Charles rewarded him with the Irish Earldom of Castlemaine.

One practical effect of the relationship between the new King and the new Earl was the introduction of pineapple culture to England. Charles, eating one that had been brought from Barbados, gave its fronded, spiky top to the new Earl. Roger—so tradition relates—had it planted at Dorney. It grew; a fruit was proudly presented to the king, and thereafter the pineapple became the unofficial badge of the period.

Roger's wife, however, was even closer to the king than her husband, for she was the alluring Barbara Villiers, future Duchess of Cleveland and royal mistress for over ten years. Charles used to meet her at Dorney and she bore him several children. Was her first child also his? The truth is not certain, although Charles himself said so. The subject of the disagreement is shown, stiff in her ruffled sleeves and apron, in a portrait in Dorney's Parlour: Lady Anne Palmer, aged—perhaps—six.

DRUMLANRIG CASTLE

DUMFRIES & GALLOWAY

Drumlanrig Castle, with its fairy-tale skyline ornamented with shining lead domes, is a Scottish palace of hearts. Everywhere, outside and in, the heart motif reappears, surmounted by a crown. Modern visitors might guess at a tale of long-dead lovers or—knowing that the Young Pretender stayed here during the '45—surmise that the hearts are an emotional memorial to the Jacobite cause.

However, the love here commemorated is much older, and of a more austere nature.

When, in the High Middle Ages, the Scottish noble Sir James Douglas departed with his contemporaries for the Crusades, he took more with him than his panoply of war and a militant soul. He had also been entrusted with a sacred duty: that of bearing with him the heart of Scotland's great hero, King Robert the Bruce. The King, a good friend of the Douglas family, had died without fulfilling his deepest desire of fighting for the Cross against Islam. Now Sir James—known as 'the good Douglas'—was helping his lord to make the journey posthumously.

The loyal exercise, however, was fatal to Sir James himself. In battle against the Moors in Spain, he was mortally wounded. But, even in his last moments, he still managed to keep faith both with his dead lord and his good nature. With the cry 'Forward, brave heart!', he flung the relic in its silver casket ahead of him towards the Saracen army. From then on, the Douglas motto was 'Forwards', while the Douglas badge became a crowned heart, flanked by two spreading wings. It is this crowned and winged heart, emblem of an ancient loyalty, that appears throughout Drumlanrig—carved on stone, wrought in iron, stamped on leather, gilded and half-concealed in the frame of a mirror.

The Douglas family owed its lands in Nithsdale to the goodwill of the Bruce and, over the century that followed his death, they built themselves a castle there. Today's Drumlanrig is built on top of this earlier building and according to the same medieval ground-plan: a plain rectangle round a courtyard. It was the work of William Douglas, soon to become the first Duke of Queensberry and one of the ablest men in Scotland during the late seventeenth century.

In public life, William was his country's Lord High Treasurer; however, the figures

DORNEY COURT The whole household would have gathered to eat in the Great Hall: family on the raised dais at the far end, retainers in the body of the hall.

DUNROBIN CASTLE Portraits in the Queen's Corridor include a sixteenth-century Irish chieftain, painted by Michael Wright.

involved in his house-building operations were astronomical enough to give qualms even to his capable spirit. His misgivings were so severe, indeed, that he wrote a dreadful warning on the cover of his accounts: 'The Deil pike out his een wha looks herein.' ('May the Devil pick out the eyes of anyone who looks in this.')

Over the next century, his ducal inheritance became merged with two others that were equally noble, those of Buccleuch and Montagu, and the contents of Drumlanrig today bear witness to the wealth of all three strands in its history. Art treasures, furniture, porcelain, needlework (some reputedly by Mary Queen of Scots), an enormous silver chandelier weighing 196 pounds: they make a dazzling collection. The greatest treasure of all, however, does not dazzle; instead, it glows with the quiet light reflected off a book on to a woman's white collar. Even amongst Drumlanrig's wealth of beauty, Rembrandt's quiet portrait of an old woman reading reigns supreme.

DUNROBIN CASTLE
HIGHLAND

When viewing great houses in their groomed perfection, it is easy to forget that—like small ones—they still have to be managed in day-to-day fashion. Even in the past, when they were tended by huge staffs, they needed a considerable amount of machinery to make them work as places in which to live. Dunrobin Castle demonstrates just how considerable was that amount.

Lamps, fire buckets and gas heaters; paraffin stoves and copper cans for the gentlemen's shaving water; kitchenware and early carpet sweepers: surveyed by the glass eyes of stags shot in the neighbourhood, all are today in the Castle's Sub-Hall. Most resplendent of these memorials to unremitting labour is the estate's red fire-engine: steam-powered, fitted out in gleaming brass, and with the house's name picked out in gold on the side. Fire, however, has played an uncomfortably large part in remodelling Scotland's northernmost great house, for in 1915 a disastrous blaze wrecked the huge French-style chateau that Sir Charles Barry had created for the Duke of Sutherland the century before. Nevertheless, it spared the older parts of the Castle round which Barry's additions had been built, and the damage itself was later made good. As a result, today's Dunrobin is a castle built up piece by piece between the thirteenth and twentieth centuries. It is, in fact, one of the oldest houses in Britain to have been continuously lived in throughout its history.

Venerable though part of the Castle is, the rank of its occupying family dates back further still. The Earldom of Sutherland was created in

DRUMLANRIG CASTLE One of Rembrandt's greatest works: 'An Old Woman Reading', which hangs in the Staircase Hall.

about 1235, which makes it among Scotland's oldest. The Castle, however, does not receive a recorded mention in history until 1401, by which time four earls had come and gone, and a son of the fifth's—by a daughter of King Robert the Bruce—had just missed the chance of founding Scotland's ruling dynasty instead of the Stuarts. (Nominated the heir to the kingdom, he died of plague before he could ascend the throne.)

The Sutherland Earldom, unlike many others, can pass through the female as well as the male line and from the sixteenth century onwards women played an important part in Dunrobin's history. The ninth Earl, for example, was incapable of running his estates, so his sister Elizabeth ran them for him. When he died in 1514, she inherited his title, though not without considerable (and bloody) opposition.

Celebrated as she was in her day, the fame of the first Sutherland countess in her own right has been eclipsed by that of the second. Also called Elizabeth, the nineteenth holder of the Earldom succeeded to the title in 1766 when she was not merely a child but an eleven-month-old baby. Oblivious to the renewed wranglings to which her succession gave rise, the tiny heiress grew up to marry the hugely wealthy English landowner George Granville Leveson-Gower, Marquess of Stafford and future first Duke of Sutherland (Elizabeth would be known as the Duchess-Countess.) The match made the Marquess richer still, but it also brought a reputation that, among many Scots, remains notorious to this day. It was Lord Stafford's plans to update his vast Scottish estates that linked his name for ever to the harrowing events of the Highland Clearances.

After his death, both Sutherland titles passed on down a line of five dukes. But then, in 1963, the Dukedom passed sideways to a male relative, and a Miss Sutherland-Leveson-Gower, niece of the fifth Duke, found herself the twenty-fourth holder of the Sutherland Earldom: newly separated from the senior title and, as always, transmissible through the female line. Like both her lady–lord predecessors, she too is called Elizabeth.

DUNVEGAN CASTLE The Dunvegan Cup, given with their thanks by the O'Neills of Ulster to Chief Rory Mor MacLeod.

DUNVEGAN CASTLE

HIGHLAND

'With this banner, I can never be defeated in battle.' Even after nine centuries, the words of the great Norseman Harald Hardrada still blaze with hope. He was describing his most prized possession, captured on a raid in the Middle East and, in Nordic style, given a formal identity of its own: Landöda, or 'Land Ravager'.

Significantly, it had not been unloaded from his ship when, in 1066, he invaded England and met his death at the Battle of Stamford Bridge. After this disaster, the wonder-working fabric vanished from sight . . . and then, just possibly, reappeared. Is Land Ravager now the Fairy Flag of Skye's Dunvegan Castle?

From the super-heroics of the Norsemen to the fairy host and other mysteries of the Celts seems at first a far cry. But, at the time of

Harald's death, the two cultures were closely intertwined in the Western Isles, and men from the Hebrides were among those who escaped from Stamford Bridge. Did they take their leader's famed totem—his banner—with them? It seems possible. As to what happened, or might have happened next, accounts differ.

Dunvegan Castle enters known history in the thirteenth century, as a curtain-wall fortress of a Norse prince called Liotr, or Leod. Although he lived at the very end of Norse dynastic rule in the Hebrides, Leod was starting a dynasty of his own that continues to the present day: for over 700 years, the Chiefs of MacLeod—or sons of Leod—have led their clan from their rocky stronghold on Skye's north-western corner.

This long occupancy has given the castle a special role as a clan treasure house. Alongside MacLeod portraits, books, hunting trophies and weaponry, Dunvegan contains such precious items as the pipes of the MacCrimmons, hereditary pipers to the Chief, and the Drinking Horn of Chief Rory Mor, the vessel which each Chief's heir must drain dry on coming of age. (It holds a bottle and a half of claret.) It also contains the Dunvegan Cup; of wood mounted in filigree silver, this was given to Rory Mor in the sixteenth century by the O'Neills of Ulster, whom Rory supported in a rising against the English.

But, even amongst these treasures, the Fairy Flag rules supreme as the clan's most valuable relic. According to one legend, it came to Dunvegan Castle through the agency of a MacLeod who joined the Crusades. On his travels in the Holy Land, the clansman had to cross a mountain pass guarded by a she-devil. Called the Daughter of Thunder, she was a famed slayer of Christians; however, armed with advice from a friendly hermit, the crusader faced his adversary and triumphed over her. Before dying, the generous spirit gave him her girdle and told him to make a banner out of it for his clan.

A variant on the story has the Highlander being given the flag by a Saracen fairy. 'If danger threatens the clan,' she told him, 'wave this banner. It will bring an army to your aid.' Either way, the clansman carefully brought the supernatural present back across Europe to Skye and his chief's castle.

It is anyone's guess as to what truth lies behind these and other legends about the origin of the Fairy Banner. Do they point to re-emergence—always through the agency of a woman—of Harald Hardrada's Landöda from the obscurity in which, somewhere in the Isles, it had laid for so long? The few facts known fit the theory. The fabric has been dated to between AD 300 and 600, well before Hardrada's time. And its silk definitely comes from a Middle Eastern source, possibly Syrian.

Does it bring victory in battle? In the fifteenth century, and again in the sixteenth a sorely pressed Macleod of MacLeod waved it on the battlefield—and won. Much later, in 1939, the Chief's home and its many treasures were in desperate danger from a major fire. But, when the Flag was rushed out of Dunvegan to safety, the flames died down. And, in the years following, MacLeod pilots flying over wartime Europe would carry the Banner's picture in their cockpits as a modern-day amulet. For them, too, its message was: 'With this banner, I can never be defeated in battle.'

EARLSHALL CASTLE
TAYSIDE

'I despise with the mind what I adorn with the hand.' Thus, in austere vein, Sir William Bruce, owner of Earlshall Castle in the seventeenth century, and the man responsible for the painted ceiling in its Long Gallery. But why Sir William should have felt so ambivalent about his great work is open to question. At the time it was painted, its mixture of ornament and moral principle would have been seen as eminently worthy; today, it is an amazement and a delight.

Right down its length, it is densely patterned with an array of the ideas—spiritual and secular—that the owner thought important. The Seven Virtues are all illustrated; so are the coats-of-arms of Scotland's ruling class. And so are improving maxims such as 'A Nice Wyf And A Back Doore Oft Maketh A Rich Man Poore'.

Against the world-weary cynicism of this, however, Sir William juxtaposed the symbol of his own, much happier, experience: the 'lynkit hearts' motif that commemorated his love for his second wife, Dame Agnes Lindsay, and that is still used throughout the Earlshall estate. And, running in and out of it all, are the ceiling's main occupants: its menagerie of painted animals, real and imaginary. The elephant, the lion, and the 'Ram of Arabia'; the pelican, the ostrich, and the 'drumadarie' (with three humps). . . all parade and cavort their way down the Long Gallery's 50-foot (15-metre) length.

An element of parade is continued at eye-

EARLSHALL CASTLE Over a hundred Scottish basket-hilted swords line the walls of the Long Gallery with its painted ceiling.

level as well, for its walls are lined with the world's biggest collection of Scottish basket-hilted swords: over a hundred of them, with beautifully incised hilts and precision blades made in Germany. Nor is this the Long Gallery's only reminder that Earlshall, with its tower-house structure, was built in violent times. It contains the exit from a secret passage that starts in one of the Castle's main bedrooms, and that allowed the laird to escape if danger threatened.

Not surprisingly, a ghost hovers in the Long Gallery's vicinity: one of several that frequent the Castle. Another—or, at least, something—makes a depression every day in the bed that stands in the room once used by the visiting Mary Queen of Scots. A third takes the form of the footsteps of Sir Andrew ('the Bloody') Bruce, ruthless persecutor of the Covenanters (or Presbyterians).

The first of this trio is a benign presence, on record as having caught a passer-by to prevent her falling. Its main characteristic, however, is a tendency to collect shoes. During a ball given in the Long Gallery during the eighteenth century, a young girl left the gathering and went down a small staircase at the end of the room. The dancers were horrified to hear a sudden shriek; they found the girl halfway down the staircase, sitting in hysterics on one of the steps. Something, she said, had snuffed out her candle, and something had tried to get her shoes off. One of them was indeed missing, and remained elusive.

A century later, workmen restoring the castle under the architect Robert Lorimer opened up a small, hidden recess at the stair's foot—and in it they found one red shoe. The Castle's present owners add: 'It may be coincidence but the youngest daughter of the family, whose bedroom leads off the small stairway, cannot find a pair of her favourite red shoes.'

EASTNOR CASTLE

HEREFORD & WORCESTER

On a boiling hot day in 1821, there took place in Westminster Hall the very last staging of a ceremony that had begun at the crowning of King Richard II. In 1821, it was George IV's turn to stand before his people at his coronation banquet, while his official champion challenged all comers to deny his right to kingship. Both in Richard's time and George's, the King's Champion was a Lincolnshire landowner named Dymoke. And, in keeping with his knightly duty, he was armed *cap-à-pie*, and furnished with a gauntlet to throw down.

EASTNOR CASTLE Heraldic displays, gilding and fan tracery ornament the Gothic Drawing Room, designed for the second Lord Somers by the Victorian architect A. W. Pugin.

George's coronation banquet was something of a fiasco, being wildly disorganized and uncomfortably hot, and both this and the challenge ceremony were discontinued afterwards (though coronations still see the Dymokes playing an official role). But the fluted suit of armour in which the hapless Champion sweltered has survived. It can now be seen at Eastnor Castle, where it shares with a similar suit the distinction of dating from 1520. The probable source of the Champion's suit was the armoury of the Electors of Bavaria, whence it was looted by Napoleon.

Turkish daggers, Scottish broadswords, the remains of an Etruscan helmet (*c.* 440 BC), and over thirty Italian suits of armour from a rather later date: these are just some of the company that the Champion's armour now keeps. The setting for the whole display is an extraordinarily apt one, for Eastnor Castle is one of the biggest and most imposing fortresses to be found in Britain. But, although the military ironwork it contains has seen plenty of warfare, the building itself is—delightfully—a complete fake, and owes its origins to the preoccupation with the Gothic that grew up in the eighteenth century.

Among the Gothic style's admirers during the Regency period was the second Baron Somers: John Cocks, Lord Lieutenant of Herefordshire and the future Viscount Eastnor. The Baron wanted a new house to replace the old-fashioned one he had inherited. Coming from a banking family, he had the money; he also had a romantic mind; and Eastnor became a glorious dream of medieval chivalry, concocted by the architect Robert Smirke. However, the realities of later warfare quickly broke in when, thanks to the demands of the Royal Navy, the builders found they could not get enough timber for the roof trusses. Smirke promptly forsook traditional building methods and pioneered a new one: he had the roof trusses made in cast iron, the first time this was done in Britain. They showed themselves most commendably up to the job and, under their load of battlements, still do.

ECCLESHALL CASTLE

STAFFORDSHIRE

There is an element of farce in the history of Eccleshall Castle. In the summer of 1643 Bishop Wright, Bishop of Lichfield and lord of the manor of Eccleshall, paid for his friendship with Charles I when a Parliamentary force camped at Eccleshall church and besieged the Castle. Sir William Brereton, the Parliamentary commander, blasted the south front of Eccleshall, doing a considerable amount of damage but meeting determined resistance. He withdrew, perhaps to consider new tactics or perhaps as a deliberate bluff. Whatever the reason, the defending Royalists assumed that the danger was over and went into Eccleshall to celebrate. At this point, Brereton's forces returned and were able to take the Castle without difficulty, 'many of the Cavalier defenders', as Eccleshall's current owner says, 'being neither inside nor sober'. The Royalists paid the price: the Castle was plundered and some of its contents thrown into the moat, from which they have only in recent years been recovered. Eccleshall became a prison.

All that was in the last days of the original Castle. After the Restoration a new Bishop of Lichfield, William Lloyd, began a rebuilding programme, retaining some of the Castle walls but planning something altogether more grand. By the eighteenth century Eccleshall had become a bishop's palace worthy of the rich diocese of Lichfield, and looked largely as it does today. During the nineteenth century, Sir Walter Scott was a frequent visitor.

In 1867 the Church of England authorities disposed of Eccleshall Castle, breaking a connection with the diocese of Lichfield which went back to the time of St Chad (*c.* 670). The Castle was eventually bought round about the turn of the present century by George Carter, a Staffordshire brewer, who saw it as the setting for his considerable collections of books, porcelain and furniture. These were begun by his grandfather in the middle of the nineteenth century after he had retired from the family brewing business, and include a complete set of Dickens first editions and first editions of Thackeray, Surtees and Bram Stoker's *Dracula*. At one time the Carters were partners in a Stoke-on-Trent pottery, and this interest is reflected in the collections of Chinese and English porcelain and of items from the now-closed Hope and Carter pottery.

But the family silver is missing. It was lost with the butler and most of the domestic staff when the Humber ferry tragically capsized in 1890.

EDMONDSHAM HOUSE

DORSET

There is a strong Dutch feeling about Edmondsham House which has been preserved with some care. Dutch gables were a feature of the original house, built on a medieval site in the latter half of the sixteenth century. When the outer two wings were added two centuries later they too were given Dutch gables, with the result that, after rendering in the nineteenth century, the façade looks—deceptively—all of one period. Of the

EDMONDSHAM HOUSE The central portion and the outer wings present a united Dutch front, though built 200 years apart.

ECCLESHALL CASTLE This Derby porcelain figure is one of the many fine pieces from George Carter's collection.

interior features, probably the most interesting is the Jacobean main staircase with its adzed balustrade.

Edmondsham has been in the ownership of the same family since it was built, though it has sometimes passed through the female line. Quite early in its history the inheritance had a narrow escape when, in 1629, four-year-old John Tregonwell fell from the roof of Milton Abbey church. He was unhurt, thanks to the voluminous petticoats and skirts which were the normal dress for small boys at the time.

A later Tregonwell, Lewis, set in train a significant piece of regional development when he began the process of changing Bournemouth from a village of a few hundred people to the resort and residential town that it is today.

ELTON HALL

NORTHAMPTONSHIRE

Many country houses owe their architectural interest to the way in which they reflect the taste, self-image and ambitions of succeeding generations. Elton Hall is one such. Having been in the ownership of the Proby family since 1660, it has been much restored, refurbished and remodelled over the centuries. At one period, in the early nineteenth century, it had battlements and turrets made of wood and painted to look like stone, just as if it were a film or stage set. These sham decorations were removed and replaced with classical styling, though on the south front the Gothic effects remain.

The Proby family was prominent in the social and official life of the old county of Huntingdonshire. Indeed, the old county boundary with Cambridgeshire used to run through the middle of the large dining room—a Victorian addition—and so the family could claim that the squire and his wife dined in different counties.

The family's connection with Elton goes back to the sixteenth-century courtier and one-time Lord Mayor of London, Sir Peter Proby, who was granted the manor by Queen Elizabeth I in recognition of his services. It was Sir Peter's grandson Sir Thomas Proby who,

ELTON HALL The State Dining Room where, before county boundaries were altered; some guests dined in Huntingdonshire and others in Cambridgeshire. Today, all are united.

having married into a wealthy local family, built Elton Hall, incorporating the fifteenth-century tower and chapel—now the large drawing room—which dated from an earlier house on the site. The Gothic additions were made between 1812 and 1814, when French prisoners-of-war camping at Norman Cross, near Peterborough, worked on the house. Most of the Gothic effects were removed in another phase of building in the middle of the nineteenth century, and finally between 1868 and 1878 the central tower, a billiard room, a new kitchen and a second stable block were added.

The large drawing room is the finest room in the house and the one that received most attention from successive owners. It was formed from the medieval chapel in about 1760, and the ceiling, with its enriched cornice and frieze, dates from then. The decoration of the walls in the style of a French château was a mid-Victorian addition. There is a revealing tale attached to the unfinished Reynolds portrait of Kitty Fisher, the infamous eighteenth-century courtesan, which now hangs in the drawing room. In Victorian times this was considered unsuitable for family viewing as she offered a poor example of behaviour, and it was banished to the housekeeper's room. The house also contains an outstanding library of about 12,000 volumes, including Henry VIII's prayer book.

EUSTON HALL
NORFOLK

The Dukedom of Grafton was one of six ducal lines which began with the illegitimate sons, by various mistresses, of Charles II. The mother of the first Duke of Grafton was Barbara Villiers, Lady Castlemaine, who had five other children by the King. Henry Fitzroy, as he was christened, married Isabella, the daughter and heiress of the Earl of Arlington. Since the death of the Earl in 1685, his country seat at Euston has been the home of the Dukes of Grafton.

The Duchess's inheritance was a house built

ELTON HALL One of a pair of cabinets in the Large Drawing Room, made from a seventeenth-century Japanese lacquer box for Fonthill.

by her father in the 1660s, 'not only capable and roomsome, but very magnificent and commodious' according to the diarist John Evelyn, who visited it shortly after it was completed. Euston Hall also had the distinction of being probably the first to have a pumped water supply, a luxury that soon became *de rigeur* for the fashionable country house. Evelyn described the Euston pump as 'a pretty engine' which took water from the canal in front of the house and, as well as providing a water supply for the house, turned a corn-mill.

The first Duke did not have long to enjoy his acquisition. He died of wounds in Ireland in 1690. When his son came into possession, he commissioned a remodelling of the house, and this was carried out round about 1755. This version of Euston remained substantially unaltered until 1900, when the west and south wings were destroyed by fire. They were

EUSTON HALL The Hall as it looked throughout the nineteenth century. In 1900, fire destroyed the west and south wings. Although rebuilt, these were demolished in 1952.

rebuilt, but in 1952 the rebuilt sections were removed to leave the hall as it stands today.

The most notable feature of Euston is its unrivalled collection of portraits of the leading figures of seventeenth-century court life. Lord Arlington appears in a painting by Lely, as Knight of the Garter; his wife Isabella's portrait is by Gennari, and his daughter, also Isabella, with her son the second Duke, was painted by Kneller. The royal connection is amply represented by a series of portraits from James I onwards, which includes Barbara Villiers posed by Lely with her son, the first Duke, as Madonna and Child.

A portrait in the Inner Hall, of Anne, the first wife of the third Duke, recalls a period when Euston Hall was the centre of society scandal. Then, as now, the personal affairs of those in political life were fair game for rivals, and the third Duke's troubles began in 1763 when he first met Nancy Parsons, a London tailor's daughter who was the veteran of many affairs. Anne, the Duchess, left him and later eloped with the Earl of Upper Ossory. Meanwhile, the Duke, who was Prime Minister at the time, increasingly brought Nancy into the

public eye. She excited criticism by acting as hostess at Euston, but the last straw was her appearance with the Duke at the theatre in the presence of Queen Charlotte. Nancy became the subject of fierce attacks from, among others, Horace Walpole and the anonymous gossip-writer 'Junius', and in 1770 the third Duke was forced to resign from office. Shortly afterwards, Nancy Parsons disappeared from his life and the Duke remarried.

FAIRFAX HOUSE

NORTH YORKSHIRE

Fairfax House is a splendid town house brought back from the brink of destruction. Built in the early 1760s for Viscount Fairfax, and for many years a focal point of York social life, it had by 1981 become appallingly neglected. First a club, then a dance hall, then partly rebuilt as a cinema, it was in danger of collapse when it was rescued by the York Civic Trust. Two years' effort between 1982 and 1984 went into restoring the original interior work (much of which

FAIRFAX HOUSE *The Great Staircase, with wrought-ironwork balusters by Maurice Tobin climbing the cantilevered flight. Busts of Shakespeare and Newton survey the restored scene.*

proved to be intact under layers of paint) and the house is now furnished with the Noel Terry Collection, described by Christie's as one of the best private collections of mid-eighteenth-century furniture formed during the past fifty years.

An eighteenth-century tragedy lies behind the original building of Fairfax House. The ninth and last Viscount Fairfax was married twice: his first wife died within a year of their marriage, and two years later, in 1722, he married a distant cousin, Mary Fairfax. They had three sons and three daughters—all but one of whom died, together with their mother, in an epidemic of smallpox.

The sole surviving child was Anne. She and her father were devout Catholics, and she became engaged to William Constable, scientist, friend of Rousseau and heir to Burton Constable Hall on Humberside. The Constables were one of the old Catholic families, but it seems that William was not as devoted to his religion as Lord Fairfax and his daugher required; perhaps William's friendship with Rousseau is a clue. At any rate, the wedding was called off literally at the last minute in 1755. Perhaps it was Anne's depression brought about by this disappointment that led Lord Fairfax to set up house in York shortly afterwards, at first in rented houses before he bought and refurbished Fairfax House.

The cost was, for those days, enormous, and when the work was done Viscount Fairfax complained to his bank that 'my daughter's house, which is just finished and paid for, drains me of all my money'. This was in the autumn of 1762. His finances were evidently not too severely damaged, however, for by the following spring he could afford 'an elegant entertainment and ball' for more than 200 people. This was ostensibly to celebrate his birthday, but he no doubt hoped that it would provide a possible new consort for his daughter. In this he was unsuccessful, for she died in 1793, unmarried.

The Noel Terry Collection, with which Fairfax House is furnished, was built up by the great-grandson of the founder of the Terry chocolates business, now part of Rowntree Mackintosh. He died in 1980, leaving his extensive collection to the York Civic Trust. Among the items of furniture and pictures is an outstanding collection of clocks in which all the major English makers of the late seventeenth and early eighteenth centuries are represented.

FASQUE Built in 1809, Fasque became the Gladstone family home twenty years later. The essence of Scottish baronial style, it recalls the great, expansive days of Scottish sporting life.

FASQUE

GRAMPIAN

The particular attraction of Fasque is that it is a Scottish family home that has been virtually unchanged since the Gladstone family began to occupy it in 1829. Practically nothing has been thrown out during that time, and everything in the house 'belongs to it'. Even Victorian bathrooms and laundry equipment remain at Fasque.

The house was bought in 1829 by Sir John Gladstone, a Leith man who had travelled to Liverpool as a twenty-two-year-old to seek his fortune—and who had succeeded in making one. He became an important figure in Liverpool business life, with interests in corn supply, ship-owning, insurance and sugar. When he came to Fasque at the age of sixty-five, he brought with him three children: Thomas, then twenty-five; William, twenty and at Oxford; and fifteen-year-old Helen. His eldest son, Robertson, took over the family's Liverpool interests and remained there.

Of the children at Fasque, it was of course William—W.E. Gladstone—who made his mark nationally. His political career was of a length typical of the nineteenth century but which is unlikely to be seen again. He entered the House of Commons in 1832, when he was twenty-two, and eleven years later was a member of Sir Robert Peel's Cabinet. His first period as Prime Minister began in 1868, and his fourth ended with his resignation in 1894 at the age of eighty-four. He was thus a major political figure almost throughout the reign of Queen Victoria, who feared and disliked him.

Fasque was Gladstone's home from 1830 until his marriage in 1839, and he maintained close links with the house until his father died in 1851. After that, his increasing estrangement from high Tory views caused a break with his brother Thomas which was not healed for many years.

There are mementoes of William at Fasque, but the house is seen today substantially as it was in the time of his nephew, Sir John, who

died in 1926, and reflects conditions for residents, guests and staff in a typical Scottish sporting house. Those days virtually vanished after the First World War, but at Fasque their relics are preserved as if in amber.

FAWLEY COURT Polish swords and sabres hang in the Armoury, part of the fortified manor house built in the twelfth century.

FAWLEY COURT

OXFORDSHIRE

Below ground at Fawley Court, in the vaults that belonged to a fortified manor built in troubled times by a Norman knight, hang relics of other conflicts that are far removed in time and place from medieval Oxfordshire. Flags of the First World War, uniforms of the Second, sabres wielded at the Battle of Vienna, when Austria and European Christianity were saved from Islamic attack in 1683 by John III Sobieski, gallant King of Poland: these are what await the visitor to Fawley, now a red-brick mansion set in a

Capability Brown landscape.

Although the house at Fawley—designed by Christopher Wren in the 1680s—is closely contemporary with Sobieski's great victory, the presence of the Vienna mementoes does not date from then. The Polish element provides the key link here, for Fawley Court is owned by the Polish Congregation of Marian Fathers and it is they who have built up Fawley's museum of Polish memorabilia. The military exhibits—many of which were used by the Polish Army, Navy and Air Force in the Second World War—form only part of their display. Elsewhere in the house are maps, paintings, and documents bearing the signatures of the Kings of Poland.

In addition to building up the museum, the Fathers have also in effect created (or recreated) its home. During the Second World War, Fawley was taken over by the British Army. When the Fathers bought it in 1953 it was in a much-decayed state. Now, however, James Wyatt's classical decorations can be admired in all their delicacy, while the glory of the Drawing Room ceiling by Grinling Gibbons—one of only three in the country—matches that of the Polish heroes that the museum commemorates.

FINCHCOCKS
KENT

Finchcocks is a fine example of what can be done to restore the fortunes of a house for which, less than twenty years ago, there seemed no hope. There has been a house on the site since the thirteenth century, and it is named after the original owners, a powerful Kentish family. In 1725 the present house was built for Edward Bathurst, a barrister and kinsman of the Earls of Bathurst. The sky-ward-soaring front elevation is attributed to Thomas Archer.

In its early years the contents of Finchcocks were no less imposing than its exterior, and included paintings by the Italian primitives and by Rubens and Watteau. But everything

was sold off, and after a number of changes of owner it was bought in 1970 by the pianist Richard Burnett, who specializes in the playing of early keyboard instruments. Five years later he reopened Finchcocks as a 'living museum' of some seventy harpsichords, spinets, clavichords, chamber organs and early pianos.

More recently, Finchcocks has been developed as a study and recording centre and as a venue for recitals and concerts of chamber music. The stables have been converted to workshops where early musical instruments are restored and replicas made. Structurally, however, the house remains much as it was in its early Georgian heyday.

FINLAYSTONE HOUSE
STRATHCLYDE

In the autumn of 1555 the Protestant Reformer John Knox returned to his native Scotland on a visit from Geneva, where he had established himself with his wife Margaret. Here, with Calvin and others, he was hammering out the tenets of the new faith. He was seeking the support of the Scottish barons for the end of papal jurisdiction in Scotland, the necessary first step in the creation of the Scottish church. For six months, Knox preached in the homes of sympathetic lairds in the south of the country, and one such was the fifth Earl of Glencairn, whose houses included Finlaystone. On this visit, early in 1556, Knox gave the first Protestant communion in the west of Scotland at Finlaystone. The yew tree in the grounds was planted on that occasion, though it has since been moved from its original position closer to the house.

John Knox was received with enthusiasm in the grand houses of southern Scotland. His message was a flattering one: the lairds were masters in their own houses, and it was for them to say what form of worship they would permit their families and servants to attend in those houses. The result of Knox's six months' tour was the historic Covenant of 1577, when

FINLAYSTONE HOUSE The owner's mother, Frances, in 1904. Both doll and photograph are in the Doll Museum.

the lairds pledged themselves to the Reformation in Scotland. Finlaystone can therefore claim to be among the cradles of the kirk.

It also has a later claim to a part in Scottish culture. James, the fourteenth Earl of Glencairn, was among those who responded to the appeal of Robert Burns's poetry and of his personality, and he became one of Burns's patrons. In 1786 Burns was in despair. His literary ambitions seemed to have come to nothing, and he was working like a slave on the family farm. His proposal of marriage to his future wife, Jean Armour, had been rejected under pressure from Jean's father, and Burns had accepted a book-keeping job in the West Indies and even booked his passage. Then, in June, his first book of verse was published, containing some of what are still regarded as his best poems. At once, the course of his life was changed. His poetry struck a chord in Scotland, then emerging from the trauma of the failed '45 rebellion, and particu-

larly with the lairds. He was sent for from Edinburgh, where he was fêted. Among those who befriended him at this time was the Earl of Glencairn. Burns said later that the Earl had rescued him from wretchedness and from exile; a touch of poetic exaggeration, perhaps, but certainly he dined, and possibly stayed longer, at Finlaystone, scratching his signature on a window-pane to prove it. Burns paid the Earl the tribute—significant in those days—of giving his son James the second Christian name 'Glencairn', and when the fourteenth Earl died in 1792 the poet wrote a long lament for his patron.

Finlaystone left the ownership of the Glencairn family in the mid-nineteenth century and passed into other hands. However, by marriage it has eventually come into the MacMillan family and is now the home of the chief of the Clan MacMillan. It is good to know that a house which has been so close to two of the most vital elements of Scottish culture—the kirk and Rabbie Burns—is still a part of its national roots.

FIRLE PLACE
EAST SUSSEX

The Gage family has owned Firle Place for over 500 years, and both the house and its contents reflect the strength and stability of a family that, with one period of relative obscurity, has remained prosperous and close to the centre of power for most of that time.

The family came out of Gloucestershire to Sussex by way of marriage, and it was Sir John Gage, Governor of Calais and Constable of the Tower of London, who built the Tudor manor house in a style reflecting his high standing at court. He was a favourite of Henry VIII and one of the executors of the King's will. Sir John died in 1556, and Firle—and the Gage family—entered a difficult time owing to their adherence to the Catholic faith. The Gages were regularly fined for non-attendance at church, and during the Cromwellian period they were under constant suspicion.

FINCHCOCKS A grand piano by Clementi, 1821, one of over 70 early keyboard instruments collected at Finchcocks by the owner, pianist Richard Burnett.

With the beginning of the eighteenth century, however, the 'bad times' came to an end, and Sir William Gage, who inherited Firle in 1713, started the rebuilding of the house in the form it retains today. There was a new mood of prosperity in the air. Country society was developing, and in the south-east of England one of the expressions of the new social scene was cricket, which was developed from a vulgar game for ruffians into a suitable pastime for gentlemen. Among the leading Sussex gentlemen involved was Sir William Gage, who is sometimes known as 'the father of county cricket'. In one of the earliest county matches on record, in 1725, he captained the Gentlemen of Sussex against the Gentlemen of Kent, and it was from such regional contests that the national county-cricket network grew. Sir William did not marry, and when he died in 1744 Firle passed to his cousin Thomas, the first Viscount Gage. Records of the rebuilding of Firle have been lost, and it is not clear how much of the work was completed in Sir William's time, and how much by the first Viscount. Basically, the original Tudor house was given a Georgian interior and a formal east front which is the main elevation.

The Gages continued to play a part in affairs of state. The first Viscount's second son, Thomas, went into the army and, after serving in Flanders and at Culloden, was posted to America. He became Governor of Montreal and later of Massachusetts, and the outbreak of the War of Independence found him in command of the British forces. He survived the war and retired to England with his American wife, bringing back paintings, documents and mementoes which came to Firle with Thomas's son Henry, who inherited the title. Except for the Second World War, when it was a military billet, Firle Place has been the home of this branch of the Gage family since that time.

FLOORS CASTLE
BORDERS

Floors Castle, on its site overlooking the Tweed, is the biggest inhabited castle in Scotland. Spreading magnificently on either side of its entrance front, and crowned with a skyline as intricate as Vanbrugh's Castle Howard, it is more of a palace than a castle. Around it stretches countryside that Sir Walter Scott called a 'kingdom for Oberon and Titania'. And within its walls are treasures

FIRLE PLACE *The first Viscount Gage, who completed the remodelling of Firle Place c.1750, looks out on the Downstairs Drawing Room. Below his portrait, a rare fox console attributed to Kent.*

culled from palaces and great houses across the world, from Versailles to China.

Huge Brussels tapestries, Ming dynasty porcelain, paintings by Hogarth, Reynolds, Gainsborough: these are what today's visitor to Floors can admire. But missing from this array is what was once regarded as the jewel in the Castle's crown—the superb library built up by John, third Duke of Roxburghe and the Castle's owner in the second half of the eighteenth century. Its lack is, quite literally, the price Floors had to pay to achieve continuity in the ducal line and, ultimately, the building's palatial size.

The bibliophile third Duke came to his life's ruling passion in default of an earlier and tenderer one. He fell in love with the elder sister of Charlotte of Mecklenburg, wife of King George III, and wanted to marry her. However, the rules of the court laid down that a younger sister should not become the ruler of

FLOORS CASTLE The third Duke of Roxburghe (here painted by Hoppner), who lost a love and gained a magnificent library.

an older one. Sadly, the Duke and his beloved vowed lifelong constancy to each other; neither married, and the Duke devoted himself to his book collection, which grew to include such gems as a Caxton *Histories of Troy* and a first-edition *Decameron*.

When he died in 1804, the dukedom passed briefly to a very aged cousin and, when the latter also died childless, the ducal succession was thrown into confusion. Contenders for the title were plentiful; the House of Lords managed to winnow them down to two, but it took some years and much legal wrangling before the victor finally emerged. He was Sir James Innes of that Ilk, a baronet who could trace his ancestry back to the seventeenth-century founder of the whole Roxburghe line of peers. With the Dukedom, Sir James inherited the plain, box-like building that was Floors Castle, its distinguished contents, and a huge legal bill. To meet it, he staged the saleroom event of the period and sold off the third Duke's library; the *Decameron* alone fetched 2,000 guineas.

Nor was this the only unwelcome surprise the new fifth Duke had for those who still hoped they might one day win the title. That day, they felt, could not be long removed, since James had no children and was now seventy-six. But, to their chagrin, he and his young wife lost little time before producing a son. In 1823, full of achievements and nearly ninety, the old Duke died; the sixth Duke, also called James, was by that time seven. He was no more than fourteen years older when he married, received the first new peerage created by Queen Victoria, and started enlarging his family home. By the time his young sovereign paid him a visit there, Floors had become the palace it is today.

FONMON CASTLE
SOUTH GLAMORGAN

On 12 February 1747, the great preacher John Wesley wrote from Bristol to a widow of his acquaintance, Mary Jones of

Fonmon Castle. The subject was the education of her nine-year-old-son Robert, whom she planned to send to the Wesleys' new school at Kingswood. Something about young Robert had given Wesley the idea that there might be future difficulties. 'You will probably hear Complaints,' his letter to Mrs Jones said, 'for the Discipline is exact: It being our View, not so much to teach Greek and Latin, as to train up soldiers for Jesus Christ.'

Exact the discipline indeed was: a six-day week, and a fifty-two-week year, with the hapless pupils getting up every day at four in the morning. Such complaints as Robert doubtless made have not survived, but actions speak louder than words. He did a bunk.

Wesley's estimate of his reluctant pupil was shrewd, for Robert grew into someone for whom pleasure was a serious business. Dividing his time between Bath and London, he gambled, played tennis, attended the theatre, went to assemblies in fancy dress. A portrait of him by Reynolds shows him at one of these: an extremely handsome man, posing in the gear of a Cossack.

Trained in good taste by family tradition, he also laid the foundations for what would, in effect, be his life's work: appreciating beauty at no matter what cost. Fonmon is his crowning achievement: the conversion of the house—one of the very few extant—from a medieval castle to a rococo mansion.

By Robert's day, the family home had been in existence for over 500 years. Originally a small stone fortress, it had grown to include towers, a courtyard, an extra block at the back. For over a century, it had been in the hands of the descendants of Colonel Philip Jones, Cromwell's adviser on Welsh affairs. While distinction now marked Fonmon's contents, the building itself was more than old-fashioned; parts of it were archaic.

With great architectural tact, Robert and his Bristol-based architects transformed the Castle during the 1760s into a residence fit for a newly wed gentleman of refinement. To create a new hall and staircase, they joined four rooms together; to make a drawing room, they

FONMON CASTLE Collector, gambler and society figure Robert Jones III, here shown in fancy dress by Reynolds.

joined two (in one of which John Wesley had preached). To construct their magnificent first-floor library, they knocked down one wall of the old fortress's medieval hall, added to it, put windows in, and gave master plasterer Thomas Stocking full rein on the new walls and ceiling. The results were and are a triumph of airy, gilded elegance.

Robert did not live all the rest of his life in the lovely house he had made. Financial problems despatched him to a less costly lifestyle abroad; however, he refused to let them get him down. The family friend Wesley, still anxious for his old protégé's welfare, suggested that he should settle in the staid surroundings of Holland, but Robert would have none of it. France, headquarters of taste, was where he wanted to go, and he did. True to form, he enjoyed himself.

FORDE ABBEY
SOMERSET

The first sight of Forde Abbey makes the visitor think of prosperity and tranquillity, and indeed Forde's tranquillity goes back to 1141. In that year the Cistercian Order was offered the site for a new monastery—so that Forde predates the other great Cistercian foundation in the south of England, Beaulieu, by about fifty years.

The building was completed by 1150, with the exception of the now-demolished abbey church, and Forde soon acquired a reputation not only for its wealth but also for its learning. Visitors reported consistently on the Abbey's splendour, magnificence and culture. These qualities came together in the creation of the last Abbot, Thomas Chard, who remodelled the Abbey in the years immediately before the Dissolution. Much of his work remains today, thanks largely to the fact that, rather than see it destroyed, he handed Forde Abbey over to Henry VIII and accepted a local living in return.

For a century after the Dissolution, the Crown tenancies of the Abbey are obscure, but in 1649 it was bought by Edmund Prideaux, Cromwell's attorney-general. Over the remaining ten years of his life, Prideaux refashioned the interior in the Italian style, adapting and enlarging the former Abbot's lodging as his family living quarters, making a grand saloon of the old monks' gallery and adding a grand staircase and state apartments. The lavish effect is seen at its best in the saloon, with its rich plasterwork and Mortlake tapestries representing scenes from the Acts of the Apostles woven (apparently for this specific room) from Raphael's original cartoons for his work at the Sistine Chapel in Rome.

The Abbey remained in the ownership of Prideaux's descendants, whose alterations and additions were relatively minor, until the line died out in 1846 and the house and all its contents were sold. Among the tenants in this period was, from 1815 to 1818, the philosopher Jeremy Bentham, the apostle of utilitarianism and 'the greatest good for the greatest number'. One of Bentham's guests at Forde Abbey was the legal reformer Sir Samuel Romilly, who wrote to a friend of 'the magnificence of the house, quite a palace I should rather call it, for it is much more princely than many mansions which pass by that name'. At the 1846 sale, the house was fortunate, escaping the fate of so many great houses in the nineteenth century. Within a few years it had been bought by the Roper family whose descendants still live there and have recovered some of the contents.

FULBECK HALL
LINCOLNSHIRE

Fulbeck Hall was established by Sir Francis Fane in the eighteenth century and acquired its historical associations during the nineteenth through the personalities of two

FLOORS CASTLE Named views of Dresden decorate this Meissen travelling tea-set, or tête-à-tête, shown in the Gallery.

FONMON CASTLE The Jones family, portrayed by William Hogarth. Robert Jones III's father, Robert II, stands between his sister and his widowed mother.

people: one lived there as a child, and another who planned—in vain, as it turned out—to die there.

Harriet Fane was one of fourteen children of Henry Fane, MP for Lyme Regis in Dorset and holder of the office of Keeper of the King's Private Roads. We meet Harriet first, at Fulbeck, in 1810, when she was seventeen. She is seen in a watercolour at theatricals—the garden scene from *Much Ado About Nothing*—with her older sisters Ann and Caroline. She appears again in a miniature in the Drawing Room, and again, in the Small Dining Room, in wax silhouette.

Harriet Fane was to become Mrs Charles Arbuthnot, but it is her relationship with the Duke of Wellington for which history knows her. By the 1820s the hero of Waterloo had turned to diplomatic and political activity, and

it was in this role that he entered the Arbuthnot circle, and especially Harriet's. She was one of those nineteenth-century women who give the lie to the view that there was no female participation in politics before women had the vote. Harriet combined acute political sensibility with discretion and the ability (as her published journals show) to record and analyze contemporary affairs. Between the mid-1820s and her early death from cholera in the epidemic of 1834, she was one of the most influential women in England. Her widower became the Duke's companion in London until Wellington's death in 1852.

The Duke of Wellington also figures in another of the exhibits at Fulbeck Hall, a letter written in his middle age to another Fane, the Dowager Duchess of Westmorland. The Dowager Duchess's daughter was Lady Georgiana

Fane, whom we have already met at Brympton d'Evercy. When young, Lady Georgiana had rejected, evidently under pressure from her parents, Wellington's offer of marriage, but they continued to correspond for the rest of his life. The letter at Fulbeck was written at a time when Lady Georgiana, who never married, was making a nuisance of herself in connection with their youthful romance; the Duke wrote to her mother in the hope of silencing the gossip.

Our second Fulbeck character is Harriet's elder brother Henry. Henry had served with Wellington in the Peninsular War of 1808–14, and no doubt their friendship as senior officers in that campaign spilled over into their social contacts, bringing Wellington again into the Fane family orbit. Unlike many of his fellow-officers who found, after the Peace of 1815, that their military careers were abruptly cut short, General Sir Henry Fane went on to become, in 1835, Commander-in-Chief in India.

Before long, however, he found himself at odds with government policy over India and, with his health declining, tried to resign. His resignation was refused, but he decided to go anyway. In preparation for his return to England, Fulbeck Hall was modernized. A system of bells was installed, still to be seen on the back landing at the Hall, and there was extensive redecoration including the furnishing of a fashionable 'Tent Room'. Sadly, the General did not live to enjoy his planned retreat. He died at sea on his way from India, predeceasing both his old commander, the Duke, and the kinswoman who might have been the Duchess of Wellington.

FORDE ABBEY A view of the Abbey from the north in 1727, looking, as a later visitor wrote, 'quite a palace . . . much more princely than many mansions which pass by that name'.

FULBECK HALL Mementoes of Sir Henry Fane's service as Commander-in-Chief in India from 1835 to 1840, the last years of his life.

FURSDON HOUSE

DEVON

For over 750 years, there have been Fursdons living at Fursdon House. The first one—Walter de Fursdon—came to his Devon hillside in the mid-thirteenth century. Now David Fursdon represents the family over twenty generations later. Unusually for country-house history, there has always been a male heir to carry on the family name in direct succession.

However, today's David Fursdon (himself the father of three boys) points out that it has on occasion been touch-and-go, with the worst emergencies occurring in the eighteenth century. George Fursdon, who was responsible for giving his home much of its present appearance, had only one son, young George. Surviving all the medical ills that then threatened both children and adults, young George grew up to become High Sheriff of his county, and married a Cornish heiress, Elizabeth Cheyney. They, too, only had one son, who died as a

baby. Then Elizabeth herself died, while still relatively young.

George carried on by himself, bringing up his only daughter, Penelope, until 1770, when he married again. Though only forty-nine, he had almost left it too late. His new wife bore him a son the next year—and, in the following one, he himself died. But the new young George took care of the succession for the foreseeable future by having eight children, three of them male, and seventeen grandchildren.

In spite of the densely packed men on the Fursdon family tree, the fact that there was a Fursdon for them to inherit is probably due to the business sense of a woman. In 1628, the George Fursdon of the day married a local

FURSDON HOUSE The court dress of Elizabeth Fursdon, née Cheyney, who may have worn it for her wedding in 1753.

beauty called Grace Lovell. When he died at Lyme Regis fifteen years later, a Royalist victim of a Civil War engagement, Grace had his body loaded on a cart and brought home. Then she turned herself to the task of keeping the estates together till her eight-year-old son Nicholas should come of age.

The war went on; Charles I—to whom she had lent £20 to further the Royalist cause—was executed at Whitehall; Charles II returned to his Kingdom and repaid the widow Fursdon with a gift of pewter. Through it all, Grace worked on at preserving the Fursdon fortunes and, indeed, augmenting them. After her loan to Charles, she lent money to many other people. The luckless Nicholas reached his majority but, even then, she refused to let go: perhaps wisely, for in 1664 he spent some time in prison. (He had an unpleasant stay there, being—as a contemporary said—'for want of clothes and sustenance . . . forced to live on the charity of others and full of worms'.) Only when Grace died in 1691 could Nicholas start running his own estate; he found that his tough, possessive, clever mother had left him a rich man.

Her portrait by Lely, which hangs in Fursdon's Hall today, shows a woman with the fashionably heavy jaw of the period, beautiful hands, and huge, slightly slanting eyes. It comes as no surprise to hear that her ghost walks abroad on the night of 30 January every year: anniversary of the day her former debtor, King Charles I, met his death.

GAULDEN MANOR
SOMERSET

The plaster work at Gaulden Manor is among the house's most interesting features, and one item in particular, an Elizabethan frieze round the hall, is said to depict the life story of an earlier owner, James Turberville.

The Turbervilles were a West Country family—said to have been the model for the D'Urbervilles of Hardy's *Tess*—who produced, among other distinguished members, the Elizabethan poet George Turberville and James, Bishop of Exeter. Imprisoned for refusing to take the Oath of Supremacy acknowledging Queen Elizabeth I, James spent four years in the Tower of London and a further period under house arrest before being released. These events are symbolically represented in the frieze, which shows the scales of justice, the Tower, and a strongly Catholic image of Virgin and Child. Perhaps not surprisingly after these experiences, ex-Bishop Turberville retreated into an obscure country life, most probably at Gaulden. 'He was', according to a memoir, 'a gentleman born of a good house, very gentle and courteous.'

After the ex-Bishop's death Gaulden Manor was sold to a succession of owners, none of whom stayed long. One of the most interesting of them was Christopher Wolcott. His son Henry, after making an exploratory trip in 1628, emigrated to America with his wife and three children two years later. The Wolcotts settled in New England, and became one of America's leading founding families. Henry's son was a signatory to the Connecticut charter in 1662, and his son, Roger, helped to found the town of Windsor, Connecticut, which had been settled by a group of migrants from

GAULDEN MANOR The ornate sixteenth-century ceiling and plaster frieze, featuring religious scenes, in the Great Hall.

GLAMIS CASTLE The fourteenth Earl and Countess of Strathmore, parents of the Queen Mother, in the Drawing Room. The large picture shows the third Earl.

Dorset. A later Wolcott, Oliver, became state governor in 1817. There is a Society of the Descendants of Henry Wolcott in the United States whose members pay frequent visits to Gaulden Manor, and which presented to the Manor the window in the Turberville Bedroom.

In 1639 Gaulden Manor was bought back again by James Turberville's great-nephew, John, who restored (or perhaps added to) the plaster work. After the mid-eighteenth century the Turberville connection ceased—leaving, so it is said locally, only a few spectral reminders such as the ghostly coach that calls at the front door when a Turberville dies, a grey lady who sits by one of the fireplaces, and sundry knocks and footsteps.

GLAMIS CASTLE

TAYSIDE

Glamis thou art, and Cawdor; and shalt be What thou art promised. Yet do I fear thy nature . . .

Shakespeare gives Glamis and Cawdor to his Macbeth a good two centuries before the rank of thane was created. But Glamis itself was there, even then: a place frequented by royalty, a repository for its dying breaths, a setting for both hospitality and grief.

A royal hunting lodge built on a sacred Celtic site, it was probably no more than a simple stone tower. The walls and ceiling of one of its rooms were the last things seen on earth, not by Macbeth's royal victim, but by his grandfather: in 1034, King Malcolm II of Scotland was wounded at a nearby battle and brought to his former pleasure-house to die. Macbeth was another of Malcolm's grandsons, and both he and Duncan would have been familiar with the royal hunting lodge. When, at the hands of his cousin, King Duncan also met his death in battle, it was perhaps inevitable that some of those who recalled the event should transpose it to Glamis from its real scene at Elgin, much further to the north.

Duncan's murder is, indeed, only one of the legends that Glamis has attracted to itself. Several others concern its famous secret chamber, where the Devil is reputed to have played cards on a Sunday with a Lord of Glamis and his gambling companion, an Earl of Crawford, nicknamed the 'Tiger'. (The psychic energies released by this satanic encounter were so formidable that the room had to be sealed.)

However, by Shakespeare's time, the reality of Glamis was as filled with ancient horror as any legend of regicide would have it. If anything, the reality was actually worse, for the victim of the royal murderer was a totally loyal subject, and the end she met was much worse. The true tragedy of Glamis concerns the widow of John Lyon, sixth Lord Glamis. She was born a member of another great Scottish family, that of Douglas, and so—to her ill-doing—was the second husband of the Scottish Queen, widow of James IV. The old King's son, James V, had in his youth had a hard time at the hands of his stepfather and his followers. Later, James's misery came into a dreadful flowering, for he set himself to persecute the entire clan.

The integrity of the beautiful and much-loved Lady Glamis was beyond question, but

GLYNDE PLACE The first members of the Trevor family, from North Wales, to live at Glynde. The Trevors continued to occupy the house until the line died out in 1824, when the Brands succeeded.

this did not prevent her being swept up in her sovereign's campaign of vengeance. Accused of the twin crimes of witchcraft and plotting to poison the king, she was first incarcerated in a dungeon and then, all but blind, led out on to Edinburgh's Castle Hill to be burnt alive. Her young son was also imprisoned under sentence of death, and her castle was seized by her sovereign and his wife, Mary of Guise.

For five years, this ruthless pair held court at Glamis; an end was only put to their rule by James's death and the succession of his daughter, the infant Mary Queen of Scots. The young Lord Glamis, who had managed to survive, was let out of prison and had his estates restored to him. When he came back to Glamis, he found that James and his wife had stripped it bare.

Although the future never held anything worse than this for the Lyon family, Scotland's violence-ridden history ensured further reverses in their financial fortunes. The ninth Lord Glamis, who was created first Earl of Kinghorne by Mary Stuart's son, was rich enough to rebuild parts of his medieval stronghold; the second one lost all this wealth—and more—during the Civil War. The third, who succeeded in 1646, was left with debts totalling £400,000.

The impoverished new holder of the Kinghorne title (to which the Earldom of Strathmore was later added) was another man who—like James V—had suffered for much of his childhood at the hands of his stepfather. Far from becoming a murderous paranoid, however, he grew up to be a gifted, humorous and totally determined man who, with his wife, finally managed to clear the family of debt. It took him forty years; he managed so admirably, however, that he was able to make major alterations to his home as well. A portrait now hanging in Glamis's Drawing Room shows him in classical garb, pointing with justifiable pride to the collection of towers and turrets he had created. In most essentials, the Glamis he was pointing out is the Glamis we see today.

One thing that the painting does not show

is the Castle's atmosphere. In spite of its grim historical connections, both real and legendary, its rooms breathe hospitality and welcome. It was in these happy surroundings that Her Majesty Queen Elizabeth The Queen Mother spent her childhood, and it is in them, too, that the Bowes-Lyon family lives today, six centuries after one of their number became the first Thane of Glamis.

GLYNDE PLACE
EAST SUSSEX

A bishop of legendary kindliness, a Speaker of the House of Commons who decided that the talking had to stop, and the illegitimate daughter of a prime minister and a scandalous duchess are among the characters associated with Glynde Place.

An Elizabethan manor house on what looks like a perfectly sheltered site, Glynde's apparent cosiness has proved deceptive. Generations of those who have lived there, up to the present century, have complained of the cold, which neither 'turning the house round' so that the front was on the opposite side, nor the search for the latest efficient 'warming apparatus' seemed to cure. This appears to have caused something of an obsession with health. Originally, the main rooms of the house faced north because it was considered that if they faced the Channel, and therefore the Continent, they would be vulnerable to the plague.

In the eighteenth century the threat of smallpox shook the village of Glynde. Glynde Place's owner at that time was Richard Trevor, Bishop of Durham. The Bishop was a kindly man who arranged for a supply of ale from his brewhouse for any labourer or carter toiling up the notorious hill past his house. The story goes that, to protect the villagers from the scourge of smallpox, the Bishop ordered that the population should be isolated, half at a time, in the stable block for six weeks.

After the Bishop's death, Glynde Place passed to the Brand family, which provided it with its most distinguished nineteenth-

GODOLPHIN HOUSE The Godolphin Arabian stallion, one of the founding fathers of the Stud Book of British racing. It was brought from Paris in 1728.

century inhabitants: Henry Brand, first Viscount Hampden, and his wife Eliza. It was Eliza who brought to Glynde the story of the romantic duchess and the future prime minister.

The duchess was the beautiful and talented Georgiana, Duchess of Devonshire. Having had three children by the Duke, she had an affair with Charles Grey, who was already well up the ladder that was to lead eventually to 10 Downing Street. In 1791 she gave birth to a daughter, Eliza, who was brought up as Eliza Courtney by Grey's parents. Eliza's own daughter, known in the family as Eliza Eliza to distinguish her from her mother, became the wife of Henry Brand.

Henry Brand entered Parliament in 1852, and twenty years later became Speaker of the House of Commons. The key political issue during his period as Speaker was Home Rule for Ireland. There were then no rules for ending a debate in the Commons. On a February afternoon in 1881, MPs began a debate on the Irish question which was still going on, after two all-night sittings, on Wednesday morn-

ing. At this point, Speaker Brand decided that enough was enough, and declared that the debate must close. This led to the introduction of rules for the formal closure of debates.

Henry's life at Glynde Place with his Eliza seems to have been particularly happy. There still exists a collection of letters between them written between 1839, the year after their marriage, and 1859. It was Henry, too, who started a journal, which he called 'Glyndiana', in which the everyday doings of the house and estate were recorded. 'Glyndiana' is still kept up by the present Lord and Lady Hampden.

GODINTON PARK
KENT

The story of Godinton Park—built in the Middle Ages and the home of the Toke family for over 400 years—is above all the story of one man, Captain Nicholas Toke. In the seventeenth century, he remodelled his house, set the stamp of his distinctive personality on it and, to ensure that it should be passed to a son of his, married no less than five times. All attempts failed, however; the Captain's line remained a female-only one, and he finally had to leave Godinton to a nephew.

The house acquired by his heir, another Nicholas Toke, was well worth inheriting. At its heart was a fifteenth-century Great Hall, held together by a vast and even older tie beam of local chestnut. Just outside the building was a tree that was more ancient still: an oak that, so local memory maintained, had been there since the Norman Conquest. Captain Nicholas had improved the Hall by adding a ceiling, but his masterpiece of interior decoration lay elsewhere in the house. As his name implied, he had a passion for things military, and a similar one for hunting and its extensions. He celebrated both in his freshly panelled Drawing Room or Great Chamber, where the intricate carving over the fireplace shows the

GODINTON PARK The Staircase with its carved figures is one of Captain Toke's most spectacular achievements.

stag of the hunter's patron saint, St Hubert, and scenes from pastimes such as pig-sticking and bear-baiting. The carved frieze round two walls of the room, though military in inspiration, is far less barbaric. Movement by movement and in meticulous detail, it shows exactly how skilled musketeers and pikemen should wield their weapons.

Although later Tokes added their own embellishments to Godinton, Captain Nicholas's carved woodwork has remained unscathed by later changes in taste. The Tokes of the Victorian period even went so far as to add some more—without, however, ruining the general effect. Though Godinton passed to other owners in the late nineteenth century, the Captain's musketeers and the rest of the Tokes' work can still be admired today, but another of Godinton's most famous features is now—in its original form—missing from the list. On 3 September 1939, at the very moment that Neville Chamberlain was broadcasting the news of Britain's state of war with Germany, its great 'Domesday Oak' was suddenly riven in two.

GODOLPHIN HOUSE

CORNWALL

It sounds like a quiz question: what have tin-mining, a seventeenth-century poet and a world-famous horse in common? The answer is Godolphin House.

One distinctive feature of Godolphin House strikes the visitor straightaway: it is the colonnaded North Front, supported by six stout granite columns—an indication, if ever there was one, that the owners were people of power and substance. And so they were. The Godolphins' money came from tin, and had done since pre-Norman times. In the sixteenth century the traveller Leland could still report 'no greater tin works in all Cornwall than be on Sir William Godolphin's ground'. Sir William was, at that time, Lord Warden of the Stannaries—the overseer of the unique and separate legal system of the tin-mining communities. His nephew, Sir Francis, built up the family fortunes still further by introducing new technology and bringing German mining expertise to Cornwall, and it was his grandson, also Sir Francis, who added the impressive front to the original house built round about 1475.

The Godolphins were passionate Royalists. Sidney Godolphin, born in 1610, was killed fighting for the King's men in the Civil War, but not before he had left behind some limpid poems. A second Sidney Godolphin, a generation later, became Lord High Treasurer to Queen Anne and in this capacity was, in effect, the paymaster of the great John Churchill, first Duke of Marlborough. He was created first Earl of Godolphin. However, when the Queen turned against the Marlboroughs the association proved to be politically damaging and Godolphin was sacked.

There is a touching story about Margaret, Countess of Godolphin, whom the Earl married in 1675. Margaret's saintly life, according to John Evelyn who was a friend and wrote a memoir of her, stood out like a beacon against the scandals of the contemporary court. She spent her life in London, but had often heard her husband speak of his Cornish home, and no doubt cherished hopes of visiting it one day, or perhaps even settling there. Sadly, it was not to be. She died in 1678, giving birth to their only son; but in her will she asked, if her husband could afford to take her body so far, to be buried in his beloved county. Her wish was granted.

Their son Francis achieved distinction in a quite different sphere. He married Henrietta Churchill, eldest daughter of the Duke of Marlborough and Duchess in her own right, and his main interest in life was racing. When he built a house of his own, he not surprisingly chose a site near Newmarket, and it was here that he came into possession of a horse which is legendary in the annals of English racing. It was a brown bay standing about fifteen hands, and was discovered by Thomas Coke (the builder of Holkham Hall) in Paris in 1728. The story goes that it had been used as a draught horse. Coke brought the stallion back to England and gave it to a friend, who passed it on to the Earl of Godolphin.

The Godolphin, as the stallion became known, was one of the three horses—the others were the Byerly Turk and the Darley Arabian—from which all thoroughbred racehorses are descended, and whose direct line can be traced to the present day. The interbreeding of the offspring of these three produced the classic Eclipse, Matchem and Herod lines which are the outstanding families in the Stud Book of British racing.

With the death of the second Earl, leaving no surviving children, Godolphin House passed by marriage to the Osborne family, who demolished part of it and let the rest as a farmhouse. Restoration of what was left was begun in 1937 when the house was bought by S.E. Schofield.

GOODWOOD HOUSE
WEST SUSSEX

The Dukes of Richmond have always liked to be in at the beginning of things. The first Duke—another of Charles II's illegitimate children, this time by Louise de Kerouaille—was Master of England's first hunt, the Charlton Hunt. His son, the second Duke, introduced a menagerie to Goodwood, one of Britain's first. The third Duke campaigned for electoral reform, and introduced racing to Goodwood. The tradition of innovation continued down to the present century: the ninth Duke was a motor-racing champion in the Brooklands era, and his son has made Goodwood the home of international dressage.

At the centre of all these developments has stood Goodwood itself, bought by the first Duke in 1697 as a hunting lodge. Part of the house as it was then—a Jacobean reconstruction—survives in the present Long Hall, but it was the third Duke who created Goodwood as it exists today.

He was born in 1735 and followed an army career. Among his achievements was the creation of the Martello-tower defence system round the south and east coasts of England. There were two phases in his rebuilding of Goodwood. First, round about 1760, he commissioned Sir William Chambers to extend the Long Hall with wings to right angles at each side. Later, he became more ambitious, and James Wyatt designed for him a house in the shape of an octagon. In the event, only three sides of this were completed, but even these left the family heavily in debt when the third Duke died. Away from the house, he built the Stable Block and new kennels for the Goodwood Hunt and, in 1802, set up the original Goodwood racecourse.

The third Duke's attempts at electoral reform were less successful. In 1780 he introduced in the House of Lords a bill for manhood suffrage, annual parliaments and equal electoral districts, proposals that were to be among the demands of the Chartists fifty years later. As it happened, he chose to introduce his bill on the day that the Gordon Riots began, and even as he was speaking the mob could be heard outside the Chamber. Peers arriving for the debate were forced from their carriages, robbed and assaulted. The debate was eventually adjourned and resumed the following day, but the Duke's bill was heavily defeated. Nine years later the French Revolution spread fear throughout British political life and made the time inopportune for democratic reform. The Duke lost interest in the subject and retired to Goodwood to spend the remainder of his life on further improvements to his estate.

Although Goodwood had hardly shrunk from society in the past, the new century was the cue for a sparkling era in the history of the house. In 1818 work was completed on the ballroom which had been planned by the third Duke as a picture gallery, but never finished. The occasion was marked by a ball and supper for some 700 guests, with a bonfire on a hill in the park and illuminations among the trees. From then on, the ballroom was a focal point for the festivities surrounding Goodwood's July race week, which became a fixture in the calendar of King Edward VII and has remained a royal favourite ever since.

The successive Dukes of Richmond have all been keen collectors, and the contents of Goodwood today are the accumulation of 400 years of this tradition. There is virtually a complete catalogue of family portraits going back to Charles II and Louise de Kerouaille. The third Duke contributed, among other things, the collections of Sèvres porcelain and Louis XV furniture and the Gobelin tapestries. The fifth Duke, through his uncle, brought into the family the possessions of the Dukedom of Gordon, many of which came to Goodwood when the Gordon Estates were dispersed earlier in the present century. The result is a collection that provides the visitor, again and again, with the pleasure of recognizing the originals of pictures which have become familiar through reproductions.

But Goodwood is about people as well as artefacts, and there are many good stories told about the Dukes of Richmond and their families who have lived here. Perhaps the most remarkable is that of the second Duke, who was married at eighteen to Sarah, the daughter of the Earl of Cadogan, in settlement of a gambling debt between their fathers. Immediately after this enforced marriage, Charles, the second Duke, left for a three-year Grand Tour, and on his return to London was much struck by the beauty of a young woman he saw at the theatre. He made enquiries about her—to be told that she was his estranged wife. They resumed their marriage, and she bore him twelve children.

The fourth Duke, nephew of the third, is remembered for his cruel and untimely death in 1818 at the age of fifty-four. He had been appointed Governor General of Canada and opened his period of duty by making an extensive tour of the hinterland by horse and canoe. At one point he paused to stop a fight between a dog and a pet fox, and was bitten for his pains. The tour went on, but a week later the Duke began to develop an obsessive fear of water—the first symptom of rabies. He struggled to continue his tour, but had to be restrained in the end and died agonizingly at a farmhouse to which he had been taken.

GORHAMBURY

HERTFORDSHIRE

In 1652, not long after the execution of Charles I, the Essex Royalist Sir Harbottle Grimston backed his faith in a rather doubtful future, and risked £10,000 in a property near St Albans that had illustrious connections.

Called Gorhambury, it had not long before been owned by the former Lord Chancellor, Francis Bacon, one of the most influential men of his times. During the frequent periods when he had been in residence—so a later commentator recalled—'St Albans seemed as if the court had been there, so nobly did he live.'

GORHAMBURY *Sir Nicholas Bacon, father of the future Lord Chancellor, and the builder of the Tudor Gorhambury.*

But, for the purchaser, the fame of Gorhambury's previous owner was only part of the point. Sir Harbottle's real aim was to be close to London, pending such time as Charles I's son returned to his Kingdom.

The gamble paid off. The monarchy was restored, and Harbottle—who had been closely involved in helping Charles II return—immediately rose to illustrious status himself. He became Master of the Rolls and Chief Steward of St Albans. At home, his flourishing fortunes were reflected by additions to Gorhambury's contents. His wife, herself born a Bacon, had brought many of the Bacon family possessions back to the old family house; Sir Harbottle proceeded to add to them by having his portrait painted. Indeed, he had it painted three times, and his heirs followed his general example.

In every generation, the Grimstons commissioned portraits of themselves to hang at Gorhambury; meanwhile, the Bacon connection had seen to it that portraits of the house's former owners were also present in quantity. In the end, the Grimstons simply ran out of space. In 1773, the third Viscount Grimston (the family's fortunes had continued to prosper) decided that a new house was needed. With his wife, Harriot, he built a new Gorhambury in the modern Palladian manner and moved his family and his picture gallery into it. The succession of portraits continued undisturbed, but the old Tudor building that had housed so many of them fell into dereliction.

Fragments of it can still be seen today but, in the present as in the past, the great distinction of Gorhambury remains its contents. The family portraits, surveying the Gorhambury rooms, now run with scarcely a gap from the fifteenth to the twentieth centuries.

GOSFORD HOUSE

LOTHIAN

It is only in the past few decades that Gosford House has come into its own, for the first time in its 200-year life. For most of that time it was unloved, variously regarded as an ugly duckling, a pointless extravaganza, or simply damp and uncomfortable. Built in the last decade of the eighteenth century in the grounds of the Old Gosford House of a century earlier, it was not actually lived in until 1890. Even before it was completed, it had its critics. The Duke of Rutland thought the site 'objectionable in the highest degree'. Lady Louisa Stuart commented that the house looked from

GOODWOOD Canaletto's painting of the Thames seen from Richmond House, the Duke of Richmond's London home, hangs in the Main Entrance Hall at Goodwood together with three other Canalettos.

a distance like 'three great ovens'.

Robert Adam's design was certainly remarkable. The main house was flanked by two wings, or pavilions, and all had huge windows facing west across the sea. It was these windows that gave rise to Lady Louisa's jibe about ovens. When the house was completed in 1800 the seventh Earl of Wemyss, who had commissioned it, refused to live there, declaring it to be damp. He was succeeded by his grandson as the eighth Earl in 1808, but he likewise declined to use Gosford House as a home, though he did hang his pictures in the main

rooms in the centre block, demolishing the two pavilions. A further insult to the new house was the restoration of its predecessor by William Burn in the 1830s. The ninth Earl, who succeeded in 1853, could see no merit in the new house at all, and proposed to pull it down completely. Gosford House had become a total white elephant by the time the tenth Earl succeeded in 1883.

At this point, the Hall's fortunes briefly changed. The tenth Earl was an ardent collector of Italian Renaissance paintings. The surviving central block of Gosford House had already proved its merits as a picture gallery, and its new owner decided to replace the two missing wings, extending the gallery space and adding living accommodation. After three sets of plans had been submitted, building at last got under way and was completed in 1890. Its *pièce de résistance*—fortunately still surviving the later misfortunes of the house—is the Marble Hall in Italianate style, three storeys high, with its Palladian gallery and magnificent central dome. The towers on each side of the Hall have their own staircases leading to suites of rooms on each floor. It is hard now to realize, from the inside, that this is only one-third of the house of 1890.

Gosford's full glory was, however, short-lived. In 1914 the tenth Earl died, and after that the house was used only intermittently, including a period as an hotel. In the Second World War the contents of the entire house were stored in the south wing and the remainder was requisitioned by the Army. In 1940, fire destroyed much of the central block, and shortly after the war serious dry rot was found in the north wing, and the roof was taken off. The twelfth Earl returned to Gosford in 1951 to re-establish his family in the undamaged south wing, which he has done with conspicuous success.

And so, at last, Gosford House has found a caring owner.

GOSFORD HOUSE Robert Adam's grand double staircase. Despite such glories, Gosford remained unloved until recently.

GREAT DIXTER First a medieval manor house, then a farm; then, as here, rescued and restored by Sir Edwin Lutyens.

GREAT DIXTER

EAST SSUSSEX

To British gardeners, Great Dixter above all means gardens, Christopher Lloyd and clematis. To architects, however, the name stands for a triumph of sensitive restoration.

At the end of the nineteenth century, Great Dixter was no more than a large farmhouse, surrounded by outbuildings. Today, visitors can see its oldest part much as it originally was: a timbered Great Hall that had been erected for the lord of the manor at some point in the mid-fifteenth century. In its earliest days, the building had an earth floor and an open fireplace in the middle. Both have now vanished, but the great beams that span the hall still show where the smoke from the fire once blackened them.

The house owes its rescue and its transformation to the architectural historian Nathaniel Lloyd, who bought it in 1910, and to Sir Edwin Lutyens, who restored it for the Lloyd family. In the former farmyards and round the outbuildings, Lutyens also laid out part of Great Dixter's famous gardens, while Nathaniel himself designed a further portion.

As a finale to the restoration work—one

that is breath-taking in its audacity—Lutyens joined the house at the back to another building that had been transported to the site piecemeal. It was a Tudor yeoman's hall that Nathaniel had discovered, neglected and derelict, in Benenden. Great Dixter celebrates the rescue, not just of one house, but two.

GRIMSTHORPE CASTLE

LINCOLNSHIRE

'An extempore building set up of a sudden by Charles Brandon Duke of Suffolk', was how, in the 1600s, Grimsthorpe Castle was described by a visiting authority. Today's building, with its elegant railings and its entrance front by Vanbrugh, looks neither extempore nor, indeed, very like a traditional castle. Behind the Vanbrugh front, however, arrow slits in a corner tower proclaim distant but definite warlike origins, while the Castle's Victorian restorers found the 'extempore' label all too true. Grimsthorpe, once a medieval fortress, was given much of its present shape by a Tudor courtier in a hurry.

Like many of his contemporaries, Charles Brandon—who was a brother-in-law of Henry VIII—profited handsomely from the Dissolution of the Monasteries. Among his gains was the Cistercian abbey of Vaudey, which stood close to where Grimsthorpe's lake is today. When, in 1540, Charles wanted to provide his sovereign with a resting-place on a journey north to York, the materials for building it were right to hand: Vaudey Abbey came down and speedily went up again as a handsome house with a double courtyard, surrounding and incorporating the old Castle. Its hurried builder skimped, however, on the foundations: a fact that gave the restorers a considerable headache.

Although Charles was responsible for much of Grimsthorpe's physical fabric (or the lack of it), the fortunes of the family it housed were really founded by his wife, Katherine. Katherine—a woman full of charm and character—entered the ranks of the nobility at the age of seven, when she inherited the Barony of Willoughby de Eresby from her father. Brandon, many years her senior, tried to win her hand in marriage for his baby son; then, his third wife dying in 1533, he married the young heiress himself.

GRIMSTHORPE CASTLE The Vanbrugh Hall recalls the architect of the castle's present entrance front, built by the second Duke of Ancaster around 1725.

HADDON HALL Painted by Rex Whistler, the ninth Duke of Rutland—Haddon's restorer—surveys what an earlier observer called a 'good old house, all built of stone'.

In 1545, the Duke also died; both Katherine's sons were carried off by illness not many years afterwards. This was the period when English religious beliefs were being plunged into turmoil; the widowed Duchess of Suffolk supported the reformed Protestant church, and received Bishop Latimer as a guest at Grimsthorpe for three months. She later sent him money when, before his death at the stake, he was imprisoned in the Tower of London. Nor was this her only defiant move.

In 1553, the year of Mary Tudor's accession, the widowed Duchess of Suffolk broke all the rules that forbade noblewomen to wed beneath them, and married her gentleman-usher, one Richard Bertie. (To do it, she turned down the hand of no less a person than the King of Poland.) The following year, the Berties' ideas on religion came under the hostile scrutiny of the authorities, and the pair fled to Europe. Returning after Elizabeth I came to the throne,

they found Grimsthorpe a wreck, and in a poverty-stricken state it continued for some years: when Elizabeth sent the sister of Lady Jane Grey there for a period of house imprisonment, Katherine had to ask for extra furniture to be supplied as well.

In spite of all difficulties, however, Grimsthorpe and Katherine survived. So did her barony which, in 1580, was inherited by her son, Peregrine Bertie. He was the twelfth in the baronial line; its latest holder, Baroness Willoughby de Eresby, is the twenty-seventh.

HADDON HALL
DERBYSHIRE

Five hundred years ago, what were kitchens like? What happened if, at a banquet of the same period, a guest opted out of a measure-for-measure drinking bout? And what sort of objects, throughout the centuries, have people habitually lost in the course of their daily lives? The answers are all at Haddon Hall: extraordinary Haddon, with its maze of grey battlements, its glinting diamond panes, its buttresses shrouded in roses.

Early in the eighteenth century, the type of partial neglect that spelt the ruin of so many other houses handed Haddon the key to its splendour. From then onwards, it stood idle for 200 years—uninhabited and untouched. When, in the early twentieth century, the ninth Duke of Rutland decided to restore the property he had inherited from his ancestors, he found that the house presented a coherent, unspoiled progression of building styles and patterns of life that stretched from the Norman period to the Jacobean. And then, quite suddenly, its continuity stopped, frozen for ever in time by the owners' inheritance of an Earldom and Belvoir Castle.

When, consequently, the Duke's restoration teams moved in, they were presented with—for example—a range of kitchens built in the Middle Ages and still containing fixtures used by Tudor cooks. There, in the bakery, were the meal-chests; there, under a window in the main kitchen, were the big stone troughs for holding water. Log box, chopping-block, salting trough and 'dole cupboards' (portable larders with pierced doors for ventilation): Haddon's kitchens still contain them all.

Not far away is the banqueting hall, built by a Crusader owner of Haddon in the fourteenth century and added to in the fifteenth. Servants coming from the kitchens entered the hall through the carved wooden screen at one end, and it is fixed to this that today's visitor finds the punishment that awaited unwilling drinkers. It takes the form of an iron fetter: the killjoy had one hand imprisoned in this, while the drink he'd refused was tipped down inside his sleeve.

The Chapel with its paintings, the Dining Room with its heraldic ceiling; the Long Gallery from which Dorothy Manners, most celebrated daughter of the house, allegedly escaped to join her lover, and the steps down which she ran: every step through Haddon brings some evocation of the past. But it is in its Museum that the presence of its former inhabitants crowds most closely, for the display includes what the ninth Duke's workmen found under floorboards and behind wainscots as work progressed.

Who were the people who kept losing their pipes, knives, dice, small change? How hard did the owner of that ring or those scissors hunt before giving up the search? What chaos did the loss of the exhibited keys entail? And what happened to the child who, at some point in the seventeenth century, lost its shoe? Haddon, having answered some questions, gently poses others.

HAGLEY HALL

WEST MIDLANDS

No visitor would suspect that Hagley Hall is a house rescued from disaster. But in 1925 three-quarters of it was destroyed by fire, to be painstakingly restored by the ninth Viscount Cobham.

The Cobham title came to the Lyttelton family late in the nineteenth century. The Lytteltons first came to Hagley in 1564. The present Hall replacing the original house was the creation of the first Lord Lyttelton who, like many young noblemen of his time, had visited Italy on the Grand Tour and fallen in love with Italian art and culture. He returned to England with a very clear idea of how he wanted Hagley to look, and indeed with some objects—such as the marble busts of Roman emperors that adorn the White Hall—which would in due course take their place in it. At this stage, however, all this was a young man's dream. Before he could start building or even planning to build, Lyttelton had to make his way in the world, and Hagley Hall, like those at Houghton and Burghley, was to be built with the rewards of public service.

By 1756, with ten years as a Lord Commissioner of the Treasury, a brief period as Chancellor of the Exchequer, and a lucrative court appointment as Cofferer to the Royal Household behind him, Lyttelton retired from public life and set about turning the older family house at Hagley into a Palladian mansion. His father had died in 1751, and work had already started on landscaping the grounds.

Under the influence of Horace Walpole, whose advice he sought, Lyttelton's first idea was to build a Gothic house, but he was apparently dissuaded by his second wife, Elizabeth, who had firm views and an equal firmness in making them known. She is thought to have been responsible for the appointment of Sanderson Miller, a local gentleman-architect, to design Hagley. From 1752 onwards, Lyttelton wrote to Sanderson Miller with a continuous stream of instructions, many reflecting Lady Lyttelton's opinions. 'We are pretty indifferent about the outside,' he wrote on one occasion. 'It is enough if it is nothing offensive to the eye.' Another letter went into detail about the internal arrangements. The custom of the ladies withdrawing after dinner, leaving the men to their wine in the dining room, was then relatively new, but the noise of the men still at the table could be a distraction. At Hagley, Lady Lyttelton wanted (and achieved) the division of dining room and drawing room by a staircase, 'to hinder the ladies from the noise and talk of the men, when left to their bottle'.

Building began in 1756, and was completed by 1760. Craftsmen were brought from Italy to create the ceilings and chimneypieces. Lord Lyttelton's Grand Tour treasures were brought out of store and put in their appointed places; they were joined by copies of figures he had admired in the Pitti Palace. Rysbrack contributed busts of Rubens and Van Dyck. It was in this setting, in the White Hall at Hagley, that the completion of the house was celebrated in 1760 at a house-warming party that went on for three days.

The Lytteltons have combined generations of public service—in Parliament, in government, in colonial administration and in the Church—with the rearing of large, rumbusti-ous families and a certain amount of cheerful irresponsibility. The second Lord Lyttelton, one of the founder-members of the infamous eighteenth-century Hellfire Club, staked Hagley Hall against the picture of 'The Misers' in a card game, which he won, thus bringing Hagley's most celebrated possession into the family. The fourth Lord had fifteen children, who all distinguished themselves in their various fields, and the tenth Lord Cobham had eight, the eldest of whom is now the owner of Hagley. Among the Lytteltons' claims to fame is their service to cricket. Three successive generations of the family were presidents of the MCC, and Hagley Cricket Club, founded in 1834, was one of the earliest in the Midlands. The tenth Lord Cobham, in 1945, remembered his uncles practising cricket in the Gallery, to the great detriment of the furniture and woodwork, though signs of this damage have now been eliminated. These uncles showed a fine disregard for the valuables of the house, using piles of priceless books from the library over which to play leapfrog.

The fire which nearly destroyed Hagley broke out on Christmas Eve 1925. Much of the library and many of the pictures were destroyed, but, despite showers of boiling lead from the roof, there was no injury or loss of life. 'My life's work destroyed,' the ninth Lord Cobham was heard to mutter as the flames surged and roared, but before he died in 1941 he had time to enjoy his restored home.

HAMMERWOOD PARK
EAST SUSSEX

Hammerwood Park shares with the Capitol and the White House, together with Baltimore Cathedral, the University of Virginia, and a number of other American public and commercial buildings, the distinction of having been designed by Benjamin Latrobe.

Latrobe, born in England in 1764 but educated in France, returned to England at the age of twenty to study architecture under Samuel Pepys Cockerell and engineering with

HAMMERWOOD PARK Male and female revellers cavort across this bas-relief, copied from the Borghese vase in the Louvre. The bas-relief is in Coadestone, an artificial composition material.

the lighthouse-builder John Smeaton. Latrobe designed only two buildings in England: Hammerwood Lodge, as it was then known, and Ashdown House two miles (three kilometres) to the south, now an independent school.

Hammerwood's façade is perfectly symmetrical, an effect Latrobe achieved partly by the use of false windows. He was commissioned by John Sperling, a member of an Essex county family, and started building in 1792. Not long after completion, however, family duties called John Sperling back to Essex. Meanwhile Latrobe's wife had died and he had decided to emigrate to America. Hammerwood Lodge passed into the hands of a succession of banking families who occupied the house throughout the nineteenth century.

The most interesting occupants of Hammerwood Park were the Whidbornes, who moved there in 1901. George Whidborne was a clergyman, and his Edwardian family seems to have stepped straight from the books of E. Nesbit. The children wrote copious letters and

poems, and produced numerous sketches, depicting the happy family life of the house and the teeming wildlife of its surroundings. After the First World War, in which the eldest son, George, was killed, the family drifted away from Hammerwood and it and its contents were sold in 1922, a sadly familiar story for the period. After long years of neglect, restoration began in 1982 with the purchase of the house by its new owner.

HAREMERE HALL
EAST SUSSEX

Britain's Prince Regent and future King George IV visited many homes belonging to his subjects, but few of his drinking companions—a remarkable crew though they were—can have been as wildly individual as the tiny Sir John Lade of Haremere Hall.

Sir John, who combined wildness with considerable (if rapidly diminishing) wealth,

HAREMERE HALL Haremere's exterior dates from two distinct building programmes, in the early and late seventeenth century.

lived both in the real world and in an overlapping fantasy one. Oddly, his dream ambition was not to be richer, grander or more handsome than he was, but the reverse. In the real world, he was nicknamed the 'Gentleman Whip', and was capable of performing such feats as driving a four-in-hand from Bath to London in eight hours. In his imagination, he really was a coachman: a robust, earthy character, whose delicate touch on the reins was equalled only by the indelicacy of his manners. He went to some lengths to achieve a considerable degree of vulgarity, such as having his teeth filed down so that he could spit better. Less informal characters, like Lord Chancellor Thurlow, saw and shuddered.

The Prince Regent, however, had no objection to his horsey friend's manners. Nor, indeed, was he much worried by those of Sir John's wife: Lady Laetitia Lade, *née* Smith. Lady Letty was another manifestation of Sir John's instinctive love of the vulgar: she was a former prostitute's maid, and had changed little since her working days. 'Swearing like Letty Lade' became the Prince Regent's phrase for any spectacularly bad language used in his presence.

The future King joined with a will in the revels staged by Letty and Sir John at Haremere, but—as far as the hosts were concerned—the good times were not to last. In the end, with all his wealth spent, Sir John did

time in a debtor's prison. On emerging, he was forced to become . . . a coachman.

Horses are still a feature of life at Haremere, with exhibitions now being given by the stables' modern inmates. These, like their predecessors of the Regency period, also display the powers and skills of the horse as a working animal. But the Suffolk Punches and the huge Shires that can be seen today at Haremere Hall are far removed in time and style from the carriage-horses that once won wagers for their sporting owner-driver.

HAREWOOD HOUSE
WEST YORKSHIRE

Royal patronage, income from land, the redistribution of wealth after the Dissolution of the Monasteries—these are the factors that have helped create so many British country houses. Harewood is different. It was a creation of successful commerce.

Henry Lascelles was an eighteenth-century merchant engaged in the lucrative West Indian trade, and from the profits he set himself up with a country seat at Gawthorpe Old Hall, on the opposite side of the valley to Harewood. His son Edwin, who became the first Lord Harewood, inherited the adjoining estates of Gawthorpe and Harewood on the death of his father in 1753, and devoted much of the rest of his life to establishing Harewood as one of the major seats in the north of England. The key to this plan was the building of Harewood House to replace the Old Hall.

Although Harewood today—little changed from Lord Harewood's vision—gives an impression of 'no expense spared', Edwin Lascelles was a true Yorkshireman with a keen sense of the value of money. He considered commissioning designs for Harewood from Sir William Chambers, the King's architect, but settled for the local, and less expensive, John Carr of York. The millstone grit of the exterior was quarried on the estate, where the bricks for internal walls were made, and raw materials for the stucco also came from Lascelles land.

HAGLEY HALL 'The Misers', *painted by Marinus van Reynerswaele, came to Hagley after the second Lord Lyttelton won the painting at cards. If he had lost, the Lytteltons would have lost Hagley.*

Edwin Lascelles went to Robert Adam for the interiors, but instructed him to keep a close eye on costs.

Harewood House was occupied in 1771, some fifteen years after work on it had begun. Thomas Chippendale was commissioned to furnish it. He too was a local man, coming from Otley, though by the time he started work for Harewood he was well-established in London. His reputation did not, however, help his relations with Lord Harewood, who was a notoriously slow payer of bills. By 1777, after Chippendale had completed eight years' work to the value of some £7,000, practically nothing had been paid. Lord Harewood forged ahead nonetheless: Gawthorpe Old Hall was demolished and Capability Brown was engaged to landscape the park and grounds at Harewood.

Harewood was one of the first houses in Britain to have a bell system fitted so that servants could be called by pulls on a network of ropes. This was a great advance, as before it had been necessary to station servants at various points round the house so that they could give service when and where it was required.

It is generally agreed that nineteenth-century alterations by Sir Charles Barry spoiled the classical perfection of the original house, and the addition of a third storey of bedrooms certainly added to the problems of later generations of the family struggling to keep Harewood together. By the beginning of the twentieth century the Lascelles fortunes were on the wane. The fifth Earl of Harewood's heir, Lord Lascelles, was struggling to live the life of an officer in the Grenadier Guards on an income of £600 a year. It was in February 1916, on leave from France where he had won the DSO and bar and the Croix de Guerre, that Lord Lascelles, at the age of thirty-three, had a remarkable stroke of luck.

In his London club he fell into conversation with his great-uncle, the Marquess of Clanricarde. What was remarkable about this was that the Marquess was a noted recluse and was not often seen in London. He devoted his life to his collection of Italian and Flemish art. However, the old man and the young officer evidently saw eye to eye, for when the Marquess died a few months later he left Lord Lascelles his paintings, a fortune of £2,500,000 and an estate in Ireland. Lascelles used some of the money to start his own collection, part of which can now be seen in the Rose Drawing Room at Harewood. The final seal was placed on the renewed fortunes of the Lascelles family when, in 1922, Lord Lascelles married the Princess Royal, only daughter of King George V and Queen Mary. Lord Lascelles—who became the sixth Earl of Harewood on the death of his father in 1929—lived on until 1947.

James Lees-Milne's diary gives an interesting account of a visit he made to Harewood for the National Trust in 1947, shortly after the death of the sixth Earl.

Lees-Milne found the Princess Royal living in her private apartments while workmen repaired the ravages to the state rooms caused by the house having been used as a hospital during the Second World War. Two things were on the Princess Royal's mind: the political uncertainties associated with the post-war Labour government—Her Royal Highness wondered whether there might be pressure for the Royal Family to emigrate—and which items from the house might have to be sold to meet the £1 million death duty demand. As it turned out, she need not have worried; after a massive sale of land she lived on at Harewood, surrounded by the things she loved, until her death in 1965.

HARLAXTON MANOR
LINCOLNSHIRE

A stranger coming across Harlaxton Manor by chance might well wonder what unknown royal palace this is. It is, in fact, a remarkable Victorian Gothic confection, whose appearance in the Lincolnshire countryside is as remarkable as the mystery of its building and the story of its subsequent owners.

It was built between 1832 and 1851 by a man named Gregory Gregory, of whom little is known except that he came from a family with money in coal, canal and railway companies. He left no record of his life, no heir, and the documentation of the building of Harlaxton Manor has not survived; but it seems that he created the house as a setting for the collection of objects on which he had spent a lifetime. What this collection contained can

HARLAXTON MANOR Detail of the plasterwork that looks down on the Great Hall—a mere fragment of Harlaxton's rich interiors.

now never be known, for it was broken up in a sale in 1877—a sale which, so litigious were the remote members of Gregory Gregory's family to whom his estate had passed, had to be specially authorized by Act of Parliament. Over the next fifty years the manor itself passed this way and that between various remote cousins until, in 1937, it was sold and the contents again cleared.

This was very nearly the end of the story of Harlaxton, for a contract had gone out for the

demolition of the house when, at the last moment, it was saved by an eccentric millionaire, Mrs Violet Van der Elst. Despite her name—which came from her second husband, a Belgian artist—Mrs Van der Elst could not have been more English. She was the daughter of a Middlesex coal-porter and a Quaker washerwoman, and had made a fortune from toiletries, including the first brushless shaving-cream, Shavex—a business she began in her kitchen. She poured money into Harlaxton Manor, as indeed she needed to since it was uninhabitable, lacking both the telephone and electricity and having only one bathroom, the last owner lagging not far behind Mrs Van der Elst when it came to eccentricity. Mrs Van der Elst renamed the house Grantham Castle, and set aside its library to house her collection of over 3,000 books on the occult, and as a setting for the séances at which she tried to contact her dead husband. Her only impact on public life was her long-standing campaign against capital punishment, which brought her into conflict with the law on many occasions and ultimately ruined her. She died penniless in a nursing home in 1966, having sold Harlaxton in 1948 for less than she paid for it.

The Jesuit Order bought the manor as a seminary, but stayed for only a few years. The house was then leased to Stanford University and finally to the present occupants, the University of Evansville, Indiana.

HARRINGTON HALL
LINCOLNSHIRE

'Come into the garden, Maud . . .' The garden into which Tennyson invited his beloved still exists, and has done since the seventeenth century. It belongs, in fact, to Harrington Hall in Lincolnshire; Somersby, Tennyson's birthplace, is less than two miles away, and it was at Harrington that, as a young man, he courted a real-life Maud.

In the late eighteenth century, the brick manor house with its oddly tall Elizabethan porch passed to a family that frequently let it

out to rent. Among the occupants who leased it in the last years of the Georgian period was an Admiral John Eden, stepfather and guardian to a young woman of wealth named Rosa Baring. Around 1834, Tennyson met her, was attracted, and fell in love. On his visits to Harrington, he would meet her in its morning room; then, going out through its garden door (now a window), the couple would wander up and down the Jacobean terrace with its herringbone-brick path.

Tennyson's poem is fundamentally tragic in tone: the hero slays a hostile brother in a duel, and the heroine dies. Happily, Rosa and Tennyson brought matters to a less gloomy, if more banal, end: the poet grew tired of his wealthy lady-love, and was soon courting someone else. His fictional love for her, however, has survived and so—despite an emergency in 1930, when Harrington was nearly demolished—has its setting.

HARRINGTON HALL A dummy-board mounts guard over the Hall, a room that was familiar to Tennyson and his Rosa.

HARTLAND ABBEY

DEVON

One of the abiding interests in life is how other people live. And so it was when Lady Borington spent a night at Hartland Abbey in 1810 as a guest of Colonel Paul Orchard and his family. Hartland seems to have been as isolated socially in those days as it was, and is, geographically. Set in a narrow wooded valley running in from the wild Atlantic shore, it was far from the nearest town, and, it may be supposed from Lady Borington's account of her stay, out of touch with changing social usage.

At that time, Hartland Abbey had only relatively recently been rebuilt in a Strawberry Hill style; it involved the demolition of the old Great Hall, the lopping-off of various other medieval bits and pieces, and the creation of three new reception rooms with bedrooms

HAREWOOD HOUSE Winterhalter's painting of Adelina Patti marks the involvement of Lord and Lady Harewood in opera.

above. The Colonel had completed this work in 1779. But although the setting was fashionable, the life of Hartland evidently was not. By the beginning of the nineteenth century entertaining at country houses had settled into a recognized pattern. The guests would assemble in the drawing room for dinner as it came up to seven o'clock. They would then process into the dining room, where a sumptuous and lengthy meal would be taken, after which the ladies would withdraw to leave the men to their drink and conversation until perhaps eleven o'clock or so.

Not so at Hartland Abbey, Lady Borington reported with some wonderment. The style of life there reminded her of what used to happen two centuries before. Meeting in the drawing room, the guests sat on high-backed chairs until ten o'clock, when a bell announced that dinner was served. This proved to be a meal of cold cuts. There was no question of social contact afterwards; when the meal was over, the assembly processed out of the dining room again and each person was ushered to the bedrooms by 'an old grey-headed domestic'. It does not sound a particularly enjoyable stay.

The reason for the archaic arrangements at Hartland may have been that Colonel Orchard was then very near the end of his long life; he was seventy-one when Lady Borington was a guest. He had inherited the Abbey from his father, who had come into it by marriage. Until the early years of the eighteenth century the building was very much as it had been since the Abbey was founded in 1160. There were some alterations in 1705, but it was the Colonel who altered the character of the place from medieval holy house to Georgian country seat. Later, in the mid-nineteenth century, there were further alterations when Sir George Gilbert Scott, the eminent architect of the Albert Memorial, provided Hartland Abbey with a new front hall and entrance. There are thus four distinct periods reflected in the house; the interiors are, however, largely Victorian and include the panelling of the dining room and inner hall with panels from the demolished Great Hall, and the treatment of the drawing room with linenfold panelling, which had been made newly fashionable

HARTLAND ABBEY The vaulting and decoration of the Alhambra Corridor, by Sir George Gilbert Scott, was inspired by a visit to the Alhambra Palace in Granada.

through its use by Pugin for the interiors of the new Houses of Parliament.

One of the interesting features of Hartland Abbey is the display of a virtually complete collection of documents tracing its history back to 1160. There is a remarkable story attached to these documents, which had not been seen for over two hundred years until, one day in 1952, the owner and his daughter were foraging in the Abbey cellar and came upon them. The find—consisting of several thousand items—included much material of county significance which is now in the care of the Devon County Records Office. However, the items displayed in the house include the original grant of the Abbey by Henry VIII to the present owner's ancestor, William Abbott, and a document bearing the seal of James I which is still in the original container in which it was brought from London by King's Messenger.

HATCH COURT Here drawn by an artist of the 1820s, Hatch Court was designed by the gifted amateur architect Thomas Prowse.

HATCH COURT

SOMERSET

A four-square country house in Somerset, built of Bath stone for a Georgian family that had grown rich in the wool trade, seems on the face of it an unusual home for a Canadian military museum. But the link between Hatch Court and Princess Patricia's Canadian Light Infantry was provided early this century when Andrew Hamilton Gault married Dorothy Shuckburgh, niece of the house's owner.

The wedding took place in 1922 and, compared to the pace of his life in the previous decade, ushered in a period of (relative) calm for the groom. An English-born Canadian, he had fought as a very young man in the Boer War. At the outbreak of the First World War, he had gone one better than merely offering himself; he raised and—at his own expense—equipped a whole regiment.

Recruiting started only two days after war was declared and, in the incredible space of seventeen days, the outfit was ready to sail from Canada. Named after the daughter of the

Canadian Governor General, the Duke of Connaught, it was trained and stationed in France by the end of 1914. The 'Patricias' saw their first action at Ypres, and their last—on 11 November 1918—at Mons. For the first year, Andrew was their commander; although invalided out of the front line, he stayed on in France to the end and, at last, took the regiment triumphantly back to Canada.

Rather in the manner of Buchan's Richard Hannay, Andrew settled after the war into the typical life of an English country squire, but his temperament continued to lure him into heroic adventure. In this—again as in the Hannay books—he was joined by Dorothy. However, it was not international skulduggery that frequently took them into the unknown, but flying. In tiny aeroplanes such as the De Havilland Moth, the aviators would take off for destinations all over Europe and beyond. Between flights, they were claimed by the somewhat soberer existence of MP for Taunton and his wife.

At Hatch Court today, the 'Patricias' museum built up by the present owners is also a memorial to the man who brought the regiment into being. It includes photographs, one of the original recruiting posters, the battalion's nominal roll—and, in a commanding position over the fireplace, the propeller from a Gipsy Moth. On it, in closely written ranks, are the names of all the places to which Andrew and Dorothy ventured.

HAUGHLEY PARK

SUFFOLK

In July 1553, King Edward VI of England died, and his last breath was the starting-signal for a brief contest for the throne between the supporters of Protestant Lady Jane Grey, who was to reign for nine days, and those of Catholic Mary Tudor, daughter of Henry VIII and Catherine of Aragon, who was eventually to reign as Mary I. Both unhappy women were mere pawns in a hard-fought political game, and when it became clear that Lady Jane's supporters were about to win the day Mary escaped with her retinue to the protection of the Howard family at Framlingham in Suffolk. The nephew of a county family, John Sulyard, there provided her with men and horses to continue her journey and she was also helped by his neighbour, Henry Jerningham. The Sulyards and the Jerninghams were destined to be united again.

The Sulyards were already, by that time, owners of the manor of Haughley. It was John Sulyard's grandson, Sir John, who consolidated the family's growing status by building Haughley Park in about 1620. The family remained at Haughley for nearly two hundred years, but towards the end of the eighteenth century the male line died out, leaving three daughters, of whom the youngest was Frances Sulyard.

Frances was a noted beauty, and in 1800 she married Sir George Jerningham of Costessey. This was no marriage of convenience between the families of East Anglian worthies. It was clearly a love-match. Visiting Haughley Park in 1799, Sir George wrote to his mother of Frances's beauty and charm. 'I think if possible,' he wrote, 'she is still more handsome in

HAUGHLEY PARK The East Front, from a drawing by Frances Sulyard about the time of her marriage to Sir George Jerningham. The couple spent the first nine years of their married life here.

the morning than by candlelight, which is rather uncommon with the modern belles.'

Frances and Sir George lived happily at Haughley Park for nine years, during which time they had five children. Then, when Sir George's father died, the young couple moved to the Jerningham family home at Costessey Hall near Norwich and Haughley was sold. Ultimately, however, its fate was happier than Costessey's, which was finally demolished, a victim of neglect, in the 1920s. Haughley, by contrast, went on being home to a succession of families.

The present owners bought Haughley Park in 1957, but four years later there was a serious fire which gutted half the house. The damaged portion was restored in period style. The staircase, the plaster cornices of the four reception rooms and the hall fireplace are among the items replaced during the rebuilding and they elegantly refute the claims of those who say that the old craftsmanship is dead.

HEDINGHAM CASTLE
ESSEX

Even today, with only the Keep left standing, there is no mistaking the purpose of Hedingham Castle. It is sternly defensive, dominating the Essex countryside. The fine wooded hill on which it stands is now one of its most attractive features, but when Hedingham Castle was fulfilling its defensive role the hill would have been kept clear of trees and undergrowth to give a full field of fire.

Aubrey de Vere was one of William the Conqueror's ablest lieutenants, and he was rewarded after the Conquest with land in various parts of southern England and lordships of no less than fourteen Essex manors. Hedingham was one of these. It was his son, also Aubrey, who built the Castle in about 1140. It was conceived on an ambitious scale. The ashlar stone used for the facing was brought from Northamptonshire—a considerable and expensive feat of transport for those days—and the walls were 10–12-feet

(about 3·5 metres) thick, and even thicker on the east face. Signs of the prodigious defences, such as the groove for the portcullis in the main doorway, together with slots for reinforcing bolts, can still be seen.

The entrance leads to the Guard Room on the first floor, from which a 13-foot-wide (4 metres) spiral staircase leads to the Banqueting Hall, whose arch, rising to 20 feet (6 metres), is said to be the largest Norman arch in Europe. In the twelfth and thirteenth centuries, this Hall would have been the social and political focus of the neighbourhood.

The de Veres were created Earls of Oxford in the twelfth century and became enthusiastic Crusaders. The third Earl took part in the Anglo-French struggles during the reign of King John, supporting the barons' offer of the English crown to the French Prince Louis; when an invading French army landed at Colchester John's royal forces put Hedingham Castle under siege. The third Earl's men resisted fiercely, as they did when the Castle was again attacked in the following year. Temporarily disgraced, the Earl soon had Hedingham and his other lands restored to him.

The thirteenth Earl of Oxford, after long service in the Wars of the Roses that ended with a period of twelve years' imprisonment in France, returned to Hedingham towards the end of his life. He restored it to such a state that it was fit, in the 1490s, to receive a visit from Henry VII. The visit did not go well for the Earl, however. The story goes that when the King came to depart, all the Earl's servants lined up in full livery. There were strict controls on the number of men a noble might put into livery, in order to prevent the stealthy build-up of private armies, and the Earl had gone too far. 'I may not have my laws broken in my sight,' said the King, and the Earl was heavily fined.

During the fifteenth century, Castle Hedingham seems to have been overtaken by the changing needs of its owners. Country gentlemen came to favour mansions rather than castles, and the Castle was pillaged for further building. A house with attendant stables,

HEDINGHAM CASTLE Changing tastes and the depredations of later builders have left only the great Keep of the Castle still standing—but still dominating the Essex countryside.

pantries and a bakehouse was built on the outer bailey in Tudor times, no doubt with Castle stone—and the same stone was used again when the existing eighteenth-century house on the adjacent site (not open to the public) was built. But by this time the illustrious de Veres had left Hedingham Castle. Henry, the eighteenth Earl of Oxford, was the last de Vere to own and live at Hedingham, and he died in 1625. With the death of the twentieth Earl in 1703 there were no further heirs. The Earldom died out and the Castle was sold to the Ashurst family, whose descendants still own it.

HELLEN'S

HEREFORD & WORCESTER

Some houses, irrespective of their age, have an extraordinary talent for attracting occupants of note. But age undoubtedly helps, and this is where Hellen's scores. Tucked away though it is at Much Marcle (or March) on the Welsh border, Hellen's has never had a dull existence. Built by a woman whose very name—Yseult—is the stuff of legend, its appearance coincided with the events leading up to King Edward II's hideous end at Berkeley Castle.

The house takes its name from the steward, Walter Helyon, that Yseult Mortimer Audley put in charge of her property. She was the sister of Roger Mortimer, lover of Isabella, Edward II's Queen. The adulterous pair were to stage a successful *coup d'état* against Isabella's husband and sovereign.

In November 1326, Isabella and Roger made 'Helyon's home' a base for themselves and the insurrectionist army they had gathered. They caught the wretched Edward, and finally had him despatched to Berkeley, where he was murdered. Not long afterwards, Roger Mortimer himself met the horrible death prescribed for traitors when Isabella's son, Edward III, ousted him. But Isabella, curiously enough, emerged from the affair relatively unscathed, and so did her one-time hostess, Yseult.

Indeed, the mistress of Hellen's even managed to have James, her son, accepted by Edward III (who had come with his mother to Much Marcle during the coup) as a companion and schoolmate for his own son, the Prince of Wales. The two young men became the closest of friends; they fought at Crécy together in 1346 and, when the Black Prince passed through the Welsh Marches the following year, it was inevitable that he should stay at Hellen's. To do his friend honour, James Audley had a new fireplace built in the little banqueting hall of his home, and over it put the crest that the prince had won on the Crécy battlefield: the three white feathers, with the motto *Ich dien* (I serve). The crest—which has been borne by all Princes of Wales ever since—is still there, and so is the stone table at which the Prince dined.

In James's time, Hellen's was still a castle, and recognizably grand, but after the Tudor period the house began to decline and the family fortunes to take a downward turn. As Catholics, they favoured the wrong religion; as Royalists, they found themselves backing the wrong side. In the 1650s, patrolling Cromwellian soldiers raided the house and killed its chaplain. Its Royalist master, Fulke Walwyn, became a road-sweeper in Hereford, and never came back to live in his home again.

Equally sad was the story of Fulke's granddaughter, Hetty—or Mehettable—Walwyn. After running off with a farm-worker, Hetty did indeed come back, but lived to regret it. Her mother sentenced her to semi-imprisonment in an upstairs room with a strongly barred window. Like James Audley before her, she too left a memorial to her love. With the one possession that remained to her, a diamond ring, she wrote on the window's glass:

It is a part of Virtue to abstain
From what we love if it shall prove our bane!

She signed it with her name. And outside, on a pane close by, her lover signed his: John Pearcel.

HEMERDON HOUSE
DEVON

The archetypal English country house is set in its park among the rolling farmland which has historically provided the owners with their wealth. But not all country houses

HEMERDON HOUSE James Northcote's 'Worthies of Devonshire', painted in 1824, presides over the Drawing Room at Hemerdon.

are like that, particularly in the west of England. There estates have tended to be smaller, and their owners dependent not on the land but on professional incomes.

One such is Hemerdon, on the outskirts of Plymouth. Hemerdon House is now surrounded by about 500 acres of its own land, but at its largest it was never the centre of a viable agricultural estate. As a result, the Woollcombe family, which has owned Hemerdon since 1790, has relied on external sources of income, principally from the family law business that still flourishes in Plymouth.

There seems to have been no grand scheme behind the building of Hemerdon House. The building records have not survived, but it seems that, though generally Regency in style, the house was run up bit by bit at some time in the 1790s, with later embellishments and additions. Initially, it was a wedding present for Maria Woollcombe from her father, when she married her cousin George Woollcombe,

HELLEN'S The banqueting hall that was refurbished for the Black Prince's visit, with the stone table at which he dined.

the son of a Plymouth surgeon, in 1792. They had two sons; one died as a young man, and Hemerdon passed to the younger son, another George, who chose the navy as a career. The pictures in Hemerdon House came mainly from an uncle, Henry Woollcombe, who died in 1847 and who founded the solicitors' practice.

Striking proof that Hemerdon was not viable solely as a country estate came in the early years of this century when George Woollcombe, who inherited in 1902, tried to make it work in just that way. The times were against him in any case, but the fact was that there was simply not enough land to support a squire without other means of income. It was evidently touch and go in the twenties and thirties, and when George died in 1947 the house was split into flats. It has been brought together again by the present Woollcombe owner, who has retired there after a career in commerce. And so Hemerdon House has once again become what it was built to be, a solid home for a middle-class family.

HEVER CASTLE
KENT

In 1522 the English ambassador to France, Sir Thomas Bullen, returned to his Kent home after four years' service, bringing with him his lively and sophisticated fifteen-year-old daughter Anne. The ambassador's return was to change the course of English history.

Anne Bullen is known to us by her 'court' name of Anne Boleyn, and shortly after her return to Hever Castle she began the long journey that led her first to the throne as Queen of England and finally to the executioner's block. She became a lady-in-waiting to Henry VIII's first Queen, Catherine of Aragon, and in that position she caught the King's eye. He already knew the Bullen family well; Anne's mother, Elizabeth, had been his first mistress, and he had moved on to, among others, Anne's elder sister Mary. Henry's plan was to add Anne to his collection of Bullens, but meanwhile Anne had fallen in love with a young courtier, Lord Henry Percy. She was banished from the court, and shortly afterwards her father took her abroad again, this time to the Netherlands. She returned, eighteen years old, in 1525.

The King now began to make frequent visits to Hever, and, although still married to Catherine, proposed to Anne in 1527. She refused him on the ground that he was already married, and refused to be his mistress. Her response set in train the separation of the Church of England from Rome, the suppression of the monasteries, and many of the civil and military troubles of the next century. The rest of Anne's story is well known: her three-year marriage to Henry produced one daughter, the future Queen Elizabeth I, and ended with her own execution and those of five of her alleged lovers. After her father's death, Henry VIII appropriated Hever and passed it to his fourth wife, Anne of Cleves.

Although there were many subsequent changes of ownership until its purchase in 1903 by the American millionaire William

HEVER CASTLE Romantic but ruinous: Hever as it was about the time William Waldorf Astor discovered it, its past forgotten, its fabric in decay, its gardens sown with potatoes.

Waldorf Astor, many mementoes have returned to Hever of the days when the Castle was at the centre of political and court intrigue. On the mantelpiece of the Inner Hall is a copy of the clock which was Henry VIII's wedding present to Anne Boleyn, and in the same room are portraits of the King, Anne, and her sister Mary. In Anne Boleyn's room, which she occupied as a little girl, is the prayer book which she carried with her to her execution. In the Rochford Room—named after Anne's brother, who was alleged to have been among her lovers—is the original Papal Bull confirming Henry VIII's marriage to Catherine of Aragon.

The Astor family is descended from a German emigrant, Johann Jacob Astor, who arrived in America in 1783 and set up a fur-trapping business which, when he died in 1848, had made him the richest man in the United States.

William Waldorf Astor was Johann Jacob's grandson. After a brief political and diplomatic career—three years spent as US ambassador to Italy helped to form his taste as surely as did the Italian tours of eighteenth-century English aristocrats—he became disenchanted with America and removed himself, and his fortune, to England. He took out naturalization papers in 1899, and bought first the Cliveden Estate in Buckinghamshire and, in 1903, Hever Castle.

Hever Castle's fortunes had dramatically declined since Henry VIII's day. At one time it became a smugglers' hideout. By Victoria's reign it was tenanted as a farm. The original Great Hall (now the Dining Hall) was the farmhouse kitchen. The Guardhouse was used as a toolshed, the gardens were laid down to potatoes, and geese swam in the moat. Thousands of craftsmen were employed to refurbish the Castle itself and build the mock-Tudor 'village' which was, in fact, a hugely extravagant set of guest rooms. The present contents of the house reflect a diligent search all over Europe and beyond by Astor and his agents for furniture, paintings, furnishings and *objets d'art* suitable for the restored Castle. The result

HEVER CASTLE William Waldorf Astor, who bought Hever in 1903 after settling in England. The picture is dated 1919.

is an eclectic collection, though with a bias towards the period that gave Hever its fame. However, the lavish Edwardian style could not last, nor indeed could the Astors' wealth. First Cliveden, then Hever, was sold. The Tudor 'village' built to house the Astor guests has been adapted to more contemporary usage as a conference centre, and Hever has been owned since 1983 by a Yorkshire-based property company. Hever's treasures, however—one of the last great private collections—remain.

HIGHCLERE CASTLE
BERKSHIRE

'How scenical! How scenical!' was Disraeli's comment when he saw what the third Earl of Carnarvon, with the help of the architect Sir Charles Barry, had made of Victorianizing the Georgian house the Earl had inherited. Disraeli was not a man to use words imprecisely, and his true reaction to the new Highclere Castle must remain in question. But there is no doubt that the Earl was given what he wanted, for the remodelling was Barry's third attempt to please his client. It was what Barry wanted too; his son said that the transformation of Highclere was one of his father's favourite works, a remark not to be discounted from a man whose commissions included the Houses of Parliament.

The design of the two works—the Hampshire castle and the Mother of Parliaments—went on at the same time. But neither the Earl nor Barry was to see the completion of the remodelling. The Earl died in 1850 and Barry ten years later, leaving almost all the interiors to other hands. Nevertheless, the succession of Victorian interiors is astonishing, not to say heady, culminating in the drawing room redecorated at the turn of the century by the fifth Earl. He had already developed the interest in Egyptology which was to lead, in 1922, to the opening of the tomb of Tutankhamen. His interior makes an interesting contrast to the embossed leather panels of the saloon, the library reminiscent of the Reform Club in London (another Barry building), and the Gothic fantasies of the entrance hall. As a celebration of Victorian taste throughout the Queen's reign, Highclere Castle is unique.

HOAR CROSS HALL
STAFFORDSHIRE

At first sight, Hoar Cross Hall, golden-red and four-square, looks like an Elizabethan manor house straight from the history books.

In fact it's a Victorian confection, built between 1862 and 1871 in the high noon of nineteenth-century confidence, with seventy rooms, richly ornamental plasterwork and an impressively castellated entrance archway, flanked by lodge and gatehouse. There is even an attendant church, a memorial to Hugo Meynell Ingram, for whom the Hall was built but who died in the hunting field in the year it was completed. The design is by the great Victorian architect G. F. Bodley.

There can have been no doubt in the mind of Hugo Meynell Ingram and his wife that their new house would be a fitting setting for many generations of family history. Indeed this was probably the thought that led them to choose a design based on the Meynell family's genuinely Elizabethan Temple Newsam House near Leeds, now a municipally owned museum. Alas, it was not to be. The first steps were already being taken in the historical process which spelt the end of the lifestyle represented by Hoar Cross Hall, with its indoor and outdoor staff of fifty. Its life as a family country house in the style for which it had been built lasted for only about eighty years, and it has been rescued slowly and painfully—but successfully—from decay by the present owners.

HOAR CROSS HALL The oak-panelled Long Gallery, with ornamental plasterwork to the design of G. F. Bodley.

HOGHTON TOWER Like its hilltop site, the house's massive Gate House strongly proclaims the defensive intentions of the builder.

HOGHTON TOWER

LANCASHIRE

Hoghton Tower, halfway between Preston and Blackburn, is the archetypal house on the hill. Now shorn of the great tower that first gave it its name, it still broods on its hilltop overlooking the Lancashire plains: a stone manor house with courtyards and battlemented walls, built to last by Thomas Hoghton in the reign of Queen Elizabeth I.

Hoghton's impressive appearance is enhanced by the way one reaches it. Like a castle in a child's drawing, it is approached by half a mile of ruler-straight road, going directly up the slope to its gatehouse. When, in 1913, the de Hoghton family was visited by King George V and Queen Mary, the whole slope was lined with well-wishers but, on an earlier royal visit, the Hoghton welcome was more sumptuous still. In 1617, the first Hoghton baronet, Sir Richard, entertained King James I.

On their approach to their host's home, James and his glittering retinue of nobles are said to have progressed, not over the stones and dust of a summer road, but along half a mile of red velvet carpet specially woven for the occasion in the Netherlands.

For both the King and Hoghton itself, it was an action-packed visit. James hunted, visited his host's alum mines, touched local people for scrofula (then known as the King's Evil), and knighted two worthy Lancastrians. Hoghton and its occupants, meanwhile, sweated to provide the settings and food for the celebrations. Menus from the King's visit are still preserved, and the work involved must have been enormous.

In the manner of the day, a meal consisted of only two courses, but what courses they were: beef, mutton, pork, venison, fowls, game, rabbits (boiled, fried, and cold), peas with butter, mince pies, custards. When one course featuring many of these foods had been eaten, another would come to the table. A full day after the sovereign had left, the revellers were still 'as merry as Robin Hood and all his fellowes'.

During one of the enormous meals, King

HIGHCLERE CASTLE The impressive Entrance Hall by Sir George Gilbert Scott carries on the Gothic magnificence of Sir Charles Barry's pinnacled exterior.

James was particularly struck by the quality of the loin of beef he was eating. He had knighted two local notables already; why not a third? And so, on 17 August 1617, the beef on its dish received the ceremonial tap with a sword. From then on, the cut of beef between the ribs and the hindquarters has always been known as the 'Sir Loin', or sirloin. And today's de Hoghtons can still point to the massive oak table on which the noble beef had lain.

HOLKER HALL

CUMBRIA

HOLKER HALL Along with its 3,500 books, the Library contains the microscope of the famous scientist Henry Cavendish.

With its dormers and bays, its square tower and its eye-catching cupola in pale-green copper, Holker Hall looks quintessentially Victorian. Victorian it is in part but, like many other British country houses, its Victorian dress cloaks an earlier base. It is a base that goes back to before the early eighteenth century, when a young baron called Sir Thomas Lowther lived there with his musical and energetic wife, Elizabeth. Daughter of the second Duke of Devonshire, she was also of grander status than her husband. Not surprisingly, the Lowther's Jacobean home acquired an up-to-date Georgian look, to be embellished later in the century by an even more up-to-date Gothic one.

Always inherited and never sold, Holker holds memories of over 250 years of continuous family life, with the two families involved being those of the Lowthers and the Cavendishes, to whom Holker passed in 1756. Enter the Dining Room, and there many of them are, surveying diners from their gold frames. One of the family portraits on display shows Lady Elizabeth herself, holding the score of *Tamerlaine* by Handel, and looking uncharacteristically placid; an ardent walker, she is believed to have brought an attendant footman to such exhaustion that he expired. There, too, is William Cavendish, father of the seventh Duke of Devonshire, who was killed in the Holker grounds after being thrown from a dogcart. The only non-member of the family visible is Van Dyck, painted by himself.

It was in the seventh Duke's time at Holker that the building received its first remodelling at the hands of the Victorians; not surprisingly, they reinforced its Gothic look. But more work was to come, for in 1871 the building was struck by what is probably the greatest enemy of all houses: fire. The alarm was given in time to the sleeping household by the Duke's son, Lord Frederick Cavendish (later to be the victim of political assassination by the Fenians in Dublin's Phoenix Park), but nothing could be done to save the west wing of the blazing building. Duke, family, servants all flung themselves into a frantic effort to contain the damage, the Duke sawing away at picture cords as a beam roared into flames above his head. When the fire was finally under control, it was obvious that a complete new wing was needed and, without hesitation, the Duke set to his building plans again.

As Duke of Devonshire, Holker's owner was, of course, also owner of Chatsworth, his ducal palace in Derbyshire. Shy and retiring, however, William did not care for its baroque splendours, and he remained faithful in his affections to his Lakeland home. Spencer

Compton and Frederick, who were brought up at Holker, also loved it and went on living there after their father had sadly taken charge of his massive (and money-eating) Derbyshire residence.

As the present Cavendish owner comments: 'For four hundred years, my ancestors felt that for them, Holker was more desirable, more favoured by Providence and more enhanced with natural beauty than any other place on earth. With my family, this feeling persists today . . .'

HOLKHAM HALL
NORFOLK

'I would definitely put Holkham among the first twenty great houses of England,' wrote James Lees-Milne, who had seen all of them. 'With its collections it forms one very great work of art indeed.' Holkham's secret is not only its perfect reflection of the early-Georgian age in which it was built, but also the fact that it has hardly been touched since. Yet its site was chosen almost by chance, and the estate whose income has sustained it for 250 years was, in 1720, a virtual wasteland where, as one visitor commented, two rabbits would fight each other for a blade of grass.

The Thomas Coke who built Holkham Hall inherited the estate at the age of ten. In 1712, when he was fifteen, he embarked on the Grand Tour, then an essential part of a young nobleman's education. He was abroad for seven years, during which he struck up friendships with William Kent, the painter, architect and landscape gardener, and Kent's patron Lord Burlington, a great connoisseur and collector. Kent and Burlington between them fashioned Coke's taste, and when Coke returned to England he brought with him a considerable collection of books, paintings, sculpture and other objects. He was then faced with the problem of where to house them.

The site he chose did not meet with the approval of all Coke's friends. 'A very un-pleasant place,' snorted one, and many others agreed that the windy north Norfolk coast was a strange place for a mansion inspired by the very different climate of Italy. At first, even fate seemed to be against Thomas Coke, for his fortune suffered badly from speculation in the South Sea Bubble and it was not until 1734 that work began on the house. He did not live to see the interior finished.

The second personality associated with Holkham, Thomas Coke's great-nephew, was 'Coke of Norfolk', the great agricultural improver, who was created Earl of Leicester. Holkham Hall became the centrepiece of a prosperous stretch of north Norfolk, with productive stock and a tenantry of farmers educated into the ways of 'high farming'. His annual Holkham Sheep Shearings—Britain's first agricultural shows—were held at the Hall, and several hundred guests were entertained there. The plaque over the door of the Marble Hall neatly encapsulates Coke's achievement: 'This Seat,' it says, 'on an open, barren estate, was planned, planted, built, decorated and inhabited the middle of the XVIIIth Century by Thos. Coke, Earl of Leicester.'

Many people had a hand in Holkham. The plans were William Kent's, though based on designs by Inigo Jones and Palladio. Burlington contributed ideas. Matthew Brettingham of Norwich supervised the work (and was not above trying to pass it off as his own). And then there was the figure of the Earl himself, determined to 'keep everything under my eye which alone I can trust'. It took from 1734 to 1761 to complete Holkham Hall, and it was perfection: the Derbyshire alabaster in the Marble Hall, the statuary in the Gallery, the furniture to William Kent's designs, the Inigo Jones ceilings and chimneypieces, the paintings in the Landscape Room, the tapestries. But where there was magnificence in the State Rooms, there was also convenience in the guest rooms. Admiral Boscowen visited in 1757 and reported to his wife that 'the apartments are elegant, and very convenient, a dressing-room to every bedchamber, with servants room to each, and water closets to most of them.' In the private apartments there was a library for the amusement of guests.

The State Rooms have an atmosphere of timelessness which has been preserved by disturbing Coke's original intentions as little as possible. One of the features of the Hall is the constantly changing perspective of the views of one wing from another, seen through the central block, a triumph of William Kent's original design.

Although a man of discrimination and scholarship, Coke of Norfolk also had the robust tastes of a country gentleman of the time. He drank prodigiously, enjoyed a cock-fight and hunted with enthusiasm. There was, too, a 'no nonsense' side to his character. In 1782 it fell to him, as MP for Norfolk, to propose the motion in the Commons for the ending of the American War of Independence. The King wanted hostilities to continue, and so it was Coke's duty to present the views of the Commons (which had voted for peace by a majority of one) to him. To some shock and amazement, he waited on George III in his country clothes, which, although this was his right as a Knight of the Shires, looked very much like insouciance, especially as Coke was only twenty-eight at the time. The incident caused a good deal of comment, and it is commemorated in the picture by Gainsborough which hangs in the Saloon, showing Coke as he was dressed before the King.

The domestic quarters below the State Rooms have been restored and preserved as they were in the inter-war period of this century. Among their curiosities is the only private post office in England, a relic of the first Earl of Leicester's term of office as Postmaster-General. The post of sub-postmaster at Holkham has been hereditary ever since, and is currently held by the present Viscount Coke.

HOLME PIERREPONT HALL

NOTTINGHAMSHIRE

Holme Pierrepont was built—unusually for the time and region, of red brick—in the reign of Henry VII, and it was built to impress. The Pierreponts were a substantial family of Conquest origins, and they were proud to entertain the King in their new house in June 1487. They became Earls and eventually, in 1715, Dukes of Kingston. By the eighteenth century Holme Pierrepont was a

HOLME PIERREPONT HALL *A view of the South Front in about 1780. At this period the Duchess of Kingston was in exile following her trial by the House of Lords for bigamy.*

rarely used subsidiary house, the main seat of the family being at Thoresby Hall. At this point the family had a brief spell of notoriety.

The scandal began when Evelyn Pierrepont, second Duke of Kingston, took as his mistress Elizabeth Chudleigh, who was a maid of honour to the Princess of Wales. She was already married to Augustus John Hervey, heir to the Earl of Bristol and conveniently away at sea a good deal of the time; but the marriage had been kept secret so that Elizabeth could keep her post at court. It was one thing to keep a marriage secret; divorce was quite another matter, and when Hervey indicated that he wanted a divorce Elizabeth refused, seeking instead a court order that Hervey's assertion that they had been married was false. This indeed she obtained, and in 1769, twenty-five years after her first marriage, she embarked on her second with Pierrepont. He died four years later, leaving her all his property.

HOLKHAM HALL Gainsborough's portrait—one of his last works—of the first Earl of Leicester, 'Coke of Norfolk.'

Not surprisingly, the second Duke's family took all these machinations badly, and his nephew, Evelyn Meadows, preferred a charge of bigamy against her. In 1776 the Duchess was found guilty by the House of Lords; but, evidently wily in the ways of the law, she claimed immunity as a peeress and beat a hasty retreat to the Continent. For her remaining twelve years of life she drifted from Calais to Rome, to Paris, to St Petersburg, and finally back to Paris, where she died. Meanwhile, she was lampooned by London gossips as 'Kitty Crocodile'; however, she was sustained in her exile by the rents of over £4,000 a year from the Holme Pierrepont estate.

The Hall retained its subsidiary status throughout the nineteenth century, being used by the Pierreponts—now given the Earldom of Manvers—while Thoresby was repaired and rebuilt. At some point early in the century the Gothic embellishments were added. The present owners, Robin and Elizabeth Brackenbury, who are engaged on a massive programme of restoration, are relatives of the Manvers by marriage, and include among their forebears another lady of some notoriety—the suffragette Georgina Brackenbury.

HOPETOUN HOUSE
LOTHIAN

In the State Dining Room of Hopetoun House hangs a portrait of Charles Hope, Hopetoun's first Earl. Clad in his scarlet peer's robe, he turns briefly aside from the work that has been occupying him: an architect's plan taken from the bulging portfolio on the floor. For the onlooker, however, the real point of interest is neither the plan nor the Earl, but the view stretching out behind him.

For there is Hopetoun House itself, seen from an unusual angle across its curving front, with scaffolding erected on the roof. The great Adam family of Scottish architects—the father, William, and his sons John and Robert—is at work.

Both majestic and graceful, Hopetoun is

HOPETOUN HOUSE Cheered by local gentry and tenantry on the roof, King George IV arrives to take lunch at Hopetoun House on his state visit to Scotland in 1822.

generally accepted as William Adam's ultimate masterpiece. Part of his mastery, however, lay in the way he superimposed his own work on an earlier and smaller mansion, and still achieved a harmony of design. The front of Hopetoun is the Adam family's work; the central block at the back, however, was the original house, built by Sir William Bruce. But Bruce, like the Adams, also had Charles Hope as his employer, and Bruce's mansion was only eighteen years old when the Adam remodelling began. Why did the first Earl change his mind so drastically, so soon?

As often happens where building fashions are concerned, the reason lies in a change in the patron's status. What made the Hope family unusual, however—even tragic—was the cause of their social elevation. Originally descended from one of Mary Queen of Scots'

French attendants, the Hopes entered the second half of the seventeenth century rich, well respected and possessors of a baronetcy. The second baronet's son, John, took part in a disastrous journey with the future King James II, then Duke of York. The ship they were travelling in was wrecked, and John Hope lost his life. Did he lose it while trying to save that of his future King? The truth is not known for sure, but a clue perhaps lies in the speed with which John's son, the infant Charles, was created the first Earl of Hopetoun almost as soon as he had reached his majority.

Finished in the year of Charles's ennoblement, the first Hopetoun House belongs in conception and planning to his long minority. When, soon after coming of age, he came into his Earldom as well, the new peer inevitably began to think in terms of something even better, and was urged on in his plans by the Marquess of Annandale, a connoisseur of the arts and his brother-in-law. (Much of Annandale's superb art collection is in Hopetoun House today.) In the 1720s, William Adam was brought in on the remodelling scheme, followed by his sons.

Among the interiors created by the Adam family was a range of state apartments, with specially made furniture and glorious gilded ceilings. It was here that, the century afterwards, Hopetoun welcomed its most distinguished guest, King George IV. By 1822, the Prince Regent had at last succeeded to the throne, and—impelled by an excess of romanticism—was making a state journey north to show himself as the true descendant of the Jacobite royal line.

On his visit to the fourth Earl's home, guards of honour filled the Hopetoun courtyard and local residents cried 'Huzzah!' from the roof. Sad to relate, the lunch the new monarch took seems a subdued affair; indeed, he himself had nothing more than three glasses of wine, with some turtle soup. It is to be hoped that, for all those looking on, the grandeur of the visit's setting made up for the visitor's uncharacteristic lack of party spirit.

HOUGHTON HALL

NORFOLK

Between the flat coastland where Holkham stands and the even flatter land of the Fens, there is an area of rising land known as 'high Norfolk'. High Norfolk's most significant house, and indeed the largest country house in Norfolk, is Houghton Hall.

It was built between 1721 and 1735 for the Prime Minister, Sir Robert Walpole, on the site of the two earlier houses. To make room for the house and its park, the village of Houghton was cleared and rebuilt outside the park gates as New Houghton. This has given rise to the theory that Houghton was the setting of Goldsmith's poem *The Deserted Village*, but there is no real evidence, and the

removal of whole villages to please the whim of the local landowner was a common enough practice at the time.

A fine house, Houghton Hall is also the expression of an eighteenth-century power struggle between Sir Robert Walpole and his neighbour, brother-in-law and protégé Charles, second Viscount Townshend—the agricultural reformer 'Turnip Townshend' of the history books. The Townshend seat was (and still is) Raynham Hall, ten miles to the east of Houghton and regarded by the Townshend family as 'the metropolis of Norfolk'. Meanwhile, in London, Walpole, having nurtured Townshend, proceeded to push him out of the corridors of power, and by 1730 had succeeded. Townshend retired, bitter and defeated, to Raynham to concentrate on turnips.

HOUGHTON HALL The peak of William Kent's achievements at Houghton, the Green Velvet Bedchamber with its velvet State bed.

At this point Houghton Hall was nearing completion. Its splendours were greater than Raynham ever knew. Townshend was so piqued by all this that not only did he refuse to be entertained at Houghton, but he withdrew from the neighbourhood whenever Walpole was at home. He died in 1738.

Colen Campbell was the architect of Houghton Hall, though his design was modified somewhat by Walpole's clerk of works, Thomas Ripley. William Kent was brought in to design the interiors, and his work is still to be seen at Houghton in abundance. On the practical side, the latest appointments were installed. A horse-powered pump brought water to a tower, from where it was fed by gravity to the house, a system which continued to work until the 1920s.

Walpole, who remained Prime Minister until 1742, had little opportunity for the private enjoyment of his new house, but his 'Congresses' at Houghton were notable occasions. Twice a year, in the summer and during the Christmas recess, the great and good of government, together with local worthies, would gather at Houghton Hall to eat, drink, hunt and talk politics. These were 'men only' occasions spent, according to one observer, 'up to the chin in beef, venison, geese, turkeys etc. and generally over the chin in claret, strong beer and punch.'

But all was not meat and drink at Houghton in those days. Walpole had filled the Hall with treasures: Kent's furniture, sculpture and a collection of pictures valued at the time at £40,000. This collection graced Houghton for only about thirty years. After Walpole's death in 1745 his estate passed quickly to his grandson. By this time the Houghton estate was in trouble, with mounting debts, and the situation was not helped by the heir's feckless and dissolute character. To keep the place afloat, the heir sold most of his grandfather's pictures in 1779 to Catherine the Great of Russia, and these now form part of the collection of the Hermitage Museum in Leningrad. Kent's original hangings and furniture, however, escaped a similar fate and remain to

delight present-day visitors to Houghton.

In 1791 Houghton passed to the literary Horace Walpole, Earl of Orford. He was an old man by this time, settled comfortably in the villa he had built for himself at Strawberry Hill in Twickenham, and with the famous collection of paintings sold—to his great disgust—he had little interest in Houghton. He was owner of Houghton for six years, dying without an heir in 1797, and ownership then passed by marriage into the Cholmondeley family, whose descendants live at Houghton today. The Cholmondeleys' primary interests, however, were in Cheshire, and for more than a century or so the Hall was unoccupied by members of the family. Towards the end of the nineteenth century, when the agricultural depression was biting hard, Houghton had the ignominy of being put up for sale without finding a buyer. Although the house remained intact, it was in need of restoration by the time the fifth Marquess of Cholmondeley moved in in 1913, and thereafter the fortunes of the house were revived. Although there are gaps in the original collections which must be traced to Leningrad, the fifth Marquess took care to fill them with objects of comparable taste, and Houghton today faithfully reflects its eighteenth-century glory.

HUTTON-IN-THE-FOREST

CUMBRIA

In country houses as in everything else, fashions change, and nowhere is this more evident than in the history of Hutton-in-the-Forest. The forest concerned was the Royal Forest of Inglewood, and Edward I is known to have visited Hutton-in-the-Forest in 1292. At this time, the manor was owned by the de Hutton family, who later built the fourteenth-century pele tower which is the oldest part of the present house. This was a fortified keep built as a refuge from raiders from across the border. By the seventeenth century the fear of border raids had passed, and when Hutton-in-

HUTTON-IN-THE-FOREST Detail from one of the series of Mortlake tapestries known as 'The Playing Boys'.

The contents of Hutton-in-the-Forest are largely family mementoes derived from the ancient and far-flung Vane family. They include a collection of pictures which were formerly in the home of a senior branch of the family at Fairlawne, near Tonbridge in Kent. The effect as a whole is that of a family faithfully guarding the pieces that came into their possession; notably, a Mortlake tapestry from the series known as 'The Playing Boys', a collection of eighteenth-century Chinese porcelain and some good eighteenth-century English furniture.

INVERARAY CASTLE

STRATHCLYDE

Massive without, exquisite within: the extreme contrast between the exterior of Inveraray Castle and its interior never fails to astonish. Even today, the painted rooms of Inveraray dazzle in their sophistication. In the period when they were created—the late eighteenth century, very few years after a road had been brought to the area—they must have seemed little short of magical. Indeed, the whole experience of visiting the Castle would have produced one culture shock after another. First, there would have been the hours spent travelling on a military road, heading ever further into the back of beyond; then, on arrival, there was the contrasting civilization of an aristocrat's great house. And then there was the spectacle of the most refined, ultra-fashionable settings in all Europe.

The inspiration behind them was French: the very latest decorative styles to have emerged from France in the 1770s. France was also the country of origin of Girard and Guinand, the artists who put the inspiration into effect on the walls and ceilings, and it was the home of the weavers who—working to given measurements—produced the tapestries with their pastoral scenes that hang in Inveraray's Drawing Room.

However, much of the talent that made Inveraray was British-born, from the London

the-Forest was bought in 1605 by the Fletcher family, rich merchants from Cockermouth, the moat was filled in and the process of converting a castle into a country house began. About 1680 the transformation was continued with the building of the courtyard and its baroque central façade.

The next significant phase in the development of the house came in the nineteenth century, by which time it was owned by the Vane family, the present owners. There were two aspects to the nineteenth-century work. To designs by Anthony Salvin, the pele tower was battlemented and the tower on the south front was built, together with other additions. Meanwhile, Lady Vane came under the influence of William Morris and the early arts and crafts movement, and this is reflected in various parts of the house, most notably in Lady Darlington's Room.

architect Roger Morris, who designed the original building, to the local tailor who tacked the French tapestry-work into place on the seats of the gilt chairs. But even between London and the old county of Argyll there is a gulf, and the real magic of Inveraray lies in the fact that it succeeded in being built and furnished at all.

The team responsible for this astonishing feat was headed by Archibald, third Duke of Argyll, Earl of Ilay, and Chief of the Clan Campbell. He inherited Inveraray in 1743, when he was sixty. In spite of his age he threw himself into building plans. With the help of Morris, he conceived the awesomely difficult plan of rebuilding his ancient clan fortress in a completely different spot—and of moving the whole of Inveraray town to do it.

To supervise the work, Morris in his turn secured the help of the celebrated Adam family and, although building operations were doubtless hampered by the '45 Rebellion, the work went ahead surprisingly fast. The new Castle walls went up, John Adam designed buildings for the new town, the Castle's central tower was built, and the surrounding land was groomed into a civilized state.

Although the third Duke did not survive long enough to live in his creation, he at least had the satisfaction of seeing how it would look, for the basic building—minus the turrets it wears today—was finished in 1758. During the fourth Duke's lifetime, work halted; but, with the arrival of his successor, John, the whole operation started again.

John was a connoisseur of beauty in all its forms. His wife, the former Elizabeth Gunning, was acclaimed as the most beautiful woman of her day, and his new Castle in the Highlands was to attain a similar status. It was

INVERARAY CASTLE The Tapestry Drawing Room still contains the Beauvais tapestries that John, fifth Duke of Argyll, ordered for the apartments he was planning in 1785.

KENTWELL HALL Secure within its broad moat, Kentwell is a classic Elizabethan manor house. Behind it is a walled garden, a fish pond, a Victorian vinery and a fine yew walk.

John who brought in the French painters who created the State Dining Room's ceiling; it was John again who masterminded the cooperation of the Edinburgh carpenters who made the chairs for the Dining Room, the Beauvais weavers who produced their coverings, and the Inveraray carpenter who tacked them into position.

Unhappily for both the Duke and Inveraray, the Duchess Elizabeth died in 1790, before work on the French-inspired Drawing Room was finished. With its completion, the Duke himself stopped working on the Castle. The Duchess's amazing looks, however, survived in her sons—who both became Dukes in their turn—and her husband's love of perfection survives, too, in the rooms he made for their family home.

KENTWELL HALL
SUFFOLK

Rising impressively behind its moat at the end of an avenue of limes almost a mile long, Kentwell Hall is in the classic symmetrical Elizabethan style. It looks like the kind of house that must have entertained monarchs, been a centre of conspiracies, seen unbelievably lavish scenes of entertainment. In fact, Kentwell has lived a quiet life for 400 years, in the ownership of a succession of Suffolk worthies of whom, by coincidence, no fewer than four (including the present owner) were lawyers.

The house was begun in the 1560s by William Clopton, whose family had acquired the manor of Kentwell two centuries before. Building seems to have proceeded over several decades under William and then his son Thomas: first the centre block, then the west wing, and finally, to make up an E-shape, the east wing, towers and porch. In 1618, however, the male Clopton line died out and Kentwell passed by marriage into the D'Ewes and later the D'Arcy families. This succession is chronicled in the castings of the hoppers of the rainwater system, which carry all three families' coats of arms.

There was evidently considerable investment at Kentwell during the first century of its life, for in 1676 it was described as 'a very fair brick house with twelve wainscot rooms, the park stocked with above 150 deer, a double dovehouse, fish ponds and other conveniences'. In that year the estate was sold to Sir Thomas Robinson, who created the lime avenue. He did not live to enjoy it, however, falling to his death from the window of his London chambers while trying to escape from a fire.

In 1826 the house was, apart from some

KINGSTON HOUSE The Dining Room, whose oak panelling dates from 1728. The grandfather clock shows the phases of the moon.

trifling Georgian alterations, substantially as it had been built, both inside and out. But then fire struck, gutting the centre block though leaving the fabric standing. The shell was bought by the then High Sheriff of Suffolk, Robert Hart Logan, who engaged Thomas Hopper to undertake an ambitious restoration. The interiors of the Great Hall, with its minstrels' gallery, and of the Main Dining Room, in which the apparently grained wood panelling is in fact plaster, are Hopper's work. Although not affected by the fire, the east wing was evidently also remodelled during this period. Like Sir Thomas Robinson, however, Logan was not to enjoy his house for long, and following his early death in 1838 Kentwell was sold again.

A succession of ownerships and tenancies followed until, in 1971, Patrick Phillips bought the Hall, by then in a serious state of decay and bereft of its estate. A steady programme of restoration has taken the house back towards its Tudor prime.

KINGSTON HOUSE

OXFORDSHIRE

The exact date of this modest but satisfying manor house is not known, but it was built in the mid-seventeenth century for the Latton family who had been Lords of the Manor of Kingston Bagpuize since 1543.

As often happened to suit changing tastes, at some point in its history—probably in mid-Victorian times—Kingston House was 'turned round'. The old front entrance, through what is now the saloon, led to an inner hall and staircase, with a drawing room on the first floor in the present Rose Room. The present cantilevered staircase and gallery from the new entrance hall would date from that time.

Kingston House was, from 1939 to her death in 1976, the home of Miss Marlie Raphael, who gave devoted attention to the garden. She extended the formal garden (now being recreated) to make a woodland garden with grass walks which, carefully planned to bloom throughout the year, is one of the main attractions of the house. The older trees—yews, Wellingtonias and cedars among them—survive from earlier periods in the history of Kingston.

In 1976, Kingston House was inherited by Miss Raphael's niece, Lady Grant, now Lady Tweedsmuir, who has deployed sixteenth- and seventeenth-century furniture to recall the house's beginnings. The present ownership seems peculiarly apposite, for Lady Tweedsmuir is married to a son of John Buchan. The atmosphere of Kingston House strongly recalls that of the fictional Fosse Manor, which Buchan admirers will remember as the country house to which Richard Hannay has retired at the beginning of *The Three Hostages*.

KINGSTONE LISLE PARK
OXFORDSHIRE

To enter the hall at Kingstone Lisle Park is an inspirational experience. The idea, as the owner explains, is that you 'come through an Italian palace, eyes uplifted, to an English country house'. Everything leads the visitor upwards and onwards: the fluted pillars, the classical figures that crown them, the glittering chandelier and—at the end of the hall—the wonderful flying staircase, curling and crossing up out of sight without any pillars to support it. Kingstone Lisle's hall is a triumph of interior design; the extraordinary thing is that no one knows who the designer was.

Superb craftsmanship is a hallmark of Kingstone Lisle. Starting in the hall, it pervades the whole house, from the antique Irish glass to the modern hand-made carpets on each of which twelve girls worked for two years. Among its most charming manifestations is a display of cabinet-making in miniature: pieces made by apprentice craftsmen and used as portable samples. The collection fits easily on to the top of a piecrust table.

The house also contains the work of two further craftsmen—in fact, craftswomen—who are much nearer in time than the

KINGSTONE LISLE PARK 'An inspirational experience': the Staircase Hall, designed by a genius whose name has been forgotten.

miniaturist 'prentice boys. The stools and fire screen in the drawing room, the morning-room chairs, the dining-room carpet, were all embroidered by Kingstone Lisle's owner or her mother. The embroiderers' triumph comes in the octagonal sitting room. The difficult shape of its floor imposed only one real solution: a carpet specially designed for it. A flower-garden in gros and petit point, it took its creator seven years of stitching.

KNEBWORTH HOUSE
HERTFORDSHIRE

In the minds of many people in Britain, the invention of printing is summed up less by the huge intellectual and social changes that it brought about than by one frequently reproduced painting. In a gloriously romantic jumble, it shows medieval courtiers, knights, apprentices, printing equipment, one noble lady and one dog, and illustrates a visit paid by King Edward IV to the printing press set at Westminster by William Caxton.

Although it found its way into a million history books, the painting's value as historical evidence is fairly minimal; it was, of course, painted long after the event, and is the work of the Victorian artist Daniel Maclise. Artistically, however, it is a splendid example of Victorian Britain's interest in the glories of its island history and—for the initiated—it also possesses a real biographical interest. One of its armoured knights is a portrait of the nineteenth-century novelist, poet, politician and baron, Edward Bulwer-Lytton. The picture

hangs in the State Drawing Room at Knebworth House, which Edward inherited in 1843, and which he turned into a superb temple of high Victorian Gothic.

In its origins, the building that the romantically minded Edward acquired was not in fact very far removed in time from Caxton's printing press at Westminster. The man who first put it on the map, Sir Robert Lytton, was a friend and comrade-at-arms of Henry VII, founder in 1485 of the new royal dynasty of Tudor. Sir Robert's fortunes prospered with those of his royal patron, and so did those of the medieval castle that he bought in 1490. By the time he died, he had turned it into a large brick residence well stocked with windows.

Oddly, the Tudor mansion escaped radical

KNEBWORTH HOUSE Victorian Knebworth: the State Drawing Room, redesigned in High Gothic style by Edward Bulwer-Lytton. The Caxton picture hangs in the far corner.

change for over 300 years. However, by the time it reached the hands of the formidable Elizabeth Bulwer-Lytton in 1810, it was falling apart. It needed drastic reduction and a new look. Elizabeth supplied both and turned it into a stucco Gothic castle.

Meanwhile, her son Edward was going through school and university before emerging as something of a dandy. He married a beautiful Irish girl called Rosina; his mother, hotly disapproving, cancelled the allowance she made him, so, to support himself, he started writing. Soon he was the author of a torrent of novels.

A miniature of Rosina at Knebworth shows her in a charming guise, holding the baby Robert Lytton (one day to be Viceroy of India) in her arms. Reality, however, was less idyllic. Robert's sister—the adorable 'Little Boots', also drawn by Edward's friend Maclise—died. Edward and Rosina bickered, rowed and split up. Later, when he was standing as a Parliamentary candidate for Hertfordshire, she turned up and denounced him in public at the hustings.

Difficult though Edward's private life may have been, his public and creative one clearly helped make up for it. He travelled; he wrote. He became a friend of Charles Dickens, who often visited him at Knebworth and who used a miniature pagoda in Knebworth's Falkland Room as the original of the 'Chinese house for Jip with little bells', to which Dora Copperfield tried to accustom her dog. And, above all, he turned his romantic love of the past into visible effect by altering Knebworth yet again.

It had been Gothic before; within a year it was super-Gothic. Sprouting fantastic towers and spires, it was—and is—much more attractive than the rather glum pile constructed by Elizabeth. Indoors, the transformation of the State Drawing Room was just as startling, and just as delightful. Surviving where his novels have not, this and the rest of Edward's architectural creations in the Romantic tradition are probably his real masterpieces.

LAMPORT HALL
NORTHAMPTONSHIRE

In 1846 Lamport Hall came into the possession of Sir Charles Isham, latest in a 300-year-long chain of Ishams to have lived on the top of their Northamptonshire hill. A spiritualist and a vegetarian, he was a charmingly offbeat character who combined high principles with a weakness for fun. 'In things transitory,' ran the comment he inscribed over Lamport's front door, 'resteth no glory.' At the same time, he good-naturedly pulled up the stone floor of Lamport's High Room and replaced it with parquet, so that his daughter could dance happily at the ball held for her coming of age.

LAMPORT HALL Sir Thomas Isham, here painted by Lely, acquired many treasures for Lamport on his Grand Tour.

LAVENHAM PRIORY
Parts of the original hall
house, dating from the
thirteenth century, are
now incorporated in the
Great Hall. The huge
brick fireplace was added
in about 1530.

His most unusual achievement, however, is to be found outside, in the Lamport Hall grounds: the twenty-foot-high rockery that he built, one of the first in Britain. An inspired gardener, he cleverly sited his baby Alp to face north, thus ensuring the necessary cool growing conditions for its mountain plants. But, not content with mere practicality, he added to the mountain scene an unlikely flourish of his own, the first garden gnomes to be imported into England.

One of their number now stands in the house's library. It is, perhaps, an object of lesser importance than some of the room's other paintings (they include a Bible that belonged to King Charles I). However, as the oldest garden ornament of its sort in the country, it deserves the special protection given it by its glass dome.

LAVENHAM PRIORY

SUFFOLK

Lavenham, a former centre of the Suffolk wool trade, is the county's architectural jewel, and has been described as the finest medieval town in England. It owes its charac-

ter to its timber-framed houses, of which the Priory is one.

The name of the house is deceptive; there is no evidence that it was ever used for religious observances, though in the thirteenth century it was owned by the Benedictine Order and was possibly used as a staging-post for monks on their way to the monastery at Earls Colne. It was built as a hall house, remnants of which now form part of the Great Hall. There was considerable expansion over the succeeding two centuries, which—together with the Lavenham woolmark on the exterior—strengthens the view that the building was of significance in the wool trade. By 1580, ownership had passed to Henry Copinger, the rector of Lavenham, who brought up twelve children there and farmed the estate.

Almost at once, Copinger became involved in a dispute over tithes with the major landowner, the Earl of Oxford—the kind of dispute between land and church which plagued English country life until well into the present century when the tithe was finally abolished. The Earl of Oxford declined to pay the tithe on his park, whereupon Copinger threatened to resign from the living, which was in Oxford's gift. The quarrel was temporarily patched up, but the dispute rumbled on to the end of Copinger's life in 1622, by which time he had spent £1,600 defending the rights of the Church.

The Priory continued as a working farm well into the present century, and older Lavenham residents can remember buying milk at the dairy door. Later, it was left to become derelict until it was bought for restoration by the present owners in 1979. Their aim has been to reinstate the structure of the Priory as it was in Henry Copinger's time.

LAYER MARNEY TOWER
ESSEX

There are many examples in Britain of houses that are but a shadow of their former glory, cruelly cropped by fire, time or death duties. Examples of houses that never were—proud beginnings robbed by circumstance of their flowering—are rarer. Layer Marney is one such.

Rising surprisingly from the flatlands of Essex, Layer Marney Tower was to have been the centrepiece of a large mansion which was never completed. Its ambitious creator was Henry, first Lord Marney: 'a person,' according to one commentator, 'of great wisdom, gravity and of singular fidelity.' He was also evidently a man with a keen instinct for survival, or perhaps exceptional charm, for, having been a privy councillor to Henry VII, he went on to perform the same office for Henry VIII and also become Chancellor of the Duchy of Lancaster, Vice-Chamberlain and Captain of the King's Guard, and a host of other titles. Honours came to Lord Marney like moths to a candle, and it is not surprising that, probably about 1520, he decided to build himself a suitably grand house.

The visitor can only speculate on the wonder of the house that might have been. In the event, all that was built was the great gatehouse—the Tower itself—with its east and west wings and a separate range, built as stables and now used for functions and as an art gallery. The grand courtyard that Lord Marney clearly envisaged was not to be; fate, in the person of the Grim Reaper, was to intervene.

The first Lord Marney died in 1523, and his son John followed him to the grave only two years later, at the age of thirty-two. Neither of John's marriages gave him sons. The Marney line died with him.

It has to be said that, unfinished though it was, Layer Marney was sufficient for many people's purposes. Indeed it was grand enough to be a suitable lodging for two days for Queen Elizabeth I on a progress through Essex in 1579, by which time it had been acquired by the Tuke family. Less exalted times were to come: when one of a long line of owners bought the Tower in 1904, he had to unstop the bricked-up windows, renew the staircase, and comb the country for panelling contemporary with the building of the house.

The present owners bought the tower in 1959. Of the two eight-storey turrets, each 80-feet (24 metres) high, only the lower two storeys are in use, the floors of the others having collapsed or been removed. However, the staircase of the west turret can be climbed to give a marvellous view from the roof. Until 1900, the present main entrance was an arch which provided carriage access to what, if the house had ever been finished, would have been the courtyard. The first Lord Marney was a man who, over 400 years ago, had a vision of the house he would like to live in. What that vision was, no one will ever know.

LEEDS CASTLE
KENT

Two flags, not one, are flown from the masthead of Leeds Castle. Turn and turn about, they show the gold and indigo lions of a medieval queen, and the silver eagles of Leeds' last and longest individual owner, who bought it—practically uninhabitable—in 1926.

This dual proclamation of identity is an intentional one, for it signals the most salient fact of the castle's nine centuries of history.

LAYER MARNEY TOWER *The great Gatehouse of a house that never was. Two deaths in quick succession robbed Essex of the house to which the twin towers were to have been the centrepiece.*

Just as A La Ronde is a woman's house, so Leeds—ancient and bristling with strength though it is—can claim to be called a woman's castle. For many years at the height of the Middle Ages, English kings gave this strategic fortress to their wives. In our own time, it was again a woman owner who rescued it and made its future secure. It is in honour of all the ladies of Leeds that the two flags fly.

In its earliest days, however, such compliments would have been far from the minds of the owners of Leeds Castle. Indeed, its very name commemorates a male occupant rather than a female one: Ledian, chief minister of a Saxon king of Kent. Ledian—also called Leed—owned lands on the bank of the River Len, which at one point forms a lake. In the lake were two islands; Ledian took advantage of this unrivalled opportunity this and used them as the site for a modest wooden 'castle'.

When the Normans came, the Saxon occupiers of Leeds were rudely elbowed out of the way, and the wooden building met the same fate. The two islands offered a perfect site for the sort of impregnable stone fortress the conquerors needed to maintain their grip on their new lands. Not long after the start of the twelfth century, one Robert de Crèvecoeur (in English, Robert Heartbreak) started building a stone version of Leeds. Five generations of his family followed him until, around 1260, a mistake over a matter of loyalty brought them low. They were forced out, and Leeds finally ended up in the possession of King Edward I and his wife, Eleanor of Castile.

The royal couple often stayed at Leeds, and the King finally gave it to his Queen. Although a hard man and a ruthless monarch, Edward adored her, and was desolate when she died. 'My harp,' he wrote afterwards, 'is turned to mourning, in life I loved her dearly, nor can I cease to love her in death.' Each stage in the progress of her bier from the Midlands to Westminster was marked, by his orders, with a memorial cross (London's Charing Cross is a Victorian version of the final one). And Leeds itself is also her monument: in the Middle Ages, a mass was said daily there for

LEEDS CASTLE Carved oak beams form the ceiling of the 75-foot-long Henry VIII Banqueting Hall, with its ebony floor.

her soul, and it is her flag that displays its lions to the Leeds battlements today.

Edward gave Leeds to his second wife and, in the years that followed, the Castle became the property of four more royal wives. One was Isabella, widow of Edward II: adulteress, murderess, and born survivor. Another, in contrast, was Anne of Bohemia: the fifteen-year-old bride of King Richard II, she spent her first weeks in England at Leeds. They, too, were devoted and Leeds was as popular with Richard as it had been with Edward.

Its status at the time is indicated by the contemporary French chronicler Froissart, who visited the English court in 1395: 'I heard,' he wrote at one point on his travels, 'that the King had gone into a beautiful palace in Kent called Leeds Castle.' Indeed, so palatial was it that, when Queen Anne's brother in turn visited England, Leeds became his lodging for a month. He was no less a personage than the Holy Roman Emperor.

By this time, Anne herself had been dead for

over twenty years, and her husband for ten. The Emperor's host was the next king but one: Henry V, fresh from his victory at Agincourt. Hero of England though Henry was, he was far from heroic in his dealings with his step-mother, the fourth queen-occupant of Leeds. In accordance with tradition, Queen Joan had for a while owned the Castle. Shortly after the imperial visit, however, Henry had her charged with one of the worst crimes in the medieval canon: plotting to bring about his own death by means of witchcraft. She was lucky to escape with her life; as it was, however, her wealth was seized (the probable aim of the whole sorry manoeuvre) and she was imprisoned in the Castle over which she had once ruled.

Modern visitors to Leeds can inspect Joan's household expenses at Leeds for part of the year 1422: a momentous one for herself, the Castle and for England, for it saw King Harry's death. He freed his stepmother just before he died, and gave her back her property. Leeds, however, went to his own widow: Catherine, heroine of the rather puzzled courtship immor-talized by Shakespeare.

Joan moved out, doubtless with relief; the widow Catherine (aged twenty-one) moved in, and proceeded to make her presence felt at Leeds in the most spectacular manner. She repaired the building's fabric; she had a clock put up—one of the first in Britain. And she rocked the nation by falling in love.

Her lover was her Clerk of the Wardrobe, one Owen Tudor. In spite of the appalling difficulties involved, the relationship blos-somed and they made a secret marriage. Just in time, for their guilty secret was soon to be discovered: Owen was sent to the Tower, and his wife was also imprisoned. However, the resourceful pair at length managed to extricate themselves, and went on to have five children. Without knowing it, they also founded a dynasty, for their grandson became the first of England's Tudor monarchs, Henry VII.

With Henry's own son, Henry VIII, the connection between Leeds and royal women failed, and so in the end did that between Leeds and royalty itself. It is possible that the

Maids of Honour housed in the new Maidens' Tower included Anne Boleyn; traces of the presence of Henry's other wives have so far remained invisible. Henry himself made major improvements to the Castle but he finally gave it away to one of his statesmen.

From then on, its fortunes varied; at one time a prison, it was also the home of the only peer to emigrate to America. It was damaged by fire, Gothicized, returned to a medieval appearance. The appointments, however, also remained medieval; by the 1920s, when it changed hands for the penultimate time, bathrooms were still non-existent, while ser-vants were lodged in what one potential buyer called the dungeons.

However, these drawbacks did not dismay its final lady owner. Occupying Leeds Castle for only two years short of a half-century, the Hon. Olive Lady Baillie—whose ancestors were themselves courtiers of the Tudor monarchs—made caring for it her life's work. Thanks to her, it is again a 'beautiful palace in Kent'.

LEIGHTON HALL

LANCASHIRE

The name of Gillow is well-known among connoisseurs of English furniture. Robert Gillow set up business in Lancaster in about 1730, and the firm prospered to the extent that by 1761 it had opened premises in London's Oxford Street, employing designers like Shera-ton and Hepplewhite. Responsible for such milestones in furniture-making as the billiard table and the telescopic table, Gillow's went on to become the firm of Waring and Gillow. Few large country houses, especially in the north of England, are without items of Gillow furniture, but the most notable collection is at Leighton Hall.

Leighton Hall was built in the mid-eight-eenth century on the site of an earlier house, and later Gothicized by Harrison of Chester. In 1822 it was sold to Richard Gillow, grandson of the founder of the Gillow business, who retired to the house. He brought with him a number of mid-Georgian Gillow pieces, including an expanding table, now in the Dining Room, which is thought to have been the prototype of this style. The wealth of furniture from one maker's workshop undoubtedly gives Leighton Hall a unique sense of coherence and completeness.

Most of the owners of Leighton Hall have been Roman Catholics, and this tradition was continued by Richard Gillow's marriage to a daughter of the staunchly Catholic Stapleton family from Carlton Towers. Richard died in 1849, leaving Leighton Hall to his son, also Richard. This Richard had early intimations of mortality that proved to be false. At seventy, he decided that as he had not much longer to live it was not worth doing anything more than trivial repairs at the Hall. In the event, he lived to the age of ninety-nine, and when he died in 1906 the Hall was in a very poor state.

LEIGHTON HALL This early eighteenth-century games table, its chessboard inlaid in the lid, is among the Gillow collection.

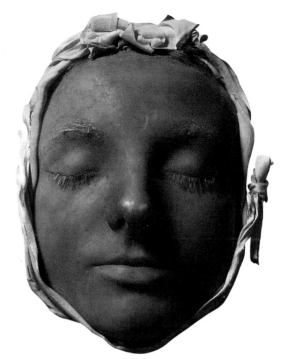

LENNOXLOVE The death mask of Mary Queen of Scots, taken from her severed head after her execution in England in 1587.

It was brought back to life by his grandson and is still owned by Gillow descendants.

LENNOXLOVE

LOTHIAN

So much has been written about the fascination of Mary Queen of Scots; so many pictures exist that show her as far from fascinating. It is therefore something of a shock to find that she was indeed beautiful.

The evidence is of the most incontrovertible type, and also the grimmest. It is her death mask, taken from her severed head after her execution in England. It is now on display in the Great Hall of the Scottish castle of Lennoxlove—in the same room as the silver box that gave its name to the Casket Letters, apparent proof of Mary's involvement in the murder of her second husband, Lord Darnley. Mary was forty-four when she died, but the mask seems to show a younger woman: one with a short upper lip and a delicately curving chin.

By a curious coincidence, Lennoxlove has two connections with someone who could lay claim to the title of 'la belle Stuart'. Indeed, the building takes its name from this second beauty—or, rather, from her love for her short-lived husband.

In 1662, a fifteen-year-old granddaughter of the first Lord Blantyre entered the household of King Charles II's queen as a royal maid of honour. Called Frances Teresa, she was dazzlingly pretty and, inevitably, Charles expressed extreme interest. But the unbelievable happened: Frances turned him down. Instead, she wanted her cousin: Charles Stuart, Duke of Lennox. And, in spite of the King's displeasure, she got him. The impetuous couple fled Charles's wrath, and married in secret.

The storm blew over in the end. The court painter Sir Peter Lely produced portraits of them both, and his picture of Frances shows that the 'Belle Stuart' nickname bestowed on her by society was fully justified. Sadly, however, their happiness was short-lived. Lennox, appointed Ambassador to Denmark, died there in 1672. Frances, meanwhile, contracted smallpox, and was the 'beautiful Stuart' no longer. Much to King Charles's credit, he came to the young widow's rescue and gave her a new post of honour at court, that of Lady of the Bedchamber.

When, in the early eighteenth century, the Duchess died, the instructions she left to her trustees revealed a charming plan for commemorating her late husband. They were to buy the castle of Lethington and present it to her cousin, the Master of Blantyre. There was just one condition attached; its name was to be changed from Lethington to Lennoxlove. The Master was happy to accept, and Frances's memorial to her Duke was assured of safe passage into the future.

LEVENS HALL

CUMBRIA

Levens Hall, like several other houses, bears the sign of the heart. But the gilded hearts that decorate the down-spout by the front door

LEVENS HALL The complete set of Charles II chairs in the Dining Room is believed to be the finest one in the country.

do not recall any sentimental attachment; they refer, instead, to the way Levens allegedly changed hands in the 1680s. It was, so the story runs, gambled away by its owner on the turn of a card: the ace of hearts.

The facts of the matter remain somewhat obscure but, however the conveyance was made, it brought nothing but good to Levens itself. It was the new owner—a Colonel James Grahme or Grahame—who provided the element of the Levens scene that was to make it nationally celebrated: the superb garden with its population of topiary shapes.

Both garden and park were the work of one of the greatest landscape gardeners of the time, Monsieur Beaumont. Former garden adviser to King James II, he came to work at Levens when the fall of the last Catholic ruler of Britain brought his royal appointment to an abrupt end. Happily, the fame of his new garden creation near Kendal both restored and enhanced his reputation: by the turn of the seventeenth and eighteenth centuries, Londoners were making the then horrendous journey north to the county of Westmorland, just to view M. Beaumont's works.

It was this same reputation that has ensured

LILIES An aerial view. During World War I the then owner, Vernon Brittain, drilled troops on the lawn. Later, the house became a training school for nursing students.

the survival of his garden today. Colonel Grahame's daughter, to whom Levens passed later in the 1700s, resolutely refused to allow any landscaper of the Capability Brown school to sweep away her old-fashioned topiary—it had been part of her childhood, and so had the genial figure of its creator.

By an equally happy chance, the house was also left as its pre-Palladian owners had created it. Like many buildings in the Border Country—then a highly flexible zone, depending on the relative powers of the English and Scots—Levens has at its heart a medieval pele tower, built at a period when defence was a day-to-day necessity. An owner of the Elizabethan period enlarged and gentrified his tower home, and Colonel Grahame added a service wing. However, the Colonel's greatest achievement (other than the gardens) was his furnishing schemes—especially that of the Dining Room, with its Cordova leather hangings and its Charles II chairs.

Levens' ghosts include a disconcertingly bouncy black dog that appears from nowhere and trips people up, but the most imposing of the building's spectres is its Grey Lady: an eighteenth-century gipsy who was turned away from the Hall's door and died of starvation. Her dying curse, so the story runs, foretold

that Levens would never pass to a son of its owner until the River Kent stopped its flow, and a white fawn was seen in the park.

In the nineteenth century, both phenomena were observed: a white fawn appeared, and the river froze. And Alan Desmond Bagot was born—the first male heir in the direct line for over a century.

LILIES

BUCKINGHAMSHIRE

The present house of Lilies was built in 1870 to replace an earlier, part-Tudor building which was burned to the ground. It is set in that part of Buckinghamshire which was virtually appropriated by the Rothschild family, who built their large mansions at Mentmore, Waddesdon, Halton and Ascott, and Baron Ferdinand de Rothschild was the first tenant of the rebuilt Lilies, which he took while waiting for Waddesdon to be completed.

Later owners, in the Edwardian period, were the rich and eccentric Brittain family. One of these, Vernon, rode into the village of Weedon each morning with half-a-crown for every man who touched his forelock and a florin for every woman who curtsied. When the First World

War broke out, he drilled soldiers on the lawn at Lilies. Perhaps it was as well that Vernon Brittain did not survive the war; he would not have liked the less feudal world that emerged after it.

It is an interesting comment on changing standards of comfort that when Lilies was advertised for sale in 1894, after Baron Rothschild had left, it had nineteen bedrooms but only two bathrooms. There is now a catholic collection of pictures, books, letters, documents and *objets d'art* ranging from arte-facts from early Egyptian tombs to the first television tube and the first issue of *TV Times*. There are over 800 pictures and posters, the Victorians being particularly well represented with oils and drawings by Ruskin, Rossetti, Lord Leighton and Etty. A further pre-Raphaelite connection is that many of the carpets now at Lilies are from the home of Holman Hunt.

LITTLECOTE

BERKSHIRE

On a stormy night in 1575 old Mother Barnes, midwife of Great Shefford in Wiltshire, lay in her bed and was glad that she knew of no young woman in the neighbour-hood likely to go into labour that night. Old Mother Barnes dozed, and dreamed. She dreamed of horses' hooves, the rattle of carriage wheels in the lane outside her house. But this was no dream—there was someone hammering on her door. 'Mother Barnes! Mother Barnes!' a voice shouted above the wind and rain.

She pulled back the bolt and opened her door, and there, framed in the light of a lantern, were two men. She had never seen them before.

'You are Mother Barnes?' said the taller of the men. She nodded. 'Then there's work for you,' he went on. 'And a fine reward—if you can hold your tongue.' He quickly spelt out what they wanted.

Perhaps frightened of what would happen if she refused, Mother Barnes agreed to go with them. She was blindfolded and taken some eight miles to what she could tell was a big house. She was led up a staircase to a bedroom, and there her blindfold was removed. In front of her, in labour, was a young woman she did not recognize. Mother Barnes called for water and spare sheets, and in due time the baby was delivered. She took the child and handed it to a tall, slender gentleman who was standing near. To her horror, instead of holding the baby close as she had expected, he held it up and dashed it into the fire.

She smothered her protests and allowed herself to be blindfolded for the return jour-ney. But before she went she cut a small piece of material from the bed-hangings, and as she was led down the stairs she counted them and fixed the number in her mind. The two men were as good as their word: they delivered her safely home and pressed coins into her hand. No doubt she had little more sleep that night, or for many nights after. At length, she told her story to the magistrate, producing the scrap of cloth she had brought away with her and telling him of her counting of the stairs.

Shortly afterwards, 'Wild' William Darrell of Littlecote, locally notorious for his sexual exploits, came to court on a charge of child murder. He was convicted on old Mother Barnes's evidence, though he did not serve his sentence. Instead—these were not sweet-smelling times where justice was concerned—the sentence was commuted in exchange for the acquisition by his prosecutor, the Attorney General Sir John Popham, of the manor of Littlecote. 'Wild' Darrell went free—but not for long. Riding on Littlecote land a few months later, his horse shied, Darrell was thrown, and his neck was broken.

But who was the young mother? This did not come out at the trial and has never been satisfactorily explained. One theory is that it was Darrell's sister Ada, with whom he was known to have had an incestuous affair. Another is that she was a Miss Bonham, whose brother was a guest at Littlecote on the fateful night. The diarist John Aubrey alleged that the mother was one of Darrell's servants—

though, being the kind of man he was, would he not have been more likely to turn her out of the house to face her trouble on her own?

Whatever the answer, the story has left its mark on Littlecote. It is said that the bloodstains of the murdered baby appear on the floor of the room where it was put to death; that Mother Barnes is seen with the baby in her arms; that Darrell himself appears, still trying to make peace with his conscience; that the mother and baby are seen outside the fateful room; and that mysterious footsteps are heard. Some of these reports are as recent as 1969.

Littlecote's more tangible contents today include the arrangement of some rooms to represent a day in the life of the house in July 1642, when the then owner, Sir John Popham's brother Alexander, evacuated his family in advance of the threatening Civil War. In the Great Hall hang the arms and armour of the local contingent of the Parliamentary Army. But nothing teases the imagination so much as the events of that night over 400 years ago when old Mother Barnes heard a knock on her door, and a baby briefly lived.

....

LITTLE MALVERN COURT

HEREFORD & WORCESTER

....

Little Malvern Court can best be summed up by stating the obvious. It is a house by a church, the church of Little Malvern Priory, first established a century after the Norman Conquest, and surviving until Henry VIII closed the monasteries.

But the relationship between church and house is a closer one than even appearances indicate, for the Court contains some of the monastery itself, and its first occupants were the Prior and his ten or twelve monks. They fished their fast-day meals from one of Little Malvern's five surviving monastic ponds; they ate them in the Prior's Hall, or refectory, which also still survives within the body of the house. And, for the main business of their lives, they went to the church that loomed over the complex of buildings.

By the end of the Middle Ages, the community had become rather a flaccid one, for the Bishop of Worcester concluded an inspection by condemning the 'great ruin of the Church and place'. The neglectful monks were sent off to Gloucester for two years to atone for their ways, and the Bishop instigated repairs in the 1480s. Some of his restoration work also survives, but the outwardly religious function of the buildings was cut short by Henry VIII's Dissolution of the Monasteries, and Little Malvern passed to a layman called Henry Russell.

However, even this did not break the relationship between church and house. It merely went underground. The Church of England was established in the country at large, but the Russells were recusants: they refused to attend its services. Where they did worship was in a secret chapel—a Roman Catholic one—under the roof. Only when official opposition to Catholics was relaxed in

LITTLECOTE The severity of the Cromwellian chapel—the only survivor of its period—reflects the stern purpose of its time. —

the late eighteenth century were the Russells' descendants able to set up a more public place of worship in the old Prior's Hall.

At the same time, they sold some of their land to the monastery of Downside, for eventual use as a site for a Roman Catholic church. Built half a century later, its graveyard now contains the remains of the Malvern Hills' most famous son: Sir Edward Elgar.

LLANVIHANGEL COURT
GWENT

Many of the houses discussed in this book were owned by Catholic families which performed miracles of faith—and survival— during the two centuries and more when to be Catholic was, at best, socially and politically crippling and, at worst, fatal. In the history of Llanvihangel Court was an owner whose exploits illustrate the tensions of those times.

In 1665, John Arnold inherited Llanvihangel Court from his father Nicholas. He was a rabid Protestant which, living as he did in the territory of the Catholic Herbert family, inevitably brought him into conflict with his neighbours. In 1678 he committed what looks like a deliberately malevolent act. He sent to the Speaker of the House of Commons a list of local recusants, which resulted in the closure of the Jesuit College near Monmouth and the hounding of a number of priests who escaped. One of these, Father David Lewis, was captured near Abergavenny and taken into the town to be held overnight. His captors feared a riot, and so Father Lewis was taken on to Llanvihangel Court where he was hidden in an upper room. Next day, he was taken to Monmouth and to his eventual execution.

It could not be expected that such an act would go unavenged, and indeed John Arnold evidently did not expect so, for he took to wearing armour on his visits to London. He was dressed thus one day in April 1680 when he was attacked in Bell Yard, in the City, by a would-be assassin named John Giles. Giles's dagger was deflected, and he was later arrested

LLANFIHANGEL COURT, ABERGAVENNY

LLANVIHANGEL COURT The two stained-glass windows on the Main Staircase commemorate the visits of Elizabeth I and Charles I.

and brought to trial. His punishment, a £500 fine, seems relatively light given the offence and the climate of harsh sentences at the time, but perhaps there was a feeling that few would have mourned if Giles had been successful. Shortly afterwards, there was a change in the political climate and John Arnold found himself in the dock for conspiracy. His own fine was £10,000, a sum he was unable to find. He spent several years in prison as a result. His death, it appears, was not greatly regretted.

These days, Llanvihangel Court is more at ease with its environment, having, after a succession of owners, come into the hands of a descendant of the fourth Earl of Worcester, who sold the house to the Arnolds back in 1627. John Arnold would not have enjoyed the irony.

LONGLEAT

WILTSHIRE

Opened to the public in 1949, Longleat was one of the first country houses to invite visitors and to organize additional attractions. One of these, as a million car-stickers testify, is 'The Lions of Longleat'—but the wildlife park and other attractions are complementary to a visit to one of Britain's most spectacular domestic buildings.

The original Longleat was an Augustinian priory founded in the thirteenth century, but the present house dates from the 1570s, when the estate had been acquired, following the Dissolution of the Monasteries, by Sir John Thynne. The resources of the estate provided timber, bricks and ironwork, and Sir John bought a quarry at Box to supply Bath stone. Sir John died in 1580 with Longleat still unfinished, though building operations had not deterred Queen Elizabeth I from visiting Longleat in 1574—the first in a long line of royal guests which extends to the visit of the present Queen Elizabeth in 1980.

Though the Thynne family played only a minor part in court and political life, their private life had its rich moments. Sir Thomas Thynne was the grandson of Sir John and the third owner of Longleat. His first wife, Maria Audley, dreamed that she would die in childbirth and asked for her portrait (now in the State Dining Room) to be painted so that there would be some record of her life left behind. She did indeed die in childbirth. Their son, Sir James, married Lady Isabella Rich, who was a centre of scandal at the court of Charles I. Later in the seventeenth century Sir Thomas Thynne came to a cruel end in what might have been a crime of passion or, alternatively, of politics.

Sir Thomas had married, as her second husband, Lady Elizabeth Percy, heiress to the Northumberland estates. She was first married when she was twelve, but her husband had died six months later, and before marrying Sir Thomas she had been pursued by a Swedish diplomat, Count Charles Königsmark, who was bitterly disappointed at her choice of Sir Thomas. The Count's first thought was to challenge Sir Thomas to a duel, but he was persuaded that if he killed his rival his marriage to the widow would not be countenanced. Another means must be found of disposing of Sir Thomas.

On the evening of 12 February 1682 Sir Thomas was entertained to supper by his wife's guardian, the Dowager Duchess of Northumberland. His carriage had just left her house in London's St James's Square when, near the present site of the Reform Club in Pall Mall, it was attacked by three men. One forced his way inside and shot Sir Thomas at point-blank range. The assassins were caught, tried and hanged, and shortly afterwards, as he was about to leave the country in disguise, Count Königsmark was captured. He was acquitted of the murder, however, and was allowed to return to the Continent, where he not many years later died a soldier's death.

But was it Königsmark who had hired the assassins? The jury, which may or may not have been corrupt, decided not. This left the question of who else might have had a motive to kill Sir Thomas, and on this the finger could be pointed at the King, Charles II, or his associates. Sir Thomas was a friend and supporter of the Duke of Monmouth, the illegitimate son of Charles by Lucy Walters and disputed claimant to the succession. Charles was approaching the end of his life. Three years before he had been seriously ill. Monmouth had already been gathering support in the West Country. It would have done the King's party no harm to have one of Monmouth's chief agents out of the way.

The matter has never been settled, but it is interesting to speculate on what might have been had Sir Thomas not been assassinated. Given what happened to Monmouth's West Country supporters three years later at Judge Jeffreys's 'Bloody Assize', Sir Thomas would probably not have survived. But if he had, and his marriage to Lady Elizabeth had produced an heir, the estates of the Thynnes and Percys would have made a formidable combination.

There was more scandal for the Thynne family in the eighteenth century, by which time they had acquired the Weymouth title. The second Viscount Weymouth took as his second wife Louisa Cartaret, a member of the Cartaret family which was among the founders of New Jersey. Viscount Weymouth surprised Louisa with her lover in an upstairs gallery at Longleat, and killed him. The gallery is now known as 'The Grey Lady's Walk', and it is said that Louisa's ghost is still to be seen there. Portraits of all these characters from the Thynne family history are still at Longleat.

The third Viscount Weymouth was created Marquess of Bath in 1789, though his ownership of Longleat was apparently a difficult period. His house, reported Horace Walpole, was often 'full of bailiffs'. Despite this, he managed to find the money to commission Capability Brown to lay out the park between 1757 and 1762. After his death in 1796 the family fortunes seem to have been strong enough, for shortly afterwards there began the first of two nineteenth-century transformations of the interior of Longleat. Between 1800 and 1810, Sir Jeffrey Wyatville was commissioned to create the present Grand Staircase, replacing a Wren original, and carry out various other improvements. Later in the century, the artist John D. Crace designed the exotic Italianate decorations which light up several of the rooms, including the 90-foot-long Saloon, with its fireplace copied by Crace from the Doge's Palace in Venice and its ceiling based on that of the Palazzo Massimo in Rome.

LOSELEY PARK
SURREY

Many family portraits have an uncanny power to act as a looking-glass, reflecting the genetic persistence of dark eyes or long fingers down through the generations to that of the present. Less often do they act as a physical reflector of the surroundings in which they now hang. One place where this dizzying shift of perception is achieved, however, is the

Great Hall at Loseley Park.

Here, from their gigantic group portrait, ten members of an eighteenth-century More-Molyneux family survey their home and their present-day descendants. At the centre, surrounded by the billowing skirts of some of her daughters, sits Cassandra More-Molyneux. Beside her stands her husband, in full-bottomed wig; sons James and Thomas stand at either end of the canvas. And the floorspace that, 250 years ago, they all occupied for the picture is the same as that occupied by the picture's observer today: the portrait was painted in the room where it now hangs, and which is still used by the More-Molyneux family today.

At the time the picture was produced, the double element of the family name was extremely new; it had been brought to Loseley only a generation before, by the husband of heiress Margaret More. The house they lived in

LOSELEY PARK Carved out of chalk, the ornamentation of the Drawing Room's unique chimneypiece has the look of fine lace.

already contained some notable portraits, including those of King James I and his wife. They were presented by the King himself in return for hospitality bestowed; he visited Loseley twice. His predecessor, Elizabeth I, had marked up yet another visit, and her host's descendants still possess the crisp instructions that on one occasion preceded her arrival.

The orders received by Sir William More, Loseley's builder, covered three points in all. He was to make room for the royal servants by clearing out his own. He was to ease the jolts of the royal carriage by covering the drive with straw. And he was to ensure his home got a good cleaning first; the last time round, it had apparently been deficient in this respect.

Illustrious though the royal visitors were, however, even they have to compete hard for our interest with a much more modest occupant of Loseley: Sir William's granddaughter, Ann. In the face of frenzied parental opposition, she became the wife of the great metaphysical poet John Donne. The marriage took place in secret and, when it was found out, Donne suffered considerably for his love: Sir George More, Ann's father, had the poet and aspiring man of affairs clapped in the Fleet Prison. He was soon released but, even though the Mores forgave him, his career hopes were dashed. Ann bore him twelve children and, to John's lasting grief, died after giving birth to the twelfth. It is to her inspiration that English literature owes some of his most beautiful work.

LUTON HOO

BEDFORDSHIRE

A fish, a crouched bear, a tiny elephant, a frog climbing its way up the former handle of a parasol: add the fact that these little creatures are carved out of jade or obsidian, with eyes of precious stones, and the name of their creator leaps immediately to the mind. All four were made by Peter Carl Fabergé, jeweller to the last of the Russian tsars. All four are now in a country house in Bedford-

LONGLEAT Jan Siberechts' painting of the house in 1675, which hangs in the Bedroom Corridor. It shows that there has been little change since except for the new front entrance of about 1800.

shire, where they keep company with such other Fabergé objects of art and practicality as a tray of jade and rose diamonds and a diamond-encrusted cigarette box ornamented with the portraits of their doomed Imperial Majesties: Tsar Nicholas II and Tsaritsa Alexandra Feodorovna.

From the imperial court of pre-revolutionary Russia to the outskirts of Luton seems a far step. But the link between St Petersburg and Luton Hoo is a direct one, and has given Britain an unequalled collection both of Fabergé's works and of relics of the Russian court in general. In 1903, the house was bought by the art collector Sir Julius Wernher; in 1917 his son Harold married Lady Anastasia, daughter of the Grand Duke Michael Mikhailovitch of Russia.

On one side of her family, Zia Mikhailovna could include Tsar Nicholas I, who ruled Russia at the start of the Crimean War. On the other, she could count the poet Pushkin, her mother's grandfather. It was her mother who loved Fabergé's miniature animals, and these and many other specimens from the master's workshops in St Petersburg came into the family as presents. Lady Zia inherited them from her father and, since the Grand Duke and his wife were English residents, the collection was complete: the convulsions and confiscations of the Revolution had not touched it.

A further family link—operating through Lady Zia's aunt—provided some of the portraits in Luton Hoo's Russian Rooms. The whole portrait collection runs from the father of Catherine the Great (a Prussian duke) to Lady Zia's father, and includes two of Catherine herself, draped in the massed diamonds of the Chain of St Andrew.

Three portraits of a slightly different sort survive in the original state robes worn by three women in the imperial circle. For the coronation of the British King Edward VII in 1902, the Baroness de Stoëckl wore a pink dress, made to Russian court pattern by Worth. Her daughter, maid of honour to the

Tsaritsa, had a version in red velvet; Lady Zia's own mother had one in pale blue. The occasion of the blue dress's appearance was earlier, probably at Queen Victoria's Diamond Jubilee in 1897; the rapturous celebration of a monarchy that, unlike the Russian one, has survived.

LYME PARK

CHESHIRE

Much is left—as we shall see—of the history and traditions of Lyme Park, but of one aspect of Lyme's past there is now, regrettably, no living trace. The venerable breed of Lyme mastiffs, at least one of which went into battle with its master Sir Piers Legh at Agincourt, made suitable and welcome gifts to the royal courts of Europe before dying out shortly before the First World War. They can, however, still be admired in the collection of paintings in the former knights' bedrooms at Lyme and in the adjacent corridor.

The Leghs were fighting men. They served the Black Prince in the Hundred Years War; there was a Legh, as we have seen, at Agincourt; Leghs fought at Hutton Field, at Flodden, at Edinburgh; one of them died in a duel before he was of age. Had the reigning Legh not been a minor at the time, no doubt Legh blood would have been spilt in the Civil War. But this pause in the letting of blood seems to have calmed the family down. From the seventeenth century on, the Leghs became more interested in building, exploration and, later, the political life of Victorian times.

Most male Leghs in direct line, and there were eleven of them, were christened Peter (or Piers), and so are referred to by Roman numerals, like popes. It was Peter X who, at the start of the eighteenth century, created the Lyme Hall of today from earlier seats and who stamped upon it the mark of the fashionable architect of the day, Giacomo Leoni, one of the inventors of the Palladian style as interpreted

LYME PARK The richly ornamented Drawing Room, a survival from Lyme's Elizabethan period, provides a profusion of effects.

in Britain. His treatment of Lyme, where he started work in 1725, can be regarded as a text for the many imitations that followed—especially since, like his followers, he faced the problem of incorporating his new (and in their time alien) ideas into the fabric of earlier houses. So he left the Elizabethan Long Gallery as it was: his own gallery, called the Bright Gallery, runs round three sides of the courtyard at first-floor level and, although it trumps the Elizabethan work, does not diminish it.

There was, later in the Leghs' family history, a curious *volte-face* on the question of Leoni's and later contributions to Lyme. In 1898 the second Lord Newton, later to achieve minor ministerial status, succeeded to the title. (By this time the Leghs, rather late one might think, had acquired a peerage.) He and his wife took a strong line against any suggestion that the family should have come so low as to need to take regard of fashion. The Leghs went back hundreds of years; they lived, as Lord and Lady Newton saw it, in an Elizabethan house; they went to some lengths to recapture Elizabethan effects. In the Great

LUTON HOO The Grand Stairs, curving round Bergonzoli's 'The Love of the Angels', were created by Sir Julius Wernher, who brought to Luton Hoo most of its art treasures.

Hall, for example, Leoni's huge stone chimneyplace was replaced, and the mahogany doors, like the rest of his colour scheme, painted over. The original colours have now been restored.

Their heir, the third Lord Newton, was of a different cast, or alternatively had had the stuffing knocked out of him by the vicissitudes of war and inheritance. When James Lees-Milne, on behalf of the National Trust, met him in 1943 he saw a man defeated by the burden of Lyme. 'The world is too much for him, and no wonder,' Lees-Milne wrote in his diary. 'He just throws up his hands in despair.' A great house, still filled with the contents of generations of Leghs, was clearly going to pot. Lees-Milne, spending a night at Lyme, plugged in his electric bed-warmer: 'Instantly there was a loud sizzling sound and a blue flash ran round the cornice of the room.' Lyme Park— which, in truth, had never quite lived up to its outward splendour—was near the end of the road. Lord Newton was prepared to give it to the National Trust and to leave much of the furniture there on loan; but there was no endowment for maintenance, and only the involvement of Stockport Corporation and the Greater Manchester Council enabled Lyme to be saved.

Lyme Park is now a treasure-house whose contents include much from the days of private ownership as well as items on loan from the National Portrait Gallery and other sources. The restoration work that has been carried out so far has aimed to return the house as far as possible to its early-eighteenth-century state and recapture the gracious style of living that was then possible for the old and wealthy English families.

MANDERSTON

BORDERS

A precise moment: 7 November 1905. There is great excitement and activity among the gentry of the Border counties. Dresses have been anxiously ordered and even more anxiously fitted. Carriages, and the occasional motor, rumble through the evening. Old friendships will be renewed tonight, old rivalries pursued, new matches made. Sir James and Lady Miller are giving a ball to celebrate the completion of Manderston.

The walls of the ballroom are hung with embossed velvet in primrose and white, Sir James's racing colours. The curtains are woven with gold-and-silver thread. From the central panel of the ceiling, Apollo looks down on the scene, flanked by paintings of Venus in the long panels. The room is furnished in the style of Louis XVI. The drawing room, lined with silk brocade and curtained in white silk, is also to be used. A marquee on the terrace awaits, hung with antique tapestries. Downstairs in the kitchen and scullery an army of staff beavers away, the women hoping, later on, for

MANDERSTON The main staircase, copied from the Petit Trianon at Versailles. The rail is solid brass, the balustrade silver-plated.

MAXWELTON HOUSE Anna—or 'Annie'—Laurie, heroine of the ballad and victim of her father's political beliefs.

a glimpse of the fine ladies from behind a convenient curtain.

It is not hard for the visitor to Manderston to imagine the scene, for the ballroom is decorated and furnished as it was on that night, and the drawing room, kitchen and even the scullery are little changed. The ball was the first and last that Sir James and Lady Miller ever gave at Manderston. Within three months, at the age of forty-two, Sir James was dead. But our point in time has a larger significance. The style of life epitomized by the ball was already doomed. There had been other events in 1905: in April, *The Times* had published an important article on the possibility of a German invasion of France, and what Britain's attitude should be; in January, on 'Bloody Sunday', Tsarist troops had fired on their own people in St Petersburg; everywhere one looked, the spirit of the nineteenth century was being broken. Manderston, a house rebuilt between 1903 and 1905 under specific instructions to the architect that no expense was to be

spared, was among the last of its kind. It is a monument to the kind of prosperity, in relation to the cost of living and service, that will never be seen again.

There was a house on the site of Manderston in the 1790s, but in 1855 the estate was bought by the Miller family, whose fortune came from Russian trade in hemp and herrings. In 1893 Sir James Miller, noted as one of London's most eligible young men, married a Curzon daughter. Shortly afterwards he began improvements to the Manderston estate to bring it up to the standard appropriate to the family's enhanced status. Work on the stables and home farm came first. It was followed by the remodelling—or rather, virtual rebuilding—of the house. One of the features is a staircase, closely modelled on one in the Petit Trianon at Versailles, with a silver-plated balustrade and a solid brass rail. Another, of course, is the ballroom. There are architectural fancies: in the anteroom to the dining room, a false door for the sake of symmetry; in the crimson library, a concealed door among the bookshelves. A visit to the house is truly proof that even the relatively recent past is another country.

MAXWELTON HOUSE
DUMFRIES & GALLOWAY

Maxwelton Braes are bonny,
They're a' clad ower wi' dew.
Where I and Annie Laurie
Made up the promise true.

Annie Laurie, heroine of one of the best known of British love songs, really existed. So did—and does—her home at Maxwelton, an early-Renaissance house on three storeys. And the original words of the song, quoted above, were written by her lover, William Douglas of Fingland.

Her real name was Anna. Born at Maxwelton House in 1682, she was the daughter of well-to-do Robert Laurie, soon to be created Sir Robert Laurie of Straith. Sir Robert is the third key personage in the tale of his

MELBOURNE HALL In Lord Melbourne's room on the first floor, below a portrait of the Prime Minister, is the round library table at which he wrote when at home.

daughter's romance, for he and William Douglas were—quite literally—at daggers drawn. After getting his baronetcy for helping to put down the Covenanters (the Presbyterians), Anne's father later took an equally uncompromising line over the Jacobites. Young William, however, supported the Jacobite cause and saw no reason to keep his views secret. Apparently, he even fought a duel with Sir Robert, and only Annie's pleas temporarily restored the pair to sanity. Not surprisingly, Annie Laurie was not allowed to marry her William. She became instead the wife of one of his relations, Alexander Fergusson. Douglas, meanwhile, tried to ease the anguish of his forbidden love by recalling the great moments of their romance in verse.

The sequel to the story comes over a century later, when an accomplished young woman called Alicia Spottiswoode came across William's poem in a book. As was the fashion of the time, she composed a slightly more elegant version and set it to music. At the end of the Crimean War, Alicia—by then the sister-in-law of the Duke of Buccleuch—turned her copyright in the ballad over to the public: she had her version published, with all revenues going to help those widowed and orphaned by the war.

The song was hugely successful and, as a result, Annie and Maxwelton have achieved undying fame.

MELBOURNE HALL
DERBYSHIRE

The tender relationship between the young Queen Victoria and Lord Melbourne, her first Prime Minister, and the stormy relationship, earlier in his life, of Melbourne with his wife Caroline are recalled at Melbourne Hall.

The two phases, pivotal to Melbourne's life, occurred twenty years apart. It was in 1805 that William Lamb, as Lord Melbourne then was, married Lady Caroline Ponsonby, the Earl of Bessborough's daughter. He was twenty-six, newly called to the Bar, and on the verge of his Parliamentary career. Two years later, they had a son, Augustus, but from then on the marriage began to disintegrate. By 1813 Lady Caroline's behaviour, and in particular her pursuit of Lord Byron, had become an embarrassment, and William Lamb made his first moves towards the separation that he eventually achieved twelve years later.

Lady Caroline's obsession with Byron, her pursuit of him to the point of dressing as a page to get to his rooms, the public 'scenes' she mounted when Byron rejected her, and her subsequent willingness to vilify him were the talk of London. So, too, was William Lamb's amazing forbearance. When she died, he remarked that 'in spite of all, she was more to me than anyone ever was or will be'. He did not marry again. The popular idea that, when Victoria came to the throne in 1837 at the age of eighteen, Melbourne sublimated his feeling for his former wife in care for the young Queen is probably a romantic fiction. But the diarist Charles Greville may have been right when he suggested that Melbourne was 'a man with a capacity for loving without having anything in the world to love'. His wife had died mad. His son had died of epilepsy. He brought to the task of training the young Queen a degree of devotion and affection which she had lacked in her own life and which she reciprocated until he was ousted from her affection by Prince Albert. It was somehow right that Melbourne's name should have been given to the chief town of the Australian state named after Victoria.

Lord Melbourne's room at Melbourne Hall contains, among other mementoes, the round library table that he used as his writing-desk, and elsewhere in the house are former possessions of Lady Caroline Lamb and gifts made to Lord Melbourne by Queen Victoria.

The links at Melbourne Hall between Queen Victoria and her prime minister do not, however, end with the departure of Melbourne from the political scene. His sister, Emily Lamb, became the wife of Lord Palmerston. It was a romantic story. Palmerston, though a notorious and freebooting womanizer, had for years cherished a passion for Emily, who was married to the fifth Earl Cowper, and his feelings were reciprocated. When the Earl died, Palmerston and Lady Cowper lost little time in going to the altar, though they were by that time both middle-aged. Queen Victoria did not think much of it, and refused to send Lady Cowper, whose daughter was one of her ladies-in-waiting, a message of congratulation. All this was at the time when Melbourne had influence at court, but it does not seem to have ruffled his relationship with the Queen. In this period Emily was the owner of Melbourne Hall, and her bedroom in the oldest part of the house is still known as Lady Palmerston's Room.

MELLERSTAIN
BORDERS

Seldom can the founders of a great house have met under such unpropitious circumstances as the makers of Mellerstain. Grisell Hume had fled from Scotland to Protestant Holland with her family to escape the power of James VII (who ruled as James II in England)—the last Catholic monarch in Britain. The man she was to marry—another Protestant refugee, George Baillie—was in even worse straits. His father belonged to the Covenanter movement, which in 1637 had pledged itself to resist the re-introduction of Roman Catholicism to Scotland. In 1679, it had staged a rebellion against James's brother,

Charles II, which failed. Robert Baillie survived, but was later accused of high treason and executed. George, landless and penniless, fled.

In fact, Grisell and George knew each other already from their time at home in Scotland. Both George's dead father and his uncle had had a talent for trouble and, in 1676, Baillie senior had been imprisoned in Edinburgh's Tolbooth for saving his brother-in-law from like imprisonment. While he was there, he had a surprising visitor in the shape of a small girl of twelve. Sir Patrick Hume, Grisell's father, needed to contact him secretly and had employed his eldest daughter as go-between.

George Baillie naturally met the Humes—Grisell included—and, when he fled the country after his father's second arrest and death, it was equally natural that he should join them in the Netherlands. He found a new career as an officer in William of Orange's Horse Guards, and he and Grisell fell in love.

Since the refugees had no money other than what they could earn, the young couple's prospects looked somewhat bleak. However, this was the 1680s and George was in the right place at the right time. Both he and his prospective father-in-law accompanied William of Orange on his triumphant 'invasion' of Britain in 1688, when—as the Protestant husband of James II's Protestant daughter Mary—he yielded to England's urgent invitation to save the country from James. Both Scots had their lands restored and, in 1691, George brought his bride Grisell home to his family estate of Mellerstain and the house that stood on it, called Whiteside.

Under the new regime, the Baillies and the Humes prospered, with Grisell's father becoming a peer. George, meanwhile, became an MP and helped devise the treaty that, in the early years of the eighteenth century, formally united the countries of England and Scotland. As the family's aspirations rose, so did its standards and, by 1725, the time had come for a new home that matched its status. The result was Mellerstain itself.

To begin with, however, it was only half a house—or, rather, two quarters of it. William Adam, the architect the Baillies employed, clearly intended to build a mansion with two projecting wings. The wings were constructed, but the central block that would join them never saw the light of day. One wing was devoted to stables; George, Grisell, and their two daughters Grisell and Rachel lived in the other, although they may have had an annex in the shape of fast-crumbling Whiteside.

It was not till Rachel's son, another George, inherited his mother's old home that Mellerstain was finished, and became the masterpiece it is today. George employed William Adam's son Robert for the work, and Mellerstain's Library and Music Room are among this architect's greatest achievements. High up above the Library doors, the marble busts of two women face each other: they are of Rachel and her adventurous mother.

MENTMORE TOWERS
BUCKINGHAMSHIRE

The landscape of European architecture is dotted with hunting lodges that, enhanced by taste and money, went on to better things. But, even amongst this company, Mentmore Towers is surely unique. Nor did it grow into glory: it was glorious right from the start when, in 1850, Baron Meyer de Rothschild decided to build a new house for himself in the Vale of Aylesbury.

Although the Baron had just married, the first impetus for his plans had come, not from his wife, but his mother Hannah, the widow of Nathan de Rothschild, the founder of Rothschild's Bank in England. Nathan had bought a country house near London in rural Gunnersbury, and Hannah de Rothschild, aware of the virtues of country air, later implored her City-bound sons to respect their health and do a little hunting. To make sure her advice was taken, she bought the young de Rothschilds some land in the best hunting country Buckinghamshire could provide.

Meyer was the first to jump at the tempting invitation. He first built a small house (later

MELLERSTAIN *One of Robert Adam's masterpieces: the Library, where the ceiling is decorated in the original pink, blue and almond-green that he chose for his design.*

used as a laundry), then started planning a very much larger one. The architect he called in, Sir Joseph Paxton, is today better known for his associations with gardens and glasswork. However, the results—the only domestic ones surviving from Paxton's drawing-board— show how nobly the former gardener at Chatsworth rose to the Baron's challenge. With the flamboyant, spiry towers that give it its name, Mentmore has been hailed as the finest neo-Jacobean building in the country.

Following the Mentmore sale of 1977 (see page 84), many of the superb works of art that filled the house at that period were dispersed, but the magnificent interiors still combine to fill the observer with delight and admiration. Their fittings include, for example, the Grand Staircase of white Sicilian marble, the panels of Genoese velvet that line the Dining Room, gilded woodwork, huge mirrors, and the Grand Hall fireplace with its white marble rams, believed to have been designed by Rubens for his own home in Antwerp.

Although the Rothschilds have departed, Meyer's one-time hunting lodge still displays *le goût Rothschild* at every turn.

MENTMORE TOWERS *The Grand Staircase, built of white Sicilian marble, leads up from Mentmore's arcaded Grand Hall.*

MEOLS HALL
MERSEYSIDE

Sheer bad luck, death duties, and a variety of other causes have brought about the breakup of many of Britain's great estates. In the case of the Hesketh family, owners of Meols since King John's time, disaster struck as a result of an ambitious and far-sighted scheme which simply didn't come off.

Early in the eighteenth century the Heskeths married into the Fleetwood family and so became owners of the Rossall estate, stretching across the northern half of the Fylde peninsula. The country seat was Rossall Hall. Meols Hall, which had been the Hesketh family home, was let first as an agent's house and later as a farm.

In 1836 Peter Hesketh—later to become Sir Peter Hesketh-Fleetwood—conceived the grand design of establishing a new port and town at the mouth of the River Wyre, to be called Fleetwood. It was an enterprise in the spirit of Robert Owen's New Lanark and, later in the century, Sir Titus Salt's Saltaire. At first, things went well. By 1841 there was a railway line from Preston, and the new port was used to provide a sea link between Fleetwood and Ardrossan for passengers travelling from London to Scotland on the west-coast route. Then money began to run out, and within a few years Sir Peter was forced to sell most of his estates. In 1844 Rossall Hall became a public school. Much of the Hall's contents were sold, but many of those that survived can now be seen at Meols. Sir Peter himself retired to the south of England, where he died in 1866. Meols Hall was rescued from the wreckage of the estate by Sir Peter's younger brother Charles, who was rector of North Meols, and so was kept, and remains, in the Hesketh family.

Earlier, however, at the end of the eighteenth century, the Hesketh family had been more successful in creating the resort of Southport, the site of which was part of the Rossall estate. This was the work of the romantically named Bold Fleetwood Hesketh, not a tribute to his character but merely the combination of three family names. He combined enterprise and public duties with a talent for painting and drawing, and some of his work can still be seen at Meols Hall.

MICHELHAM PRIORY
EAST SUSSEX

The Augustinian Priory at Michelham was established in the thirteenth century, enjoying apparent prosperity until the Black Death of 1349, after which it became increasingly difficult to staff the extensive farms. Only fragments of the original Priory remain, including the shell of the refectory, parts of the arches of the lavatorium and the ground floor of what may have been the original Prior's lodging. In the fifteenth century, bishops were reporting after their visitations that the Priors of Michelham were incompetent or worse, the buildings in decay, the vows and services of the Church ignored, and the canons immoral.

After the Dissolution the Priory had a chequered history, mainly one of debt and dilapidation. In a drawing made in about 1830 it looks like a run-down farm building, with walls crumbling, roofs agape and a general air of neglect. Michelham's rescue began in 1897, but a fire in 1927 and military occupation during the Second World War left the Priory once again in need of expensive attention. This was begun in 1959 by a new owner, Mrs R. H. Hotblack, who, after carrying out a good deal of work, presented the building to the Sussex Archaeological Society. Within the Priory ruins, pre-Dissolution settings have been re-created, and are revised annually to provide a changing insight into the historical life of the site. A watermill produces stone-ground wholemeal flour and a 'Physic Garden' on the sixteenth-century model was created in 1981.

MILTON MANOR HOUSE
OXFORDSHIRE

In December 1688 William of Orange was in the final stage of his triumphal 'invasion' of Britain. He had landed at Brixham and by the night of 11 December he was close to Oxford. He stationed his troops at Abingdon and elected to spend the night at a comfortable modern house at Milton.

It was at Milton that he heard that his

MILTON MANOR The Roman Catholic chapel, which contains the chalice and missal of Bishop Challoner, first priest to celebrate Mass there.

MICHELHAM PRIORY A view of the South Front from across the moat. Overlaid but not entirely concealed by Tudor alterations, the arched windows of the original refectory can still be traced.

invasion had succeeded without a shot being fired. James II (James VII of Scotland), the last Roman Catholic ruler of Britain, had fled the country. Unfortunately, he was caught by some of his angry subjects and brought back, and William himself had to arrange secretly for his rival's departure to succeed. But James's rule over Britain effectively ended on the night that William stayed at Milton Manor.

The house that received him had been finished only twenty-five years earlier and, in its trim, brick-built symmetry, must have looked as comfortable then as it does today. However, there was less of it than there is now, since its wings were added in the following century. But these were not the only alterations to overtake Milton, for the man responsible—Bryant Barrett, lacemaker to King George III—was a friend of a friend of Horace Walpole, creator of Strawberry Hill. A clear link runs between Horace's Gothic fantasy at Twickenham and Barrett's delightful Gothic library and private chapel at Milton.

By an odd twist of circumstance, the house that once welcomed Protestant William became, with the arrival of the Barretts, a Roman Catholic one. The first priest to celebrate mass in the new chapel was Bishop Challoner, who was also one of the country's first Roman Catholic bishops to be appointed since the time of Mary Tudor.

MIREHOUSE
CUMBRIA

If, in the nineteenth century, the Lake District attracted literary figures, Mirehouse attracted most. Tennyson, Carlyle, FitzGerald of *Omar Khayyám* fame all stayed there. The

Poet Laureate Robert Southey lived not far away, at Keswick; Wordsworth lived rather further off, at Rydal.

Of them all, FitzGerald perhaps best summed up the essence of Mirehouse in the 1830s. In a letter written half a century later, he remembered sitting at the little chess table that now stands in the Mirehouse Dining Room, 'playing chess with Dear Mrs Spedding, in May, while the Daffodils were dancing outside the hall door.'

It was the Spedding family—particularly John Spedding and his sons Thomas and James—who presided over this springtime paradise. A Lake District landowner, John Spedding, inherited the seventeenth-century house with its Georgian additions in 1802, and moved in. With him he brought a family friendship that had started in the schoolroom at Hawkshead. For six years, he had shared a bench there with William Wordsworth. William's schooldays were unhappy, but he must have found some consolation in his school-mates: when he moved back to the Lake District in 1799 with his sister Dorothy, the classroom comradeship was renewed, and they became close friends of John's sisters.

In the next generation, John's younger son James, though not a poet himself, was head of his own younger literary circle that contained stars as bright as the great Lakeland poet. The greatest of all was Alfred Tennyson, whom he met at Cambridge in 1829, along with Tennyson's closest friend Arthur Hallam. James drew portraits of them both (plus another of Fitz-Gerald, head deep in a book).

Hallam died tragically young, in 1833, and Tennyson, to whose sister Hallam was engaged, was distraught at the loss. He unsuccessfully sought comfort in his affair with Rosa Baring of Harrington; he sought it more lastingly in his poem 'In Memoriam'. In 1835, still grieving, he raised £15 by selling a gold medal he'd won for his verse (he was chronically poor), and used the cash to get him to the safe retreat of Mirehouse.

Here, a new friendship would claim him: that of FitzGerald, whom he met for the first

MEOLS HALL Fleetwood Hesketh, whose parents' marriage united the Meols and Rossall estates, painted by Joseph Wright in 1757.

time. And here, too, he felt serene enough to continue working on poems such as 'The Daydream' and 'The Lord of Burleigh'. A further boost to his spirits came when James took him to Rydal Mount to meet Wordsworth, who formed a high opinion of him.

Although the Tennyson–Spedding association had its roots in serious matters—they had both been members of the Cambridge debating society called 'the Apostles'—the two young men clearly had a lot of fun, at Mirehouse and elsewhere. 'Smokeable with J.S.', was how Tennyson thought of James. Spedding, in his turn, spiced his generosity with wit. In 1851, the newly married poet brought his wife Emily to stay at Mirehouse. Laid out on the bed they found an array of old socks with holes in them, all Tennyson's discarded property. James had collected them over the many years he had given the poet guest-space in the north and in London; now, to remind Tennyson that the bad times were behind him, here they all were.

James shared with his brother Tom a friendship with another great Victorian man of letters, Thomas Carlyle. Carlyle's family home was just over the Border, at Ecclefechan. Mirehouse was a convenient stopping-off place and, between visits, Carlyle kept Tom up to date with his literary work. On one occasion, when he was deep in his six-volume book on Frederick the Great of Prussia, he wrote: 'If I

MIREHOUSE The poet Tennyson as a young man, drawn by his host and friend, 'smokeablewith' James Spedding.

live to get out of this Prussian Scrape (by far the worst I ever got into) it is among my dreams to come to Mirehouse.'

Come he did—and again, and again. As with Tennyson, Mirehouse became part of the background of his life. On his last visit, when he was seventy, he had difficulty recognizing the middle-aged man shown in a portrait in the library. 'What creature', he inquired, 'is this?' It was himself.

MOCCAS COURT

HEREFORD & WORCESTER

Moccas Court is a house with a strong musical tradition. 'There was always music in the house,' one former resident remembered, speaking of the end of the eighteenth century. And music at home was taken seriously in those days. An opera singer would come in the summer to stay and teach. All the women at Moccas, it seems, sang, one specializing in ballads. They also played the harpsichord, though some better than others. The other instrumentalists in the household included a cellist, a violinist and an organist. The South Drawing Room was in those days, as its gilded frieze of musical instruments indicates, dedicated as a music room.

This musical family was the Cornewalls, who appear as owners of Moccas Court in the mid-seventeenth century. The present house—in which the musical gatherings described above took place—was completed in 1783. It was the fruit of a marriage between a wealthy London banker of Huguenot descent, Sir George Amyard, and the sole heiress of Moccas, Catherine Cornewall, whose portrait hangs in the entrance porch. Under the terms of Catherine's inheritance, Sir George took the name and arms of Cornewall. Perhaps his ambitions for Moccas Court outstripped his pocket, despite his wealth, for after commissioning designs from Robert Adam he employed a local architect, Anthony Keck, to see the work through. However, he later consulted both Capability Brown and Humphrey Repton for advice on the grounds and park.

The letters and diaries of the Cornewall family give a detailed picture of the kind of life that was lived at Moccas Court in the period following the completion of the new house. Apart from music Moccas Court had a well-stocked library of over 3,000 books. No Cornewalls have lived in the house since 1916, but it is pleasant today to stand in the South Drawing Room and listen for the music of nearly two centuries ago.

MUNCASTER CASTLE
CUMBRIA

In 1464, at the time that England was embroiled in the complex struggles of the Wars of the Roses, a group of Cumbrian shepherds found a weary, half-demented man wandering on the hills near the coast. For refuge, they took him to the strongest place on the landscape: the 200-year-old Muncaster Castle, constructed over the remains of a Roman fort. Sir John Pennington, its owner, welcomed the wanderer in and cared for him and, eventually, the fugitive's identity was revealed.

He was the former King Henry VI: last of the Lancastrian monarchs, on the run after the Battle of Hexham. Dull of intellect though he may have been, Henry was aware of his obligations. He arranged for Sir John's kindness to be thanked with a gift: an enamelled drinking bowl, made of glass and therefore fragile. Appropriately, the poor Holy Fool added a prophecy: as long as the bowl remained intact, so would the Penningtons stay both in luck and in their Castle.

Revived and refreshed, Henry returned to

MOCCAS COURT The bow-fronted porch was a later addition to the house designed by Anthony Keck and completed in 1781.

the turmoils of his own family and their dynastic war. In 1470, he would win back his crown; in 1471, he would lose it again. And by the end of that year, he would be dead: murdered in the Tower of London. At Muncaster, however, no such abrupt end awaited his glass drinking bowl. It survived; so did the Castle, and so did the Penningtons themselves. Over 500 years later, they are all still together, and the bowl has earned its traditional title of 'Luck of Muncaster'.

Although the oldest of Muncaster's treasures, the bowl is certainly not the only one. From the Tudor chimney pieces to the pseudo-Titian that Gainsborough painted for a bet, it is full of delights. Over the stairs, Canova's 'Dancing Hours' skip for joy; in the Drawing Room with its barrel ceiling, a naked Renaissance lady in alabaster kneels with mock modesty on her plinth.

Slightly less elevated in tone is the background history of a silver-mounted goblet in the Dining Room. Its body is a gourd, found in 1648 after a shipwreck on the nearby coast. The Pennington of the day, one William, devised a handsome use for this curiosity but was also plagued with an economical mind: to make the silver mount, he had the silver buttons cut off his pageboys' liveries and melted down.

Muncaster also houses a long and elegant line of family pictures, but its most striking portrait is neither elegant nor family. For this the visitor has to go upstairs, to the passage that's illumined by the celebrated presence of Thomas Skelton, manager and 'late Fool' of Muncaster. It was Thomas who, with his monkey face and chequered robe, has given the English language 'tomfoolery': an achievement as enduring as the defeated King's gift.

NAWORTH CASTLE
CUMBRIA

At Naworth Castle we again meet the Howard family, whose acquaintance we have already made at Arundel and elsewhere.

MUNCASTER CASTLE *The Drawing Room, with its barrel-vaulted ceiling, houses both family portraits and Gianbologna's 'Alabaster Lady'.*

The Howards spent much of the sixteenth century making dynastic arrangements which ensured their collective prosperity. It was Thomas Howard who made the link between two of England's great landowning families by taking as his first wife Lady Mary Fitzalan. Altogether he produced three sons, including, by his second marriage to Margaret Audley of Audley End, Lord William Howard. The stage was set for another Howard coup, bringing into the family the estates of the once powerful and still wealthy Dacre family, owners of Naworth Castle, Greystoke Castle and much more.

The fourth Lord Dacre had a son, George, and three daughters. George died as a child after a fall from his rocking horse, and the Dacre estates were divided among the three daughters, Anne, Mary and Elizabeth, much to the resentment of Lord Dacre's brothers, both of whom unsuccessfully contested the inheritance. At this point the Howards moved in: Philip Howard married Anne Dacre, Thomas married Mary and William married Elizabeth. This exceptionally neat arrangement was decided upon in 1571 when William Howard was only fourteen and his bride-to-be

a mere eight years old.

Lord William, or 'Bold Willie' or 'Belted Will', as he was variously known, had married into some extremely prosperous parcels of land in Yorkshire, Northumberland and Cumberland. One of these was Henderskelfe Castle near Malton, and another was Naworth Castle. True, Naworth Castle was not much to look at. Before and during the protracted period of litigation by the two Dacre brothers opposed to their nieces' inheritance, the Castle had fallen into decay. Furthermore, it was a fairly rudimentary border fortress lacking the trappings of fashion and convenience that a rich young couple might expect. Soon after the turn of the century, therefore, Lord William embarked on a programme of improvements at Naworth. This work cannot be dated precisely, but the year 1602 appears on a lead waterspout. Lord William had joined the Church of Rome in 1584, and as a result had forfeited some of his, or rather his wife's, estates to the Crown. They were restored on payment of £10,000 in 1601, and it seems probable that Belted Will felt, by this time, secure enough to start work on Naworth.

Lord William lived on until 1640, and

Naworth became a happy family home for this branch of the Howards. There is a story that towards the end of Lord William's and Lady Elizabeth's lives there were no fewer than fifty-two Howard relatives living in the Castle. It is pleasant to think of the aged couple sitting at the head of this gathering as they sat to eat in the magnificent Great Hall, with their portraits—still there, one each side of the door—staring down the length of the room.

It was Lord William's great-grandson who brought ennoblement to this branch of the family as the Earl of Carlisle, for services rendered to Charles II. But some fifty years after Lord William's death the great days of Naworth Castle as a family home passed when the third Earl of Carlisle decided to rebuild Henderskelfe as Castle Howard and use this as his principal seat. Consequently Naworth escaped eighteenth-century fashions, though unfortunately it could not escape fire, which struck in 1843. Only Lord William's Tower escaped completely, but the Castle was faithfully restored and the Stanley wing added.

The Great Hall, 78-feet long and 24-feet across, is still the Castle's centrepiece. Its greatest treasures are the early Gobelins tapestries bought by the fifth Earl of Carlisle at the time of the French Revolution, and originally intended for Castle Howard. They once belonged to Henry of Navarre, and bear his monogram. There is a story in the family that shortly before the outbreak of the First World War the tenth Earl was offered £100,000 for them by the French government. He might very well have accepted, for the Naworth estate was in poor shape at the time and the money would have been useful; but war broke out, and the offer was not repeated.

NETHER WINCHENDON HOUSE

BUCKINGHAMSHIRE

Medieval, or Georgian Gothic? Tudor, Jacobean, or nineteenth-century reconstruction? Nether Winchendon House beguiles the eye and teases the mind to equal degree. Its interior fittings do the same: how

NETHER WINCHENDON HOUSE The Great Hall with, on the left, the only tapestry portrait of King Henry VIII to be made during his lifetime.

many of them are imported, how many are seen in the settings for which they were made? And who is the man with the beard in the Drawing Room frieze?

The frieze is as good a place as any to start unravelling Nether Winchendon's playful tangles. It was commissioned by a senior civil servant of Henry VIII, Sir John Daunce. He had rented the house from nearby Notley Abbey, to whom the property had belonged since the time of Thomas à Becket 400 years before. Today's Drawing Room was part of Sir John's plans for making his medieval house more comfortable; by building an extension, he was giving himself an elegant parlour. So that it would be up to date as well, he ordered the upper walls and ceiling to be ornamented with a densely patterned frieze of cherubs, arabesques and Green Men of the Woods. And, quite naturally, he had his own portrait included, with his initials.

During the sixteenth century, Nether Winchendon acquired some patterned Tudor chimneys in addition to the parlour wing. Apart from adding a cupola, the seventeenth century left the house more or less alone, but the eighteenth saw the dawn of major changes.

Its most famous Georgian owner was Sir Francis Barnard, who became governor of New Jersey and Massachusetts. The US town of Winchendon commemorates to this day his old home in England, but he seldom lived in the house. It was his son, Scrope, who took it on himself to bring the neglected building back to shape. With great enthusiasm, he set to work and added Strawberry Hill Gothic to its mixture of styles. His last addition was the entrance hall, completed in 1820.

NEWBY HALL

NORTH YORKSHIRE

The Scottish architect Robert Adam has many shrines to his genius, ranging from a military base on the Moray Firth to the

NAWORTH CASTLE *Four heraldic beasts—the Dacres' red bull and gryphon by the fireplace, the Greystoke dolphin and a mysterious sheep at the door—guard Naworth's 78-foot-long Great Hall.*

grandeur of Syon. But perhaps the most important shrine of all is a room lying roughly midway between the two in distance.

As its name implies, Newby Hall's Tapestry Room was created round its tapestries; the furniture, in turn, was made to go with the room. Three agencies in all were involved—Thomas Chippendale, the Gobelins factory where the tapestries were woven, and Adam himself—and their influences intermesh to an extraordinary degree. Adam started work on the designs once most of the tapestries had arrived. It is possible that he influenced the decision to have further Gobelins work for upholstering the chairs and sofas; he must certainly have been involved in having their frames made by Chippendale. The overall result is a pinnacle of harmonious design.

It is remarkable that all three of its original main elements—tapestries, decoration and furniture—are still together. Indeed, Chippendale's contribution is his only one known to have its original upholstery: a fact that makes the Tapestry Room unique.

The inspiration behind this room was William Weddell, Newby's owner in the mid-eighteenth century. In 1765, William started on the Grand Tour that was standard practice for young men of means and breeding. By contemporary standards, his inspection of Europe's beauties was rather short, but he used his time to great effectiveness. When he returned in 1766, he brought back nineteen chests of classical sculpture from Italy. And, behind him in France, he had left an order for a complete set of tapestries depicting 'The Loves of the Gods', as designed by Boucher.

Obvious priorities led him to build a sculpture gallery first and, by 1767, work on this at Newby was forging ahead. But Weddell didn't like it, and it was at this point Adam was called in to complete the scheme. The architect can scarcely have drawn breath for, in the same year, the first—and main—batch of Gobelins' tapestries turned up.

The first designs for the Tapestry Room were laid before its future owner in 1769. Two years later, the rest of the tapestries arrived

and, while William was arranging his statues in the new gallery (they are still just where he placed them), the rest of the planning fell into place. By 1776, the Tapestry Room was ready to be used and admired.

William and his wife Elizabeth lived to enjoy their wonderful home for another sixteen years. But then, near the end of the century, William rashly took a cold dip in the Roman Bath in London, caught a cold and died—childless. He left Newby to his cousin and fellow connoisseur, Lord Grantham.

Later that year, Elizabeth sadly handed Newby's contents, with an inventory made by Chippendale's son, over to the wife of her husband's heir. One wonders what she can have thought at leaving them.

NEWHOUSE *The arms of Newhouse's unusual Y-shaped formation, extended in the eighteenth century, appear to welcome the visitor.*

NEWHOUSE

WILTSHIRE

There is a most extraordinary painting at Newhouse. Called 'The Triumph of The Hares' and painted by an unknown artist, it shows the bitten biting. Across the scene, hares are depicted hunting their human prey, toying with the victims and finally feasting upon them: a hare's-eye view of a just heaven, perhaps. It is not a mere joke; the message is too forceful for that. What is the picture doing there? What does it mean?

There are two hypotheses, which may be linked. The picture has been dated to about 1640, which would make appropriate the theory that it depicts allegorically the political turmoil surrounding Charles I at that time: an early example of political satire. But satire is a notoriously perishable commodity, and one would have to be a reincarnated member of Charles's court, and so able to identify personalities and situations, to pursue this theory to its conclusion. An alternative idea is that the hares are, in fact, 'Eyres'—members of the family that owned Newhouse then and whose descendants own it still. There was indeed an Eyre in Parliament at that time, and his kinsman became a formidable Lord Chief Justice a century later. But the mystery of 'The Triumph of the Hares' remains.

Newhouse is unusual in another respect as one of the few country houses to have been built in a Y-formation, a fashion of late Elizabethan times that was apparently short-lived. The two wings which extend the arms of the Y were added in the eighteenth century. Shortly after that, Newhouse acquired its associations with one of the most tragic minor figures in English history.

On 30 January 1801 Emma Hamilton, wife of Sir William Hamilton, former British Ambassador to Naples, gave birth to a daughter. She made little attempt to conceal whose child it was: she named the baby Horatia, after the father, Horatio Nelson. To judge from their letters, Nelson, Emma and Horatia lived very happily, in between his tours of duty, at the house he had bought for his mistress at Merton in Surrey. But after Nelson's death at Trafalgar in 1805, his country did not honour his deathbed plea that it should look after Emma and his child. Debts mounted; Merton was finally sold and Emma drifted away to die the death of an alcoholic in France. But Nelson's family did what England failed to do: his nephew George Matcham had become owner of

Newhouse by marriage to an Eyre heiress, Susannah, and his mother Catherine took on the responsibility of Horatia's upbringing. The dark shadow over the little girl's life passed, and she grew up to become the happy wife of a country clergyman. Catherine Matcham's portrait hangs above the chimneypiece in the Drawing Room at Newhouse, and there are other Nelson memorabilia in the house to record the part played by the family in redeeming the nation's neglect of the natural daughter of one of its greatest heroes.

NORTON CONYERS
NORTH YORKSHIRE

In 1644, one of the great battles of the Civil War was fought at Marston Moor near York. Among those who fought for the Royalists, who were heavily defeated in the encounter, was Sir Richard Graham of Norton Conyers. Like so many of his fellows, he was badly wounded. Sir Richard escaped—thanks, so the story goes, to his horse. He was carried home

NORTON CONYERS The Hall with, beyond, the staircase—the scene of the noble ride by Sir Richard Graham's horse.—

NEWBY HALL The Sculpture Gallery, planned by John Carr and completed by Robert Adam to house Weddell's great collection.

NUNWELL HOUSE 'See thy grounds well-stocked . . .': Nunwell House as it looked in the early nineteenth century, by which time it had received some Georgian additions.

some thirty miles, and his horse did not stop until it had crossed the hall—in those days paved with flagstones—to the staircase, where it placed a hoof on the bottom tread. Its shoes had become so hot from the ride that the mark was burned into the wood. By way of evidence, the scarred piece of wood from the step can be seen displayed on the landing at Norton Conyers.

As it stands today, the house is largely Jacobean, as is suggested by the curved gables added in 1632. There is brick beneath the roughcast, but when the roughcast was removed some years ago to improve the appearance it had to be hastily replaced because of problems with damp.

The Graham family has owned Norton Conyers, with a brief interval in which it was sold out of the family and subsequently bought back, since 1624. The house was to achieve fame of a quite different kind two centuries later.

In 1839, when she was twenty-three, Charlotte Brontë was working for a short period as

governess for a family named Sidgwick who were related to the then tenants of Norton Conyers. According to Charlotte's closest friend, Ellen Nussey, she visited the house and was told the legend of 'Mad Mary'. In the eighteenth century, a mad woman—reputedly a Lady Graham—was kept as a virtual prisoner in a remote attic room. The room still exists, but the floor is too unsafe for visitors to be admitted. When Charlotte Brontë came to write her first and finest novel, *Jane Eyre*, in 1847 she used the story as the basis for the mad Mrs Rochester, who eventually burns Thornfield Hall to the ground.

Norton Conyers is one of at least three candidates for the model on which Thornfield Hall is based. There are certainly similarities but, as the present owner generously says, 'it is more likely that Charlotte drew on her memories of several houses than that she relied exclusively on one'.

In the early nineteenth century the Grahams were enthusiastic huntsmen, and Sir Bellingham Graham was Master of the Quorn Hunt at the time when John Ferneley's picture of the Hunt to be seen in the hall was painted. Sir Bellingham is pictured on a bay horse beneath the left-hand branches of a tree. There is a story that when the picture was finished its ownership was decided by throwing dice. Sir Bellingham was not present, but he nominated a proxy to throw for him, and the proxy threw double six, thus bringing one of Norton Conyers's most striking pictures to the family.

NUNWELL HOUSE
ISLE OF WIGHT

In the early 1640s, an Isle of Wight diarist called Sir John Oglander wrote a touching recipe for happiness: 'Fear God as we did; marry a wife thou can'st love; keep out of debt; see thy grounds well-stocked; and thou may'st live as happily at Nunwell as any Prince in the world.'

Where grounds were concerned, Sir John was talking in the full flush of justified enthusiasm, for he had just laid out a garden for his family home. With his own hands, he had planted two whole orchards, one for stone fruits and the other for apples and pears. There were 'all sorts' of French flowers and tulips, too; 'I have been so foolish,' the diarist went on, 'as to bestow more money than a wise man would have done in flowers for the garden.'

Foolish, perhaps, but this generosity of both spirit and purse was to do Sir John worse harm than encroach on his gardening budget. He was writing on the eve of the Civil War, and he was soon to know more about the happiness of princes than he could have wished.

Devotedly Royalist, the family nearly ruined itself in support of King Charles I. Nonetheless, Sir John still contrived to fill a purse with gold that, on bended knee, he could offer his monarch when Charles visited Nunwell late in the hostilities. When the forces of Parliament caught up with him, the loyal knight was imprisoned for the role he had played in the war. It was, however, the scaffold

that awaited Charles, and he may even have spent one of his last nights of freedom at Sir John's home before being taken away to custody, trial, and death in Whitehall. The room the King and his equerry occupied at Nunwell are still used as bedrooms today, and often slept in by the present owner's guests.

OAKLEIGH HOUSE
NORFOLK

In the mythology of dreams, a famous place is occupied by John Chapman, the Pedlar of Swaffham. According to legend, he once dreamed that he should go to London and stand on London Bridge, where a man he met would have good news for him. John did as his dream directed. As it foretold, he fell into conversation with a stranger on London Bridge and, inevitably, the talk turned to dreams.

OAKLEIGH HOUSE The regularity of the Georgian façade hides evidence of a past that dates back to the Elizabethan period.

The stranger mentioned that he'd had an odd dream of his own, which directed him to go to the home of a John Chapman in Swaffham. Under the trees in Chapman's garden, a great treasure lay hidden. . . .

The outcome was equally inevitable but, oddly, there was a sequel. On the pot of gold coins that John dug up behind his house was an inscription in a foreign tongue. A visitor translated it for him, and he learned that another pot, 'twice as good', lay hidden under the first. And it did.

OTLEY HALL The Screens Passage originally divided the Great Hall, on the right, from the kitchens, stables and servants' quarters, and is still the entrance to the house.

True or false? As local records show, John Chapman certainly existed and, in the second half of the fifteenth century, he certainly came into considerable wealth. He himself paid for major improvements to Swaffham's church; in the century following, his descendants were financially secure enough to have the pedlar's old home completely rebuilt in the latest style.

Behind its Georgian facade, Oakleigh House still retains evidence of its Elizabethan and early Jacobean past. Its oak-and-softwood staircase predates the one at nearby Blickling Hall built in the 1620s. The doors in the attics, formerly the servant's quarters, are of the same period. The present walled garden—probably once a courtyard—is overlooked by the outlines of Elizabethan windows, now filled in.

Evidence of the truth or otherwise of the treasure-trove legend is, by contrast, non-existent. From the pedlar's point of view, the dream story would have made an excellent explanation for gold gained by less honest means. However, a Roman road is close by,

and modern finds of antique coins and jewels are by no means infrequent. Could Oakleigh and the wealth that helped build it have their origins in the hoard of some Latin-speaking Romano-Briton, who abandoned it over a thousand years earlier?

OTLEY HALL

SUFFOLK

Many of the English families prominent in Tudor and Elizabethan life have retained their position to the present day, and the homes of some of them feature in this book. Other families, with equally distinguished histories, have sunk without trace. In some cases, their fortunes were gambled away, either at the tables or in ill-fated business ventures. One such family, the Gosnolds of Otley Hall, simply backed the wrong side in the Civil War. There were families that did this and survived, but not the Gosnolds. Quite simply, the Civil War ruined them.

At the beginning of the seventeenth century, there was no reason for the Gosnolds to doubt that their descendants would go on enjoying the family prosperity. Heads of the family had held court appointments to four successive kings. A judicious marriage had united the Gosnolds with the Naunton family, enabling further extensions to be made to Otley Hall. Moreover, Bartholomew Gosnold had played a leading part in the settlement of New England.

Friend of Raleigh and the Earl of Essex, Bartholomew Gosnold was the captain of *Concord*, which sailed in 1602, under Raleigh's patronage, for the New World. He explored the coasts of what are now Maine and New Hampshire. The Martha of Martha's Vineyard was his daughter and, having named Cape Cod, he called Cape Cod Bay 'Gosnold's Hope'—'one of the stateliest sounds I ever was in'. Bartholomew Gosnold's ecstatic reports when he returned home led directly to the foundation of Jamestown, Virginia—the first permanent English settlement in North America—in 1607. Bartholomew himself died of swamp fever in Jamestown after only four months.

It was not this, however, that dealt the final blow to the family fortunes. That lay fifty years in the future. Colonel Robert Gosnold fought gallantly in the Civil War for the Royalists. Besieged in Carlisle, he and his men lived for nine months on meal, rats, dogs and, as a rare treat, horsemeat. But when Cromwell won, Gosnold's reputation for daring and fierce loyalty told against him: he was imprisoned at King's Lynn, heavily fined, and his estates—including Otley—confiscated. He spent all he had in buying them back and died in poverty. All his possessions, down to his prayer book and his tobacco box, had to be sold off, and Otley was bought by an Essex family and let on a series of farming tenancies.

The revival of Otley Hall dates from early this century, and the process has gone on fitfully, under various owners, since then. Today, the house has been restored to the grandeur it knew in the Gosnold period, though the only personal mementoes of this prosperous past are to be seen in the arms and initials to be seen here and there. For the rest, the Gosnold heritage is to be found in the records of the early settlement of Virginia.

PARHAM PARK
WEST SUSSEX

ON 28 January 1577 a small private family ceremony was held in the grounds of a house in Sussex. Thomas Palmer, aged two-and-a-half years, toddled out to lay the foundation stone of his new home to be. For the Palmers, well-to-do mercers and freemen of London, the starting of the new house was a crowning achievement. They had acquired the manor of Parham at the Dissolution, but its existing house proved too small. By 1577 they felt confident enough to build a large gabled Elizabethan manor house.

Young Thomas Palmer grew up to be a sailor, and went to sea with Drake. Perhaps a landsman's life was not to his taste, for he was still in his twenties when he sold the estate to Thomas Bysshopp of Henfield for £4,500. Descendants of Thomas Bysshopp were to live at Parham until well into the present century.

In 1922 Parham Park was sold to the newspaper-publishing Pearson family, and although some of its contents were removed, the Bysshopps and their descendants still look down on the interiors that they knew so well. Most of the pictures and much of the furniture, however, have been carefully chosen by the Pearsons to reflect the original Elizabethan form of the house. The furniture is mainly early English. Of the extensive collection of royal and family portraits, more than twenty date from before 1600. The output of the tireless fingers of the gentlewomen of earlier centuries—gros point; petit point, stump work and tapestry—adorns every room in the house in bed hangings, samplers, chair covers, wall hangings, carpets and cushion covers, brought up to date by the late Mrs Pearson's own needlework. The Pearson family have successfully reawoken the house of Thomas Palmer's childhood.

PARNHAM

DORSET

Many houses, old and new, contain antiques of the past; Parnham—home and workshop of furniture-maker John Makepeace—contains the antiques of the future. Where other historic houses are receptacles for craftsmen's work, Parnham is the setting for its creation.

It has, naturally, also been furnished from its owner's workshop. One corner of its Tudor Great Hall, for example, is dominated by a seat that is neither Tudor nor even traditional: named the 'Desert Island Chair', it combines function with the most dream-like, exotic of landscapes. Again, a Parnham bedroom houses a four-poster the like of which Queen Elizabeth I never knew. Also a product of the Makepeace

workshop, it is fashioned from the wood of a single yew tree and, with its slender curved uprights, gently embowers the sleeper.

However, this same room also provides a link with past woodworking traditions in the shape of a lively carved-oak overmantel. Aptly for a bedroom, it shows a seventeenth-century Joseph, in the toils of Potiphar's wife. And the room's name, too, relates to the past rather than the future. As the Strode Bedroom, it commemorates the family who, during the sixteenth century, turned the old medieval manor into the basis of the house we see today.

Its first modernizer, Robert Strode, built the Great Hall; his grandson William added wings to the south and north, plus two porches. Within a hundred years, however, their beautiful new home was smirched with an act of violence that, in its barbarity, seems more in keeping with the harsh life of the

PARHAM PARK *In this painting of the Great Hall, Joseph Nash (1808–78) recaptured the splendour of Parham in its Elizabethan days. Queen Elizabeth is said to have visited the house in 1593.*

A link with earlier traditions in woodworking: the Strode Bedroom's overmantel that illustrates the story of Joseph and Potiphar's wife.

Scottish Borders than that of rich Wessex.

With the Civil War, the Strodes found themselves divided. The residents of Parnham were Royalists (and sheltered King Charles), while their cousins were Parliamentarians. Soon, the political bitterness spilled over into concerns even closer to the heart: the question of who should inherit Parnham itself. Matters rose to a bloody climax when, as a result of the dispute, Lady Ann Strode was taken into the Great Hall of her family home and there beheaded.

In spite of this dreadful event, the Strodes continued living at Parnham until 1764. Then they abandoned it. When, at the beginning of the nineteenth century, the family came back, the occupiers found themselves starting a process of remodelling and restoration that has—off and on—lasted almost ever since.

In the Regency period, John Nash added Gothic battlements and chopped a bit off the Great Hall to insert a dining room. Just before the First World War it was bought by a Tudor enthusiast, who painstakingly reinstated the interiors and put back the Elizabethan garden. (A slightly earlier memory of Parnham's grounds is enshrined in the famous Sherlock Holmes story, *The Hound of the Baskervilles*; Conan Doyle had the idea for his plot when, as

a visitor at Parnham, he woke one night to hear hounds baying in the moonlight.)

In the Second World War the house saw another notable set of occupants: General Eisenhower and the 16th US Infantry Division. The invasion of Normandy was initially planned from Parnham. Not long afterwards, however, the estate and house were split up, and the former HQ became an old people's home for a period. It was finally bought by John Makepeace in 1976.

PENCARROW

CORNWALL

In the summer of 1882, the composer Arthur Sullivan and the writer W. S. Gilbert—whose operetta, *Patience*, had already taken London by storm—were working on its witty successor, *Iolanthe*. Initially, Sullivan was slow to keep pace with the song scripts that his partner sent him but then, suddenly, his adored mother died. Overwhelmed by his loss, he found some relief in starting to set *Iolanthe* to music. Further help came when Lady Andalusia Molesworth invited him to leave hot, dusty London to seek both inspiration and

PENCARROW 'Poised for ever in mysterious calm': the Misses St Aubyn, painted in 1754 by Arthur Devis. St Michael's Mount is in the background.

solace in the calm of Pencarrow.

With its Palladian front and rococo plaster-work, the Georgian house that welcomed the composer breathes an atmosphere of confident serenity. Reynolds's portraits stare graciously down from the walls. Pencarrow's greatest treasure, a large Ch'ien Lung bowl, displays a quirky realism. Its interior is decorated with English huntsmen in full cry across the lawns of Pencarrow House itself, while the exterior shows scenes of busy Chinese peasants. All were portrayed by an artist in China, who had probably been sent a sketch to copy from the other side of the world and had filled in the detail from his own surroundings.

The builders of Pencarrow were two Sir John Molesworths, the fourth and fifth baronets of that name. Lady Andalusia, widow of the eighth, was a brilliantly tactful hostess. She allowed no one to bother her guest. Pencarrow's piano was put at Sullivan's disposal and he spent most of his time at it, in the drawing room overlooking the Italian garden, with its subtle changes of level and flights of steps.

By degrees, the notes began to fit them-selves to the words:

Bow, bow, ye lower middle classes!
Bow, bow ye tradesmen, bow, ye masses!

sang Gilbert's disdainful peers as, in their procession, they made their way down the steps that Sullivan's musicality conjured up.

Sullivan was only one among thousands of Victorians, eminent or no, to feel the blessing of the Molesworth presence. As a radical MP, Andalusia's husband, Sir William, had been an ardent and tireless reformer, and it was mainly thanks to him that penal transportation to Australia was halted.

The unconventional Molesworths were not always popular among their local circle. But if Andalusia had not barred the door to the local gentry during Sullivan's rest cure, the world would arguably have been considerably poorer. And the contents of today's Pencarrow would not have included, alongside its unrivalled family portraits and its Chinese porcelain, the original costume of *Iolanthe*'s Lord Chancellor.

PARHAM PARK The Long Gallery was used as a drill hall during the Napoleonic era. Oliver Messel painted the ceiling in 1976.

PENHOW CASTLE

GWENT

Neatest and cosiest of little castles, Penhow has stood on its mound in the Welsh Marches since the twelfth century. For the first part of its life, it fulfilled the defensive (and oppressive) role for which its builders intended it. As time went on, its function became more and more domestic until, by the end of the seventeenth century, one end of it had become a handsome—and completely indefensible—house, with rows of windows.

In the early 1700s, its role started changing once again. The former fortress became a farm, with the animal population competing for space with the human one. By the time the present owner found it in the early 1970s, the farmer was living in the former dining room while the block that had once housed the Great Hall was occupied by stabling and chickens. The chickens have now gone and, restored, Penhow is once again a moated, fortified home.

Among the finds made during the restoration work was an inscription scratched in the ancient plaster over a fireplace: 'Sir Thomas Bowles—forget me not.' Even without his plea to the future, there is now small risk of forgetting him, since he was one of Penhow's main builders. A beneficiary of Richard III, he used his extra wealth to improve the Great Hall of his home, with its retainers' hall below. In this he was following his family's example, for it was probably his grandfather, John Bowles, who had built the Hall in the first place.

With its space and height, it would have made a huge difference to a home that, until then, had been basic in the extreme; a little rectangular tower, over 200 years old, with two storeys and a look-out post on top. But, crude though its amenities may have been, they were not without a certain strategic sophistication. The stair from the lower chamber to the sleeping quarters above contained (and still does) the subtlest of booby traps. One step is an inch higher than all its fellows: for the unwary attacker, a stumble and a yell would inevitably have led to outraged discovery.

As a family, the tower-dwellers who installed this brilliantly simple device were to go on to much higher things than a rough fortress in Wales. Penhow Castle was the first home in Britain of the Norman line of St Maurs—or Seymours. John Bowles was a Seymour son-in-law; so, somewhat later, was the ultimate power in the land, King Henry VIII. As today's castellan of Penhow points out, the dynasty that gave a Queen to England began in the upper bedroom of the Castle's keep, protected by its cunning stairway.

PEOVER HALL

CHESHIRE

Of the fifteen manors that Ranulph Mainwaring was given as a reward for his part in the Norman Conquest, it was Peover that he chose for his personal use. In so doing, he founded a dynasty that lived at Peover for nearly 900 years.

The first house at Peover was a moated manor, of which the moat is all that survives. In the 1580s the Mainwarings built themselves a splendid new house. This Elizabethan building forms the core of the present Hall. The stable block, built for Thomas Mainwaring in 1654 by his mother, with its remarkably elaborate interior and mullioned windows, is a perfect example of Carolean exuberance.

The remodelling of the house by the present owners has included the adaptation of the old kitchen—with its original two great fireplaces and fine timbered ceiling—as a Great Hall, from which the original sixteenth-century staircase ascends.

Peover Hall is a house full of nooks and crannies. A priest's hole of prodigious proportions extends the whole height of the house from the cellars to the top storey, with exits at each level. At the end of the Long Gallery is a low door leading into the so-called Priest's Room, and a hidden door in the panelling of the former dining room leads into another small bedroom which has a strategic view over the park in two directions.

The Mainwaring family sold Peover Hall in 1919 and it eventually came into the hands of the present owner. Meanwhile, it served during the Second World War as the headquarters of General Patton of the US Army. Subsequently, a new neo-Elizabethan elevation replaced the decayed Georgian wing, and with the help of panelling and other features rescued from other demolished houses Peover is being returned to its sixteenth-century glory.

PLAS GLYN-Y-WEDDW

GWYNEDD

Built in 1857 as a Gothic-style dower house for the Madryn estate, Plas Glyn-y-Weddw has been used since 1896 as a public art gallery. It was set up in this role by Solomon Andrews, a prosperous Cardiff businessman who bought parts of the Madryn estate in that year.

The scheme was an admirable one, in keeping with the wider educational ideals of the times. There was a tramway connection with Pwllheli, unfortunately wrecked in a storm in 1927. Bands played in the grounds of Plas Glyn-y-Weddw three afternoons a week. It is pleasant to think of families combining the pleasures of the tram ride and the gardens with the more serious inspection of what was claimed to be Wales's finest and largest collection of indigenous paintings and drawings.

After a period of neglect, artists Gwyneth and Dafydd ap Tomos bought the house in 1979 with the intention of reviving its former function, though in more contemporary style. There are now paintings, ceramics and sculpture from all over Wales on exhibition. The style of Solomon Andrews's philanthropy is evidently still maintained.

PLAS GLYN-Y-WEDDW
The entrance hall and staircase are the most distinctive features of the Victorian Gothic house. The effects include the generous use of stained glass.

POUNDISFORD PARK

SOMERSET

The owners of country houses have tended to be either Anglican—in Scotland, Episcopalian—or Roman Catholic. For a period in the eighteenth and nineteenth centuries, the owners of Poundisford Park were, unusually, followers of a new nonconformist sect, the Countess of Huntingdon's Connexion.

The long-lived Countess of Huntingdon was an early follower of John Wesley and George Whitefield, and in her widowhood set up a network of sixty-four chapels and a theological college to supply them with ministers. Later, she broke away from the Methodists to pursue a more Calvinistic line than was favoured by Wesley. Among the members of her sect was the Welman family of Poundisford Park.

A characteristic of Methodism and its offshoots is the combination of faith with practical good works, and indeed John Wesley found time among his preaching activities to organize pharmacies for the poor. Rebecca Welman, who lived at Poundisford with her brother Thomas and his wife, followed a similar line of thought by setting up a herbal dispensary, though one of her more famous local remedies, 'Miss Rebecca's Drops', are said to have been based less on the flowers of the hedgerow than on brandy and laudanum. With the continued support of the Welman family, the dispensary continued in operation until the mid-1860s.

Meanwhile, the Welmans built a Countess of Huntingdon's chapel at Fulwood, across the park. They were a devout family. Rebecca's sister-in-law Charlotte helped with the herbal remedies and, after her first husband's death, married Thomas Thompson, treasurer of the Methodist Home Missionary Society. Charlotte's stepdaughter, Jemima Luke, taught in Sunday School and wrote evangelical hymns. Altogether, they were representative of the 'comfortable' wing of the Methodist movement which was later partly submerged by the more fundamentalist Primitive Methodists.

After a chequered career in the late nineteenth century in the hands of various tenants, Poundisford was bought in 1928 by the father of the present owner, and restoration

PENHOW CASTLE The marks over the fireplace in the Lower Hall were made by heated pokers used for warming drinks; they were first wiped clean on the lintel.

PEOVER HALL Tuscan columns and arches give distinction to Peover's stable block, built in 1654 for the enthusiastic horseman and squire, Thomas Mainwaring, by his mother.

was begun under the guidance of the Hon. Anthony Methuen. It has been returned to its Elizabethan state, to show off, for example, the mid-Elizabethan ceilings and friezes which represent the early work of West Country plasterers.

POWDERHAM CASTLE

DEVON

The oldest inhabitant of Powderham Castle lives in the garden. He is at least 150 years old, and his name is Timothy. He is a tortoise. Even this great age is as nothing compared with the occupancy of the Courtenay family, which has lived at Powderham since about 1400 and had been established in the district for two centuries before that. It was

Sir Philip Courtenay, second Earl of Devon, who started the building of the Castle round about 1390.

Not that all has been plain sailing for the Courtenays. They have had their share of misfortune, some of it brought upon themselves. In 1525 Henry Courtenay was created Marquess of Exeter by Henry VIII, but it was always hazardous to be smiled upon by that mercurial king. By 1538, Courtenay was languishing in prison; he was eventually found guilty of treason and executed, and his estates were forfeited. His son Edward was imprisoned in the Tower with him, and not released until 1553, when Queen Mary pardoned him, restored his land, and recreated the Earldom of Devon for him. He did not last long in favour, however, and he was exiled in disgrace to Italy, where he died in 1556. With his death the least he achieved the revival of the Earldom of Devon, though he did not assume the title himself. On his death it passed to his cousin, William Courtenay, who became the tenth Earl. He celebrated the restoration of the title by adding the Victorian courtyard.

Despite these vicissitudes, the Courtenay family has managed, over the centuries, to make alterations and extensions in keeping with the times. The eighteenth century brought a series of changes, of which the third Viscount's Music Room was the last. These and subsequent changes have enhanced rather than disrupted the history of the Castle. The portraits and artefacts collected by the family over many generations add to the sense of continuity, to which Timothy the tortoise is a dignified, if somewhat unexpected, adjunct.

POUNDISFORD PARK George Vivian, *an ancestor of the present owner, in the costume he wore to visit Pasha Ali in Albania in 1819.*

Earldom of Devon disappeared from view for nearly 300 years.

Strangely enough, the Courtenay who eventually successfully claimed back the title seemed to bring the family no better luck. He was the third Viscount Courtenay, a glittering youth whose coming of age was celebrated at Powderham in 1791 with a masquerade ball of which the centrepiece was a marquee decorated with hundreds of pink-silk roses. Later, he added the exquisite Music Room to the Castle, designed by James Wyatt. What happened to the third Viscount is not clear. There are hints of a scandal in his extreme youth involving the eccentric collector William Beckford. Another account says that he found 'sufficient reasons' to remove himself from the reach of English criminal law. At all events, he went to live first in New York and later in Paris, where he died unmarried in 1835. Ten years earlier his debts had brought about the sale of a large proportion of the contents of Powderham. But at

PRIDEAUX PLACE

CORNWALL

Unite and unite, and let us all unite,
For summer is i-comen today,
And whither we are going we will all unite
In the merry morning of May. . . .

It is the morning of 1 May, and we are at Padstow in Cornwall. The townsfolk have gathered by the harbour and danced their way through the streets, behind the 'Obby 'Oss, singing alternately the 'day' and 'night' Padstow May Songs. They will end up on the castellated terrace at Prideaux Place, where the 'Oss will dance.

Rise up, Mr Prideaux, I know you well and fine,
For summer is i-comen today.
You've a shilling in your purse, I wish it was in mine
In the merry morning of May. . . .

What we are seeing is the survival of a ritual whose roots are lost in the mists of time, but about which some intelligent guesses can be made. There are elements of fertility rites and of ill-concealed sexuality. There is the medieval custom of wassailing the master for alms, more usually associated with Christmas but often practised at other times of the year.

Until 1914, the signal for the start of the Padstow 'Obby 'Oss ceremonies was a morning fusillade from the terrace of Prideaux Place. That year, one of the cannon split—some may have seen it as a warning of things to come—and the practice was abandoned. But the celebrations still reach their climax at Prideaux Place, which is appropriate enough since the Prideaux family has owned and sustained Padstow since the Dissolution, thanks to a sharp operator among the Prideaux ancestors.

In 1536 Nicholas Prideaux was assistant to the Prior of Bodmin, then the owner of the manor of Bodmin. In advance of the arrival of Henry VIII's assessors he persuaded the Prior to lease his lands so that the Crown could acquire only the freeholds. The lease of Padstow and its already prosperous port went to Joan Munday, who married Nicholas Prideaux's nephew and heir William. Later, the family acquired the freehold, and the stage was set for it to settle at Padstow for good. A manor was built in Elizabethan times, to be followed over a century later by Georgian extensions and improvements. A Victorian Prideaux Gothicized the house, so that it now contains elements of three distinct phases of country-house development.

Prideaux Place and its owners have never played a part in national politics, probably because, in the past, distance from London was against them; but they have made some notable contributions to cultural life. Dean Humphrey Prideaux (1648–1724), born in the house, distinguished himself as a theologian and Oriental scholar. His books included a *Life of Mahomet* and *The Old and New Testament connected with the History of the Jews*. A later Humphrey, in the eighteenth century, was a patron of the arts and in particular of a local painter, John Opie, who was brought up on the estate. As a young man he painted portraits of Humphrey, his wife Jenny and their dogs which are to be seen in the drawing room of the house. The £25 and a new suit of clothes that he earned for this work enabled Opie to

set off for London at the age of twenty to try his luck as a fashionable portrait-painter. For a time, his style pleased the town, and he later became a member of the Royal Academy and an accomplished painter of historical scenes.

Another artist for whom Humphrey sat was Rosalba Carriera, whose pastel portrait of him is also in the drawing room. There was a touching sequel to this sitting which did not emerge until about 150 years later. When the picture was being cleaned in 1914, a love letter from Rosalba to Humphrey was found sealed into the frame. As the letter was replaced in its hiding-place, we do not know whether it was a one-sided appeal or whether the otherwise upright Humphrey shared her passion.

QUEX PARK Detail of the 'African Plains' diorama. It was painted by a patient when the house was a World War I hospital.

QUEX PARK
KENT

Major Percy Powell-Cotton was essentially a Victorian (though he lived on until 1940) who devoted most of his life to exploration and travel. He made twenty-eight expeditions to Africa and Asia, risking frequent discomfort and occasional danger. Even his honeymoon was spent on safari in central Africa, living with a tribe of pygmies. He was

PRIDEAUX PLACE
*Strong, dark colours and
stained glass make the
Library a fine example of
late Gothic style, reflected
also in much of the room's
furniture.*

a fervent collector, note-taker and photographer. He was also, and this must be mentioned straightaway, a big-game hunter. His approach to wildlife would find markedly less sympathy today than it did in his lifetime. Nevertheless, those who disapprove of his hunting will find much else to interest them at Quex Park, and it is worth remembering that the conditions of exploration in the nineteenth century, when it was not possible to observe

POWDERHAM CASTLE The exquisite Music Room, designed by James Wyatt in 1794 for the ill-fated third Viscount Courtenay.

wildlife from the safety and comfort of a jeep led inevitably to a less sensitive approach.

Major Powell-Cotton's collections are brought together in the eight galleries of the Powell-Cotton Museum adjoining his family home in Quex Park. Taken together, they reflect the interests of a man possessed of a boundless curiosity and an instinct to preserve and record his findings. Here, a set of dioramas, 70 feet long, showing over 500 animals in their natural settings; there, one of the world's finest collections of African and Asian ethnographical items; again, the most important collection outside London of Chinese

Imperial porcelain of the Ching dynasty. It is an astonishing assemblage, reflecting with accuracy the spirit of an age when acquisition was nothing unless underpinned with knowledge and understanding. Much of the value of the exhibition lies in its creator's meticulous note-taking and scholarship.

Percy Powell-Cotton was born in 1866 and set out on his first expedition when he was twenty-one. In 1905 he married, and his honeymoon expedition with his wife to central Africa provided the newspapers, on their return, with much vivid copy about 'the first white woman in the land of the pygmies'. The same expedition almost brought his collecting activities to a close. He was charged from dense grass by an angry and slightly wounded lion. He fired both barrels of his .400 rifle, but missed. The lion was on top of him by the time his porters arrived to help. Using a heavy club and a whip, two of them managed to distract the animal's attention long enough for a third to shoot it at close range. The major escaped with seventeen claw wounds and the severely mauled suit which is today on display in the entrance hall at the Quex Park museum.

The rifle was, however, not Powell-Cotton's only weapon. The invention of photography had signalled the start of the modern attitude to wildlife: from the mounting of dead specimens to the observation of living ones. Powell-Cotton was a pioneer of wildlife photography, using glass-plate negatives and the long-distance binocular camera. Later, when cine-film became available, the Major took to it with equal enthusiasm.

Quex Park is a Georgian mansion on the site of an earlier manor house, and was built for John Powell, an ancestor of the Major and the present owner. The Powells were Kentish county worthies who perhaps, if it had not been for the Major, would be forgotten today. Their house, much altered in Victorian times, is precisely of their class and lifestyle. It reflects their family interests, their collection of good individual pieces of furniture and their taste in reading, furnishing and leisure pursuits through the generations.

RABY CASTLE
COUNTY DURHAM

The history of Raby is no less than the history of the struggle for ultimate power over England: particularly the England of the north, far away from London and its influence. Invasions, royal marriages, uprisings, civil wars, great political shifts: the owners and occupants of Raby were involved in them all, from the eleventh-century Norseman King Cnut to the third Earl of Darlington, who supported the 1832 Reform Bill and was made a duke for it.

Through it all, the walls of Raby Castle dominated their northern setting with massive assurance. The only real threat to their existence was posed, not by attack or financial ruin, but by family ill-will. The first Lord Barnard, disliking his son-and-heir's choice of a wife, tried to disinherit the pair by making sure they would have nothing to inherit. Selling Raby's contents, he started to pull the Castle down and it took a court ruling to make him stop. When, in 1723, his heir finally succeeded to the barony and the Castle, the steps he took to make good the damage were also an exquisite form of revenge on the past. He set a major programme of restoration under way and replaced Raby's ravaged woodlands (his father had cut all the timber as well) with an elegantly landscaped park.

Although Cnut—King of Denmark, Norway and England in the early eleventh century—had a provincial base close to Raby, at Staindrop, he was not responsible for fortifying the manor house that stood where the Castle does now. This was the work of the great northern family of Nevill, which frequently dictated the fortunes of medieval England. In 1378, John, the third Lord Nevill, was permitted to add battlements to his Raby stronghold.

In the last years of the fourteenth century, Raby came into its golden age. With consummate skill, John's son Ralph threaded his way through the tortuous and bloody politics of the period and always ended up the winner. From

Richard II, he accepted an earldom; as the first Earl of Westmorland, he helped depose his benefactor and install the first Lancastrian King, Henry IV, on the throne. For this service he became Earl of Richmond and Earl Marshal of England, but these were not the only advantages accruing from his dubious role. The new King was more than benefactor; he was also now a relative, for Lady Joan Beaufort, the Earl's wife and the eventual mother of fourteen Nevill children, was his sister.

Of the troop of royal nieces and nephews that briefly occupied Raby Castle, it was the youngest—beautiful Cicely—who became the most celebrated. Known as the 'Rose of Raby',

she helped her family make yet another shift of allegiance from losing to winning side, for she became the wife of the Duke of York, leader of the Yorkist faction in the Wars of the Roses. The Yorkists finally won: Cicely's eldest son became King Edward IV, while her third briefly reigned as Richard III. And her granddaughter, Elizabeth, became the wife of the first Tudor king, Henry VII, and ancestress to the entire royal line of Britain.

Although the arrival of the Tudors and the defeat of Richard III had, on the face of it, wrong-footed the Nevill family, they recovered with their usual skill and were soon backing Henry VIII in his divorce from Catherine of

Aragon. It was, however, one of the consequences of this divorce that finally brought down the Lords of Raby. During the Reformation, they stayed faithful to the Old Religion. They supported Mary Tudor; much more unwisely, they also supported the next Roman Catholic heir to the Kingdom of England, Mary Queen of Scots.

By 1569, Mary's active career was over. Deposed from her throne and a refugee, she was now a prisoner of her cousin, Queen Elizabeth. But she was both Elizabeth's heir and—in the eyes of all Catholics—already their Queen, for the Pope had excommunicated her English rival. Plot after plot was hatched against Elizabeth and, for a while, Raby became the centre of the Catholic stage. In its great hall—capable of holding 700 knights, all Nevill men—the Nevill Earl of Westmorland and his fellow peer, Percy of Northumberland, planned what would become known as the Rising of the North. However, the rising failed, and, for the Nevills and many others, that was the end. Raby's owner fled the country and, after 400 years of Nevill occupancy, Raby was taken over by the Crown.

In the following century, the Crown sold it again to the politician Sir Henry Vane. But, with the turbulence of the Civil War not far ahead, the history of the Lords of Raby was to remain troubled. Sir Henry became a Parliamentarian and was appointed Lord Lieutenant of a strongly Royalist county; to add to his difficulties, he also opposed the execution of Charles I. But, invidious though Sir Henry's public position appeared, it was ease itself compared to that of his son. Sir Henry Vane the Younger experienced a similar alienation from the forces and ideals of Cromwell and was for a time imprisoned. After Cromwell's death in 1658 he re-emerged, but was again incarcerated when the monarchy was restored in 1660. Hopelessly trapped between two camps, he was finally executed in 1662.

It was Sir Henry's fifth son, Christopher, who at last placed Raby and its occupants firmly back in the monarchy's favour. Originally a supporter of Charles's brother,

James II, he switched allegiance to William of Orange and, just before the close of the seventeenth century, was made a baron. It was this same Christopher who took such drastic steps to cut his heir out of his inheritance.

The curmudgeonly first Lord Barnard's descendants continued over the next two centuries to be highly active in politics, and to profit by them. They became Earls of Darlington, then—thanks to Earl William Henry's support of the 1832 Reform Bill—Dukes of Cleveland. But the atmosphere of Raby was politically less electric than it had been. Instead, the process of restoration and remodelling started by the second Lord Barnard went purposefully ahead in successive waves, each one leaving the Castle more magnificent—but, at the same time, more comfortable—than before.

With its exquisite Octagon Drawing Room, its Entrance Hall cunningly adapted to allow carriages to enter, its Blue Bedroom with Gothic bed and mahogany bidet, much of Raby's interior today is more reminiscent of the world described in Trollope's 'Palliser' novels than that of Froissart's medieval *Chronicles*.

Elsewhere in the Castle, however, the Middle Ages continue to make themselves felt. The medieval Kitchen still has its service passage that could also be used by defence forces, and its eight-sided ventilation lantern. The Servant's Hall now lacks the arrow slits that gave on to the outside world, but its vaulted roof still betokens its ancient origins (it was once probably the Castle's guard room). And the current owner, though descended from the Vanes, can also—thanks to his paternal grandmother—take his ancestry back to the family who first built and ruled Raby: the Nevills.

RAGLEY HALL
WARWICKSHIRE

It is not every family that can claim descent, even if tongue in cheek, from King Solomon and the Queen of Sheba, but such a claim

RAGLEY HALL The Great Hall's baroque plasterwork was added by James Gibbs in 1750. Symbolic figures of War and Peace face each other from the fireplaces.

exists in the history of the Seymours. The name, it is said, is a corruption of 'St Maur', which in turn derives from a Moor of the seventh century who claimed Solomon and Sheba as ancestors. Be that as it may, the Seymours' pedigree is long enough in any case, starting before the Conquest.

The story of the present Ragley Hall, however, begins in 1595, when Sir John Conway of Conwy Castle in Wales bought Ragley Castle and its land as a home for himself and his local bride. A century later his great-grandson was created Earl of Conway and began to plan a new house in keeping with his new station in life. His architect was Robert Hooke, a distinguished scientist as well as an architect who applied scientific principles to his designs; Ragley is the only surviving example of his work. Hardly had the plans been drawn up, however, than the Earl died, leaving an only daughter who soon followed him to the grave. Ragley passed to a cousin, Francis Seymour. Because of these challenging

circumstances, it was not until the middle of the eighteenth century that the roof was finished and the interiors by James Gibb were begun.

The second phase of Ragley's development followed close on the heels of the first. Towards the end of the eighteenth century it was thought that George III might be coming to call—in the event, he did not, though the Prince of Wales (the future George IV) did—and James Wyatt was commissioned to augment and enhance the state rooms. The three rooms on the garden front, including the Red Saloon, date from this period.

The family had two black sheep, both of whom, however, had their redeeming sides. The family had now acquired the title of Marquess of Hertford, and in 1777 Francis, who was to become the third Marquess, was born. He grew up to become a great friend of Prinny, and hence the latter's visits to Ragley. The third Marquess, aided no doubt by the double fortune brought to him by his marriage with Maria Fagniani (who had inherited from each of two nobles who believed her to be his daughter), joined with a will in the extravagances of the Regency. However, he combined this, as was not exceptional in those days, with a rare taste and discrimination in works of art. In later years his gross debaucheries caused him to appear in fiction as Lord Steyne in Thackeray's *Vanity Fair* and Lord Monmouth in Disraeli's *Coningsby*.

He was succeeded by Richard, the fourth Marquess, who lived not at Ragley but in Paris and was something of a chip off the old block. He built on his father's art collection, to the neglect of his estates and himself. He died unmarried, but not without issue; and he left his art collection to Richard Wallace, his illegitimate son.

Richard Wallace, later knighted, gave his name to this collection of paintings, furniture and antiquities, now housed in the former London home of the Hertford family in Manchester Square.

The lifestyles of the third and fourth Marquess appear to have weighed heavily on the family, for in the 1930s, when it seemed that Ragley would be inherited by George, the seventh Marquess, his father disinherited him, apparently on the grounds that he was financially irresponsible. George's major interests were in the theatre and the arts, and perhaps this reopened painful memories of a century before. At any rate, George's younger brother, Henry, died before he could inherit and so his son, whose home Ragley still is, came into ownership at the age of nine. Death duties had by this time taken their toll on the estate, the 24,000 acres of the Edwardian period having been reduced to 6,000 by the Second World War. There was an even worse threat: the trustees of the young Lord Hugh, the present owner, were planning to sell Ragley Hall for demolition. Fortunately this was averted, but it meant, for the eighth Marquess, taking on a lifetime commitment of restoration.

Today, Ragley's contents have been carefully replaced or reassembled so that the rooms on view accurately reflect the taste of the times when they were built. Distinguishing additional features are two large and striking modern paintings. Ceri Richards's 'The Defeat of the Spanish Armada' (1964), and Graham Rust's mural 'The Temptation' (1983) on the ceiling and walls of the South Staircase Hall. It is satisfying to see the artistic traditions of a great house not only preserved but continuing into the present day.

RIPLEY CASTLE
NORTH YORKSHIRE

Sir Wharton Amcotts, a wealthy Lincolnshire landowner, decided in 1780 to travel north to the spa town of Harrogate to take the waters. He took with him his only daughter and heiress Elizabeth. For twenty-three-year-old Sir John Ingilby of Ripley Castle, four miles from Harrogate, it was evidently love at first sight; he and Elizabeth were married in the October of the same year. But, regrettably, Sir John would repent the marriage at leisure.

The castle that Sir John had inherited from his father was not in good shape. It was rambling, uncomfortable and, in Sir John's words, in 'wretched condition'. It was the newly married couple's—or, at any rate, Sir John's—expectation that Elizabeth Amcott's dowry would enable Ripley Castle to be largely demolished and rebuilt according to plans that its owner had already drawn up. But it was not to be: Sir Wharton refused to part with any of his money. Perhaps the fact that Sir John was not his father's legitimate son, but had taken the family name by Act of Parliament, had something to do with it. Neither the couple's attempt to charm themselves into his favour nor the comments of society on his failure to do his duty by his daughter had any effect, and Sir John was forced to borrow £12,000 to finance the work at Ripley.

This was not the end of it. When work began, it was discovered that the condition of the old fortified manor house was worse than had been thought. The budget was quickly overspent, and perhaps the situation was made worse by Sir John's determination to save as much of the old house as he could. However, the new Ripley Castle was completed by 1786, and over the next few years it may have seemed that the couple's troubles were over. Sir John spent a year as High Sheriff of Yorkshire. In 1790 he was elected to the House of Commons. By 1794 the Ingilbys had six children, and although four more had died in infancy this was not unusual at the time, or seen as particularly tragic. Then, in the late summer of 1794, the blow fell.

Sir John's creditors indicated that they could wait for their money no longer and that they were seeking his arrest as a debtor. Sir John faced ruin. Leaving their children behind in the care of various relatives, the couple fled to Switzerland. It was to be nine years before Sir John would feel it safe to return. Things went from bad to worse. It was not even a settled exile. The Revolutionary War with France had begun, and Sir John and his wife had to be constantly on the move. Another child was born in 1795 and had to be left with a nurse. Sir John and Lady Elizabeth were unsuited to such an existence: he was obstinate and strong-willed, she short-tempered. In 1800 Elizabeth left him to live with her aunt in Lincolnshire, vowing never to return to Ripley. Finally, having settled his debts, Sir John was able to return to England in 1804.

He found Ripley in a terrible state. The windows had been bricked up to avoid William Pitt's window tax. The interiors were in disorder. Thanks to a good manager, the estate was in good heart, but the Castle was dismal. Sir John was now in his late forties. His wife had left him. His eldest son had died at eighteen. No doubt he felt the need to rebuild his life, and he chose as his partner Martha Webster, the daughter of one of his tenant farmers and twenty-three years his junior. He lived on until 1815, giving her five children but not, even after Elizabeth died in 1812, offering her marriage.

The house that Sir John returned to in 1804 consisted of the surviving tower of the old Castle, dating from 1555, plus the new rooms added on to the old foundations in the 1780s.

Splendid though the newer rooms are, it is the three tower rooms that are of most interest. At the top is the Knight's Chamber, still with its original 'waggon roof' ceiling and sixteenth-century panelling. The panelling conceals a priest's hiding-hole. The Ingilbys have been unwavering Catholics, and several members of the family have distinguished themselves in piety. One was Francis Ingilby, who, as a French-trained priest, was hunted through the north of England in Elizabeth's reign and was finally executed at York in 1586. He is known to have used the hiding-hole in the Knight's Chamber on his visits to Ripley.

Below the Knight's Chamber is the tower room, the main bedroom of the old Castle. Its decorations, heavy with royal symbols, are relics of a visit to Ripley by James I in 1603, for which they were hastily created. On the ground floor is the library, the scene of a courageous encounter between an Ingilby lady and Oliver Cromwell. It seems that after the Battle of Marston Moor in 1644 Cromwell came to the Castle in search of Royalist Sir William Ingilby. Sir William was in hiding, some say still close to the battlefield, others that he was in the priest's hole upstairs.

Sir William had a sister, Jane, who had also been at Marston Moor, dressed in full armour as a trooper. When Cromwell turned up at the Gatehouse, demanding lodgings for the night (and perhaps hoping that Sir William would return home, or reveal himself) Jane reputedly greeted him with a pistol in each hand and refused him admittance. It must have been a remarkable confrontation. Eventually, a compromise was reached: Cromwell stayed but Jane remained armed and kept an eye on him. They are supposed to have spent the night one at each end of a large table, with Jane's pistols on her lap, at the ready.

There is a postscript to the story. The following morning Cromwell, cheated of his prey, ordered the revenge killing of Royalist prisoners who were in the area, and some of them were lined up and shot against Ripley Castle's Gatehouse wall. The marks of the musket balls can still be seen in the wall today.

RIVERHILL HOUSE

KENT

Riverhill House has the distinction of having been chosen as a home for a specific purpose: to establish newly introduced trees and shrubs. It was Riverhill's sheltered position on a lime-free hillside that attracted thirty-three-year-old John Rogers there in 1840. Scientist, botanist, Fellow of the Royal Society and friend of Darwin, John Rogers was the only son of prosperous parents, and able to devote his life to his personal interests. His family, descended from the Protestant martyr John Rogers who was burned at the stake in 1555, established itself in the City of London as merchants and brokers. By the end of the eighteenth century it had been able to afford a move to then fashionable Streatham. The move to Kent of 1840 marked a definitive break with London life.

The house looks more 'all of a piece' than it really is. It began as a Queen Anne house built on the site of a Tudor farmhouse. The site itself is of historical significance: an ancient track runs through the grounds, its path marked now only by a stone bridge which spans it. The track is known as 'Harold's Way', and is said to have been used by the Saxon army on its way to confront William the Conqueror at Hastings in 1066.

In Georgian times a third storey was added to the new Riverhill House and, later, the porch. When John Rogers bought Riverhill in 1840 he enlarged it further, and so did his successors up to about the turn of the century. But his predominant interest was the garden, and by 1842 he was ready to start planting. His planting records from those days still exist, and so it is possible to date accurately all the specimen trees and shrubs.

The collection of family memorabilia dates back 400 years but is chiefly concerned with the history of the family since Riverhill House became its base. Among the most interesting items are the scrapbook and commonplace book of Muriel Rogers, the wife of Colonel

RIPLEY CASTLE Sir William Ingilby (1594–1652), who was pursued to the Castle by Cromwell after the Battle of Marston Moor.

Rogers, who lived at Riverhill before the First World War. These records of social events and party cooking give an intimate picture of that vanished age.

ROCKINGHAM CASTLE

LEICESTERSHIRE

For 500 years a royal residence, and for 450 years the possession of one single family, Rockingham Castle is the contemporary of the Tower of London. After conquering England in 1066, William of Normandy moved swiftly to secure his gains by, among other measures, ordering the construction of unassailable strong points. One site that offered itself immediately—as it had done, much earlier, to tribesmen of the Iron Age—was on the brink of the Welland Valley escarpment, and Rockingham Castle was among the first stone fortresses that the Normans built.

King William and his successors saw it as

more than a centre from which to hold the hinterland in terror; it was also a place of pleasure. Rockingham's complex of Great Hall, chapel, garrison, keep and surrounding curtain wall doubled as a royal hunting lodge. And, because the new rulers enjoyed being there, they were also happy to use it as a place of peaceful state business.

In 1095, for example, the Castle became the setting for the Council of Rockingham, at which King William II and his train of bishops and nobles met the Archbishop of Canterbury in an effort to resolve long-standing differ-

RIVERHILL HOUSE A view of the house in 1839. The next year Riverhill was sold to the Rogers family, who still own it.

ences. In 1194, it was the scene for a kind of medieval summit conference between two heads of state, Richard I of England and William the Lion of Scotland. Between 1204 and 1216, King John signed document after document there. In 1375, King Edward III gave his approval to the Treaty of Bruges, drawn up with the King of France.

Through and behind all the statesmanship, the domestic life of the Castle went on. The Conqueror's third son, King Henry, ordered a vineyard to be planted at Rockingham, and spent twenty shillings on the exercise. On each of his fourteen visits, King John would issue forth from the Norman gateway to hunt in the thick forests of the neighbourhood. (One of the most frequent of the Castle's royal visitors, he is believed on one occasion to have left a round-topped iron chest behind for safe keeping. Then he set off on the unlucky journey that took him across the Wash. In spite of losing the rest of his baggage there, he never re-claimed the box deposited at Rockingham.) And Edward I, while updating the same gateway's defences, also had the living quarters modernized and installed a bedroom for his beloved Queen, Eleanor of Castile.

Although Rockingham now lacks its Norman keep, it is easy to trace the outlines of the structure that Henry, John and the others knew. In the garden with its elephant-shaped yew hedgework, a circular rose plot shows just where the keep stood, while the Tilting Lawn indicates the position of one of the Castle's two baileys, or courtyards. The other bailey, whose limits are equally discernible, contained Rock-ingham's Great Hall and its other domestic buildings. By the end of the Middle Ages, however, the time was fast approaching when these, rather than the Castle's purely defensive structures, would dominate the site.

At the start of the Tudor period, Rocking-ham went through a period of near-total eclipse. The building became so unusable that Henry VIII gave permission for another Leices-tershire landowner to cannibalize the derelict complex for stone. And then, in 1544, its fortunes abruptly changed. Edward Watson, son-in-law of England's Chief Justice, used his family connections at court to win a lease on the tattered Castle. He moved into a build-ing—another hunting lodge—in the grounds, and started to convert his new property into something that could be regarded as habitable.

It took him thirty years but, by the time his grandson bought the property outright in 1619, Rockingham was a house well worth living in. The Great Hall no longer offered

ROCKINGHAM CASTLE Victim of the Civil Wars: Sir Lewis Watson, before and (top right) *after his imprisonment.* Below: *the chest that King John may have once owned.*

communal shelter to the entire household; a ceiling, with bedrooms above, had been put in, while one end now formed a separate room used for dining. Cooking had also been revolutionized: Edward had installed a purpose-built kitchen. In keeping with current views on refined living, it was as far removed as it could be—50 yards—from the new dining quarters, so that the family would not be troubled by smells and noise. The temperature of the food was a lesser consideration.

The service area of the new Rockingham also contained a servants' hall and storehouses and utility rooms growing up along what would become 'the Street'. In the family apartments, amenities included a Long Gallery, where residents marooned by bad weather could take exercise. But, enormous change though Edward Watson had wrought in his new home, he never managed to complete this most Elizabethan of fixtures. It stayed roofless until his grandson, Sir Lewis Watson, finished it the century afterwards.

On the whole, Lewis had a hard time with his building works for, during the Civil War, Rockingham played its last military role, and was all but wrecked by it. The keep went, and so did many of the walls. Sir Lewis himself was imprisoned; later released, he spent the rest of his life trying to persuade the government to foot the bill for the damage done to his home. He used the panels from his smashed four-poster bed to make the Long Gallery's door.

Never again would the Watson family have to face such dire threats to its house. Later additions and alterations continued to be in the domestic vein. A laundry with a clock tower was added at the head of the Street; the battlemented tower over which a flag flies today was built, not by a Norman or a Plantagenet king, but by the Victorian architect Anthony Salvin.

Under its Tudor dress, however, the old royal Castle of the Conqueror still survives. And the iron chest King John probably owned still awaits collection in the Great Hall, along with a companion that bears the arms of another visitor to Rockingham—Henry V.

ROKEBY PARK
COUNTY DURHAM

In December 1731, an amateur architect, Sir Thomas Robinson, wrote to his father-in-law with a progress report on his very first project: the house he was designing for himself. It was now 'entirely fitted up' to be warm and convenient for his family, and it was handsome as well. 'My chief expense,' Sir Thomas added, with justifiable pride, 'has been in Palladian doors and windows, which I am told have a very good effect. . . .'

The building he was describing was Rokeby Park: an elegant variation on the Palladian theme. It would later achieve fame for itself in two quite separate ways, and oddly both had their origins in the same year, 1813.

By that date Rokeby had become the property of the highly cultured J.B.S. Morritt, whose friends included the poet Walter Scott, not yet a baronet, and still with his dazzling career as a novelist ahead of him. In 1813, Scott published the romance *Rokeby*, that contained the song 'Brignall Banks', dedicated to Morritt himself.

It was to Scott that Morritt later wrote with news of the painting he had acquired in the same year. The work of Velasquez, it showed a beautiful woman, gazing at herself in a mirror with her back to the artist. She was—and, indeed, still is—the 'Rokeby Venus'.

Morritt had some unusual problems over hanging his prize. He wrote to Scott:

I have been all morning pulling about my pictures and hanging them in new positions to make more room for my fine picture of Venus's backside by Velasquez which I have at length exalted over my chimney piece in the library. It is an admirable light for the painting, and shows it in perfection, whilst by raising the said backside to a considerable height the ladies may avert their downcast eyes without difficulty, and connoisseurs steal a glance without drawing in the said posterior as a part of the company.

The picture that now hangs in Rokeby's

Saloon is a copy; today, connoisseurs must go to the National Gallery in London to view Velasquez' original work. They can, however, stand entranced before the other Rokeby Venus: the blonde vision by Pellegrini that hangs opposite the bed Scott is believed to have slept in. And they can still peer at the beauties contrived by the aunt of J.B.S. and an artist of peculiar flair:

> It is impossible [wrote a contemporary of Anne Morritt] to view her works without great astonishment; for certainly the act of imitation in work is carried by her to the highest point of perfection. . . . To copy fine paintings, certainly several figures, with a grace, a brilliancy and an elegance superior to the originals, was reserved for this most ingenious lady.

However, Anne was no mere uninspired copyist of other people's work. Her great skill lay in media-crossing, for her tools were not brushes and pigments, but the contents of her embroidery box. Fruit, flowers, people: all were brilliantly recreated at the point of a needle. A portrait on Rokeby's stairs shows her at work, while the picture she is working on still hangs—with all its fellows—elsewhere in the house.

Rokeby may have lost its Velasquez but, in the shape of the Anne Morritt collection, it still possesses the testimony of a uniquely creative spirit.

ROUSHAM PARK
OXFORDSHIRE

In the Entrance Hall at Rousham Park, one element strikes an interestingly discordant note amongst the civilities of parquet and family portraits. Round the walls hang mementoes of Dormer after Dormer: Jane, friend and lady-in-waiting to Mary Tudor; the seventeenth-century Robert and his wife Anne; Robert's father, Sir Robert, who built the house around 1635. But the most striking memorial to Sir Robert is not his portrait, nor

ROUSHAM PARK 'The sweetest little groves, streams, glades, porticos, cascades and river imaginable . . .': William Kent's superb garden, here drawn by himself.

ROKEBY PARK *Rokeby's other Venus, by Antonio Pellegrini, hangs in the Bedroom opposite the four-poster bed in which Sir Walter Scott is believed to have slept.*

even the totality of the house he constructed, but its oaken front door. It is bored through with purposeful-looking holes.

Within a few years of building his new home, Sir Robert and the rest of the country were overtaken by the Civil War. Rousham's owner was a confirmed Royalist, and he also believed in being prepared. So he fortified his brand-new house in the classic manner by cutting loopholes in the door: through them any approaching Parliamentarians could be subjected to a withering hail of gunfire. Alas, the Parliamentarians caught him after all, and he was imprisoned in the Tower of Oxford.

It was left to another military Dormer to give Rousham a truly fortified look. But its battlemented skyline has never sheltered any householder armed with a musket, for it is an early flourish in architecture's love-affair with the Gothic revival. In the 1730s, General James Dormer retired and decided to restyle his family home. In this his architect, William Kent, succeeded brilliantly, for after its remodelling the building emerged looking—in the words of its current owner—rather like 'an Early Tudor palace in free Gothic style'. For the period, the new look was the ultimate in modernity.

But, if the reworked Rousham was modern, its new, 'natural' garden—also Kent's work—was positively futuristic. One of his greatest achievements, it combines ruins, statues, water and trees to stand as a milestone in the development of British garden taste. One enthusiast for Rousham's transformation was Horace Walpole. The garden was, he said, 'Daphne in little, the sweetest little groves, streams, glades, porticos, 'cascades and river imaginable; all the scenes are perfectly classic.' Then, hitting an ultimate note of ecstasy, he reached his conclusion: 'It is Kentissimo'.

RYDAL MOUNT
CUMBRIA

It was a substantial household that moved to Rydal Mount on May Day, 1813: the poet William Wordsworth, his wife Mary, their three children, William's sister Dorothy and his sister-in-law Sara Hutchinson. The next day, Dorothy pronounced the house, in a letter to a friend, 'a paradise'. The move was a turning-point in the life of this extended family. It had endured years of varying discomfort in houses at Grasmere, and in 1812 had been badly shaken by the deaths in infancy of two of the Wordsworth children. Rydal Mount offered the Wordsworths so much of

RYDAL MOUNT *William Wordsworth by Benjamin Robert Haydon. The poet lived at Rydal Mount from 1813 until his death.*

what they desired, including 4½ acres of garden which William could design to his own requirements. He built a new terrace from which he could look down on Rydal Water, and a summerhouse in which to read and work. The house was little altered while the Wordsworths were there, except for the study, which William added in about 1838.

Few poets have ever been able to make a living from their work, and the financial base of Wordsworth's life at Rydal Mount was his appointment, in the year of his move there, as Distributor of Stamps for Westmorland. He retained this sinecure until he was awarded a Civil List pension in 1842, and it enabled him and his family to live a modest but pleasant life, receiving his literary and local friends as well as more distinguished guests such as, in 1840, the widowed Queen Adelaide.

But life at Rydal Mount was not all distinguished visitors and literary conversation. The drawing room saw more social pleasures, sometimes thick and fast. On one occasion Wordsworth reported to a friend that it had held a dance for forty—'Beaus and Belles besides Matrons, Spinsters and Greybeards'—and the next day there was to be a 'venison feast'.

The last years at Rydal Mount, however, were tinged with sadness. William and Mary's daughter Dora, his assistant and companion, had contracted tuberculosis. Despite this, at the age of thirty-six she married a fairly impoverished retired officer, Edward Quillinan; six years later, she died at Rydal Mount. Meanwhile, William's sister Dorothy had for years been the victim of mental breakdown. Wordsworth's appointment as Poet Laureate in 1843, though he refused it at first on grounds of age, must have come as a welcome shaft of light through the clouds of the Lake District. He died in 1850, leaving Mary to nurse the stricken Dorothy for another five years. Rydal remains as a memorial to these quiet lives.

ST FAITH'S PRIORY

NORFOLK

Searching out the history of an old building can, as many owners know, be a long and wearisome business involving painstaking research, inspired guesswork and more than a little bit of luck. For the owners of St Faith's Priory near Norwich, the groundwork at least has been less arduous, for the story of its founding is recorded in a series of thirteenth-century wall-paintings in the refectory.

In 1105 Robert Fitzwalter, the owner of nearby (and now ruinous) Horsford Castle, set out with his wife Sybilla on a pilgrimage to Rome. On their way home through France, the devout couple were set upon by brigands who, having robbed them, imprisoned them in fetters. The Fitzwalters prayed for their release and were visited in a vision by Saint Faith, a fourth-century martyr who had died in France at the hands of the Romans. Sir Robert and Robert Haydon. The poet lived at Rydal Mount

ST FAITH'S PRIORY One of the recently rediscovered medieval wall-paintings in the Refectory. The figure is St Faith.

Sybilla regained their freedom, and went to Conques Abbey in southern France, where Saint Faith's remains were (and still are), to give thanks. While there, they agreed to take two monks of the Abbey home with them and to establish a Benedictine priory on their land.

The paintings which make up this story in pictures are not the only ones on the walls of St Faith's. Preserved under the panelling that was installed in Tudor times to conceal the illegal chapel, the wall-paintings of St Faith's are gradually being revealed and preserved. They include a huge crucifixion scene, with Christ on the cross flanked by Mary and St John, which was only discovered by accident in 1924 when lightning set fire to timbers in the roof space into which the picture extends.

Following the Dissolution of the Monasteries part of the Priory was destroyed and its stone used for other buildings in the village, but the refectory wing was preserved and became the home of Sir Richard Southwell, who with his family continued to practise the Roman Catholic faith. The conversion of the remaining wing to a house by putting a new floor into the single-storey building dates from this time. Among those who lived in the house was, as a boy, Saint Robert Southwell, born at St Faith's in 1561. In the wall of the main bedroom there is a section of Tudor plaster on which he wrote his initials as a child. After a Jesuit education at Douai and studies in Rome he returned to England in secrecy in 1586 and lived a dangerous life administering the Mass to Catholic families. Finally, in 1592, the authorities caught up with him and, after an extended period of imprisonment and torture, he was hanged at Tyburn in February 1595. He was canonised in 1970.

ST MARY'S
WEST SUSSEX

In September 1651, the attempt of King Charles II to take possession of his executed father's kingdom finally seemed hopeless. At the beginning of the month, Cromwell had defeated him at Worcester and, after the battle, Charles became a man on the run, disguising himself as a servant and—on one celebrated occasion—hiding from the Roundheads in the concealing branches of an oak tree. His one hope lay in reaching the south coast and a French-bound ship.

On the afternoon of 14 October, the fugitive at last came within a few miles of his goal. The only obstacle that lay between him and the harbour of Shoreham was Bramber Bridge. Crossing it, however, presented considerable difficulty. His companion, Colonel George Gunter, recorded: 'Being come to Bramber, we found the streets full of soldiers on both sides the houses, who unluckily and unknowne to me, were come thither the night before'. Dismayed, the escapers hurriedly revised their plans; Gunter went on to reconnoitre, while Charles took temporary refuge with a Royalist family called Gough.

ST MARY'S The fifteenth-century house is the last surviving part of a monastic inn, built on even older foundations to shelter pilgrims.

The hours he spent with them were a repetition of the oak-tree experience. The patrolling Parliamentarian soldiers frequently passed within feet of him, for the Goughs' home was St Mary's, an ancient timbered house right by the bridge. It had once served as a hostelry run by monks for travellers, frequently disreputable ones; the monks themselves were rather a rowdy lot. Now, from one of its upstairs rooms, Charles could watch both the movements of the guards on the bridge, and the approach of darkness that would cover his escape. By the end of the next day, the fugitive was finally safe and clear away, on board a ship for France.

He was not, in fact, the first royal visitor St Mary's had received, nor would he be the last. The century before, Elizabeth I came to stay with the Goughs of the time, and had a bedroom redecorated in her honour. Much later, Edwardian royalty were also guests in the medieval house. None, however, can have been quite so glad as Charles to find a welcome under St Mary's roof.

ST OSWALD'S HALL

NORTH YORKSHIRE

Remodelled or in their original state, medieval great halls survive in many houses. Comparatively few, however, are still completely furnished in a way that their medieval occupants would have recognized, with furniture that itself dates from the Middle Ages. With its early oak furniture, its medieval metalwork and embroidery, and its floor of tiles dating from the 1200s, St Oswald's Hall helps to fill the gap.

The building that houses these possessions is itself 800 years old. Oddly, however, its own history as a home is much shorter. Until the last century, it was the chapel serving the needs of the manor of Fulford, close to York. With the Industrial Revolution, the congregation outgrew its place of worship and moved to a new church. St Oswald's, through whose main doorway people have been passing since

ST OSWALD'S HALL Cornflowers and wild strawberries decorate the margins of St Oswald's Book of Hours, dated 1470.

the time of the Crusades, became derelict.

Its new owner found it when he was looking for a medieval home. With its space, its Norman door and its miscellany of windows— dating from the twelfth, the fourteenth and the seventeenth centuries—it certainly qualified in terms of age, if not function. After restoring its fabric, he used St Oswald's architectural proportions to recreate within its walls a medieval hall house, furnished in contemporary style.

SAND

DEVON

All families have their mysteries, and some hold them close. What long-forgotten quarrel, for example, lies behind the will of

SAND The house in 1834. Shortly afterwards, fire destroyed the chapel and the north-west wing. At this time, Sand was let as a farmhouse, a role which it fulfilled until 1909.

Francis Huyshe of Sand, who died in the late eighteenth century? He left all his property to be sold for the benefit of his daughters, despite the fact that he had two sons still living. Although there is fairly extensive family documentation of this period, nothing has been discovered to explain a will that would, at the time, have been considered an act of wilful malice or outstanding eccentricity.

But the Huyshe family—who at this period let Sand to tenant farmers—seem then to have been a cantankerous lot. Francis's daughters re-entailed the estate on their nephew. In 1828 we find this nephew Francis in dispute over shooting rights with a neighbouring estate, whose gamekeeper, delightfully named Amos Broom, had told the Huyshe tenants that his master proposed to shoot over their holdings. In September 1828, Francis let off a broadside to Mr Broom:

I cannot conceive this piece of insolence to be solely your own [he wrote]. My property is the miserable remains of an old family estate, which will be defended with family pride, that has

been inherited from a great many centuries previous to that possession. For every instance of your invading it a prosecution will be commenced against you; and to support those prosecutions, the coat which now covers my back will be readily pledged.

It is unfortunate that the outcome of this letter, with its masterly implication of genteel good breeding set against the impudence of a wealthy upstart neighbour, is not known.

The Huyshe family had been at Sand since the mid-sixteenth century and shortly afterwards set about building the present house. The depredations of farm tenants, and a fire in 1834 which destroyed the chapel and the north-west wing, meant that when the family took Sand back for its own occupation at the beginning of the present century considerable restoration was needed. Fortunately, a set of photographs taken in 1875 and pictures of Sand before the fire were available to act as a guide. The house is now owned by a Huyshe descendant who inherited it in 1960 and has since introduced many improvements.

SANDFORD ORCAS

DORSET

A house which has stood virtually unaltered for over 400 years, the claim made for Sandford Orcas, might be expected to have more than its fair share of ghosts. And so it seems to be. This Dorset manor house has a persistently haunted reputation which has been vouched for by the present owner, previous tenants and even a BBC television camera crew which went ghost-hunting there in the 1960s. The manifestations have been many and various, and it is difficult to pinpoint any particular incident in the history of the house to

SANDFORD ORCAS MANOR HOUSE Spared Georgian and Victorian 'improvement', the house retains its sixteenth-century features.

which to relate them. There's a local tale, not entirely verified, of a tenant farmer who hanged himself in the house—but when this was, and who he was, is not clear. Sir Mervyn Medlycott, the present owner, is however clear about the events of an evening in January 1981

when he was sitting upstairs waiting for a friend to call to do some decorating.

Sir Mervyn heard someone come in through the garden door and along the passage into one of the rooms, followed by what he took to be the noise of the decorator. After a while, he decided to go downstairs to see how things were going—and found the doors locked, the lights off, and the rooms empty.

This was a relatively mild incident compared with what happened in the 1960s, when Sandford Orcas was let to Colonel Francis Claridge and his family. There were not only footsteps, but also voices, harpsichord music, the apparition, in the middle of the afternoon, of a white-smocked figure in the garden and another of a lady in red on the stairs. The man in the white smock was also seen by a member of the BBC camera crew.

There are surviving fragments of an earlier building, but the present house dates from about 1550, when it was built for the holders of the manor, the Knoyle family. After about 200 years, it was sold to the Medlycott family who let it to a succession of tenant farmers before taking it for their own occupation from 1873 onwards. The period of tenancies was what probably saved Sandford Orcas from 'improvement' in the critical Georgian and early Victorian periods. The result is that almost everything in the house, including the ten studded oak doors with their massive locks and keys, is original.

SCONE PALACE

TAYSIDE

Scone is more than a building. It is a palace, an idea, a state of mind: the heart of Scotland and the symbol of the country's national identity. Scone is to the Scots what Tara is to the Irish. Like Tara, it was the home of a 'stone of destiny', the famous Stone of Scone. On the mound by Scone Palace, the Moot Hill, decisions of the utmost importance were taken, and kings were made. They were unmade, too; Scone was the place where

Macbeth, fatally injured by Macduff, bled to death. Scone was the ancient capital of the Picts, a royal lodging-place, and a holy site, all in one.

For something like 450 years, the Stone lay at the sacred centre of the king-making ceremony, for the kings were seated on it to be crowned. Then, in 1296, Scone and the kingdom were struck by calamity. King Edward I of England invaded Scotland, temporarily reduced it to dependant status, and robbed it of its mystical emblem: the Stone. Or did he?

According to one theory, the King and posterity were outwitted by the Stone's custodians, the monks of Scone Abbey. Faced with the appalling prospect of losing the relic, they hid the real Stone and hastily carved a substitute rock to the right size. Was it this that they presented to Scotland's invader?

Whatever the truth, the stone that the invader took south with him now lies under the Coronation Chair in Westminster Abbey. In 1603, the crowns of Scotland and England were joined in the person of King James VI and I and, from that time onwards, Scotland's rulers have again been consecrated on Edward's trophy.

Until then, however, Scotland's monarchs were crowned without it, the country's liberator, Robert the Bruce, being the first. For the ceremony, the new kings lodged in the 'House of Scone'—the abbot's own residence that now forms the core of Scone Palace—and it was from here that the last king to be crowned in Scotland set out for the Moot Hill.

The year was 1651: Charles I was dead and, in defiance of Cromwell, Scotland had hailed his son, Charles II, as king. Past hunting scenes featuring his grandfather, James I, the new monarch walked to his coronation down the oak parquet that still forms the floor of the Palace's Long Gallery. The ceremony that awaited him on the mound is unique in British history, for it is the only Presbyterian crowning ever held.

Although the Long Gallery's flooring is still as Charles knew it, the murals showing his

SCONE PALACE *A French seventeenth-century ivory of the Holy Family, part of the collection of ivories in the Dining Room.*

relative and predecessor vanished in a major remodelling programme that overtook Scone at the start of the nineteenth century. However, the loss is a small one compared to what Scone has gained. The property of the noble Murray family since the early seventeenth century, the Palace is now one of Scotland's greatest treasure houses.

No matter that it was damp and therefore disliked by David Murray, second Earl of Mansfield and one-time ambassador to the court of Louis XVI and Marie Antoinette. Many of his superb French acquisitions are now here nonetheless, and so is the ambassadorial bed, fit for a king and worked with the British royal cypher.

Beside it hangs the exquisite painting by Zoffany that the Earl commissioned of his daughter, Lady Elizabeth. Elizabeth's black maid, Dido, recalls the memory of the first Earl of Mansfield, uncle of the second and one of the greatest lawyers who has ever lived. In 1772, he made British legal history by declaring that the 'odious' institution of slavery could not be accepted in Britain, and that any slave setting foot in the country automatically became free. The Earl's housekeeper, Dido's mother, was one of those he freed.

Portraits of the first Earl are also among Scone's contents. So is the fabulous collection of porcelain that he helped amass (mainly for day-to-day use). So are the collections of his successors: the ivories brought together by the fourth Earl, the clocks, the vases and goblets in 'vernis Martin'. The latter, a process of painting and varnishing papier mâché, was the monopoly of the French Martin brothers. The items at Scone once formed half of the King of France's own collection; the other half was bought by the Tsar of Russia and has not been seen since the Revolution.

Naturally, objects with royal associations are present in quantity: bed-hangings worked by Mary Queen of Scots, Marie Antoinette's writing table, the ornamental apron that once formed part of the dress of Queen Charlotte. Meanwhile, outside, an oak planted by King James—at that point, still King of Scotland only—continues to flourish.

Can it be possible that, in some subterranean hiding-place now lost, Scone still holds fast to its most treasured royal object of all: the real Stone of Destiny, hidden by the Augustinian monks almost 700 years ago?

SHELDON MANOR

WILTSHIRE

Inside the porch at Sheldon Manor there stands a stone trough, fed by a wooden pipe from the roof, which is the original water

SHELDON MANOR Like many of its kind, Sheldon Manor had a period as a working farmhouse. This photograph was taken in 1899, when the house was occupied by the farm bailiff, George Sims.

supply. From time to time, it is said, a party of horsemen is seen to ride into the porch at night to water their horses from the trough. Who are they? No one is sure, but it seems likely that they are the remnants of the Royalist army that stared out the Parliamentary forces near Chippenham throughout one night in 1643. It was a Civil War battle that never was.

The porch is the oldest and most impressive part of Sheldon Manor, dating from the first manor house built in the last decades of the thirteenth century. Sheldon Manor has passed through many hands, and countless tenancies, since then, and shortly after the Civil War a new tenant, William Forster, took over, and obtained permission to demolish part of the old house, which was in a ruinous condition, and rebuild. The hall and probably the oak staircase date from this time.

The house passed rapidly from owner to owner, tenant to tenant, over the succeeding 250 years. No one seems to have lavished much care on the place, and its condition declined. At one time it was sub-divided into two farm dwellings. In this century, Sheldon has rediscovered stability in the hands of the Gibbs family. Filled with their early English furniture, paintings and Nailsea glass, the old stone manor with its wealth of oak panelling sleeps forgotten behind its screen of yews. Only the ghostly horsemen disturb it . . .

SHERBORNE CASTLE
DORSET

When the Civil War came to Sherborne Castle, Anne Digby—Countess of Bristol and wife of the estate's owner—received a message from the Earl of Bedford, in charge of the approaching Parliamentary troops. Their orders, he said, were to demolish her property. The Earl was the Countess's brother. Anne speedily took advantage of the situation, and demanded an interview with him. Neither she nor her mother-in-law, she told him, were going to move a step from their home at Sherborne Lodge; if he carried out his

orders, it would be over her dead body.

Her determination had its effect; Bedford gave his sister a safe conduct, and his troops were called off. Three years later, the medieval castle at the heart of the estate suffered renewed attack by Cromwell's army, but Anne and her house continued to be protected. It is to her that we owe the survival of the home built and adored by one of the most remarkable figures in English history: Sir Walter Raleigh. Like its ruined fellow a quarter-of-a-mile away, it too now goes under the name of Sherborne Castle.

Soldier, sailor and semi-pirate, Raleigh came to the court of Queen Elizabeth I in 1581. The epitome of the Elizabethan gallant, he made an enormous hit with the Queen, and quickly became one of her favourites. It is possible that, to attract Elizabeth's notice, he inscribed a hopeful epigram on a palace window: 'Fain would I climb, yet I fear to fall.' (Elizabeth appended a graffito of her own: 'If thy heart fail thee, climb not at all.')

By the end of the decade, however, he had been supplanted in Elizabeth's affections by the Earl of Essex, and his time in the sun was nearly over. Indeed, he helped speed the rate of his own eclipse, for he became the lover of one of the Queen's ladies-in-waiting, Bess Throckmorton. In 1591, the pair were secretly married and, from then on, it was merely a question of time before the fall he feared.

Before then, however, Raleigh was able to seek one final favour from the Queen. He now needed a home and, returning to London from Plymouth, he had seen the one he wanted: Sherborne, with its medieval castle, its stretch of the River Yeo, and its secondary home, the lodge. The whole complex belonged to the Bishop of Salisbury. Not surprisingly, the Bishop was not especially willing to give them up, but at Raleigh's request the Queen—still ignorant of her favourite's marriage to Bess—engineered the transfer. Soon afterwards, Elizabeth's ignorance was dispelled, and she reacted with fury. Both Raleigh and Bess spent five anxious weeks in the Tower of London. After their release, they were banished from court and it was from this enforced absence that the second Sherborne Castle was born.

In place of the old lodge, the exiled courtier built a splendid new one. Efforts to make a home in the Norman castle had come to nothing, but the house Raleigh created was close to being a castle in its own right. Tall and narrow—it owes its H-shaped ground plan to later Digby additions—it was guarded at each corner by a hexagonal turret. But, instead of the battlemented skyline an earlier castle would have had, that of Sherborne was broken into an array of balustrades, chimneys, and sweeping curves in the Dutch style. Somewhere just below, on the topmost of the Castle's four floors, was the equipment for supplying water: sophisticated by the standards of the day, it consisted of a lead cistern and pipes carrying water up from its source in the park. Raleigh called his home 'fortune's fold'. The life he led there was in marked contrast to the glamorous comings and goings of his days at court. He farmed, wrote, entertained his friends both intellectual and worldly, and landscaped the grounds with orchards and water gardens. He included a stone viewpoint where he could sit and smoke. One of his servants—so the well-loved story goes—was totally unfamiliar with the new habit of smoking a pipe (it was Raleigh who had popularized the use of tobacco amongst the English nobility). Seeing his master apparently on fire, the unfortunate man came racing up with a bucket of ale, and doused him.

Much as Raleigh loved his wife and his Dorset home, his restless spirit did not allow him to bury himself there for long. In 1595, only a year after his son Wat was born, he set off in an unsuccessful attempt to find gold in South America. By the end of the century, he was back in the Queen's favour and by a strange stroke of fate he even supervised the execution of the man who had once ousted him from the Queen's side, the disgraced Essex.

Within a few years, however, he himself faced execution; indeed, he was actually led to the scaffold, only to be sent back to his cell.

Elizabeth had died and her place on the throne was now occupied by the nervous, stubborn, superstitious James I. By both temperament and policy, James was no friend of Raleigh. Raleigh became involved in plots against James, was arrested in 1603 and—in a trial that showed a monstrous degree of bias—was found guilty of treason.

Although he was not executed, his days of freedom were effectively over. He was kept in the Tower for no less than thirteen years. Sherborne was confiscated. Bess came to live near at hand; their second son was conceived and born during Walter's imprisonment. Finally, in 1616, James let him out to go on another ill-fated hunt for gold up the Orinoco. But, in defiance of royal orders, Raleigh's party attacked a Spanish settlement. It was the end of everything: his son Wat was killed in the attack and Raleigh himself was executed on his return home.

The following year, Sherborne Castle and its surroundings were given to the Digbys. In their resourceful care, it from then on survived all the tricks and turns of fortune—unlike its brilliant but unlucky builder.

SHIPTON HALL
SHROPSHIRE

In the Queen's Room at Shipton Hall there is a touching recollection of a troubled but ultimately triumphant romance. It was between the daughter of the house, Harriott Mytton, and Thomas More, the son of a neighbour. The year was 1792, and Harriott's parents, disapproving of the affair, locked her in the room which had been named to commemorate Elizabeth I's visit to Shipton two hundred years before. Slowly, it seems, the attitude of the Mytton family softened, for Harriott grew sufficiently confident of the future to engrave on the glass of one of the windows the reflection: 'Hope travels thro' not guilt now.' The hope was apparently well-founded, for in 1795 Harriott and Thomas were married. Their son, Robert, finally

SHERBORNE CASTLE The pole screen before the fire in the 'Strawberry Hill Gothic' Library protected the wax-based make-up of Georgian women from the heat.

brought together the Mytton estate at Shipton and that of the More family at Larden Hall.

Such neighbourly arrangements were of course commonplace in rural England, and perhaps especially so in Shropshire, which until the coming of the railways was a remote region in which social opportunities and communications were difficult. Indeed, Shipton Hall itself was built as a dowry for just such a marriage. The couple on this occasion, *c.* 1587, were Elizabeth Lutwych of Shipton and Thomas Mytton, both children of local worthies. The house—which replaced an earlier black-and-white timbered building destroyed by fire—was evidently quickly established, for

it was not long before Elizabeth I visited Shipton Hall and so gave the room where Harriott was to be immured its name. The date of her visit is not known, but it may well have been in 1589 to inspect the chancel of the parish church, which had been rebuilt by the Lutwych family.

The style of both house and garden at Shipton Hall is unmistakably Elizabethan, and there were few external alterations during the 300 or so years of the Mytton family's ownership. A good deal of internal refurbishing was done during the Georgian period, but the panelling of the bedrooms and of the former Solar, and the window-glazing, date from the sixteenth century. The dovecote in the grounds predates the present house and was possibly built in the thirteenth century at the same time as the original house. But it is perhaps that engraved message on the glass of the Queen's Room that calls most hauntingly across the centuries.

SLEDMERE HOUSE
NORTH HUMBERSIDE

In the early morning of 23 May 1911, disaster struck Sledmere House. Unnoticed in the kitchen chimney, a protruding beam started to smoulder, then to blaze. The fire crept upwards till it reached the roof, where it turned into an all-consuming inferno. Sledmere and its contents seemed utterly doomed.

Yet they survived: the pattern of the fire gave teams of salvage workers the time to empty one room after another; even the doors were taken off their hinges and lugged downstairs. Contemporary photographs show everything piled up on the lawn.

The heaps of furniture and *objets d'art* included Sledmere's most precious possession: a brilliantly enamelled tea table from Canton, dating from the early eighteenth century. They included the Romney picture of one of Sledmere's builders, Sir Christopher Sykes (1749–1801), and his wife Elizabeth. There was also the self-portrait by Joseph Rose, the plasterer of genius whom Sir Christopher commissioned to decorate the house he was improving. Significantly, Rose's original designs for the plasterwork also survived.

A further picture that was rescued and stacked with its fellows on the grass showed a quintessentially English group of two country gentlemen and one handsome gentlewoman: Sir Christopher's two sons, Mark and Tatton, and Mark's wife. Both brothers became owners of Sledmere, and both contributed to it greatly.

Mark filled Sledmere's gigantic library with a bibliophile's dream collection; regrettably, Tatton sold it but made up for the loss in another direction. Like his brother, he bred racehorses and, under his direction, Sledmere became for a while the biggest racing stud in England. Before every Derby Day, he would without fail ride all the way from his northern home to Epsom to watch the race. He also attended seventy-four St Legers, and one of the paintings hanging today in Sledmere's Horse Room shows him with the St Leger winner of 1846: also called Sir Tatton Sykes.

Although all Sledmere's contents were saved from the 1911 conflagration, the interior of the house was gutted. But the lucky rescue of Rose's designs, plus that of a collection of Victorian watercolours, helped the Sykes family to restore Sledmere's decorated rooms to their previous glory.

As a flourish, the sixth baronet, Sir Mark Sykes, added a decorated room of his own. Designed for him by an Armenian artist, Sledmere's blue-tiled Turkish Room is based on a sultan's apartment in an Istanbul mosque. In an exotic way, it complements the intricacy of the plasterwork elsewhere in the house that—destroyed in its first version—has still been saved for posterity.

SMEDMORE
DORSET

Twice in its 350-year history, Smedmore has almost slipped away into oblivion: first through commercial failure, and the second time by the threat of a forged will.

Present-day oilmen are not the first to cast greedy eyes on Kimmeridge Bay and the profits that might be made from its natural resources. They have a predecessor in Sir William Clavell, the owner of Smedmore in the early seventeenth century. Having built himself a house, Sir William filled his time with schemes for exploiting the resources of the neighbourhood. First, it was extracting alum—then essential for the processes of tanning and dyeing—from the Kimmeridge cliffs. Unfortunately, he was beaten to it by a rival. Then he turned to the idea of making salt by boiling sea water. This was a commercial failure. Finally, Sir William set up a glassmaking industry, using the bituminous shale of the area as fuel. This too was a failure. When Sir William died in 1644 he left behind him a considerably impoverished estate and a long list of creditors.

Smedmore passed to a cousin of Sir William's, Roger Clavell, who with his grandson managed to pay off the debts and even, by the early eighteenth century, to begin extending the house. The south-west façade was added, to be followed in the next generation by the rooms on the north-west front.

Smedmore came into the ownership of the present family—just—by the fortunes of law. It was owned by a John Clavell who died intestate in 1833. His next of kin was his niece Louisa, who was married to Colonel John Mansel, but three months after the funeral, just when Louisa was about to take possession, former servants of John Clavell produced a will leaving the house to them. Fortunately, the courts found for Louisa, and Smedmore has been in the Mansel family ever since. Its furniture and *objets*, which have a distinctive Dutch flavour, come largely from an ancestor who was a member of the Ginkel family of Utrecht. The Ginkels' fortunes began when Godart van Ginkel, later first Earl of Athlone, fought with William of Orange in Ireland.

....

SOMERLEYTON HALL
SUFFOLK
....

Many country houses are monuments to loyal service to the Crown, given hundreds of years ago. By contrast, Somerleyton Hall celebrates early Victorian enterprise. It was created, on the base of a Jacobean manor house, by one great entrepreneur, and sustained by another.

Morton Peto was one of the great names of the early phase of British railway building. He started out as an apprentice in his uncle's small building firm, in which his uncle left him a half-share at twenty-one. That was in 1830—a

SMEDMORE *A nineteenth-century Italian painted cabinet in the Drawing Room. It has a companion piece, a bureau bookcase.*

significant year in railway history, for it was the year of the opening of the Liverpool & Manchester Railway, the first completely steam-hauled passenger line. It was the dawn of the railway age, and Morton Peto set himself to take full advantage of it. His enterprise became a legend, as did his generous and humane treatment of his employees, rare among railway contractors. From East Anglia, where he was responsible for the creation of the basic rail network as well as many branch lines, he extended his business overseas. He was made a baronet in 1855 as a reward for building thirty miles of track in the Crimea to take British forces to the battlefront. Unlike most other railway contractors, who sub-contracted heavily, Peto believed in employing his men direct, and at one time he was the largest employer of labour in the world.

In 1843 the Jacobean mansion of Somerleyton came up for sale with 4,500 acres. It was in the heart of the country Peto had made his own, and he bought it. The next year work began on the new Hall. It is said that Peto's aim had been to enhance the original house, but in the event Somerleyton turned out to be almost entirely an early Victorian invention, built without regard for expense. The facing stone was brought from France. Italianate and French Renaissance effects were applied with abandon. A now demolished winter garden—an enormous iron-and-glass structure, over 40-yards square—contained sculpture and vases for which Europe was scoured. Paintings were specially commissioned for the house.

The new Somerleyton Hall was finished in 1851. Peto was still riding high, and with the contract for the Crimean railway and his subsequent knighthood, he looked unstoppable. But—such was the volatility of the railway age—within ten years he was forced to put Somerleyton and all its contents on the market, and within a further five he was ruined. The bankers, Overend and Gurney, and a labour force of 30,000 men, went down with him.

Peto's successor at Somerleyton was a man from the same mould. Francis Crossley was one of three sons of an ambitious Halifax carpet-weaver who had worked his way up to owning his own mill. Francis and his brothers de-veloped the business further by using steam-powered looms which enabled them to cut prices and so take carpets into the mass market. Like Peto, the Crossleys were philan-thropic chapelgoers, rather paternalistic but nevertheless caring and generous to the under-privileged of their day. Francis Crossley—created a baronet in the year he moved to Somerleyton—took over the house lock, stock and barrel, and it is his descendants who live there today. Sir Francis's son was created Baron Somerleyton in 1916.

Apart from the demolition of the winter garden in 1914, the only major change since 1863 has been the horizontal division of Peto's huge (and impractical) banqueting hall. Its ground floor is now the library and the first-floor additional bedrooms. What is now called the Oak Room is the surviving drawing room of the pre-Peto house, with a carved chimney-breast attributed to Grinling Gibbons. The extravagant spirit in which Somerleyton was rebuilt is seen at its peak in the Ballroom, with its crimson damask wallcovering and curtains, its gilded ornamentation and its multitude of mirrors.

Of no less interest are the gardens, which include glasshouses designed by Sir Joseph Paxton of Crystal Palace fame and a clock tower designed by Vulliamy. The clock is a model submitted for a competition to design a clock for the new Houses of Parliament, for whose building Peto was the main contractor. The Vulliamy clock was rejected as too costly, whereupon Peto bought it and erected the clock tower at Somerleyton for it.

SOUTHSIDE HOUSE
LONDON

On special written request, visitors to Southside House may be shown the last necklace Queen Marie Antoinette ever put on. Picked up from the scaffold after she was guillotined, it now forms part of the contents of Southside's special treasure chest: its fabul-ous Cabinet of Curiosities.

The necklace's companions behind the Cabinet's barred glass are almost as extra-ordinary. One of them is Anne Boleyn's vanity

SOMERLEYTON HALL The Winter Garden *stood on the north side of the Hall, overlooked by the windows of the Ballroom, which now survey the loggia and sunken garden created in its place.*

case, rescued with her other personal effects from the Tower of London after her death. Another is the Queen's ivory comb, which also appears hanging opposite in the portrait of Philadelphia Carey, lady-in-waiting to Elizabeth I (Anne was Philadelphia's aunt).

A third exhibit has altogether happier and more recent associations: it is a silver snuff box lent by the house's owners to the future Edward VII, then Prince of Wales, when he visited Southside House during military manoeuvres on Wimbledon Common. It was a cold day, and the Prince obviously had a sore throat. His hosts kindly pressed a supply of cough pastilles on him, enclosed in the snuff box. At the end of the day, he gave the box

back; some of the cough pastilles are still in it.

Any one of these treasures would be fascinating; together, the effect is dizzying. But, even amongst such peers as these, Marie-Antoinette's pearl necklace still reigns supreme in its hold on the imagination. Its story did not end when the executioner salvaged it from beside the guillotine. Very briefly, it became the property of the government representative who had supervised the execution, Paul François Barras. Then, over dinner that night, he gave it to his mistress, Josephine Beauharnais. Several months later, Josephine found herself closely affected by the Terror. A near relation had to leave France fast and secretly and, being a friend of the British Ambassador's wife,

SLEDMERE HOUSE Sir Christopher and Lady Sykes, painted by Romney. Sir Christopher redesigned Sledmere *in the 1780s, and employed Joseph Rose to redecorate it.*

SOUTHSIDE HOUSE Thirty-two family portraits hang in the oldest part of the house, now its Dining Room.

Josephine took him and his family to the British Embassy. For their clandestine voyage to Britain, the Ambassador entrusted them to a junior—indeed, sixteen-year-old—member of staff, John Pennington. He was also a member of the family that, over a century before, had created Southside House out of a rambling farmstead near the then country village of Wimbledon.

In spite of his youth, John acquitted himself brilliantly on his mission, and was given several more like it—all with Josephine as their ultimate instigator. Her courier read of her marriage to the celebrated General Bonaparte, but never met her until, one day, the Ambassador sent for him. He was to dress in his best uniform and make his way to the Bonaparte home of La Malmaison, so that

Mme la Générale could thank him personally for his help. On his arrival, John was disappointed not to find the General there. However, it soon became apparent why he had been summoned during Bonaparte's absence. Nothing, Josephine said, could really repay the young man for what he had done—but, as a token of her gratitude, she wanted to make him a present. And she handed him the pearl necklace.

On hearing its history, John was dismayed. The gift was much too good, he said. How could she part with it? For answer, Josephine led him out into the park. There, away from listening ears, she told him the truth: Napoleon would not allow the necklace to be kept in the house. When, on her marriage, she had shown it to him, his reaction had been one of horror. *'Ah, ça—non!'* he had exclaimed, retreating from the object. *'Ça, non!'*

John took the pearls back to England. After his marriage, his wife—who was not afraid of the invisible blood still clinging to them—wore the necklace regularly. It has since been restrung from time to time but, on each occasion, a little loop of six pearls has always been kept separate.

As Josephine explained to young Pennington, their history is more poignant still. Marie-Antoinette had used them as a bribe for one of her wardresses. Her young son, the Dauphin, was also a prisoner; what the six jewels bought was the chance of a last glimpse of him, being exercised in a prison courtyard.

SOUTHWICK HALL
NORTHAMPTONSHIRE

West of Peterborough and the A1, the land begins to rise away from the Bedford Levels and East Anglia merges slowly into the East Midlands. The country hereabouts is haunted by one tragic figure: that of Mary Queen of Scots. A road-sign points to Fotheringhay, the site of the now demolished Fotheringhay Castle where Mary spent her last months. A little further on is the small village of Southwick. It is said that walled up somewhere in Southwick Hall is Mary's burial certificate.

It was in September 1586 that Mary was brought to Fotheringhay Castle for her trial. In October, she was found guilty. On 7 February 1587 her death warrant arrived at Fotheringhay, and at eight the next morning she went bravely to the block. Five months later her body was buried at Peterborough Cathedral, from which it was taken twenty-five years later to Westminster Abbey. At the Peterborough burial, one of the eight men who carried Mary's funeral banner was George Lynn, the owner of Southwick Hall.

The Lynns had bought Southwick in 1441 and a century later built, on the foundations of a medieval hall, the main south front of the present house, retaining the two towers and the rooms adjoining which dated from the medieval house. In the eighteenth century there were extensions on the west side and improvements to the interior such as the panelling in the Parlour and Middle Room and the chimneypiece in the Study. In 1841 the Hall was bought by the Capron family, which still lives there.

The owners of Southwick Hall have generally been quiet East Midlands gentry going about their local and county affairs, and in a way the house reflects this. The fourteenth, sixteenth, eighteenth, nineteenth and—in the alterations made in recent years to accommodate more modern needs—the twentieth centuries are all represented. There have been no dramatic refurbishings, no wings thrown out as a mark of prosperity, but quiet adaptation over the years to the needs of the owners and of

SOUTHWICK HALL From the fourteenth century onwards, successive owners of the Hall have made additions and alterations to meet the changing needs of the times, a process that has continued until today.

*SQUERRYES COURT The first **Wardes** to live at Squerryes, painted in 1735 by Wootton. George Warde, James Wolfe's boyhood friend, is shown on the far left in a red coat.*

the times. It is entirely in keeping that Southwick Hall's one brush with history, in 1587, should have been a matter of duty quietly done.

SQUERRYES COURT

KENT

When to old England you do return,
Tell all my friends I am dead and gone,
And tell my tender old mother dear
No tears to shed,
No tears to shed,
For a hero's death awaits me here.

Thus commemorated in a contemporary ballad, General James Wolfe died in 1759 on the Heights of Abraham, at the moment of his triumph over the French. If ever sung in the hearing of the Warde family of Squerryes Court, the words recalling the great soldier must have had an extreme poignancy.

The Wolfes were neighbourhood friends of the Wardes, and James Wolfe and George Warde had been close companions from childhood. The future hero of Quebec, then aged fourteen, had even received his first commission from the hands of the Whitehall courier while standing in the Squerryes garden. And now, for all that Canada had been secured for Britain, the price exacted for the victory came to those at Squerryes as a personal blow.

To help ease their immediate grief, the Wardes set up a special 'Wolfe Cenotaph' in the garden on the very spot where the courier had once handed the fourteen-year-old his commission in the Marines. It is believed that the monument's inscription was written by George Warde himself; later, he certainly commissioned Benjamin West to paint a posthumous portrait of his friend, at the age when they were both boys together.

He also remained a friend of the 'tender old mother dear' of the song, Mrs Wolfe, helping her with her affairs and finally acting as her executor. In return, she left him the letters her son had written her, together with both his and her husband's commissions. Both are still at Squerryes, along with the sword Wolfe wore at Quebec, the first (and only) portrait ever painted of him from life, and another picture of Mrs Wolfe herself.

STANFORD HALL

LEICESTERSHIRE

As anyone who has tried it will know, running wires under floorboards is a tedious business. At Stanford, however, the problem was overcome—and overcome brilliantly—at the very dawn of the age of electricity, scarcely before the difficulty had defined itself.

The house itself was built in the 1690s for Sir Roger Cave to the designs of Francis Smith of Warwick. It is a typical William and Mary house with hipped roof and dormers over two rows of prominent windows.

In the 1890s, Adrian Verney Verney-Cave —son of Stanford's owner, Lord Braye— decided to bring his family home up to date by installing electric light. Being an amateur engineer of some distinction, he rigged up his own supply, damming a section of the nearby Avon to provide hydro-electric power. Stanford's gleaming floorboards temporarily baffled him but then, aided by memories of rabbit-catching, inspiration struck.

The engineer armed himself with a reeking bit of rabbit flesh . . . and a ferret. At each end of the room to be wired, he drilled a hole in the floor. At one, he put the rabbit. Down the other went the ferret, with one end of the electric flex tied to its collar. The ferret vanished, reappeared, devoured its reward; the flex it had trailed behind it was detached and pulled through, ready for the connection to be made. It needed two ferrets to wire Stanford Hall in its entirety. But, in the end, the job

was done and the lights switched on: a tribute to the application of both high and ultra-low technology.

Exploiting the uses of ferret power was only one aspect of Adrian's passion for solving problems of movement. By 1897, he was driving one of the first cars known in Britain, a Mercedes-Benz, and he was working on a still more challenging method of travel: flight.

His friend, ally and guide in this was Lieutenant Percy Pilcher of the Royal Navy, pioneering constructor of flying machines and one of the very first people to take—however briefly—to the air. Adrian worked as his assistant and also helped to fly the gliders his fellow-enthusiast devised.

Percy's involvement, however, came to a

STANFORD HALL Pictures hanging in the Old Dining Room include this portrait of Margaret Beaufort, mother of Henry VII.

tragically sudden end. While flying the machine called 'The Hawk' over Stanford's park in 1899, he got into difficulties and crashed, killing himself. The spot is now marked by a monument put up by the Royal Aeronautical Society of Great Britain, while Stanford's stables contain photographs of Pilcher in flight and a full-sized replica of 'The Hawk' itself.

STANSTED PARK

HAMPSHIRE

Queen Elizabeth I was not a lady famous for her jokes, which is perhaps understandable when one learns of one of her few essays at humour. It is said that when she passed through Stansted in 1591 on her way to Portsmouth she cried out 'Stand steed!'. Whether the horse obeyed her is not known, but we may be sure that her courtiers fell about at this rare example of royal wit.

STANSTED PARK A collection of mainly Dutch bird pictures, bought by the tenth Earl of Bessborough, hangs in the Stairway Hall.

Throughout 900 years of history and many changes of ownership, Stansted has maintained royal connections. It once stood on the edge of the royal hunting forest of Bere, and King John and Henry II were frequent visitors. Up to Georgian times members of the royal family were often at Stansted, one attraction perhaps being that Stansted was a convenient retreat after inspection duties at Portsmouth. Less welcome visitors were the 2,000 horse and foot of the Parliamentary Army under Sir William Waller, who was responsible for largely destroying the house in 1644.

The present house dates from the late eighteenth century, when Stansted came into the hands of Richard Barwell, a rich merchant in the East India trade. He went to the leading men of the day: James Wyatt and Joseph Bonomi for the house and Capability Brown for the park and gardens. When Barwell died in 1804 the house was sold to Lewis Way, who had a curious single-minded obsession with the conversion of the Jews. His first plan was to obtain a charter to turn Stansted into a college for this purpose, but he was unsuccessful. However, he restored the chapel, incorporating various Jewish symbols in the window above the altar to assist in the conversion of any Jewish members of the congregation. As the present owners say, 'Stansted chapel is probably the only one in England in which can be seen plaques showing the Ten Commandments written in Hebrew.' John Keats was a member of the congregation on one occasion. He attended the reconsecration in 1819 and is said to have been inspired by the experience to write the unfinished 'The Eve of St Mark'.

Disappointed in his ambitions, Lewis Way sold Stansted, which passed through various hands until it was bought in 1924 by the ninth Earl of Bessborough. Meanwhile, in 1900, a disastrous fire had destroyed Stansted's main block, which was rebuilt to plans by Arthur Conran Blomfield. The present contents are drawn from the Bessborough family's collections, including those saved when its Irish home, Bessborough House near Waterford, was burned down in 1921 during the Troubles.

STANTON HARCOURT

OXFORDSHIRE

Guests at large houses in medieval times would have been well-advised not to visit the kitchens, not that it would have occurred to them to do so. The heat, smoke and dirt produced by spit-roasting, the favoured method of cooking, were barely tolerable. Through the murk, the scullions could fitfully be seen at their labours, fearsome in appearance and dreadful in language. Conditions in the kitchen were in sharp contrast to those in the great hall, though sometimes the torments of the kitchen tended to filter through to the diners.

In an attempt to improve matters, medieval kitchens began to be built on a grander scale, with lofty ventilated roofs to take away the heat and smells. One of the few such kitchens to survive can be seen at Stanton Harcourt. Its octagonal roof is made up of banks of shutters which can be operated individually to suit the state of the wind. Below, open fires were set in bays against the wall; the soot can still be seen high above. Even in this 'improved' kitchen, the preparation of a banquet must nevertheless have made an impressive sight.

Stanton Harcourt's kitchen, Gatehouse and Tower are all that is left of the original medieval manor house; the remainder was pillaged in the eighteenth century to provide stone for nearby Nuneham Courtenay. The Harcourts were of Norman origin, and members of the family pursued distinguished military and political careers until the reign of George I, when Simon Harcourt, the first Viscount, was dismissed from office. He retired from London to entertain literary society

STANTON HARCOURT MANOR HOUSE The poet Alexander Pope described the tower as 'like Vulcan's forge', but it provided a haven where he completed the translation of Homer which made his name.

in the company of such men as Jonathan Swift and Alexander Pope, and to enjoy his new mansion at Nuneham Courtenay.

The first Viscount was particularly kind to Pope, who, at the age of twenty-five, had undertaken a translation of Homer which was to be published by subscription. Part of this work was done in what is now called Pope's Tower at Stanton Harcourt. The Tower was by then ruinous but secluded, and entirely suited to the needs of a poet. Visiting the kitchen, Pope declared that it was like Vulcan's forge and, according to villagers, witches were feasted by Satan there.

Stanton Harcourt was abandoned by the family in the eighteenth century, but came back into favour after the Second World War when the late Viscount decided not to return to Nuneham Courtenay but to settle at Stanton. The enlargements to the Gatehouse date from this period, as does an extensive programme of garden remodelling which has now reached maturity.

STANWAY HOUSE
GLOUCESTERSHIRE

In the Audit Room at Stanway House there takes place, four times a year, a ceremony which is now almost unique but which was once commonplace in every manor in England. It is the rent audit, carried out on Quarter Days—those days marked faithfully year after year in our diaries but which now have no significance for most of us. Tenants come in person to pay their dues at the eighteenth-century rent table, the rent books being kept in the drawers of the revolving top and cash placed in the well in the centre. The procedure is not merely a picturesque survival; it is a reflection of the fact that the owners of the estate have managed to keep it together. The rent audit also provides an opportunity for the voicing of any complaints by the tenants.

Stanway is an Elizabethan manor house in golden Cotswold stone, built for the Tracy family who came originally from nearby Tod-

dington. Earlier there had been a small monastery at Stanway, and the tithe barn close by dates from the fourteenth century. In 1817 the house came by marriage into the ownership of the Earls of Wemyss.

The Wemyss family divided its time between Stanway and its home in Scotland, and there is a charming vignette of early-nineteenth-century life at Stanway in the diary of the Reverend Francis Witts, a local parson. 'Nothing could be more pleasing and cheerful,' he wrote in 1826, 'than his lordship's manner among his friends and relatives at Stanway. . . . A noisy but not unskilled band of music from Broadway played most of the evening in the hall, and a promiscuous dance among the gentry and domestics was kicked up . . .' The band would have been installed in the minstrels' gallery above the screen passage; it was walled in to make an extra bedroom at some point in the mid-nineteenth century.

Another popular manor-house entertainment is recalled by the shuffleboard table along the west wall of the hall. This dates from about 1620. Shuffleboard (shovelboard) is a version of shove-ha'penny in which the ten brass counters are 'shuffled' from one end of the table to the other. The maximum score for a round is twenty points, but the owners at Stanway say that the maximum score for many years there has stood at fifteen. House guests bored with shuffleboard could divert themselves by riding the Chippendale exercising chair which stands in the hall's bay window—something like an early version of the exercise bicycle—or, if they felt less energetic, retire to the Chinese Chippendale day beds in the Drawing Room. Stanway House tells not only of its architecture and its family heirlooms, but also of the pleasant family lives passed there.

STEVENSON HOUSE
LOTHIAN

In popular imagination, large Scottish houses are either castles or mansions got up in Victorian Scots Baronial style. Stevenson is a

STANWAY HOUSE The Drawing Room or Great Parlour saw the lying-in-state of Lords of the Manor. The 'Chinese Chippendale' day-beds were made c.1760 for the Earl of Wemyss's seat at Amisfield House in East Lothian.

fine example of a Scottish house in a style which was once fairly commonplace, but which has rarely survived: the 'grange' or large farmhouse arranged round a central courtyard for the cattle.

Much of the present house, replacing an earlier one demolished by an invading English army in 1544, dates from the late sixteenth century. In 1624 it was bought by John Sinclair, a merchant and former Lord Provost of Edinburgh who was later given a knighthood, and it remained in the Sinclair family until the line died out in 1931.

Stevenson was built for entertaining, and its most epic days seem to have been in early-Victorian times when Admiral Sir John Gordon Sinclair was head of the family. It was not the only Sinclair house. There was another in Caithness where the family spent the summer, returning to the more comfortable environs of Stevenson for the winter months and providing hospitality in true Scots fashion. The Admiral had been a young officer on the *Victory* at Trafalgar, and went on to a distinguished naval career, but this did not prevent him from giving legendary dinner

parties at Stevenson. Here, the story goes, his habit was to lock the dining-room door once the ladies had withdrawn and throw the key out of the window so that drinking could continue uninterrupted. It was among the butler's duties to retrieve the key afterwards and, much later, to unlock the door and see how host and male guests had fared. Those who were not fit to mount the stairs were attended to by a boy whose job was to loosen their collars. Some guests unused to this procedure are said to have been alarmed to awake in the small hours with fingers fumbling at their throats.

Our own times are quieter ones for Stevenson. With the death of the last relict of the Sinclairs in 1931 the house was bought by William Brown Dunlop. However, he did not live there and it was not until his death in 1946 that Stevenson was again occupied as a family home. It had been virtually untouched—although it suffered from the depredations of troops billeted there during the Second World War—since 1907. Lighting was still by candles and paraffin. It was still a house designed for an army of servants, and

STONELEIGH ABBEY The banquet held in the Saloon in 1858, when Queen Victoria visited Stoneleigh. She slept in what Mrs Austen had called the 'Breakfast Room'.

wildly unsuited to more straitened times; the dining room, for example (now the main bedroom), was several minutes' walk away from the old kitchen. Conversion to suit modern conditions was begun in 1948 and completed by 1950, and since then Stevenson House has become the focal point for a group of family houses fashioned out of the laundry wing, coach house and other outbuildings.

STOCKELD PARK

NORTH YORKSHIRE

The most striking feature of Stockeld Park is the staircase leading off the white-painted Oval Hall: it is a so-called 'crinoline' staircase, and the rounded shape of the iron balusters indicates why as it bulges like the skirts of Victorian belles.

Stockeld Park was built in the mid-eighteenth century for the Middleton family, who, like so many of the Yorkshire gentry, had retained their Catholicism. The architect was the Yorkshire-born James Paine. A century later the house was bought by the Fosters, a wealthy Bradford mill-owning family, whose premises included the Black Dyke Mills of brass-band fame. Robert John Foster added another wing and a porch on the north side, and in 1895 the chapel, designed by Detmar Blow, was built on the site of the former orangery. The stables also belong to this period.

After being used as a maternity home during the Second World War Stockeld Park returned to its role as a family home, and is now lived in by the granddaughter of Robert John Foster.

STONELEIGH ABBEY

WARWICKSHIRE

Jane Austen was not the only woman in her family who could write. In 1806 her mother Cassandra wrote a letter from Stoneleigh Abbey to Jane's sister-in-law: it clearly shows from whom the great novelist derived her powers of minute observation.

'This is an odd sort of letter. I write just as things come into my head,' Mrs Austen started. Then, obviously describing the scene as it unreeled in her mind's eye, she launched into a room-by-room guide round her host's enormous home.

I will now give you some idea of the inside of this vast house, first premising that there are forty-five windows in front (which is quite straight with a flat roof), 15 in a row. You go up a considerable flight of steps (some offices are under the house) into a large Hall; on the right hand is the dining parlour, within that the Breakfast room, where we generally sit, and reason good 'tis the only room (except the Chapel) that looks towards the River.

Mrs Austen's companion in the breakfast room was Jane herself, and the pair were in fact on a family visit. Stoneleigh's owner, James Henry Leigh, was Cassandra's cousin, and the two Austens had come to help him and his family settle into the house he had just inherited. The note of slightly tense exploration is evident in Mrs Austen's next passage:

On the left hand of the hall is the best drawing room, within that a smaller; these rooms are rather gloomy Brown-wainscot and dark Crimson furniture; so we never use them but to walk thro' them to the old picture gallery. Behind the smaller drawing room is the state Bed Chamber with a high dark crimson Velvet Bed; an alarming apartment just fit for a Heroine. . . .

Like her daughter (by then the author of *Northanger Abbey*) Mrs Austen had an ironically keen appreciation of the Gothic.

The decoration scheme of the room that startled her did not, with the passage of time, become notably brighter; indeed, with the return of a missionary Leigh to England in the 1830s, it became entirely fitted out in Coromandel ebony. However, it has lost its alarming bed, for it is now a library, presided over by the portrait of Byron (for whom James Leigh's son fagged at Harrow).

The bed for which—among other things— Stoneleigh is now famous is a very different object indeed: a charming gilded fourposter,

used by Queen Victoria when she visited Stoneleigh in 1858, and covered with a bed-spread worked for her by the women of Coventry. The room in which it stands is the same as Mrs Austen's breakfast room, so Victoria—like Jane and her mother—enjoyed an early morning view of the River Avon close below her.

STONOR PARK

OXFORDSHIRE

When, in the 1530s, the traveller John Leland visited Stonor Park, he found a medieval flint-and-chalk building which, thanks to the efforts of the owner Sir Walter Stonor, proudly wore an up-to-date dress of Tudor red brick. The general effect was comfortable, prosperous, full of assurance. 'Ther is,' Leland wrote, 'a fayre parke, and a waren of connes [rabbits], and fayre woods . . . the mansion place standithe clyminge on a hill and hathe two courtes buyldyd withe tymber, brike and flynte.' Like many other homes of comparable size, it also had dovecotes, deer in the park and—typically, but in this case very significantly—a chapel.

Without knowing it, the traveller was seeing Stonor during its very last years in the sun. Starting shortly after Sir Walter's time and lasting right up to the nineteenth century, the house and the family that had built it went under the blackest of clouds. The key to this eclipse lay in the modest consecrated building at Stonor's eastern end.

When Henry VIII broke with Rome and established himself as head of the Anglican church the Stonors refused to accept the new order. They became recusants, keeping faith with the old religion and paying the price: huge fines, sequestration of lands, loss of civil status and—frequently—loss of liberty as well. As evidenced by Stonor's Georgian front and Georgian Gothic interiors (its first altera-tions since Tudor times), the family's difficul-ties lessened in the eighteenth century. But it was not able to take a full part in public life again

STONOR PARK Redecorated in fashionable Gothic-revival style in 1757, Stonor's Great Hall dates from the time of its owners' growing prosperity in the Middle Ages.

until the Catholic Emancipation Act of 1829.

The blackest year—though also the most gloriously defiant one—came in 1581, by which time the Stonors were paying annual recusancy fines equivalent to £50,000 in modern terms. Led by the phenomenal Dame Cecily Stonor, the family was totally unyielding in its refusal to accept the monarch as head of the English church. Meanwhile, Cecily's son John was an assistant to the English-born Jesuit, Father Edmund Campion, on his mission to the country of his birth.

Stonor was, naturally, one of the Catholic houses where Campion and his fellow missionaries could feel safe, and it was in the attic room high over Stonor's front door that they set up their secret printing press. Here they printed their book *Decem Rationes*, or *The Ten Reasons for Being a Catholic*; in the late June of 1581 400 copies were distributed at the University of Oxford.

The resulting furore quickened the hunt for the 'seditious Jesuits' and, within a few weeks, they were run to earth. The press at Stonor was discovered and seized, Dame Cecily and her son arrested. Campion himself was taken while preaching in Berkshire. Imprisoned in the Tower of London, he was personally examined by Queen Elizabeth, tortured three times, produced at four public hearings, and finally found guilty of treason, with its dreadful penalty. He was martyred on 1 December.

On learning his fate, the future saint declared: 'If our religion do make traitors we are worthy to be condemned; but otherwise are and have been true subjects as ever the queen had.' This summed up the recusants' standpoint and, in spite of persecution, the family at Stonor Park succeeded in living by it.

The fines and imprisonments went on (Dame Cecily, though she survived the involvement with Campion, was particularly stubborn in her recusancy), and all the Stonors' considerable possessions vanished except for Stonor Park itself. Not surprisingly, the physical fabric of the house had to be left unattended but Stonor did become one of England's leading centres of Catholic thought.

In the eighteenth century the tide at last started to turn and, following the Act of 1829, Thomas—or 'Old Tom'—Stonor made history by becoming the Member of Parliament for Oxford. Within the first year of Victoria's reign, he was also granted the barony of Camoys. It is the seventh Lord Camoys who lives at Stonor today: the latest of a line of resident Stonors that stretches back over at least 800 years. The chapel attached to their home is one of the tiny handful in England where Mass has been celebrated without a break since the Middle Ages.

STOWE

BUCKINGHAMSHIRE

It was the sale of the century. The Rothschilds were there. So were the Duke and Duchess of Bedford. So was a vast assortment of mid-nineteenth-century society, from the cream of London's nobility to parties of the vulgar who arrived, as the *Morning Post* snobbishly noted, in such conveyances as butchers' carts. The second Duke of Buckingham and Chandos was bankrupt to the tune of £1½ million, and the contents of Stowe were up for sale. It was a case of (almost) 'everything must go'. The year was 1848.

The Temple family, which had achieved dukedom only twenty-six years previously, was an example of the adage 'the higher they climb, the harder they fall'. Its advancement, originally based on sheep-farming, had been pursued single-mindedly by way of judicious marriages and political jobbery. When Richard Temple Nugent Brydges Chandos Grenville was created first Duke of Buckingham and Chandos in 1822, even the 'Chandos' part of his title was (as were most of his forenames) the fruit of marriage. Few people can have been so successful at disposing of a fortune in the shortest possible time, though his father had set him a good example.

The story of Stowe begins with Sir Richard Temple. One of Marlborough's generals, he married a rich heiress in 1715, was created

Viscount Cobham in 1718, and devoted the remainder of his life to the improvement of the estate he had inherited from his father. Stowe was already a handsome enough house, built only about fifty years earlier; but the Temples seem to have had a demonic, and ultimately ruinous, drive to get rid of money. Vanbrugh was engaged to remodel Stowe. When he died, he was succeeded in turn by James Gibbs, Giacomo Leoni and William Kent; and it was in Stowe's gardens that Capability Brown established his reputation. When Viscount Cobham died, Stowe passed to his nephew Richard Grenville, Earl Temple, who continued with the work, engaging Robert Adam to design the South Front. By 1790 the new Stowe was complete, and ready to fulfil its destined role as a centre of Whig politics and of social life.

Extravagance was a hereditary weakness, and by 1827 the first Duke of Buckingham and Chandos was beginning to feel the hot breath of his creditors. He had been too generous as a patron of the arts and literature, and too hospitable to the exiled French court. For an aristocrat of the Duke's stamp, there was only one answer to financial embarrassment—to walk, or in his case sail, away from it. He bought a luxury yacht, named it *Anna Eliza* after his wife, equipped it lavishly, and set out with a domestic staff of about a dozen, including a chaplain and a surgeon, for a two-year cruise in the Mediterranean. When he returned, the estate was still heavily in debt but the immediate crisis had passed.

The second Duke inherited in 1839 and was no better at managing money. Broke though he was, he had Stowe equipped with the latest in plumbing—water closets, showers and bathrooms—which most owners of country houses were to regard as unattainable luxuries for another fifty years. His personal water closet was neatly hidden away in a cupboard which displayed a ducal coronet over the door. When Queen Victoria visited in 1845 triumphal arches were built for the occasion, bands were hired, flags were waved by 500 labourers in smocks, and hospitality was provided of the most sumptuous and competitive kind. But by

STOWE *The North Hall, decorated by William Kent, one of the succession of 'improvers' engaged to keep Stowe in fashion.*

this time the bailiffs were beginning to close in, and indeed it was said that some of them were present on the occasion of the Queen's visit, disguised in livery. At any rate, two years later the blow fell, and Christie's was engaged to conduct the auction of contents that took place in August 1848. The auctioneers were there for forty days. At the end of it all, the Duke followed his father's example and went abroad. He died in 1861, leaving behind a will worth £200.

The third Duke could not have been more different in character from his father and grandfather. He was a typical hard-working Victorian who devoted his life to pubic service

men's ball. At Stowe, the contents were dispersed in another great auction, but the house was saved by the intervention of a benefactor who presented the estate to the trustees of a new public school. Two years later, Stowe School opened. Few houses in this book can have had a closer brush with destruction.

STRATFIELD SAYE HOUSE

BERKSHIRE

In a paddock at Stratfield Saye House stands a shrine within a shrine. Shaded by a large turkey oak, it is the grave of a horse. 'Here,' reads the gravestone, 'lies Copenhagen, the charger ridden by the Duke of Wellington the entire day, at the Battle of Waterloo.' A chestnut stallion with a tendency to kick, he was named after the Battle of Copenhagen, in which Wellington took part. After Waterloo, he spent a long and domestic retirement at Stratfield Saye, being ridden by the great Duke and his children. When he died in 1836, he was buried with military honours. The turkey oak is an additional memorial, not from the Duke but from his housekeeper, Mrs Apostles; it grew from an acorn she planted on the grave.

Copenhagen's burial place in the Ice House Paddock in many ways sums up the essence of Stratfield Saye. It is both intimate and public, touching and—in its associations—fabulously august. The house is both grand and cosy in just the same way. Quite literally so: filled with the possessions of the great, including two radiators installed by the man on whom the gifts were showered.

The radiators still work—a fact that would have pleased the practical old statesman who, when Queen Victoria complained about birds in the Crystal Palace, uttered the immortal advice, 'Try sparrowhawks, Ma'am'.

Stratfield Saye was itself one of the gifts that a hugely grateful nation bestowed on Arthur Wellesley, conqueror of Napoleon and hero of Waterloo. A large sum of public money was voted to him to finance the purchase of a home

and to paying off the family debts. In five years spent as Governor of Madras he brought about considerable achievements in famine relief. He chaired innumerable House of Lords committees on matters of public concern. He also became chairman of the London & North Western Railway, a duty which he took seriously enough to monitor locomotive and driver performance by frequent trips on the footplate. But when he died in 1889 he left no male heir, and the end of Stowe as a private palace was already in sight. Eventually his daughter, Baroness Kinloss, put the estate, house and contents on the market in 1921. It was a hazardous time for country houses, especially for those as grand as Stowe. Death duties, the loss of heirs in the First World War, and the general shock to the old order were putting many of them to the demolition-

STRATFIELD SAYE HOUSE The Great Duke liked the closely packed effect of his Print Room, which celebrated his victorious career.

that was in keeping with his national status. He was, in effect, being invited to 'do a Blenheim'. Perhaps luckily (certainly where his peace of mind was concerned) the Duke declined to follow in Marlborough's footsteps by creating a palace that, once his country's gift was exhausted, he might have had to complete out of his own pocket.

When he finally decided to buy Stratfield Saye, he in fact did so with the full intention of building himself a very much bigger house in its park. A collection of architectural designs at Stratfield Saye shows the scale of grandeur he had in mind. Pillars were an important feature in his schemes and, when in Italy in 1821, he even bought some marble monsters to incorporate in his new home. By the time he had got them back, however, he had realized that—in spite of the nation's generosity—he did not have enough money to build the palace he had projected. The pillars stayed in their packing for well over a hundred years until, in 1947, they were put up in the house's conservatory.

So the Duke finally found himself with a home that was not quite what he'd wished for. He made the best of it, addressing himself to the problem with goodwill and good sense. The present Duke of Wellington takes up the tale: 'He therefore set about making his modest house convenient and comfortable, and being a practical man he was well satisfied with the results. His friends were less so and considered that Stratfield Saye was small, pokey and unworthy of so great a figure. Sir Robert Peel was positively scathing: Queen Victoria was not enthusiastic but found the house convenient, if rather hot.' (To the end of her life, Victoria preferred low temperatures; the Duke's central heating was obviously effective.)

Wellington himself, however, did not worry about what his friends said. With its characteristic mixture of the serviceable and the magnificent, Stratfield Saye speaks volumes about the extraordinary man who made it: the brilliant soldier, the friend of monarchs, and the country-house owner with his favourite horse and his modern gadgets.

Central heating was not Wellington's only venture into the latest domestic technology. He also had china water closets, elegantly patterned in blue, installed in many rooms. Guests at Stratfield Saye, used as they were to freezing cold mansions and the night-time reign of the chamber pot, could count themselves lucky on two scores.

The walls of the print-room—a modish decorative scheme—recall the struggle against Napoleon and, naturally, this theme appears again and again throughout the house. Many of the books in the Duke's Library—one of his favourite rooms—were once in the possession of his arch-enemy. So were the tricolour flags embroidered with silver that hang in the Hall.

The steps leading in the direction of the billiard room, with the first Duke's table, are decorated with the busts of Marshal Blücher, King Frederick William III of Prussia, and Tsar Alexander I of Russia. A cabinet displays some of the great Prussian china service that Frederick William gave Wellington, along with pieces from a similar present from Emperor Francis I of Austria. The Tsar's gift is in the Hall, further on: a wide, shallow urn or tazza, in bright-green malachite.

It is the Drawing Room, however, that houses what is probably the grandest present of all. At the Battle of Vitoria during the Peninsular War, Wellington defeated Napoleon's brother, the puppet king of Spain. Joseph Bonaparte managed to escape, but Wellington's forces captured his baggage train and found in it quantities of pictures from the pre-Napoleonic Spanish Royal Collection. After some fairly rough handling in the field (soldiers used some of them as shelters for their mules), they were sent back to England.

When Ferdinand VII was restored to the Spanish throne, Wellington made arrangements for the picture collection to be returned to him. However, Ferdinand declined, explaining: 'His Majesty, touched by your delicacy, does not wish to deprive you of that which has come into your possession by means as just as they are honourable.'

Part of the King of Spain's collection was hung in Apsley House in London, which the father of the present Duke of Wellington presented to the nation just after the Second World War. The rest is in Stratfield Saye's Drawing Room, along with furnishings and wallpaper chosen by the first Duke. He bought the paper and furniture himself—and, ironically, both were French.

SUDELEY CASTLE

GLOUCESTERSHIRE

Massive, sprawling, ruined at one end, Sudeley is a phoenix among castles. More than almost any of its fellows, its history has been crowded with dramatic swoops and dips of fortune. It has survived them all.

Rich with the spoils of war, the builder of Sudeley Castle was one Ralph Botelar, Admiral

SUDELEY CASTLE Katherine Parr, sixth wife of King Henry VIII, who survived him to marry Thomas Seymour, Baron of Sudeley.

of the Fleet under Henry V. He made no secret as to the source of his financial success, since one of Sudeley's towers carried the name of a French admiral who was held to ransom there. Finally, however, Botelar was driven out of his grand new home by his royal master, and he was lucky to escape imprisonment himself.

Sudeley was visited by at least six kings and queens of England, but the dramatic climax to its reign of brilliance under the Tudors and early Stuarts was its occupation by Prince Rupert of the Rhine and its siege and near-demolition by Cromwell's troops.

A ruined hulk, after nearly 200 years of use by farmers, Sudeley was rescued and restored by a family of Worcester glovemakers, the Dents. Its still ruined portions—now carefully strengthened—show just how far it had gone before the Dents helped it rise again from the wreckage.

Among the occupants whose lives also shared Sudeley's switchback quality, the figure of Katherine Parr reigns supreme. Famous as the only one of Henry VIII's wives to survive him, she tends to be remembered as a sensible, managing creature who mothered Henry's children—distinctly middle-aged, and rather dull. In fact, her life was full of emotional aspirations: deferred, then granted, then cruelly disappointed.

When she married the King, she was a well-educated Protestant widow (twice over) of thirty-one. Her third husband was to have been Sir Thomas Seymour, brother of the late Queen Jane and uncle of the King's only son. However, Henry himself proposed marriage, and the wishes of Katherine and Thomas had to be set aside.

SUFTON COURT A watercolour of the house in 1795, from Humphrey Repton's 'Red Book'. Repton visited Sufton Court that year to landscape the park. The 'Red Book' remains in the house.

Not without difficulty, Katherine survived her years as Queen. Then, widowed again and free at last to exercise her own choice, she chose Tom Seymour. By now Lord High Admiral of England and Baron of Sudeley, he was, alas, not worthy of her. Initially they lived in London, at Chelsea Place. But, after her roving husband made a pass at the young Princess Elizabeth, Katherine moved away to Thomas's now magnificent home in Gloucestershire.

By this time, she was pregnant. At Sudeley, she spent the remainder of her pregnancy in great comfort and some state, waited on by a huge household of chaplains, chamberlains, doctors, ladies-in-waiting and servants. She and her husband were hoping for a son but, on 30 August 1548, their hopes were dashed: it was a girl.

In spite of all the care lavished on her, poor Katherine fell instantly a victim to puerperal fever. Five days after the birth, the thirty-six-year-old mother died in the Castle she had made her home. She was buried in the Castle church of St Mary's, where she still lies. Her husband—soon to end his own career on the scaffold for treason—did not bother to be present at the death-bed.

SUFTON COURT

HEREFORD & WORCESTER

In some country houses in the nineteenth century it was customary for servants to be required to turn their faces to the wall if they encountered the master or mistress. When James Wyatt designed Sufton Court, he went one better in his efforts to make the servants invisible: their quarters in the attic are so arranged that they cannot see or be seen from below. This can have added little joy to whatever scant leisure time the servants had.

Sufton Court is unusual in another respect. Most rebuilt houses went up on the sites of their predecessors, and frequently the old stone was used again. When Wyatt built Sufton Court round about 1790 the older house—now called Old Sufton—was left *in*

situ, and remains today. Old Sufton, though much altered and twice damaged by fire, retains some of its original thirteenth-century features.

The Hereford family has owned the Sufton Estate since the twelfth century, so the two houses taken together present a complete record of one family's life over 700 years. There was evidently a burst of prosperity late in the eighteenth century, for the then owner could afford not only to build himself a new house but also to call in Humphrey Repton to landscape the park. The 'Red Book' in which he illustrated his proposals is still in the house.

The most famous Hereford was Nicholas de Hereford, born in 1330. He was one of John Wycliffe's collaborators on the so-called 'Early Version' of the English translation of the Old Testament, made in about 1382. One of Nicholas's manuscript translations is held in Hereford Cathedral, and is known as the 'Cider Bible' because of its reference (appropriately enough for Herefordshire) to 'no strong drink or cider'. Wycliffe's followers, the Lollards, were constantly in danger of arrest and of being burned at the stake. Nicholas de Hereford was given special protection by Richard II for his support against Parliamentary opposition in 1397, which entitled him, his family, servants and property to the King's special care. It also gave him an annual load of timber (from wrecked pirate ships collected at Gloucester) and a volume of royal wines from Bristol. Thus armed, he was able to avoid the persecution which was the lot of so many Lollards.

SUTTON PARK

NORTH YORKSHIRE

Sutton Park stands, prim and correct, in the centre of the village of Sutton-on-the-Forest, an early-Georgian house built of local brick. It is a pleasant and welcoming house, but there is nothing on the outside to suggest the riches within. For the contents of Sutton Park are a kind of distillation of the possessions of many generations of the Sheffield family.

The Sheffields were courtiers, and one of them, John, was made Duke of Buckingham in 1703 (by an earlier creation than that of the Temple family of Stowe). His only son by marriage died at nineteen and his estates in north Lincolnshire and Yorkshire passed to an illegitimate son, Charles. This led to a family dispute which resulted in a split of the Yorkshire and Lincolnshire estates. Charles received the Lincolnshire land and the Buckinghams' home in London, known then as Buckingham House and now as Buckingham Palace. His descendants later built a family seat at Normanby Park to the south of the Humber.

Meanwhile, at Sutton Park, the present house was built *c.*1740 to replace an Elizabethan predecessor. Much care was taken with the interiors: the plasterwork is by Cortese and the Chinese wallpaper in the Chinese room is original, dating from about 1750. The brilliant effects achieved by the architect—believed to have been Thomas Atkinson of York—have been recently enhanced by the addition of chimneypieces by

Adam and Pietro Bosse from Normanby Park and, in the Morning Room, pine panelling from the now demolished Potternewton Hall, near Leeds. The contents of Sutton Park include many items from Normanby and some from Buckingham House, removed when this was sold to the Crown in 1762.

Sutton Park's new lease of life dates from 1963, when Major Reginald Sheffield and his wife Nancie decided to buy the house and leave Normanby Park, which was impracticably large and threatened by opencast mining. The only significant addition since then has been the Dining Room, which blends sensitively into its eighteenth-century surroundings.

SYON HOUSE

MIDDLESEX

Refuge for Charles I's children during one of London's plagues; the house from which Lady Jane Grey set out by river for her nine days' reign as Queen of England; the

SUTTON PARK Decoration representing tortoiseshell and ivory distinguishes the Tea Room. The plates on the walls are eighteenth-century Imari porcelain, contemporary with the house.

SYON HOUSE Jan Griffier's painting of the house and surroundings captures the massiveness of the sixteenth-century exterior and the busy life of the river which linked it with the other great riverside palaces.

starting point for a dramatic ride to London on the night before Guy Fawkes's Gunpowder Plot was revealed; the setting for an historic meeting with Cromwell on the eve of the Civil War: if any great house can claim to be 'steeped in history', Syon surely can.

Syon is unusual in being made up of a virtually unaltered sixteenth-century exterior clothing equally original eighteenth-century State Rooms. Taking its name from the biblical Mount Zion, Syon was founded as a monastery in the fifteenth century, with its house at Twickenham. At the Dissolution, it passed into the hands of the Duke of Somerset, Protector of the Realm during the first years of the boy King Edward VI's reign. In 1547

Somerset began to build the house which forms the present exterior. But these were hazardous times, especially for someone like Somerset, exposed at court to intense rivalries and jealousies. His particular rival was John Dudley, Earl of Warwick, to whom he was related by the marriage of their children. In 1551 the Earl, who had been created Duke of Northumberland, had Somerset indicted on a series of charges of plotting against the Crown, one of which alleged that a terrace he had built at Syon amounted to fortification. The main charge broke down at the trial, but a lesser one was substituted and Somerset was executed in January 1552. The following year Syon was granted to the Duke, but it was not his for long. He too went to the scaffold eighteen months later for his sponsorship of Lady Jane Grey, his daughter-in-law.

Poor Lady Jane was only sixteen when, sick and locked into a marriage she did not want, she was taken to live with the Duke of Northumberland. Her life, which now had only a few more months to run, had not been a happy one. The great-niece of Henry VIII, she had sought refuge from unsympathetic parents in learning, mastering five languages—a prodigious achievement for any child at that time and unheard-of in a girl. Her studies apart, she had little life of her own, for she was made the shuttlecock in a political game played by those around her. On 6 July 1553 Edward VI died, and the Duke of Northumberland announced to Lady Jane at Syon House that she was now Queen. She fainted at the news, and refused to hear any more of it; but the machinations of her father-in-law were not to be disturbed by the mere slip of a girl, and she was persuaded to accept the proclamation. A day or two later she was taken by barge from Syon House downriver to the Tower, where the proclamation was made. It was a one-way journey, and in February the following year she was at the Tower again, this time with her head on the execution block.

Syon came into the hands of the Percy family in Queen Elizabeth's reign. Henry Percy, the ninth Earl of Northumberland, was granted a lease of the estate in 1594 and this was converted to possession by James I. But it almost slipped out of his grasp when he was imprisoned for suspected complicity in the Gunpowder Plot. It was a distant cousin of his, Thomas Percy, who had taken part in the dramatic ride to London on the eve of the Plot's discovery. When he was dining at Syon, a horseman called for him, and they rode off together. Percy's companion was Guy Fawkes himself, and Percy paid with his life for his involvement. The ninth Earl endured fifteen years' confinement in the Tower of London before he bought his release.

Syon House was again at the centre of the national stage during the Civil War, in which the tenth Earl played a prominent political part. His was a voice for moderation. In 1646 Parliament approved of the evacuation of Charles I's children to Syon because of an outbreak of plague, and Charles—who was then being held at Hampton Court—was allowed to visit them there. It was the support given to Cromwell by a Council hosted by the Earl at Syon that led to Cromwell's march on London in 1647. But the Earl had no stomach for the harsher aspects of the Civil War, and he led the Lords' opposition to the trial of King Charles. (After the Restoration, he was equally critical of the harsh treatment of those who had been responsible for Charles's death.) He spent his last few years at Syon, away from court affairs of which he had become weary, taking a keen interest in his gardens and fruit trees. It is tempting to think that the tenth Earl was at heart more attuned to this activity than to the rough and tumble—and danger—of seventeenth-century politics.

The second significant stage in the building of the present Syon House came in 1748. The estate passed by marriage to Sir Hugh and Lady Elizabeth Smithson, for whom the extinct Earldom of Northumberland was recreated and who took the name of Percy on succeeding to the title. The vast estates that this couple inherited included Syon, which the Earl considered 'ruinous and inconvenient'. His solution was to commission Robert Adam, who was also working on the northern Percy stronghold at Alnwick Castle, to design and furnish the set of State Rooms at Syon which can still be seen today. The north range, which includes the Oak Gallery and the Print Room, remained unfinished to Adam's design and was completed in the nineteenth century.

Unlike Alnwick Castle, where much of Adam's work was obliterated by Victorian alterations, Syon still stands as a monument to the purity of Adam's taste and the consistency of his ideas. He understood well that although the suites of rooms he designed were for ceremonial use they also had to work in practical terms, and they had to give pleasure. The reason why the owners of Adam houses have found it easy to arrange tours of the rooms for their modern visitors is that Adam's designs were for a social system in which large numbers of guests progressed from room to room in the course of an evening's hospitality. They did not, in the modern fashion, stay put. Adam's purpose was therefore to provide them with, in his own words, 'variety and amusement' wherever they found themselves. So, at Syon, the ladies could admire his Long Gallery —with its ingenious ceiling design diverting the eye from the narrow width—which he had intended as their 'withdrawing room' away from the rough jokes, laughter and politics of their menfolk. The Gallery's strongly geometrical designs are in sharp contrast to those of the Red Drawing Room, which Adam designed as a ladies' anteroom, and to the gold-and-white splendour of the Dining Room. Adam's plans allowed for a greater or smaller number of rooms to be used according to the size of the gathering and the importance of the occasion, without breaking the 'circuit'.

Syon escaped Victorian remodelling, but one event in late Victorian times did have an effect: the demolition of Northumberland House, the Percys' town house off the Strand, to make way for what is now Northumberland Avenue. Some of the contents of this house, including later Adam pieces, are now at Syon, but Northumberland House's most important and obvious legacy to Syon is the famous lion that stands atop the east front. This had originally been erected at Northumberland House in 1749 to mark the then prestigious building with the sign of the family beast. By 1874, when Northumberland House was sold, its environs were no longer fashionable—but the lion was saved and re-mounted at Syon.

TATTON PARK

CHESHIRE

We live in an age when perspectives are foreshortened. Someone who plants a single tree, leave alone a tract of woodland, knowing that he will not live to see it to maturity, is regarded as eccentric. We have (perhaps with reason, given two world wars and the consequent social upheavals) lost faith in the future.

It was not always so. In the more leisurely past, the building of a country house could take generations. Plans might be made by one generation, altered by the next, and finally brought to fruition by a third. The early death of an heir—common enough in times when the average expectation of life was less than forty—might postpone, or even cancel, the completion of a house.

Tatton Park is a case in point. The Egerton family acquired the estate round about 1600. It was a junior branch of the family that produced the coal-owning, canal-building and immensely rich third Duke of Bridgewater, but its own money came from inheritance by marriage. In 1758 Samuel Egerton, who had been squire of Tatton for twenty years, acquired a large fortune from his mother's family. Shortly afterwards he had plans drawn up for the addition of wings to each side of the modest house that had been built for his grandfather some fifty years before. Only one of these wings was built by the time Samuel died, and the sole surviving part of it is the rococo dining room which was incorporated into the next stage of development.

In 1780 the estate passed to Samuel's nephew, William Tatton Egerton. He commissioned plans from Samuel Wyatt for a neo-Classical house, at the same time engaging the landscape gardener Humphrey Repton to lay out the park. By 1791 work on the new house was half-finished, but for some reason it was stopped and no more was done in the lifetime of either William Egerton or Samuel Wyatt. When building resumed in 1808 William's son Wilbraham had succeeded to the estate and Wyatt's nephews Jeffry and Lewis had taken over their uncle's architectural practice. It was the partnership of Wilbraham as patron and Lewis Wyatt as architect that saw through the completion of the house and the addition of such embellishments to the estate as the Triumphal Arch and the Orangery. If there

TATTON PARK Lewis Wyatt's opulent 1810 Drawing Room, with rococo sofas and chairs by Gillow. Wyatt worked on Tatton Park for over 17 years, realizing and embellishing the plans of his uncle Samuel.

had been financial constraints back in 1791, there were evidently none now; no expense was spared in furnishing the house, no less than 200 pieces being commissioned from Gillows of Lancaster alone. And so, some sixty years and three generations after Samuel Egerton first thought of improvements at Tatton, they were completed. However, two more generations were to pass before Tatton achieved the social distinction for which it had been designed.

In 1883 another Wilbraham, soon to be created the first (and only) Earl Egerton of Tatton, succeeded to the estate. Appropriately enough, in view of the traditional Egerton interest in inland navigation, he was one of the founders of the Manchester Ship Canal Company and indeed cut the first sod at Eastham in 1887. An enthusiastic traveller and collector, he was an authority on arms and armour and a lavish host. In 1887, the year of Victoria's Golden Jubilee, the social seal of approval was placed on Tatton when the Prince and Princess of Wales (later King Edward VII and Queen Alexandra) stayed there. (The Prince planted a tree on that occasion near the Orangery.) For the remainder of the Earl's life—he died in 1909—Tatton Park was a centre of social and cultural activities in the north-west of England, ranging from the holding of balls and garden parties to musical evenings and 'theatricals'. The enormous staff needed to keep the place going included a corps of twenty-four gardeners and over 100 estate workers.

The last days of Tatton as a privately owned house, under the ownership of Maurice, third Baron Egerton, could not have been in sharper contrast to those of his uncle Wilbraham. Maurice inherited the house in 1920 and continued to live in it until his death in 1958. 'I am exceptionally unsociable,' he once said. 'I never go anywhere or see anybody.' This was not exactly true, for he was a keen early motorist, aviator and traveller, but it must be admitted that his idea of a social gathering was tea with local cronies in the Saloon at Tatton or a picnic on the lawns for schoolchildren from Manchester.

THIRLESTANE CASTLE
BORDERS

The uncrowned King of Scotland, they called him. They called the first and only Duke of Lauderdale many other things as well, for even by the standards of the Restoration Court he was fairly remarkable: coarse in appearance and manner; a champion among debauchees; and, moreover, a schemer of the utmost ruthlessness.

The portrait of John Maitland in the Duke's Room at Thirlestane shows a thick-set figure, heavy-jowled, heavy-lidded, red-haired. His uncouthness was a legend. 'His tongue,' a contemporary wrote, 'was too big for his mouth, which made him bedew all that he talked to; his whole manner was boisterous and very unfit for a Court.' But at court he was, as Charles II's Secretary of State for Scotland, picking his nose and cleaning his ears in public, 'uttering bold jests for wit and repeating good ones of others and ever spoiled them in relating them', dipping his fingers in the King's snuffbox, and inviting himself to the King's private suppers.

To deter him from this last habit, the King devised a remedy every bit as coarse as its recipient. He had two syllabubs prepared, one with good wine for himself and the other made with horse urine, for the Duke. The two raised their glasses and drank; the King declared his syllabub to be excellent, leaving the Duke with no alternative but to agree. The Duke had to be carried out. After that, the King enjoyed

THIRLESTANE CASTLE Fit for a queen—and it was as Queen of Scotland that the Countess of Dysart, for whom Thirlestane was created, is reported to have behaved when she was in residence.

his private suppers in peace.

This monstrous creature carried out his duties in Scotland with a mixture of guile, deceit and, in the end, treachery. Having been a champion of Presbyterianism, he was regarded with hope by the Scots, despite his unprepossessing appearance. But the expectations of Scotland were bound to conflict with his devotion to the King, and in the end he abandoned his Presbyterian friends; his reward was his Dukedom and the Garter.

In the same year, 1672, that he received these honours he married as his second wife the formidable Countess of Dysart. A rich widow of forty-five who had had eleven children and countless lovers, she brought the Duke Ham House at Richmond and a fortune. Part of this was used to extend both Thirlestane, which the Duke's grandfather had built almost a century before, and the Maitland family's older home at Lethington (later renamed Lennoxlove). At Thirlestane the result was no less than the transformation of the house from a fairly primitive Scottish fort to a mansion fit for a queen. Instead, it was as Queen of Scotland, according to contemporary reports, that the Countess of Dysart behaved when she was in residence. The idea seems to have been to make a clean sweep of the old order at Thirlestane, for no less than thirteen wagonloads of furniture were taken from there to Ham House. It would have been fourteen had not the local people prevented the last from leaving. This denuding of Thirlestane may have accounted for a later embarrassment suffered by the Duke. It was discovered, just as a large party of guests was awaited for dinner, that there was not enough plate to go round. A man had to be sent hotfoot fifteen miles to Lethington to bring back extra.

The Duke engaged an English plasterer, George Dunsterfield, for the ceilings of the State Rooms and specified 'as fine work as is possible'. He certainly got it, and Dunsterfield's work is at its peak in the ceiling of the former State Bedroom, now the Red Drawing Room. From these palatial surroundings the Duke, when he was not at court, continued to rule Scotland for a further six years, despite all the Scottish nobles' efforts to dislodge him. At last they were successful, and he fell from the King's favour in 1678.

The last months of his life were pathetic. Suffering from paralysis, he retired to Tunbridge Wells to take the waters there. His pension was stopped, and he was forced to write to the King begging not to be allowed to die in poverty. There was no response, and the Duke died in August 1682, an embittered man. But there were not many to mourn, and no one to succeed him. With the death of the first Duke of Lauderdale, Marquis of March, Earl of Guildford, Viscount Petersham, all the honours he had amassed died with him. The State Rooms at Thirlestane are the memorial to a man who found it easier to make enemies than friends.

TIVERTON CASTLE

DEVON

For a small castle—as it undoubtedly is, its central courtyard never having been more than an acre in area—Tiverton has seen plenty of history. One of the keys is its position, dominating the river crossing of the Exe. The price paid by Richard de Redvers for being created Earl of Devon was that his benefactor, Henry I, commanded him to build Tiverton Castle and provide a force to defend it. As it turned out, its defensive role was not to be tested for over 500 years, but meanwhile it was, in 1495, to become the home of a princess. In that year William Courtenay, owner of Tiverton, married Edward IV's daughter, Catherine Plantagenet, and she settled at the Castle for thirty-two years of living in great style. Princess Catherine was, as she rightly claimed, 'aunt, sister and daughter of kings', but her marriage into the Courtenay family brought them little but pain. Her son Henry was beheaded by Henry VIII, and Henry's son Edward narrowly escaped the same fate, being sent into exile instead to Padua, where he died allegedly of poisoning. The attack. The first siege was successfully resisted, but when the Roundheads returned in the autumn of 1645 they penetrated the defences and wrecked part of the fortifications. There is an interesting gloss on this event in a showcase near the window of the Captain of the Guard's Room at Tiverton: a broadsheet entitled *The Taking of Tiverton Castle*. We tend to think of news in those days as taking weeks to travel from one part of the country to another; it's therefore something of a surprise to learn that this broadsheet was on sale in London only four days after the event over 160 miles away.

TOROSAY CASTLE

STRATHCLYDE

Torosay Castle on the Isle of Mull is a memorial to two very different men. One designed it; the other briefly did his best to get rid of it, then became its devoted servant.

Until the 1850s, the Campbells who lived there occupied a relatively modest Georgian building. By the mid-nineteenth century, however, the architecture of Scotland's remoter past had become widely fashionable. David Bryce, leading exponent of the Scottish Baronial style, was called in to remodel the Campbells' home from scratch. The result, initially called Duart House, is one of Bryce's most important works.

With its multitude of gables and towers, it is also extremely imposing, and when—several changes of owner later—the young Walter Murray Guthrie inherited it from an uncle, he can be forgiven for his immediate reaction. Sight unseen, he decided to sell it and offers were immediately invited for this 'substantial and commodious mansion adapted for a family of rank'.

Sporting facilities, the Victorian sales pitch went on, were:

> varied and unique and present a combination of attractions seldom united to such an extent in any single property, offering to the capitalist and lover of sport, an almost unparalleled opportunity of indulging his energetic proclivities.

TIVERTON CASTLE A three-quarter suit of armour from the English Civil War period, when Tiverton fell to the Roundheads.

Tudor court was hardly a safe place for anyone, but it was most dangerous of all for people like the Courtenay family, with their fickle and indecisive ways.

The Civil War found Tiverton Castle defending the Royalist cause, and twice under

TOROSAY CASTLE Murray Guthrie, sketched when he was dying of diabetes in 1909 by John Singer Sargent.

By the happiest of chances, however, Guthrie happened to visit his unwanted inheritance before it was sold and, on seeing it, changed his mind completely. He cancelled the sale, had the grounds laid out by the leading Scottish architect, Lorimer, and moved in with his wife Olive.

He also installed what is now acknowledged as the leading collection of eighteenth-century Italian statuary outside Italy. Nineteen pieces by the sculptor Antonio Bonazza, they were discovered in an overgrown villa garden near Milan; it cost Walter Murray Guthrie more to get them from Glasgow to Torosay than it had to buy them and ship them in ballast from Genoa to Glasgow.

Guthrie's wife, Olive, also had strong connections with the world of the arts (her father was the painter and horseman Sir John Leslie), and it was Olive who brought Torosay what is probably its most important picture: a drawing by John Singer Sargent of her husband, who was then terminally ill with diabetes. The disease was at that date incurable and—what was surely worse for someone like Guthrie—led to blindness before it led to death. When, in 1909, Olive Guthrie found herself sitting next to Sargent at a dinner party, she was understandably lacking in conversation. Sargent, no great talker himself, noticed her depression and asked what was the matter.

Through the rest of the dinner, he reflected on what he'd been told; then, just as he was leaving, he asked Olive if a picture would help. Delighted but dismayed by the offer, she pointed out that she couldn't afford his fees. Gruffly, the artist said there wouldn't be any; how long could the invalid sit for? Twenty minutes was about the limit so, the following day, Sargent visited the dying Guthrie and, working at high speed, sketched him in charcoal. The sketch, itself a memorial to a generous gesture, now hangs in the Library of the Castle that its subject once nearly sold.

TRAQUAIR HOUSE
BORDERS

The prince rode out one morning in the late autumn, and the gates clanged shut behind him. They would not open again, the laird promised, until the prince returned as crowned king.

It is the stuff of legend, and indeed part of the garland of legends that history has hung about the neck of the prince concerned. For he was Prince Charles Edward Louis Philip Casimir Stuart, otherwise the Young Pretender, the Young Cavalier, Bonnie Prince Charlie, and he was on his way to invade England. The year was 1745. The gates at Traquair House are still shut; for when the Prince came

TRAQUAIR HOUSE The Bear Gates, still shut to await the return of a Stuart King. The fifth Earl of Traquair paid for his loyalty to the Pretender with two years' imprisonment in the Tower.

again to Scotland he was bound for Culloden, defeat and exile.

Traquair is said to be the oldest inhabited house in Scotland, established as a hunting lodge for Scottish kings by the twelfth century. Strategically placed on the northern edge of the Border country, within riding distance of Edinburgh, Traquair and its lairds have played a leading role in the affairs of Scotland; but never more so than in the turmoil of the first half of the eighteenth century.

Traquair became a Stuart house in 1478 when sold to the Earl of Buchan, and by the beginning of the eighteenth century it was a centre of Jacobite sentiment. It was not an easy position to maintain in the anti-Catholic south of Scotland, and it brought the Earls of Traquair more than their share of trouble. It was a time of passwords, of secret toasts, of looking forward to the time when the true King would come over the water. The Traquair amen glass-

captures the spirit of the time in its engraving:

> God bless the Prince of Wales
> The true-born Prince of Wales
>   Sent us by thee;
> Send him soon over
> And kick out Hanover
> And soon we'll recover
>   Our old libertie.

This was, of course, an additional verse to 'God Save the King'. The words of the National Anthem, set to a tune by Thomas Arne, had been first published in the *Gentleman's Magazine* in London in October 1745. One of the official stanzas had urged God to support Marshal Wade, the Hanoverian Commander-in-Chief in Scotland, that:

> May he sedition hush
> And like a torrent rush
> Rebellious Scots to crush
>   God save the King!

TRAQUAIR HOUSE *Bonnie Prince Charlie, one of the many mementoes at Traquair associated with the ill-fated rising of 1745. The fifth Earl was closely involved with the organization of the Jacobites.*

So, in verse, were the battle lines drawn up.

The fourth Earl of Traquair had already suffered for his Jacobite sympathies in the 1715 rebellion. His successor was sentenced to two years in the Tower of London for his hospitality to the Young Pretender in the '45. It was the fifth Earl who had built the gates that figured at the beginning of this story: proud gates guarded by the stone bears of the family coat of arms.

Yet the life of the Stuarts of Traquair was not all stern cause-making. It had its tender aspect as well. When the fifth Earl was sent to the Tower, his wife Teresa went with him— not as a fellow-prisoner, but in order to share and dilute his punishment. It is good to know that this was not all that severe. Wine and tea were provided, warders of the Tower acted as servants, and the laird of Traquair and his lady occupied a suite of three rooms. When they were released, they returned to their home and spent another seventeen years together, happy with each other but depressed about their cause and, indeed, their estate. Scotland had become, in effect, an occupied colonial territory, controlled and suppressed by a network of garrisons linked by military roads. Much of the Traquair land had to be sold off: the '45 laid a pall of scrimping-and-saving that hung heavy over its owners until well into the nineteenth century, not helped by a succession of reckless investments both abroad and locally. The family account books at Traquair tell the dismal story.

When Scotland became a playground for rich English industrialists in Victorian times, the old Jacobite families withdrew to their own pursuits. There was no place for them in the fake-tartan world of Victoria and Albert. The lairds of Traquair drifted into an insularity of such epic proportions that one, determined not to marry, put nettles in the beds of ladies he thought had come to entice him.

Dreams fade, but they do not die; no Stuart prince will ever, now, come back to Traquair as king. But if by some miracle he did, he would find a glass still there which, moved into a certain light, reveals his portrait, and another which bears the seditious verse seeking his succession. And he would find the Bear Gates —the 'Steekit Yetts'—open for the first time these 200 and more years: opened wide for a king come, as many thought then and some still think, into his own.

TREDEGAR HOUSE
GWENT

In the late 1930s the last place, you might have thought, for a display of opulence was in the valleys of South Wales. The pit villages were dying. Thousands were out of work. But up at Tredegar House it was as if unemployment and starvation had never been heard of. Evan, fourth Viscount Tredegar, whose family had for 150 years plundered the valleys for their own advancement, lived in a kind of dream world supported by an army of servants, entertained by a menagerie, and surrounded by a selection of the glittering social figures of the day, from H.G. Wells to Lady Cunard, from the popular journalist Godfrey Winn to the black-magic dabbler Aleister Crowley.

But it was the last gasp of a dying way of life. Evan's father Godfrey, who had died in 1934 and who had favoured an even more extravagant style, had left behind enormous death duties. The income from the South Wales pits was no more satisfactory for the Tredegars than it was for their former employees, and the excesses of the house were financed by capital. When Evan died in 1949 it was decided to break up the estate, and by 1951 Tredegar House had become a Roman Catholic girls' school. The last of the Tredegar line retired with the remnant of the family fortunes to Monte Carlo, where he died in 1962. The 500 years of the family's rise and fall were over.

The Morgans came to Tredegar in the early fifteenth century and within about a hundred years had gained sufficient prestige and power to build a suitable mansion. The south-west wing of the present House dates from this period. With increasing wealth, the House was rebuilt and expanded, mainly towards the girls' school, Tredegar House was bought by Newport Borough Council as 'little more than a decaying shell'. The contents had, of course, long since been sold. The Council's aim has been to restore, redecorate and re-furnish the forty rooms of the House in styles representing successive phases in its life, partly with the help of items on loan from the National Museum of Wales. Of particular interest is the suite of a dozen 'below stairs' rooms. This illustrates the practices and structures of the domestic staff in the days when—as in Edwardian times—there were twenty-two living-in servants in the House, plus a number of daily servants and, of course, the outdoor staff in the gardens, workshops and coach house.

TREDEGAR HOUSE The spice cupboard in the Housekeeper's Room. The more expensive groceries were kept under her eagle eye.

end of the seventeenth century. By the 1720s the extravagance which was to be the hallmark of the Morgans was already becoming evident; the staff included two clarinettists and a harpist, as well as a troupe of fashionable black menservants.

It was the late-eighteenth- and early-nineteenth-century Morgans who consolidated the family fortunes by investment in coal and iron workings, in canals and railways, and in the commercial development of Newport. Some of the profits from these enterprises were used to remodel Tredegar House again, including the addition of more accommodation for servants. In 1859 the Morgans achieved something that had long been their ambition: a peerage, the reward for Sir Charles Gould Morgan's political services to Disraeli.

In 1974, following the departure of the

UGBROOKE PARK

DEVON

As you walk down the main staircase at Ugbrooke Park you see in front of you a large painting showing a nineteenth-century pope presenting Cardinal Weld with his Cardinal's hat. A routine painting of a papal ceremony? Not quite, for the figures watching the proceedings from a box at the right of the picture are Cardinal Weld's daughter, Lady Clifford, and the Cardinal's grandchildren.

There is a simple explanation. Cardinal Weld had been a Dorset landowner whose wife died young, leaving him with one daughter. He saw her safely married into the Clifford family, and then made over his possessions to his brother and joined the Church. He rose to become a bishop and ultimately, as the picture at Ugbrooke shows, a Cardinal.

The Cliffords of Chudleigh, owners of Ugbrooke, are the Devon branch of a family that claims descent from Robert of Normandy and were, in the Middle Ages, owners of vast tracts in the north of England. Thomas Clifford, the first Lord Clifford of Chudleigh, became Lord Treasurer to Charles II and one of the King's closest advisers, though at the end of his life he fell from grace as a result of his ardent Catholicism. He built the chapel at Ugbrooke

UGBROOKE PARK The staircase hall, with its gallery of portraits and other paintings of key moments in Clifford family history.

as an Anglican foundation, but it was later disguised as a hall so that the illegal Catholic Mass could be said there.

At that time Ugbrooke was a Tudor manor house, but in 1750 the fourth Lord Clifford brought in Robert Adam to re-design the house, and Capability Brown to lay out the park. Adam was responsible for the castellation —said to have been his first attempt at this style—and also for the rehabilitation of the chapel to its proper use, the law having been changed to permit private chapels provided they were part of the house. Adam's interiors for the main rooms remain substantially unaltered, despite a period in the mid-1950s when the drawing room, the morning room and the dining room were used for storing grain. This did no good at all to Adam's

original gold-and-silk damask wall-covering in the dining room, and it has had to be replaced.

Ugbrooke was again occupied as a family home in 1957 by the present Lord and Lady Clifford, and restoration of the main house is now complete. The Catholic heritage remains steadfast; the chapel is the Catholic Parish Church of Chudleigh, and Mass is said every Sunday and Holy Day.

UPTON CRESSETT HALL

SHROPSHIRE

Politics in earlier times was an exceptionally dangerous game. It demanded nimble footwork, the ability to see out of the back of one's head, and often willingness to enter into protective marriages.

The de Uptons and Cressetts, families linked by marriage who held on to the manor of Upton Cressett through nine centuries, seem to have been adept at it. In one generation Lancastrians, in the next Yorkists, accused of conspiracy and imprisoned by Henry VII, Royalists engaged in espionage, participants in prickly negotiations at court in the eighteenth century, they nevertheless (literally) kept their heads, the only recorded untimely death being that of Edward Cressett, at the time of the

UPTON CRESSETT HALL The upper part of the fourteenth-century Great hall, dominated by its mighty 14-foot arched timbers.

Civil War, who was killed at the Battle of Bridgnorth. Meanwhile, they were able to build and later to modify an outstanding, upstanding manor house deep in the quiet Shropshire countryside.

It is a house in two chapters: the medieval and the Elizabethan. The original fourteenth-century Great Hall, though divided by a later floor, can still be seen, its massive timbers meeting across a 14-foot span in a decorated crown post. The Gatehouse, with its two octagonal turrets, the distinctive Tudor twisted chimneys, and the ornamental plaster-work and oak newel staircases belong, of course, to the later period. The house is a tribute to survival on two counts: first, though its inhabitants between the Middle Ages and the Civil War sailed very close to the political wind, they and their home emerged unscathed; and secondly, the Hall largely escaped the attentions of later 'improvers'. Visitors will be thankful for these mercies.

WARWICK CASTLE
WARWICKSHIRE

When Queen Elizabeth I came to call, it was a big occasion. When she visited Warwick Castle in 1572 on her way to Kenilworth she brought with her a 400-strong retinue, for whom temporary wooden quarters were erected. There was no room for the Earl of Warwick as well as his guests, so he and his family had to lodge with a friend in the town.

Ownership of Warwick Castle was granted and withheld by the monarch with bewildering capriciousness in Plantagenet and Tudor times, possibly because of the strategic importance of its site which had been recognized by William the Conqueror. The right to the title of Earl of Warwick was similarly extinguished and re-created. At the time of Queen Elizabeth's visit in 1572 the Earl of Warwick and owner of the Castle was Ambrose Dudley, who had had a distinguished military career and became Master General of the Ordnance— Chief of Defence Procurement as he would be

known today. The Castle, which probably began life as a defensive site even before the Conquest, was by Elizabethan times a substantial fortress, but after Ambrose Dudley's death without issue it was returned to the Crown and left unoccupied for fifteen years. Part of it was used as the county gaol. (This has not been an uncommon fate for castles. Lancaster's historic castle is used as a prison to this day.) Elizabeth's successor, James I, granted the Castle to Sir Fulke Greville, who set about converting it to a country seat in the early years of the seventeenth century; the state-room interiors, however, belong to a later period and, in the second half of the eighteenth century Capability Brown was brought in to re-design the Castle grounds. Alterations continued until 1804, when the second Earl of Warwick (of yet another new creation) was threatened with bankruptcy. There is a story that some of the Castle's pictures were saved through the noble efforts of the housekeeper, Maria Hume, who contributed her savings of over £30,000—representing tips given to her over the years by visitors—to keep them from the creditors.

This crisis over, Warwick Castle entered its most glittering period since Queen Elizabeth's reign; the only blemish was a serious fire in 1871 which damaged the Great Hall and adjoining rooms. Later in the century, when the heir to the Earl of Warwick married Frances ('Daisy') Maynard, the Castle acquired one of its most picturesque occupants. Frances Maynard, who at the age of five had become one of Britain's richest heiresses in her own right, grew up to be incredibly beautiful. It was whispered that she was destined for a royal marriage, but in the event she chose Francis Richard Charles Guy Greville, heir to the fourth Earl. However, she did not suffer from lack of royal connections, for she and her husband were fully fledged members of the rackety circle of the Prince of Wales, later to be Edward VII. Indeed, it was only a family bereavement that prevented their being present on the weekend of the notorious 'Tranby Croft' gaming scandal in 1890, which led to a court case in which the Prince's lifestyle was

WESTON PARK Elizabeth, Lady Wilbraham, who was not content to leave the rebuilding of her house to mere architects.

exposed to public disapproval. The Prince of Wales was a frequent visitor to both Warwick Castle and Easton Lodge, the Countess's own house in Essex, where later in life she would show off with some pride the bed which she and the Prince had frequently shared.

Easton Lodge, now demolished, however represented the Countess's 'other life', in which she played host to intellectuals and radicals, people far removed from the Prince of Wales's set. By 1898, when her radical sympathies were already becoming evident, the Prince's attention had turned to her successor, Mrs Alice Keppel. Warwick Castle, however, continued to greet him as a guest, both before and after his accession, and went on as a national and regional centre of social life until the death of the fifth Earl in 1924.

Since 1978 the Castle has been owned by a subsidiary company of Madame Tussaud's, which bought it complete with its contents

and has since added to its collections. There has been much painstaking reconstruction—right down to such details as the replacement of modern electrical fittings with those of the type installed when the Castle's first electricity supply was introduced in the 1890s. Some of the state rooms have been restored to their late-Victorian prime; others are used as settings for tableaux recreating a typical weekend house party of the period.

What is remarkable about Warwick Castle is that, despite its changed roles over more than 900 years, every stage of its development is still represented. The original motte-and-bailey Norman style is still eminent, sur-mounted by Caesar's and Guy's Towers, added, together with the Great Hall, in the fourteenth century. The Watergate Tower, where Sir Fulke Greville lived while the Castle was being rebuilt in the early seventeenth century, is reputedly haunted by his ghost. The state rooms reflect the splendour of the eighteenth century and the social glitter of the nineteenth. And everywhere are the pos-sessions and portraits of the succession of men and women who have known and loved this historic place.

WESTON PARK

SHROPSHIRE

The year 1872 found the great Conservative leader Disraeli at a low ebb. He was in his late sixties and had been in opposition for the past four years. His asthma, always trouble-some, was getting worse, and he was martyred periodically by gout. Then came an even greater personal blow: the death of Mary, his wife for over thirty years.

Disraeli was desolate. He was now con-demned, he told Queen Victoria (who, as a widow herself, was moved) to go to a 'home-less home, alone, every night'. In his grief, he turned for platonic solace to three elderly ladies: the Queen herself; Selina, the wife of the third Earl of Bradford; and Selina's sister, Lady Chesterfield. A selection of the 1,100

Even when Disraeli returned to power for another six-year term in 1874 the letters went on undiminished, written in moments snatched from government business. They give a remarkable picture of a remarkable man.

Weston Park is unusual as one of the few country houses to have been designed by a woman. Lady Wilbraham, who in 1671 began building the present house on the site of an earlier medieval manor, was a keen student of architecture and had added her own notes to the annotated translation of Palladio's architectural manual. The house she designed shows that she profited from her reading. Her interiors have been overlaid with subsequent alterations, and the objective of the present owners, Lady Wilbraham's descendants, is to return the rooms as far as is possible to the spirit of the originals. But if some of the 'improvements' of Lady Wilbraham's successors are to be regretted, they can perhaps be forgiven in view of the treasures they have brought to Weston Park. These include a magnificent set of Gobelins tapestries specially made for the house and featuring a medallion of *Les Amours des Dieux* on each wall.

WARWICK CASTLE The sword of Guy of Warwick, shown in the hands of the Hon. Sidney Greville in 1875.

There is another souvenir of Disraeli: among the Prime Minister's gifts—and a curious one, surely—to the third Countess of Bradford was a yellow cock parrot. It survived them both, and went on to do a most remarkable thing. One day in 1903 it laid an egg, and it repeated this feat on twenty-three successive days. This achievement was, however, its parrot song, for on the twenty-fourth day it died. The amazing bird and its eggs may be seen outside the door of the First Salon. One cannot but wonder what Dizzy would have said.

letters he wrote to Selina between 1873 and his death eight years later are at Weston Park.

The old charmer had not lost his touch; he wrote sentimentally, with affection, but never crossing the delicate line which would have made a mockery of the heavy mourning border on his writing paper that he refused to allow to be narrowed. He reported to Selina on the gossip of politics, his comings and goings to royal and other stately houses, and on the reaction of the Queen—'the Faery', as he called her in a reference to Edmund Spenser's poem *The Faerie Queene*—to events of the day.

WILTON HOUSE
WILTSHIRE

Literature, carpet-weaving and nursing: in all three of these very disparate human activities the Herbert family, Earls of Pembroke, have made their mark. One Earl was brother-in-law to Sir Philip Sidney; another was a close friend of Shakespeare; another brought over French weavers to found the English carpet industry; another Herbert, then the tenant at Wilton, brought Florence Nightingale from relative obscurity to refashion the nursing profession. At the same time the family has observed a tradition of the patronage and collection of works of art.

In 1577 Henry, second Earl of Pembroke, took as his third wife Mary Sidney, sister of the poet Philip. Over the succeeding years, as mistress of Wilton, Mary made the house a centre of literary and artistic activity. Wilton House was, wrote her contemporary John Aubrey, 'like a college, there were so many learned and ingenious persons. She was the greatest patroness of wit and learning of any lady of her time.'

Nor did her interest stop at patronage. None of her brother's work was published in book form during his lifetime, being circulated in manuscript in the fashion of the period. On his death in battle in 1586—it was Sir Philip who, as he lay dying, refused an offer of water from another wounded soldier with the words, 'Thy need is greater than mine'— Mary became his literary executor and edited his poems and other works for publication. One of these was a romance he had written for her during a stay at Wilton, *The Countess of Pembroke's Arcadia*. Scenes from this work are illustrated in a series of paintings at the foot of the four walls of the Single Cube Room at Wilton. When, in 1599, Queen Elizabeth visited the House, the Countess composed a pastoral dialogue for the occasion. She also published two accomplished translations of French plays.

There is a tradition, though there is no watertight evidence for it, that Shakespeare and his company of actors played at Wilton, possibly in 1603, with either *Twelfth Night* or *As You Like It*. Shakespeare's troupe certainly toured out of London in the summer of 1603 because an outbreak of plague had closed the city theatres, and equally certainly either play would have made a pleasant summer evening's

WESTON PARK The Bag of the Great Seal of England, now doing more humble service as a firescreen in the Library.

entertainment at Wilton.

Unfortunately the story can be taken no further than that, but there was a definite link between Shakespeare and the Pembrokes. When the first folio edition of the plays was published in 1623, seven years after Shakespeare's death, the dedication was to the then Earl of Pembroke and to his brother, a 'most noble and incomparable pair of brethren . . . and our singular good Lords'. For this reason alone it is appropriate that a statue of Shakespeare by William Kent greets visitors in the front hall at Wilton.

The luck of the Pembrokes—friends of the talented, hosts to successive monarchs, yet survivors of the Civil War without damage to persons or property—must have seemed too good to last, and so it was. The seventeenth century brought two blows. First, in 1647, a disastrous fire destroyed most of the old house, which had been rebuilt less than twenty years

WILTON HOUSE The Front Hall. William Kent's statue of Shakespeare welcomes the visitor. The Earls of Pembroke were among Shakespeare's patrons, but whether Shakespeare acted at Wilton is less certain.

before; though it is to the fire that we owe the present house, designed by Inigo Jones and largely executed by Inigo's nephew, John Webb. Few English country-house interiors match the refined elegance of the Cube Room or the Double Cube Room. Then, in 1674, the Earldom and the house came into the hands of Philip, the seventh Earl, who was a ne'er-do-well. In nine years he succeeded in running up enough debts to ensure that on his death the contents of Wilton had to be plundered to pay the bills. On top of the losses by fire, this must have been a bitter blow.

But Philip's successor, Thomas, restored both the prestige of the family and Wilton's reputation as a treasure-house. It is his taste that is predominant in the present collection at Wilton. He was also responsible for a notable contribution to the economy of the town of Wilton and the surrounding countryside,

bringing in French weavers to found the Wilton Royal Carpet Factory.

It was Sidney Herbert, half-brother of the twelfth Earl of Pembroke, who made the Florence Nightingale connection. The Earl lived abroad, and Sidney rented Wilton during his absence. In 1854 he was Secretary for War, and Florence Nightingale was matron of the Hospital for Invalid Gentlewomen in central London. The newspapers were suddenly full of horror stories of conditions for the wounded in the Crimea. Florence wrote to Sidney offering her services; her letter crossed with one from him, asking her to help. Within weeks she and her staff of nurses were tending the casualties, work that was to result in the conversion of nursing to a trained profession. It is good—and right—to see her portrait at Wilton alongside those of the other people whose careers the owners of the house had a hand in shaping.

WINGFIELD COLLEGE

SUFFOLK

In 1361 Sir John de Wingfield's funeral took place in the Suffolk village of Wingfield. He had been its Lord of the Manor and was a veteran of the wars against France and a personal friend of the Black Prince. Although, thanks to ransoms he had taken, Sir John had died an extremely rich man, his royal comrade-at-arms paid for the funeral himself as a mark of honour (and probably attended it).

The following year, however, the terms of Sir John's will showed that he wished his money to be put to good use. It was to endow a college. On 8 June 1362, the Charter of Wingfield's College of St Andrew was sealed, and the establishment was set up on the site of Sir John's old manor house.

While its pupils and their teachers have long gone, the College itself remains, although for 200 years it too simply vanished from public view. There, with its squat tower, was Wingfield's Church of St Andrew; and there, next to it—where the College itself should have been—was a long, low Georgian house that was not as symmetrical as it looked. There was something odd about its windows, too; several were fakes. The disguise that had enshrouded the whole of Wingfield College for so long was effective enough to keep the building's continued existence a mystery until very recently. It was only in 1971 that the owner of the Palladian building by the church found that his home was, in fact, one of the 'earliest and rarest timber-framed buildings in England'. Its formal beginnings could be dated precisely: 8 June 1362, the day of the College's foundation. Some of it, however, was even older than that.

As more and more of the disguise—plaster, walls, ceilings—was stripped away, there slowly emerged a building that had been familiar to generations of medieval boys and their teachers. As in a modern school or college, the main room was naturally the Great Hall: a chamber that dated from the original

manor house that had once stood on the site. With its enormous oak beams and its dais, the Hall was where the whole community of Wingfield College met and ate: the boys at long benches down each side, the masters at the top table.

Living and (probably) teaching quarters were upstairs, on the first floor. The ceilings of the College's Upper Chambers were only put in during the sixteenth century, after the whole institution had been surrendered to Henry VIII; when the medieval scholars used them as dormitories and schoolrooms, they were open to the rafters. (The scholars would, however, have recognized one of the existing windows: the fourteenth-century one facing the collegiate church.)

It was here that, for almost two centuries, academic Suffolk youngsters followed a curriculum that was designed to prepare them for

WINGFIELD COLLEGE Built around 1300, the timber-framed Great Hall was where the College's staff and students dined.

university work. It involved both bread-and-butter subjects, such as reading, writing and grammar, and more advanced subjects that were directly linked to the life of the Church: copying and illuminating manuscripts, singing church services, and studying for Holy Orders. Such was the College's prowess that, by the fifteenth century, it had become one of the top three boarding schools in the whole county.

Following its closure in 1542, Wingfield College became a private house. In the early 1600s, its converter, Robert Edgar, put in a parlour (now the Old Kitchen); a later owner, one Squire Buck, took the remodelling several stages further and, with his false floors and Palladian façade, hid the College from view completely.

Now returned to public awareness, it combines its functions as a home with that of acting as host to the Wingfield Arts and Music Season, held every year. Events include exhibitions, recitals and concerts which exploit the hall's superb acoustics; Sir John de Wingfield, who 600 years ago founded his College for a broadly similar purpose, would have approved.

WINTON HOUSE Tradition passed on: Professor Blackie sings 'The Bonnie House of Airlie' to Lady Ruthven of Winton House, 1880.

WINTON HOUSE
LOTHIAN

Winton House is Sir Walter Scott's 'Ravenswood', the house around which events revolve in his sombre novel *The Bride of Lammermoor*. The novel was published in 1819, by which time Winton House would have looked much as it does today, the battlemented wings having been added round about 1800. Although Scott relied heavily for ideas on the legends associated with his chosen settings, there is no evidence that in this case Winton House was anything more than a locale.

There were three distinct phases in the creation of the house. The first fifteenth-century building was burnt by invading English troops when Edinburgh and the surrounding area was sacked in 1544. However, the ground floor and the main walls survived and form the core of the present house. Rebuilding began round about 1620 in the Jacobean style, and the east and south wings—including the library with its elaborately Royalist ceiling—belong to this period. The owners were still the Seton family, who had built the original house but whose main seat was at Seton Palace (now demolished). In the 1715 rising the Setons supported the Jacobites, as a result of which they lost Seton Palace, Winton House and their other properties to the Crown.

Winton House then passed into the hands of the York Building Company, a group of entrepreneurs who did well out of the suppression of the Scots under Marshal Wade, acting as sub-contractors and suppliers for the network of military roads built under his command. Subsequently the company bought and developed the area round Tranent for coal-mining but money ran out and the company failed. Under the next ownership the house's battlements were added and the L-shaped courtyard was filled in to form what is now called the Octagon Hall. Later changes to the house have been mainly changes of use in the various rooms to suit modern convenience. The

WOBURN ABBEY *The ultimate extravagance: Woburn's Grotto, a seventeenth-century confection where members of the family and house guests could retreat from the heat of the day.*

present Dining Room, for example, was the old kitchen, and is placed under the semi-circular barrel-vaulting of the oldest part of the house, at the base of the tower.

WOBURN ABBEY

BEDFORDSHIRE

Woburn is—there are no other words for it—a treasure-house. To the first-time visitor, it looks like a careful accumulation through generations; you can imagine each piece of furniture, each painting being carefully chosen and sited, a place for everything and everything in its place; a palace cherished by each generation that has lived there.

It comes as a surprise, then, to discover that Woburn originally came to the Russell family,

the family of the Dukes of Bedford, as almost an unwanted gift, and that only two generations ago a large piece of the house was hacked off virtually without a thought. Less than forty years ago Woburn is reported as looking like a furniture repository. There were items from the demolished half and from the Russells' other houses—including Chenies Manor House and Bedford House in London—not so much arranged as dumped wherever there was room for them. Thankfully, for all our pleasure, the house has long since been restored to order, but Woburn's story is one of personal and architectural vicissitudes.

The former Cistercian Abbey of Woburn was granted in 1547 to Lord John Russell, the courtier who had fairly recently, at considerable expense, restored and rebuilt Chenies Manor House for his own use and as a court guest house. John Russell was created the first Earl of Bedford; it was Francis, the fourth Earl, who moved the focus of Russell family life from Chenies to Woburn and who built on the ruins of the Abbey. The Woburn of today, however, is what remains of the work of the fourth Duke of Bedford, Francis's great-great-grandson, who inherited the title in 1732.

The fourth duke, John, was one of those eighteenth-century characters who seem to have never stopped moving. He was active in the Whig party and in government, his first important Cabinet post being as First Lord of the Admiralty in 1744. He was one of the signatories to the Peace of Paris in 1763, though this did not endear him to the mob, who hissed him in the streets of London. Even after he lost office two years later, he continued his behind-the-scenes activity in the party. Meanwhile, he rebuilt Woburn.

Work began in 1747, and the Duke's chosen architect was Henry Flitcroft, of the Palladian school. His work is the bulk of what now remains at Woburn, including the remarkable Grand Staircase which climbs through the house without visible means of support. The transformation of Woburn from modest country house to gilded country palace was continued by the fifth Duke, who in the 1780s engaged Henry Holland—the Prince of Wales's architect—to add the now demolished east range, together with a Riding School and (of course, Real) Tennis Court. Of Holland's work on the house itself, only the Canaletto Room, the Library and the adjoining anterooms remain.

After an early bruising brush with politics, when he was subjected to a vicious attack in print by the astringent Edmund Burke, the fifth Duke retired to Woburn to cultivate his garden, or, more accurately, his large estate. Taking Coke of Norfolk as his example, he became a great agricultural improver, building a model farm, carrying out important breeding work, and initiating the 'Woburn Shearings' in flattering imitation of Coke's.

In the nineteenth century the Bedfords remained close to Whig politics and to court life. Anna Maria, the wife of the seventh Duke, was one of Queen Victoria's ladies-in-waiting in the early years of Victoria's reign. (She complained of the Queen's imperious manner. On one occasion, when the Duchess was delayed in her attendance, Her Majesty cried out in ringing tones, 'Duchess of Bedford, I have been waiting some time for my shawl.') The appointment of ladies-in-waiting was linked to the political complexion of the government of the day and in 1841, when Melbourne's Whig government was defeated, it was necessary for the Duchess to go. As the Queen and Prince Albert had only recently been guests at Woburn, for which occasion the Duke and Duchess had gone to considerable trouble and expense, the timing was unfortunate. It is said that the Duchess considered protesting at her dismissal, but she evidently thought better of it and went quietly.

Bit by bit, however, the Bedford riches were beginning to ebb away. Bedford House in London had been sold in 1800 and its contents transferred to Woburn. In 1914 Covent Garden followed. After the Second World War it was found that dry rot had infested Henry Holland's east range, and this was pulled down along with the Riding School, the Tennis Court, and sundry other parts—in total, about half the house. It was the task of the thirteenth Duke to bring order to the chaos of Bedford family possessions that had finished up in the truncated Woburn. It must also be borne in mind that the twelfth Duke's estate had left a burden of £5 million in death duty.

His solution, much criticized at the time (though generally by people who had not had to face the same problems), was to take a commercial view of Woburn. It became one of the first great houses to be opened to the public in the modern style. Developments on the estate, such as the Safari Park and other leisure attractions, followed. These bold steps, since copied by some of the Duke's critics, have enabled the treasures of several houses to be kept together in a collection which constantly dazzles the eye, feeds the imagination, and demands more than one visit.

GAZETTEER

The Gazetteer provides the address and telephone number of properties, with a résumé of the most important contents and other attractions of each property.

The symbols give an at-a-glance indication of the comparative frequency of opening, the cost of admission for an adult, and the facilities available. The key:

○ Open every day except Christmas Day

◐ Open daily for the tourist season from May to September or longer

◑ Open at least 5 days a week between May and September or longer

◔ Open 1–5 days per week in summer

◕ Open intermittently

£ Entrance fee; more than £1 per adult

££ Entrance fee; more than £2 per adult

£££ Entrance fee; more than £3 per adult

ⵏ Guided tours

❀ Gardens

⬡ Gift shop

⌣ Teas

✕ Lunches

ⵣ Education facilities

⚖ Playground

M̱ Museum/special exhibition area

❀ Nature trail

⚘ Arboretum

✦ Bird garden

AV Audio visual presentation

P Free parking

♿ Facilities for the disabled

⇌ British Rail station

Directions to the property are given in relation to the nearest town or main road. The nearest railway station is given if less than 2 miles to house.

It is essential that prospective visitors check opening times with the relevant regional tourist board before making a journey to a house. Equally some details regarding the contents and/or facilities may change with time.

YOU ARE ADVISED TO CHECK DETAILS BEFORE VISITING A HOUSE

Bangor
Bryn Bras Castle
Bodrhyddan Hall
Tower
Mold
CHESHIRE
CLWD
STAFFORDSHIRE
GWYNEDD
Plas Glyn-Y-Weddw
Shrewsbury
Shipton Hall
Weston Park
Upton Cresset Hall
SHROPSHIRE
POWYS
Elgar's Birthplace
Chillington Hall
Worcester
Burton Court
HEREFORD & WORCESTER
Hereford
Bretforton Manor
Moccas Court
Eastnor Castle
Little Malvern Court
Sufton Court
DYFED
Hellen's
Stanway House
Sudeley Castle
Llanvihangel Court
Gloucester
Abergavenny
GLOUCESTERSHIRE
WEST GLAMORGAN
GWENT
Berkeley Castle
MID GLAMORGAN
Penhow Castle
Chavenage
Tredegar House
Newport
Sheldon Manor
SOUTH GLAMORGAN
Cardiff
Bristol
Corsham Court
Fonmon Castle
Barry
AVON
Bath
WILTSHIRE
The Bishop's Palace
Minehead
Chambercombe Manor
Barford Park
Ilfracombe
Combe
Wells
Sydenham Hall
Gaulden Manor
SOMERSET
Bideford
Barnstaple
Taunton
Sandford Orcas
Hartland Abbey
Poundisford Park
Hatch Court
Yeovil
Sherborne Castle
Edmondsham House
Tiverton Castle
Brympton d'Evercy
Bickleigh Castle
Forde Abbey
Parnham
DORSET
Fursdon House
Cadhay
Wolfeton
Athelhampton
DEVON
Exeter
Sand
Dorchester
Bournemouth
Powderham Castle
Sidmouth
Ugbrooke Park
A La Ronde
Smedmore
Prideaux Place
Wadebridge
Bowden House
Pencarrow
Torquay
CORNWALL
Hemerdon House
St Austell
Trewithen
Plymouth
Godolphin House
Falmouth
Penzance
Trelowarren House

284

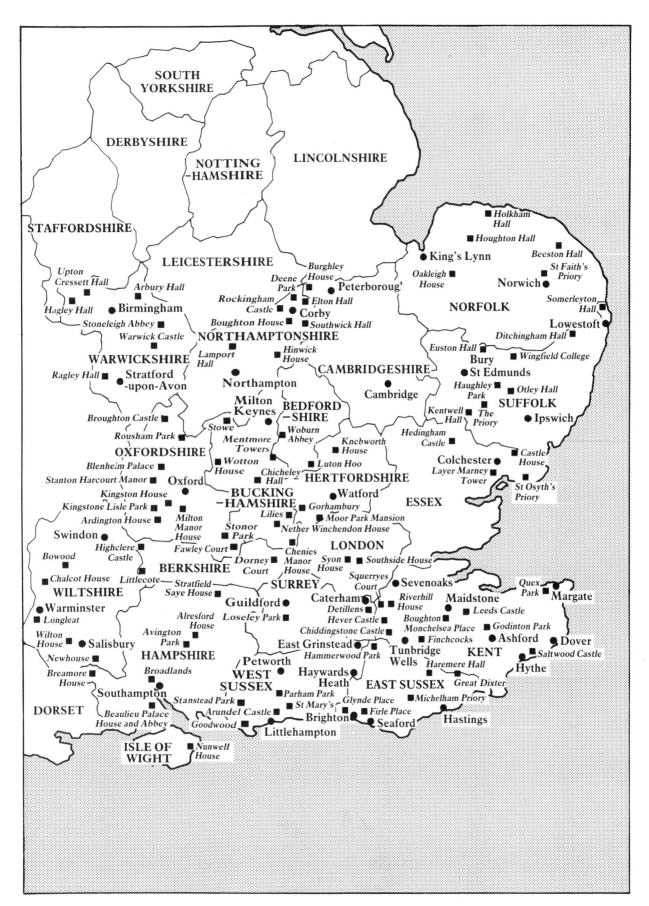

SOUTH
YORKSHIRE

DERBYSHIRE

NOTTING
-HAMSHIRE

LINCOLNSHIRE

STAFFORDSHIRE

LEICESTERSHIRE

■ *Holkham Hall*

■ *Houghton Hall*

● King's Lynn

■ *Beeston Hall*

■ *Oakleigh House*

■ *St Faith's Priory*

Norwich

Upton Cressett Hall ■

Arbury Hall ■

Burghley House

Deene Park ■

● Peterborough

NORFOLK

Hagley Hall ■

● Birmingham

Rockingham Castle ■

■ *Elton Hall*

● Corby

■ *Somerleyton Hall*

● Lowestoft

Stoneleigh Abbey ■

Boughton House ■

■ *Southwick Hall*

Ditchingham Hall ■

Warwick Castle ■

NORTHAMPTONSHIRE

Euston Hall ■

■ *Wingfield College*

Ragley Hall ■

WARWICKSHIRE

Lamport Hall ■

Hinwick House ■

Bury
St Edmunds ●

SUFFOLK

Stratford
-upon-Avon ●

● Northampton

CAMBRIDGESHIRE

Haughley Park ■

■ *Otley Hall*

Broughton Castle ■

Milton
Keynes ●

● Cambridge

Kentwell Hall ■

The Priory ■

● Ipswich

BEDFORD
–SHIRE

Stowe ■

Woburn Abbey ■

Hedingham Castle ■

Rousham Park ■

Mentmore Towers ■

Knebworth House ■

■ *Castle House*

OXFORDSHIRE

Wotton House ■

● Colchester ■

Blenheim Palace ■

Chicheley Hall ■

HERTFORDSHIRE

Layer Marney Tower ■

Stanton Harcourt Manor ■

● Oxford

■ *Luton Hoo*

St Osyth's Priory

Kingston House ■

BUCKING
–HAMSHIRE

● Watford

ESSEX

Kingstone Lisle Park ■

Milton Manor House ■

Gorhambury ■

Ardington House ■

Lilies ■

Moor Park Mansion ■

● Swindon

Stonor Park ■

Nether Winchendon House ■

LONDON

Highclere Castle ■

Fawley Court ■

Chenies ■

Bowood ■

BERKSHIRE

Dorney Court ■

Manor House ■

Syon House ■

■ *Southside House*

Chalcot House ■

Littlecote ■

Stratfield Saye House ■

SURREY

Squerryes Court ■

● Sevenoaks

Quex Park ■

■ Margate

WILTSHIRE

● Warminster

● Guildford

Caterham ●

Riverhill House ■

Maidstone

Longleat ■

Alresford House ■

Detillens ■

Leeds Castle ■

Godinton Park ■

● Dover

Wilton House ■

● Salisbury

Avington Park ■

Loseley Park ■

Hever Castle ■

Boughton ■

● Ashford

Newhouse ■

HAMPSHIRE

Chiddingstone Castle ■

Monchelsea Place ■

Finchcocks ■

KENT

Saltwood Castle ■

Breamore House ■

Broadlands ■

East Grinstead ●

Hammerwood Park ■

Tunbridge
Wells

Haremere Hall ■

Hythe

● Southampton

Petworth ●

Haywards
Heath ●

EAST SUSSEX

Great Dixter ■

WEST
SUSSEX

Stanstead Park ■

Parham Park ■

St Mary's ■

Glynde Place ■

Michelham Priory ■

DORSET

Beaulieu Palace House and Abbey ■

Arundel Castle ■

Firle Place ■

● Brighton

● Seaford

● Hastings

● Littlehampton

● Goodwood

ISLE OF
WIGHT

Nunwell House ■

Berwick
-upon-Tweed

*Bamburgh
Castle*

Preston Tower

*Chillingham
Castle*

*Alnwick
Castle*

NORTHUMBERLAND

*Naworth
Castle*

Newcastle
-upon-Tyne

Carlisle

*Hutton-In
-The-Forest*

CO DURHAM Durham

Mirehouse

Penrith

Dalemain

Auckland Castle

CUMBRIA

Raby Castle

Rydal Mount

Rokeby Park

Middlesbrough

Darlington

*Muncaster
Castle*

Kendal

Kiplin Hall

*Levens
Hall*

NORTH YORKSHIRE

Northallerton

Scarborough

Holker Hall

Norton Conyers

Newby Hall

Castle Howard

Barrow
-in-Furness

Leighton Hall

*Ripley
Castle*

Ripon

Sutton Park

Morecambe

*Stockeld
Park*

*Fairfax
House*

Bridlington

LANCASHIRE

Harrogate

*Sledmere
House*

*Browsholme
Hall*

Wetherby

York

HUMBERSIDE

Clitheroe

Harewood House

*Bramham
Park*

Kingston
-upon-Hull

*Burton
Constable Hall*

Hoghton Tower

Otley

**WEST
YORKSHIRE**

Preston

Southport

*Meols
Hall*

Goole

*Carlton
Towers*

Manchester

*Lyme
Park*

**SOUTH
YORKSHIRE**

Liverpool

CHESHIRE

Adlington Hall

Sheffield

Chester

Knutsford

*Arley
Hall*

Tatton Park

DERBYSHIRE

*Harrington
Hall*

Lincoln

Tower

Peover Hall

*Capesthorne
Hall*

Chatsworth

**NOTTING
-HAMSHIRE**

Doddington Hall

Aubourn Hall

Crewe

Haddon Hall

Fulbeck Hall

*Dorfold
Hall*

Stoke-on
-Trent

*St Oswald's
Hall*

Derby

*Holme Pierrepont
Hall*

LINCOLNSHIRE

STAFFORDSHIRE

Whitmore Hall

*Melbourne
Hall*

Grantham

Harlaxton Manor

Eccleshall Castle

*Belvoir
Castle*

*Grimsthorpe
Castle*

Stafford

*Hoar Cross
Hall*

LEICESTERSHIRE

SHROPSHIRE

WARWICKSHIRE

Stanford Hall

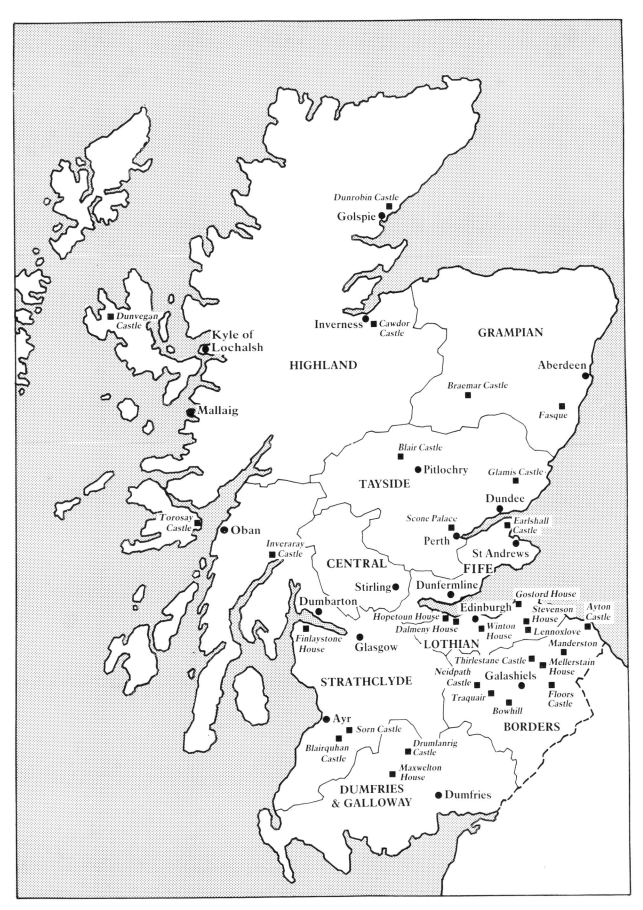

Dunrobin Castle
Golspie

Dunvegan
Castle

Inverness   Cawdor
Castle

Kyle of
Lochalsh

GRAMPIAN

HIGHLAND

Aberdeen

Braemar Castle

Fasque

Mallaig

Blair Castle

TAYSIDE

Pitlochry   Glamis Castle

Torosay
Castle

Oban

Inveraray
Castle

CENTRAL

Dundee

Scone Palace   Earlshall
Castle

Perth

St Andrews

FIFE

Stirling   Dunfermline

Gosford House

Ayton
Castle

Stevenson
House

Dumbarton   Edinburgh

Hopetoun House   Winton   Lennoxlove
Dalmeny House   House

Manderston

Finlaystone
House

Glasgow

LOTHIAN

Thirlestane Castle   Mellerstain
House

STRATHCLYDE

Neidpath
Castle   Galashiels

Floors
Castle

Traquair

Bowhill

BORDERS

Ayr

Sorn Castle

Blairquhan
Castle

Drumlanrig
Castle

Maxwelton
House

DUMFRIES
& GALLOWAY   Dumfries

287

BEDFORDSHIRE

LUTON HOO, Luton Tel: (0582) 22955
Home of Nicholas Phillips
Country house, altered by Adam and restored after 19th-century fire. Contents include: Russian collection (Fabergé items, portraits and other mementoes of the Russian Imperial family); Renaissance jewelry collection; Spanish, Italian, Flemish and British pictures (artists include Memlinc, Hals, Hobbema, Altdorfer, Bermejo, Reynolds); tapestries; the Ludlow collection (English porcelain); medieval ivories; racing trophies and paintings. Outdoors: gardens; park by Capability Brown.
◐ ££ ⌂ ⬚ ✸ P ⴺ
off A6129 Luton to Hemel Hempstead; M1 (junction 6) ⇌ Luton

WOBURN ABBEY, Woburn Tel: (0525) 290666
Home of The Marquess of Tavistock
18th-century Palladian mansion. Contents include: collection of Canaletto views of Venice; English, Continental and Oriental porcelain; silver and silver gilt; etchings by Queen Victoria and Prince Albert; 17th-century Dutch and Flemish paintings; collection of enamelled miniatures; chimney-pieces by Rysbrack; collection of Reynolds portraits. Outdoors: gardens; 3000-acre deer park with picnic areas; drive-through safari park; antiques and garden centres; pottery.
① £££ ⌂ ⬚ ✕ ⴾ ✸ P
off A5 Bletchley to Dunstable; M1 (junctions 12 and 13) ⇌ Ridgemont

BERKSHIRE

HIGHCLERE CASTLE, Newbury Tel: (0635) 253210
Home of The Earl of Carnarvon
Victorian Gothic mansion. Contents include: rich Victorian interiors; collection of Van Dyck portraits; Napoleon's chair and desk; Tutankhamun room; sculpture by Tenerani. Outdoors: park landscaped by Capability Brown; 18th-century temples and arches; walled gardens; tropical orangery; fernery.
◐ ££ ⌂ ⬚ ✸ ⚘ P
off A34 Newbury to Winchester

LITTLECOTE, Hungerford Tel: (0488) 84000
Home of Peter de Savary
Tudor manor house. Contents include: painted Dutch parlour; Cromwellian chapel; Civil War armour; Civil War tableaux. Outdoors: Roman villa and mosaic; adventure playground; 17th-century crafts village; working period farm with rare breeds; falconry; pageantry; riverside railway; wagon rides; riverside walks; knot, herb and rose gardens.
① £££ ⌂ ⬚ ✕ AV ⴾ ✸ Ⓜ ⋔ P ⴺ
off A4 Hungerford to Marlborough; M4 (junction 14)

STRATFIELD SAYE HOUSE, Reading Tel: (0256) 882882
Home of The Duke of Wellington
17th-century country mansion, with later alterations. Contents include: interior decoration, furnishings, possessions, trophies, portraits etc connected with the 'Great Duke', victor of Waterloo; family portraits by Hogarth, Hoppner, Lawrence and others; 'The Ascension' by Tintoretto; portrait of Copenhagen, by Haydon; print rooms; Prussian, Austrian, and Chinese dinner services; slate billiards table. Outdoors: gardens; wildfowl sanctuary; Copenhagen's grave; Wellington Exhibition including funeral carriage.
◐ ££ ⌂ ⬚ ✕ ⴾ ✸ P ⴺ
off A33 Reading to Basingstoke

BUCKINGHAMSHIRE

CHENIES MANOR HOUSE, Amersham Tel: (024 04) 2888
Home of Lt. Col. and Mrs Alistair Macleod Matthews
15th-century gatehouse with 16th-century wing. Contents include: medieval wine-cellar and dungeon; Persian carpets; Louis XVI furniture; collection of Staffordshire cow creamers; 16th-century tapestries. Outdoors: gardens; turf maze; medieval well and well-house with horse-driven pump; thousand-year-old 'Queen Elizabeth's oak' in the grounds.
① £ ⴽ ⌂ ⬚ ✸ P
off A404 Amersham to Rickmansworth ⇌ Chorleywood

CHICHELEY HALL, Newport Pagnell Tel: (023 065) 252
Home of the Hon. Nicholas Beatty
18th-century country house. Contents include: objects associated with the first Earl Beatty (portraits, photographs, copies of decorations, flag from HMS Lion); sea pictures; family portraits; collection of Stuart mother-of-pearl tableware; tapestries; Sir John Chester's Library.
① ££ ⴽ ⌂ ⬚ ✸ P ⴺ
on A422 Bedford to Newport Pagnell

DORNEY COURT, Windsor Tel: (062 86) 4638
Home of Peregrine Palmer
Late medieval and early Tudor manor. Contents include; Great Hall and other Tudor apartments; paintings by Lely, Kneller and others (including twelve generations of family portraits); priest's hole; the 'Palmer Needlework' (Elizabethan tapestry showing members of the Palmer family). Outdoors: gardens.
① ££ ⌂ ⬚ ✸ P
off B3026 Eton to Taplow

LILIES, Weedon Tel: (029 664) 393
Home of Mr and Mrs Peter Eaton
Late Victorian mansion. Contents include: pictures by Watts, Ruskin, Rosetti, Lord Leighton, Romney and others; collection of ephemera; Aztec remains; fossil collection; historical autograph books and documents. Outdoors: gardens; arboretum; nature reserve.
◐ ✸ P
off A413 Buckingham to Aylesbury

MENTMORE TOWERS, Leighton Buzzard Tel: (0296) 661881
The World Government of Age of the Enlightenment
19th-century 'Jacobethan' mansion, designed by Paxton. Contents include: Grand Stairs; Grand Hall (with Rubens fireplace); Dining Room (with Genoese velvet panels, gilded boiseries, paintings by Van Loo); Library (with 16th-century Italian marble fireplace). Outdoors: gardens; park with exotic trees.
◐ £ ⴽ ✸ P
off A418 Aylesbury to Leighton Buzzard

NETHER WINCHENDON HOUSE, Aylesbury Tel: (0844) 290101
Home of Robert Spencer Barnard
Medieval house, with Tudor and later additions. Contents include: Sir John Daunce's Parlour (now Drawing Room), with linenfold panelling, Renaissance frieze and armorial glass; 17th- and 18th-century furniture; Great Hall; tapestry portrait of Henry VIII (only contemporary one in existence). Outdoors: gardens, with Georgian bridge over Thame, and waterbirds.
◐ £ ⴽ ✸
off A418 Aylesbury to Thame

YOU ARE ADVISED TO CHECK DETAILS BEFORE VISITING A HOUSE

STOWE, Buckingham Tel: (0280) 813650
Stowe School Ltd
Palladian mansion. Contents include: William Kent interiors. Outdoors: landscape park; garden buildings by Kent, Gibbs and Vanbrugh; statuary by Van Nost and Rysbrack; lakes.
◑ £ 🗍 ☐ ⊛ 🥀 P
off A422 Brackley to Buckingham

WOTTON HOUSE, Aylesbury Tel: (0844) 363
Home of Mrs Patrick Brunner
18th-century house. Contents include: interiors by Sir John Soane; ironwork by Tijou. Outdoors: landscaped park.
◑ £ 𝄇 P
off A41 Aylesbury to Bicester

CHESHIRE
ADLINGTON HALL, Macclesfield Tel: (0625) 829206
Home of Charles Legh
Tudor manor house, one half timbered, one Georgian façade. Contents include: Great Hall with hammer-beam roof and murals; 17th-century organ; oak tree pillars; minstrels' gallery; paintings by Van Dyck, Lely, Kneller and others; Handel MS. Outdoors: gardens.
◑ £ 🗍 ☐ ⊛ P
on A523 Stockport to Macclesfield

ARLEY HALL, Northwich Tel: (056 585) 353
Home of the Hon. Michael and Mrs Flower
19th-century mansion. Contents include: Stephen Keene virginal; family portraits; grand staircase; collection of Piers Egerton-Warburton's paintings of buildings. Outdoors: gardens; barns; working craftsmen; plant sales.
◑ ££ 𝄇 🗍 ☐ ✕ ⊅ ⊛ P ♿
in Arley, M6 (junctions 19 & 20); M56 (junctions 9 & 10)

CAPESTHORNE HALL, Macclesfield Tel: (0625) 861221
Home of Col. Sir Walter Bromley-Davenport
Victorian mansion. Contents include: family portraits and other paintings; classical sculptures and ceramics; Gladstone roundel; Dame Dorothy's bed-hangings; collection of 18th-century American furniture; Cromwellian armour. Outdoors: gardens; theatre; nature trail; adventure playground.
◑ ££ 🗍 ☐ ✕ ⊅ 🥀 🏠 P ♿
off A34 Manchester to Stoke-on-Trent; M6 (junction 18)

DORFOLD HALL, Nantwich Tel: (0270) 625245
Home of Richard Roundell
Jacobean manor house with some 18th-century interiors. Contents include: pictures by Janssen, Morland and others; Jacobean ceiling; early Oriental and English porcelain; Queen Anne and Chinese Chippendale furniture. Outdoors: lawns; formal gardens; water garden; 1000-year-old Spanish Chestnut.
◑ ££ 𝄇 ⊛ P
off A534 Nantwich to Wrexham

LYME PARK, Stockport Tel: (0663) 62023
Stockport Metropolitan Borough for The National Trust
Palladian mansion by Leoni with 18th- and 19th-century interiors. Contents include: major English clock collection; Mortlake tapestries; major collection of portraits and other paintings; original 18th-century furniture. Outdoors: gardens; adventure playground; coarse fishing; nature trails; guided walks; deer park; orangery.
◑ £ 𝄇 🗍 ☐ ✕ ⊅ ⊛ 🥀 🏠 ♿
off A6 Stockport to Buxton ≥ Disley

PEOVER HALL, Knutsford Tel: (056 581) 2135
Home of Mr and Mrs Randle Brooks
Elizabethan manor house. Contents include: collection of arms and armour; Elizabethan ceilings and fireplaces. Outdoors: lily pond garden; rose garden; Elizabethan summer-house; topiary; stables and coach-house.
◑ £ 𝄇 ☐ ⊛ P
off A50 Knutsford to Kidsgrove

TATTON PARK, Knutsford Tel: (0565) 54822
Cheshire County Council for The National Trust
Georgian mansion. Contents include: Italian, French and English furniture commissioned or bought for the house; major collections of pictures, furniture, china, glass, silver and silver gilt. Outdoors: gardens; authentic Japanese garden; orangery; fernery; arboretum; medieval old hall; 1930s farm; fishing lake; wildfowl; village trail; deer park and rare breeds of sheep.
◐ £ 🗍 ☐ ✕ AV ⊅ ⊛ 🥀 P ♿
off A50 Knutsford to Warrington; M6 (junction 19); M56 (junction 7)

CORNWALL
GODOLPHIN HOUSE, Breage Tel: (073 676) 2409
Home of Mrs Mary Schofield
15th-century house with 17th-century colonnaded front. Contents include: pillared 17th-century colonnade; John Wootton painting of the Godolphin Arabian; family portraits; 16th-century English oak furniture.
◑ £ P
off A394 Penzance to Helston

PENCARROW, Bodmin Tel: (020 884) 369
Home of Lt. Col. Sir Arscott Molesworth-St Aubyn Bt
18th-century country house. Contents include: Chinese porcelain (incl. rare export bowl); family portraits by Reynolds, Devis and others; Nursery, with antique doll collection; Corner Bedroom (occupied by Sullivan); original costumes from 'Iolanthe'. Outdoors: gardens (with palm house, ice house, lake); children's playground and family pets corner; Cornwall Craft Association shop.
◐ ££ 𝄇 ☐ ✕ ⊅ ⊛ 🏠 P ♿
off A389 Bodmin to Wadebridge

PRIDEAUX PLACE, Padstow Tel: (0841) 532945
Home of John Prideaux-Brune
Elizabethan manor house with Strawberry Hill Gothic interiors. Contents include: 16th-century cannon; Chinese and Sèvres porcelain; rosewood and mahogany furniture; 'Ascension of the Virgin' by Guido Reni and portraits by, among others, Kneller, Dahl and Cotman; plasterwork ceiling showing tableaux of Susannah and the Elders. Outdoors: gardens; deer park; grotto; Celtic cross; Gothic dairy; stables.
◐ ££ 𝄇 ⊛ P
off B3276 Padstow to St Merryn

YOU ARE ADVISED TO CHECK DETAILS BEFORE VISITING A HOUSE

TRELOWARREN HOUSE, Helston Tel: (032 622) 366
Home of Sir John Vyvyan Bt
Tudor and 17th-century house. Contents include: paintings exhibitions; chapel.
◑ £ ⚑ ⌨ P
off B3293 Helston to St Keverne

TREWITHEN, Truro Tel: (0726) 882418
Home of A.M.J. Galsworthy
18th-century country house. Contents include: contemporary paintings and furniture. Outdoors: woodland gardens; walled gardens; landscaped park.
◑ ££ ⚑ P
off A390 Probus to Grampound

CUMBRIA
DALEMAIN, Penrith Tel: (085 36) 450
Home of Mr and Mrs Bryce McCosh
Georgian country house. Contents include: medieval hall; Chinese Drawing Room (original wallpaper, furniture of Chinese Chippendale design); family portraits; print collection; Tudor plasterwork; Westmorland and Cumberland Yeomanry museum; nursery (with 18th-century dolls' house); former housekeepers' room; priest's hole. Outdoors: countryside museum, gardens, adventure playground, garden centre.
◐ ££ ⛩ ⌨ ✕ ▨ 𝗠 ⋔ P ♿
off A592 Penrith to Ullswater; M6 (junction 40)

HOLKER HALL, Cark-in-Cartmel Tel: (044 853) 328
Home of Hugh Cavendish
18th-century and Victorian country house. Contents include: family portraits and other paintings (including works by Van Dyck, Salvator Rosa, Reynolds); 18th-century English and French furniture; Wedgwood Jasper ware collection; Henry Cavendish's microscope; Victorian and later kitchen exhibition. Outdoors: gardens, Lakeland Motor Museum; craft and countryside exhibition; baby animal farm; deer park; kitchen exhibition.
◐ £ ⛩ ⌨ ✕ ⬠ ▨ 𝖇 𝗠 ⋔ P ♿
off B5278 Cark-in-Cartmel to Haverthwaite

HUTTON-IN-THE-FOREST, Penrith Tel: (085 34) 449
Home of The Lord Inglewood
Mansion based on 14th-century pele tower with later additions. Contents include: 17th-century Cupid Staircase; English and Flemish tapestries; 16th-century needlework panels; William Morris wallpaper and other items. Outdoors; walled gardens; parkland and woodland walks; 17th-century dovecote.
◑ ££ ⚑ ⛩ ⌨ ⬠ ▨ P
off B5305 Penrith to Wigton; M6 (junction 41)

LEVENS HALL, Kendal Tel: (053 95) 60321
Home of Hal Bagot
Elizabethan country house. Contents include: Elizabethan plasterwork and panelling; carved overmantels; paintings by Lely and others (including the Rubens' copy of Mahler's 'Anne of Hungary'); miniatures and *objets d'art*, including Wellington's watch; Sèvres chocolate service; Indian chintz patchwork; 17th-century furniture. Outdoors: original 17th-century topiary gardens; park; adventure playground; model steam engine exhibition.
◐ ££ ⛩ ⌨ ✕ ▨ ⋔ P
off A6 Kendal to Milnthorpe

MIREHOUSE, Keswick Tel: (076 87) 72287
Home of John Fryer Spedding
17th-century country house, with later additions. Contents include: family portraits and other paintings (artists include Constable and Morland); manuscript poems and letters from Wordsworth, Southey, Hartley Coleridge; portraits of Tennyson, Hallam and FitzGerald, by James Spedding, and other literary memorabilia; 'Francis Bacon' collection (papers and books, collected by James Spedding for his 14-volume work on Bacon); Carlyle letters and manuscripts; chess table; Georgian/Victorian nursery. Outdoors: four age-related adventure playgrounds; walks to Bassenthwaite Lake and Norman Church of St Bega; walks to Skiddaw, Ullock Pike and Carlside.
◐ £ ⌨ ✕ 𝗠 P
off A591 Keswick to Carlisle

MUNCASTER CASTLE, Ravenglass Tel: (06577) 203
Home of Mr and Mrs Patrick Gordon-Duff-Pennington
Medieval castle, remodelled in 19th century. Contents include: 'Luck of Muncaster' bowl; family portraits and other paintings by Gainsborough, Cuyp, Reynolds, and others (including portrait of Muncaster Fool, Thomas Skelton); Elizabethan tapestries; statuary (sculptors include Giambologna); Charles II and later 17th-century furniture; Sèvres and Derby services; 16th-century panelling and carving. Outdoors: gardens and rhododendron walks; nature trail; headquarters of the British Owl Breeding and Release Scheme.
◐ ££ ⛩ ⌨ ✕ 𝖇 ▨ 🦉 𝗠 ⋔ P
off A595 Whitehaven to Broughton-in-Furness ⇌ Ravenglass

NAWORTH CASTLE, Brampton Tel: (069 77) 2692
Home of The Earl and Countess of Carlisle
14th-century semi-fortified manor house. Contents include: early Gobelins tapestries; Dacre heraldic beasts; Burne-Jones relief of the Battle of Flodden. Outdoors: gardens.
◑ £ ⛩ P
off A69 Carlisle to Newcastle

RYDAL MOUNT, Ambleside Tel: (096 63) 3002
Home of Mrs Mary Henderson (*née* Wordsworth)
16th-century yeoman's house with 18th-century additions. Contents include: Wordsworth memorabilia including family portraits; chair-seats worked by Mary and Dorothy Wordsworth; first editions of Wordsworth's works. Outdoors: gardens; terraces; water garden.
◯ £ ⛩ ▨ P
off A591 Ambleside to Grasmere

DERBYSHIRE
CHATSWORTH, Bakewell Tel: (024 688) 2204
Home of The Duke of Devonshire
Baroque palace, with later alterations. Contents include: State Apartments, with decorations by Verrio and Laguerre, Boulle furniture, Mortlake tapestries, the 'violin door'; Great Stairs by Tijou; Library (17,000 volumes); paintings by Tintoretto, Rembrandt, Hals, Giordano, Lely, Van Dyck, Sargent and others; sculpture (including the 'giant foot'). Outdoors: gardens, with Paxton's Wall, Emperor Fountain, maze, cascade; farmyard; adventure playground.
◔ £££ ⛩ ⌨ ✕ ▨ ⋔ P
off A623 Bakewell to Chapel-en-le-Frith

┌───┐
│ YOU ARE ADVISED TO CHECK DETAILS BEFORE VISITING A HOUSE │
└───┘

HADDON HALL, Bakewell Tel: (062 981) 2855
Home of The Duke of Rutland
Medieval mansion, with Tudor and Jacobean alterations. Contents
include: chapel with medieval wall-paintings; banqueting hall; dining
room with heraldic painted ceiling; long gallery; tapestries (Mortlake
and Flemish); bedroom furnishings; medieval kitchens with equipment; museum. Outdoors: terraced gardens; picnic area.
① ££ 🗂 ⊒ ✕ ⛟ ⊛ M̂
off A6 Matlock to Buxton

MELBOURNE HALL, Derby Tel: (03316) 2502
Home of The Marquess of Lothian
17th-century country house. Contents include: pictures by Lely,
Huysmans, Dahl; collection of US Sandwich glass; Lord Melbourne,
Lady Caroline Lamb and Lady Palmerston memorabilia. Outdoors:
gardens; wishing well; ironwork gazebo by Robert Bakewell; fountains
and statuary; yew tunnel; craft centre.
◑ £ 𝑘 🗂 ⊒ ✕ ⊛ P 㫈
off A514 Derby to Ashby de la Zouch

DEVON
A LA RONDE, Exmouth Tel: (0395) 265514
Home of Mrs Ursula Tudor Perkins
Sixteen-sided 18th-century 'rustick cottage'. Contents include: sitting
room with feather-work frieze; gallery with 'mosaic work' in shells and
feathers; shell and mineral collection; seaweed and sand collages; cut-
paper pictures (and the scissors used for cutting them). Outdoors:
gardens; parklands with estuary views.
① £ 𝑘 🗂 ⊒ ✕ AV ⊛ P
on A376 Exmouth to Exeter

BICKLEIGH CASTLE, Tiverton Tel: (088 45) 363
Home of Noël Boxall
Medieval gatehouse and chapel, complex of farm buildings with 17th-
century thatched farmhouse. Contents include: Tudor furniture; arms
and armour; sampler collection. Outdoors: gardens; agricultural and
domestic equipment (including period rocking horses); exhibition 'Sir
George Carew and the *Mary Rose*', plus collection of model ships;
collection of Second World War escape and spy equipment.
◑ ££ 𝑘 🗂 ⊒ ⊛ M̂ P 㫈
off A3072 Tiverton to Crediton

BOWDEN HOUSE, Totnes Tel: (0803) 863664
Home of the Petersen family
Tudor mansion with 18th-century additions. Contents include: carved
oak overmantel with Bedford crest; 18th- and 19th-century interiors;
armoury display; the British Photographic Museum. Outdoors:
grounds; dovecote; possible 13th-century lock-up.
① £ 𝑘 🗂 ⊒ ✕ AV ⛟ ⊛ M̂ P
off A38 Exeter to Plymouth

CADHAY, Ottery St Mary Tel: (040 481) 2432
Home of Lady William-Powlett
Early Tudor manor house. Contents include: numerous coats of arms
and heraldic frieze; restored Tudor hearths; chimney-piece carvings of
the traditional 'little green man of the woods' figure. Outdoors:
gardens.
◑ £ 𝑘 ⊛ P
off A30 Honiton to Exeter

CHAMBERCOMBE MANOR, Ilfracombe Tel: (0271) 62624
Home of Richard Hayward (The Chambercombe Trust)
Medieval and Tudor manor house. Contents include: private chapel;
secret chamber (the 'Haunted Room'); priest's hole; Tudor and later
furniture; armour. Outdoors: gardens.
◑ £ 𝑘 ⊒ ✕ P
off A399 Ilfracombe to Combe Martin

FURSDON HOUSE, Cadbury Tel: (0392) 860860
Home of David Fursdon
Georgian country house. Contents include: family portraits (including
Grace Fursdon by Lely); 17th-century furniture; family museum;
costume collection. Outdoors: gardens; woodland walks; children's
play area; picnic area.
◑ £ 𝑘 🗂 ⊒ ⊛ 🧺 M̂ ⚏ P
off A3072 Tiverton to Crediton

HARTLAND ABBEY, Bideford Tel: (02374) 559
Home of Sir Hugh Stucley Bt
Medieval abbey with Queen Anne, Georgian and Victorian additions.
Contents include: documents collection; paintings by, among others,
Kneller, Reynolds, Beechey and G.F. Watts; Meissen china; photo-
graphic exhibition from 1857 to 1907. Outdoors: gardens.
◑ ££ 🗂 ⊒ ⊛ P
off A39 Bideford to Bude

HEMERDON HOUSE, Plympton Tel: (0752) 223816
Home of James Woollcombe
Georgian country house. Contents include: paintings by Reynolds and
West Country artists; family memorabilia. Outdoors: gardens
◑ £ 𝑘 ⊛ P 㫈
off A38 Plymouth to Buckfastleigh

POWDERHAM CASTLE, Exeter Tel: (0626) 890243
Home of The Earl of Devon
Late medieval castle with 18th- and 19th-century additions. Contents
include: portraits by Kneller, Reynolds and other (particularly West
Country) artists; 18th-century rosewood bookcases; Regency gilt
furniture; English and Brussels tapestry. Outdoors: garden and
terrace; chapel; parkland with fallow deer.
◑ ££ 🗂 ⊒ ⊛ P 㫈
off A379 Exeter to Dawlish

SAND, Sidbury Tel: (039 57) 230
Home of Lt. Col. Patrick Huyshe
Elizabethan manor house. Contents include: early English fireplace;
heraldic stained glass; family portraits and documents. Outdoors:
gardens; late medieval hall house (Sand Lodge).
◑ £ 𝑘 ⊒ ⊛ P
off A375 Honiton to Sidmouth

TIVERTON CASTLE, Tiverton Tel: (0884) 253200
Home of Mr and Mrs Angus Gordon
Medieval castle with later additions. Contents include: international
clock collection; collection of arms, armour and militaria; family
portraits. Outdoors: gardens.
◑ £ 𝑘 🗂 ⊛ P
in Tiverton, off A373

YOU ARE ADVISED TO CHECK DETAILS BEFORE VISITING A HOUSE

UGBROOKE PARK, Chudleigh Tel: (0626) 852179
Home of the Clifford family
Castellated mansion by Robert Adam. Contents include: Catholic chapel, with original deed and licence; 16th- and 17th- century tapestries; Gillow furniture to Chippendale design; Elizabethan needlework panels; 18th-century embroidered-silk bed hangings; paintings by Siberechts, van Schooten, Huysmans and Lely; bronze by Epstein; collection of military and Diplomatic Corps uniforms. Outdoors: gardens; lakes; wagon drives; map rooms.
◑ £ ⚔ ⌨ ✕ ⚘ ⚑ P ♿
off A38 Exeter to Plymouth

DORSET

ATHELHAMPTON, Dorchester Tel: (0305) 848363
Home of Lady Cooke
Late medieval and early Tudor battlemented house. Contents include: heraldic glass; medieval art (painting, carving, tapestry, metalwork); 17th-century furniture, including Spanish walnut table; chamber organ. Outdoors: gardens with canal and dovecote.
◑ ££ ⎙ ⌨ ✕ ⚘ P ♿
off A35 Dorchester to Bournemouth

EDMONDSHAM HOUSE, Wimborne Tel: (072 54) 207
Home of Mrs Julia Smith
Jacobean house with 18th- and 19th-century additions. Contents include: walnut and mahogany furniture; lace shawls and wedding veil; Monro pistols and dirk. Outdoors: walled garden; garden walks.
◑ £ ⚘ P ♿
off B3087 Cranbourne to Verwood

PARNHAM, Beaminster Tel: (0308) 862204
Home of John Makepeace
Tudor manor house. Contents include: Tudor Great Hall; Strode Bedroom (carved oak overmantel); contemporary furniture from Makepeace workshop; collection of Victorian tools; 1920s Strode Bathroom; John Makepeace Furniture-making Workshop; Museum of Woodcraft. Outdoors: gardens, with topiary and peacocks.
◑ ££ ⎙ ⌨ ✕ ⚘ ⚑ P ♿
off A3066 Bridport to Beaminster

SANDFORD ORCAS MANOR HOUSE, Sherborne
Tel: (096 322) 206
Home of Sir Mervyn Medlycott Bt
Tudor manor house. Contents include: 17th-century stained-glass collection; paintings by Kneller, Gainsborough, Brueghel among others; Elizabethan and Queen Anne furniture. Outdoors: gardens; herb garden; bowling green; woodland.
◑ £ ⚔ ⚘ P
off B3148 Sherborne to Marston Magna

SHERBORNE CASTLE, Sherborne Tel: (0935) 813182
Home of Simon Wingfield Digby
Elizabethan mansion with later additions. Contents include: Strawberry Hill Gothic Library; family portraits; paintings by Van Dyck, Hoppner, Lely, Kneller, Gainsborough, Janssens and others (including Peake's 'Procession of Queen Elizabeth I'); 17th- and 18th-century furniture; porcelain collection; museum (in pre-Elizabethan cellars). Outdoors: gardens; Capability Brown park with lake; 'Raleigh's Seat'; orangery; ruins of old Sherborne Castle.
◑ ££ ⎙ ⌨ ⚒ ⚘ ⚑ P ♿
off A30 Yeovil to Sherborne ⇌ Sherborne

SMEDMORE, Kimmeridge Tel: (0929) 480717
Home of Major and Mrs John Mansel
18th-century manor house. Contents include: 18th-century English, Italian, French and Dutch furniture; paintings by Dutch artists; Dresden, Furstenberg and *Porcelaine de la Reine* china; 18th-century clocks. Outdoors: gardens; museum with doll collection.
◑ £ ⚘ ⚑ P ♿
off A351 Wareham to Swanage

WOLFETON, Dorchester Tel: (0305) 63500
Home of Capt. Nigel Thimbleby
Medieval and Elizabethan manor house. Contents include: Elizabethan plaster ceilings; carved panelling and overmantels. Outdoors: chapel; cider house.
◑ £ ⚔ P
off A37 Dorchester to Yeovil ⇌ Dorchester South and West

CO. DURHAM

AUCKLAND CASTLE, Bishop Auckland Tel: (0388) 604823
Home of the Bishops of Durham (The Church Commissioners)
Ancient palace gothicized by James Wyatt. Contents include: medieval chapel; Gothic throne room; portraits of bishops. Outdoors: park; 18th-century deer house.
◑ ££
in Bishop Auckland, off A688 ⇌ Bishop Auckland

RABY CASTLE, Darlington Tel: (0833) 60202
Home of The Lord Barnard
14th-century castle with later additions. Contents include: medieval Great Kitchen (with Victorian cooking utensils); Servants' Hall; Octagon Drawing Room by William Burn; Barons' Hall; porcelain collection; sporting art collection; portraits and other paintings by Giordano, de Hooch, Van Dyck, Lely, Kneller, Teniers, Reynolds and others; collection of Meissen porcelain birds by Kandler and Kirchner; the 'Greek Slave' (19th-century statue by Hiram Power); 18th- and 19th-century furniture; arms collection; taxidermy collection. Outdoors: gardens, with 200-year-old Ischia fig; deer park; carriage collection; picnic area.
◑ £ ⎙ ⌨ ⚘ P ♿
off A688 Barnard Castle to Bishop Auckland

ROKEBY PARK, Barnard Castle
Home of the Morritt family
Palladian country house. Contents include: the Pellegrini 'Venus' and other pictures; family portraits; collection of Morritt needlework pictures; Walter Scott memorabilia; giant Minton vases. Outdoors: 18th-century pleasure grounds.
◑ £ P
off A66 Scotch Corner to Brough

EAST SUSSEX

FIRLE PLACE, Lewes Tel: (079 159) 335
Home of The Viscount Gage
Mainly Georgian manor house. Contents include: extensive collection of paintings by (among others) Van Dyck, Fra Bartolomeo, Correggio, Rubens, Zoffany, Gainsborough, Reynolds, Hoppner, Kneller and Tintoretto; collection of Sèvres porcelain; English and French furniture; 15th-century Book of Hours and 16th-century Sarum Missal; American War of Independence mementoes. Outdoors: gardens, downland walks.
◑ ££ ⚔ ⎙ ⌨ ✕ ⚘ P
off A27 Lewes to Eastbourne

YOU ARE ADVISED TO CHECK DETAILS BEFORE VISITING A HOUSE

GLYNDE PLACE, Lewes Tel: (079 159) 248
Home of The Viscount Hampden
Elizabethan manor house. Contents include: bronzes by Francesco Bertos; paintings by Kneller, Zoffany, Verbruggen and others; household accounts of John of Gaunt; contemporary maps of the Battle of the Armada; William and Mary and Georgian furniture; Georgian silver; Edwardian bathroom with original fittings; Crown Derby and Meissen china. Outdoors: gardens and landscaped park.
◗ £ ➘ P
off A27 Lewes to Eastbourne

GREAT DIXTER, Northiam Tel: (07974) 3160
Home of the Lloyd family
Medieval manor house restored by Sir Edwin Lutyens. Contents include: timbered great hall; solar with original fireplace; needlework (partly the work of the Lloyd family). Outdoors: gardens tended by Christopher Lloyd; garden centre.
◔ ££ ✗ ⬦ ⊛ P
off A28 Hastings to Tenterden

HAREMERE HALL, Etchingham Tel: (058 081) 245
Home of Jacqueline, Lady Killearn
17th-century mansion. Contents include: 17th-century panelling, carvings, staircase; the Prince Regent's room. Outdoors: gardens; working shire horses.
◗ £ ⬦ ➘ ⊛ P ♿
off A265 Heathfield to Hurst Green ≷ Etchingham

MICHELHAM PRIORY, Hailsham Tel: (0323) 844224
The Sussex Archaeological Society
Restored remains of 13th-century Augustinian Priory. Displays of monastic life; excavated artefacts; musical instrument collection; 18th- and 19th-century needlework samplers; the Turner Doll's House. Outdoors: forge museum; display of Sussex wagons and ploughs; working watermill; 'physic garden'.
① £ ✗ ⬦ ▦ ➘ ✗ ⊛ ⬙ ⌂ P ♿
off A22 London to Eastbourne

ESSEX
CASTLE HOUSE, Dedham Tel: (0206) 322127
Home of the late Sir Alfred Munnings
House where artist Sir Alfred Munnings RA lived. Contents include: collection of paintings; drawings; sketches of the artist. Outdoors: gardens.
◗ £ P
in Dedham, off A12

HEDINGHAM CASTLE, Halstead Tel: (0787) 60261
The Hon. Thomas Lindsay
Norman keep. Contents include: original Norman arches and fireplace.
① £ ⬦ ➘ P
off A604 Sible Hedingham to Sudbury

LAYER MARNEY TOWER, Colchester Tel: (0206) 330202
Home of Major and Mrs Gerald Charrington
Early Renaissance gatehouse. Contents include: original terracotta mouldings; exhibitions of local history. Outdoors: terraces; church and gardens.
◗ £ ✗ ➘ ⊛ P
off B1022 Colchester to Maldon

ST OSYTH'S PRIORY, St Osyth Tel: (0255) 820492
Home of Somerset de Chair
15th-century gatehouse. Contents include: paintings by George Stubbs. Outdoors: topiary; gardens.
① £ P
off A133 Frinton to Colchester

GLOUCESTERSHIRE
BERKELEY CASTLE, Berkeley Tel: (0453) 810332
Home of Mr and Mrs R.J.G. Berkeley
Medieval castle. Contents include: 17th-century ebony furniture; paintings by Stubbs, Dankerts, Millais, Gainsborough, Hoppner, Van Dyck, Reynolds, Kneller and others; comprehensive collection of English furniture; Elizabethan embroidery; early Brussels tapestries; Godwin Cup, said to have belonged to Earl Godwin, father of King Harold. Outdoors: gardens, bowling alley, free-flight butterfly house, 18th-century kennels of the Berkeley Hunt.
◔ ££ ➘ ✗ ⬦ ⊛ P
in Berkeley, off M5 (junction 14)

CHAVENAGE, Tetbury Tel: (0666) 52329
Home of David Lowsley-Williams
16th-century Cotswold manor house. Contents include: medieval and 17th-century stained glass; original patched panelling; inlaid nine men's morris table; 1904 ballroom; early 17th-century tapestries in their original settings. Outdoors: gardens; chapel.
◔ £ ✗ ⊛ ♿
off B4014 Tetbury to Nailsworth

STANWAY HOUSE, Broadway Tel: (038 673) 469
Home of The Lord and Lady Neidpath
Elizabethan manor house. Contents include: 17th-century, Sheraton and Chippendale furniture; 17th-century shuffleboard table; portraits by Romney, Raeburn, Lord Leighton and others; George II giltwood mirrors. Outdoors: gardens; memorial pyramid; dog cemetery.
◗ £ ➘ ⊛ P
off A46 Cheltenham to Broadway

SUDELEY CASTLE, Winchcombe Tel: (0242) 602308
Home of The Lady Ashcombe
Medieval castle, restored in 19th century. Contents include: 'Katherine Parr's Nursery'; Katherine Parr memorabilia, including prayerbook; paintings by Rubens, Van Dyck, Constable, Turner and other artists (works include Eworth's 'Tudor Succession'); Sheldon tapestry; falcon mews with museum; craft workshops with exhibition. Outdoors: gardens; St Mary's Church; ruined banqueting hall; rustic adventure playground; falconry displays.
① ££ ⬦ ➘ ✗ ⬦ ⊛ ⬙ P
off A46 Cheltenham to Stratford-upon-Avon

HAMPSHIRE
ALRESFORD HOUSE, Alresford Tel: (096 273) 2843
Home of Mr and Mrs Peter Constable-Maxwell
18th-century country house. Contents include: rococo ceiling in Morning Room; private Catholic chapel; 15th-century Italian marble chimney-piece. Outdoors: gardens; beechwoods in park, French cannon.
◗ £ ✗ ➘ ⊛ P
off A31 Winchester to Alton

YOU ARE ADVISED TO CHECK DETAILS BEFORE VISITING A HOUSE

AVINGTON PARK, Winchester Tel: (0962) 78202
Home of Col. John Hickson
Country mansion, mainly 17th/18th century. Contents include: Great Saloon (plasterwork and painted decoration); library; grand staircase; paintings; French and English furniture; Bohemian glass; shell collection; orangery. Outdoors: Georgian brick church.
◑ £ ✗ ⊟ ❀ P
in Itchen Abbas, off B3047

BEAULIEU PALACE HOUSE AND ABBEY, Brockenhurst
Tel: (0590) 612345
Home of The Lord Montagu of Beaulieu
Restored medieval monastery. Contents include: collection of paintings by Canaletto's pupil Joli; Montagu and Buccleuch family portraits and mementoes; family Coronation robes; Victorian travellers' equipment. Outdoors: gardens; National Motor Museum; exhibition of monastic life; high level monorail; special events and outdoor exhibition areas.
○ £££ ⬠ ⊟ ✗ AV ⛵ M̂ P ♿
off B3054 Brockenhurst to Hythe

BREAMORE HOUSE, Fordingbridge Tel: (0725) 22270
Home of Sir Westrow Hulse
Elizabethan manor house. Contents include: paintings of the 17th- and 18th-century Dutch School; portraits by Van Dyck, Kneller and others; Renaissance fireplaces and overmantels; Brussels tapestries. Outdoors: gardens; modern maze; carriage museum; museum of countryside crafts and farm machinery.
◑ ££ ✗ ⬠ ⊟ ⛵ ❀ M̂ P
off A338 Fordingbridge to Salisbury

BROADLANDS, Romsey Tel: (0794) 516878
Home of The Lord Romsey
Georgian mansion, on earlier base. Contents include: classical statuary collection; paintings by Van Dyck, Lely, Reynolds, Romney, Raeburn, Hoppner, Lawrence and others (including 'The Iron Forge' by Joseph Wright); 18th-century plasterwork; Sèvres basin and ewer, formerly owned by Marie Antoinette; model ship collection. Outdoors: grounds; the Mountbatten Exhibition (in stable block); ornamental dairy (now visitor reception centre).
◑ £££ ⬠ ⊟ ✗ AV ⛵ ❀ M̂ P ♿
off A31 Romsey to Ringwood

STANSTED PARK, Rowlands Castle Tel: (0705) 412265
Home of The Earl of Bessborough (The Stansted Park Foundation)
Edwardian mansion. Contents include: collection of Dutch bird paintings; Brussels tapestries; Dutch, Italian, French and English furniture; Chinese and Japanese Imari porcelain; paintings by, among others, Lely, Dirk Dalens, Van Loo, and Zuccharo. Outdoors: gardens; picnic area; theatre museum; small playground; arboretum.
◐ £ ⬠ ⊟ ❀ ⋔ P
off A3 Guildford to Portsmouth ⇌ Rowlands Castle

HEREFORD & WORCESTER
BRETFORTON MANOR, Evesham Tel: (0386) 830216
Home of Derek Chapman
Tudor manor house, built on site of earlier monastery. Contents include: oak panelling; priest's hole; banqueting hall; 18th- and 19th-century cast-iron fireplaces. Outdoors: village stocks (dated 1360), dovecote; barn with horse-drawn cider mill; lake; brook with ruined mill; stables; paddocks.
○ £ ⬠ ⊟ ❀ P ♿
off B4035 Evesham to Weston sub-Edge

BURTON COURT, Eardisland Tel: (054 47) 231
Home of Lt. Cdr and Mrs Robert Simpson
14th-century Great Hall with later additions. Contents include: overmantel dated 1654; mainly Victorian furniture; costume exhibition, changed annually. Outdoors: gardens, fruit gardens.
◑ £ ✗
off A44 Leominster to Kington

EASTNOR CASTLE, Ledbury Tel: (0531) 2305
Home of James Hervey Bathurst
Gothic castle, early 19th century. Contents include: Gothic drawing room designed by Pugin; armour collection; Brussels tapestries; family portraits and other paintings (artists include Van Dyck, Lely, Reynolds, Romney, Salvator Rosa, G.F. Watts and others); carving by Grinling Gibbons; photographs by Julia Margaret Cameron. Outdoors: gardens; arboretum; deer park; lakes; views of the Malvern Hills.
◑ £ ⬠ ⊟ ❀ ♠ P
off A438 Hereford to Tewkesbury

ELGAR'S BIRTHPLACE, Lower Broadheath Tel: (0905 66) 224
Home of the late Sir Edward Elgar
Cottage where the composer Sir Edward Elgar was born. Contents include: composer's desk, family photographs, manuscripts and memorabilia. Outdoors: cottage garden.
◑ £ ⬠ ❀ P
off A44 Worcester to Bromyard

HELLEN'S, Much Marcle Tel: (0531) 84668
Home of Major Malcolm Munthe (The Pennington-Mellor-Munthe Trust)
Medieval castle with later additions. Contents include: courtroom (banqueting hall) with 'Black Prince' fireplace and stone table; Mehettable Walwyn's room; paintings by Tintoretto, Perugino, Van Dyck and others; Flemish tapestry (family heirloom of Dr Axel Munthe). Outdoors: gardens.
◑ £ ✗ ❀ P
off A449 Ledbury to Ross-on-Wye

LITTLE MALVERN COURT, Great Malvern Tel: (0684) 892988
Home of Mr and Mrs Berington
Medieval priory, with Tudor and later additions. Contents include: 14th-century monastic refectory (Prior's Hall) with timbered roof.
◑ £ ✗ ❀
off A4104 Great Malvern to Upton-on-Severn

YOU ARE ADVISED TO CHECK DETAILS BEFORE VISITING A HOUSE

MOCCAS COURT, Moccas Tel: (09817) 381
Home of R.T.G. Chester-Master (The Baunton Trust)
Georgian mansion. Contents include: 17th- and 18th-century Oriental porcelain; Hepplewhite and Chippendale furniture. Outdoors: gardens; fernery; water-garden.
❶ £ ❀ P
off B4352 Hereford to Hay-on-Wye

SUFTON COURT, Mordiford Tel: (043 273) 268
Home of Major and Mrs James Hereford
Late 18th-century Palladian house. Contents include: Repton's 'Red Book' of his landscaping work; pardon issued by Edward III and a document of protection by Richard II. Outdoors: gardens.
❶ £ ❀
off B4224 Hereford to Fownhope

HERTFORDSHIRE
GORHAMBURY, St Albans Tel: (0727) 54051
Home of The Earl of Verulam
Georgian mansion. Contents include: five centuries of family portraits (Bacons and Grimstons); books and other possessions of Lord Chancellor Bacon: Tudor windows of enamelled glass; four paintings by Sir Nathaniel Bacon (out of eight in existence). Outdoors: gardens.
❶ £ ⚲ ❀ P
off A414 St Albans to Redbourn

KNEBWORTH HOUSE, Stevenage Tel: (0438) 812661
Home of The Lord Cobbold
19th-century Gothic castle on earlier base. Contents include: 17th-century banqueting hall; State Drawing Room; Bulwer Lytton memorabilia; family portraits; paintings by Gheeraerts, Maclise, Winston Churchill and others; Mary Queen of Scots' crucifix. Outdoors: gardens; British Raj museum; narrow gauge steam railway and museum; adventure playground.
❶ ££ ⚲ ⬡ ➾ ✕ AV ❀ M̂ ⌂ P
off A1(M) (junction 7)

MOOR PARK MANSION, Rickmansworth Tel: (0923) 776611
Moor Park Golf Club
Palladian house by Leoni. Contents include: decoration by Verrio, Sleker and others. Outdoors: golf course.
❶ £ ⚲ P
in Rickmansworth, off A412

ISLE OF WIGHT
NUNWELL HOUSE, Brading Tel: (0983) 407240
Home of Col. and Mrs J. A. Aylmer
Jacobean country house, with later additions. Contents include: family portraits and other paintings; King Charles's room; collection of fans; family military museum. Outdoors: gardens; arboretum; children's nature walk.
❶ £ ⚲ ⬡ ➾ ✕ ➷ ❀ ⬟ ⚘ M̂ P
off A3055 Ryde to Shanklin ⇌ Brading

KENT
BOUGHTON MONCHELSEA PLACE, Maidstone
Tel: (0622) 43120
Home of Michael Winch
Elizabethan manor house with Regency additions. Contents include: manorial records since 1570; Mortlake tapestries; 18th-century and Regency furniture; fragmented 17th-century German stained glass. Outdoors: gardens; carriage and farm implements displays; fine views over the Weald.
❶ £ ⚲ ⬡ ➾ ✕ ➷ ❀ P
off B2163 West Farleigh to Chart Corner

CHIDDINGSTONE CASTLE, Edenbridge Tel: (0892) 870347
Home of the Misses Eldridge (The Denys Eyre Bower Trust)
Neo-Gothic castle. Contents include: Japanese collections (armour and weapons, lacquer, Haniwa figures; domestic and ornamental ironwork); Royal Stuart collections (medals, miniatures, Lely's portrait of Nell Gwynne, letters from Mary Queen of Scots and others, drinking vessel used by Prince Charles Edward, reliquary containing part of James II's heart); Egyptian collections (including probable head of Queen Cleopatra). Outdoors: grounds with lake, caves and orangery.
❶ ££ ⬡ ➾ ❀ P
off B2027 Edenbridge to Tonbridge ⇌ Penshurst

FINCHCOCKS, Goudhurst Tel: (0580) 211702
Home of Richard Burnett
Early Georgian mansion. Contents include: the Finchcocks Collection of 70 harpsichords, spinets, clavichords, chamber organs and early pianos. Outdoors: gardens; park; extensive views over Weald.
❶ ££ ⬡ ➾ ✕ ➷ ❀ M̂ P
A262 Tunbridge Wells to Goudhurst

GODINTON PARK, Ashford Tel: (0233) 20773
Home of Alan Wyndham Green
Medieval hall, with later additions. Contents include: medieval hall; Great Chamber with 'musketeer frieze'; carved staircase and overmantels; chimney-pieces of carved Bethersden marble (only found locally); paintings by Lely, Kneller and others; family portraits; porcelain collections. Outdoors: gardens; topiary.
❶ £ ⚲ ❀ P
off A20 Maidstone to Ashford

HEVER CASTLE, Edenbridge Tel: (0732) 865224
Broadland Properties Ltd
Medieval moated manor house. Contents include: mementoes of Anne Boleyn; paintings by and after Holbein; English, French and Italian furniture; Persian carpets; Brussels tapestries; collection of English porcelain; Astor family memorabilia including letters from Sir Winston Churchill. Outdoors: Italian garden with classical statuary and sculpture; topiary and maze; fountains, cascades and lake; rose gardens; rhododendron walk; open air theatre season; regimental museum.
❶ £££ ⬡ ➾ ✕ ❀ M̂ ⌂ P ♿
off B2026 Edenbridge to Hartfield; M25 (junction 6); M23 (junction 10) ⇌ Hever

LEEDS CASTLE, Maidstone Tel: (0622) 65400
The Leeds Castle Foundation
Medieval castle, with later additions. Contents include: 13th-century gatehouse and stronghold (the Gloriette); Henry VIII banqueting hall; 16th-century woodwork; Impressionist art collection (paintings by Degas, Pissarro and others); further paintings by Cranach, Tiepolo and others; French and English furniture; tapestries; mother-of-pearl collection; 'les chambres de la Reine' (reconstructions of medieval queen's apartments); dog collar museum. Outdoors: gardens; lake; duckery; vineyard; aviaries; grotto.
◐ £££ ▢ ☕ ✕ ❀ ➴ M̂ P ♿
off B2163 London to Folkestone ⇌ Bearsted or Hollingbourne

QUEX PARK, Birchington Tel: (0843) 42168
Home of Christopher Powell-Cotton (Trustees of the Powell-Cotton Museum)
Georgian mansion with adjoining ethnographic museum. Contents of house include: Kashmir walnut carved panelling; Indian and Chinese furniture and embroideries; German, Dutch and English porcelain. Museum: collection of 19th-century big game hunter, Major Powell-Cotton. Outdoors: gardens; collection of cannon; parkland walks.
◑ £ ▢ ☕ ♞ ❀ M̂ P
off A28 Margate to Canterbury ⇌ Birchington

RIVERHILL HOUSE, Sevenoaks Tel: (0732) 452557
Home of Mrs David Rogers
18th-century mansion. Contents include: engraving and painting of John Rogers, Protestant martyr; 17th-century oak Bible box; botanic library and records; Mogul ebony ivory-inlaid cabinet; Charles II high chair. Outdoors: rose walk; terraces; pleasure grounds.
◑ £ ▢ ☕ ❀ P
off A225 Sevenoaks to Tonbridge

SALTWOOD CASTLE, Hythe Tel: (0303) 67190
Home of the Hon. Alan Clark
Medieval castle. Contents include: wooden Saxon altar; weapons and armour: torture chamber (with stocks); archaeological finds; Lord Clark's study (writer of *Civilisation* TV series). Outdoors: gardens; battlement walk.
◕ £ ▢ ☕ ❀ P
off A20 Ashford to Folkestone ⇌ Sandling

SQUERRYES COURT, Westerham Tel: (0959) 62345
Home of John Warde
17th-century country house. Contents include: Wolfe portraits and other memorabilia; Soho tapestries; Chinese armorial dinner service (150 pieces); family portraits and other pictures (artists include Rubens, Van Dyck, Stubbs, Van der Helst and Romney); Queen Anne settees. Outdoors: gardens, with Wolfe Cenotaph.
◑ ££ ☕ ❀ P
off A25 Reigate to Sevenoaks

LANCASHIRE
BROWSHOLME HALL, Clitheroe Tel: (025 486) 330
Home of the Parker family
Tudor house, with later additions. Contents include: Turner watercolour of the house; family portraits and other paintings; 17th-century oak furniture; Jacobite relics: Regency furniture. Outdoors: gardens.
◑ £ 🚶 ▢ ❀ P ♿
off B6243 Bashall Eaves to Whitewell

HOGHTON TOWER, Preston Tel: (025 485) 2986
Home of Sir Bernard de Hoghton Bt
Elizabethan manor house. Contents include: Tudor and Jacobean furniture (including the 'Sir Loin' table); Gillow panelling; family portraits by Van Dyck and others; relics of King James I's visit; priest's hole; dolls' house museum; teapot exhibition. Outdoors: gardens, farm.
◑ ££ 🚶 ▢ ☕ ✕ AV ♞ ❀ M̂ P
off A675 Bolton to Preston ⇌ Pleasington

LEIGHTON HALL, Carnforth Tel: (0524) 734474
Home of Mr and Mrs Richard Gillow Reynolds
Georgian mansion with 19th-century Gothic façade. Contents include: collection of furniture by Gillow; paintings by Morland, Jordaens, Edward Seago. Outdoors: gardens, shrubbery and woodland walks; collection of birds of prey, flown daily.
◔ £ 🚶 ▢ ☕ ✕ ❀ P ♿
off A6 Carnforth to Milnthorpe ⇌ Silverdale

LEICESTERSHIRE
ROCKINGHAM CASTLE, Corby Tel: (053 6) 770 240
Home of Cdr Michael Saunders Watson
Medieval castle complex with Tudor and other additions. Contents include: Great Hall (with Elizabethan portraits); Tudor service apartments (Kitchen, Servants' Hall); the Street (laundry, brewhouse, bakery, stores, dairy etc); Long Gallery; family portraits and other paintings (artists include Zoffany, Constable, Augustus John, Sickert); medieval iron chests; porcelain collection; 'Walker's House' (with exhibition area). Outdoors: gardens (with 'elephant' yew hedge).
◑ ££ ▢ ☕ ♞ ❀ P
off A6003 Kettering to Oakham

STANFORD HALL, Lutterworth Tel: (0788) 860250
Home of The Lady Braye
William and Mary mansion. Contents include: the Cardinal Duke of York collection (Royal Stuart relics, formerly owned by the last of their line); family portraits and other paintings by Van Dyck, Jansen, Kneller and others; costume collection; tapestries; library with medieval and later documents. Outdoors: rose gardens; Pilcher Aviation Museum (with 'Hawk' replica); motorcycle museum; craft centre most Sundays; nature trail.
◑ £ 🚶 ▢ ☕ ❀ ✿ M̂ P ♿
off B5414 Rugby to Market Harborough; M1 (junctions 18 and 20), M6 (junction 1).

LINCOLNSHIRE
AUBOURN HALL, Lincoln Tel: (052 285) 270
Home of H.N. Nevile
Tudor manor house. Contents include: 17th-century carved staircase with dog gate; early oak panelling. Outdoors: park.
◕ £ 🚶 P
off A46 Newark to Lincoln

YOU ARE ADVISED TO CHECK DETAILS BEFORE VISITING A HOUSE

BELVOIR CASTLE, Nr Grantham Tel: (0476) 870262
Home of The Duke of Rutland
19th-century Gothic castle. Contents include: pictures by Van Dyck, Holbein, Hoppner, Reynolds, Gainsborough, and Gaspard and Nicholas Poussin; Gobelins and Mortlake tapestries; the regimental museum of the 17th/21st Lancers. Outdoors: gardens; statues by Cibber; adventure playground; special events in season.
◐ ££ 🗂 ⊒ ✕ ⊛ 🦋 ⋔ P ⅏
in Belvoir, off A607 Melton Mowbray to Grantham

BURGHLEY HOUSE, Stamford Tel: (0780) 52451
Home of Lady Victoria Leatham (The Burghley House Preservation Trust)
Elizabethan palace, with later interiors. Contents include: ceilings by Verrio and Laguerre; tapestries; paintings by Guido Reni, Peter Breughel the Younger, Veronese, Kneller, Lely, Gainsborough, Angelica Kauffmann, Gheeraerts, Van der Mijn, and others; collection of Chinese snuff bottles; 17th-century and 18th-century furniture; collection of Japanese ceramics. Outdoors: deer park, with lake and 'Lion Bridge' by Capability Brown.
① ££ 𝄞 🗂 ⊒ ✕ 🅼 P ⅏
off B1443 Stamford to Barnack

DODDINGTON HALL, Lincoln Tel: (0522) 694308
Home of Mr and Mrs Antony Jarvis
Elizabethan mansion. Contents include: wholly Georgian interior; 18th- and 19th-century Chinese and Japanese porcelain; Brussels tapestries; early Dutch and English furniture; portraits by Reynolds and others; 17th- and 18th-century nautical paintings; collection of English glass; pictures, sketches and woodcarvings by George Jarvis. Outdoors: walled Elizabethan garden; herb garden; croquet lawn; nature trail, collection of historic wagons
◐ ££ 🗂 ⊒ ✕ ⅋ 🦋 P ⅏
in Doddington, off B1190

FULBECK HALL Tel: (0400) 72205
Home of Mr and Mrs Michael Fry
18th-century house with later additions. Contents include: pictures by Zuccarelli, Nazzari, Lorimer and others; Coalport china; oriental porcelain. Outdoors: gardens.
◐ £ ⊛ 🦋 P ⅏
off A607 Grantham to Lincoln

GRIMSTHORPE CASTLE, Bourne Tel: (077832) 205
Home of The Lady Willoughby d'Eresby (Grimsthorpe and Drummond Castle Trust Ltd)
Tudor mansion on medieval base, with later additions. Contents include: family portraits (including two of Katherine, Duchess of Suffolk); tapestries; furniture. Outdoors: gardens, nature trails.
◐ £ ⊒ ⊛ P ⅏
off A151 Colsterworth to Bourne

HARLAXTON MANOR, Grantham Tel: (0476) 64541
University of Evansville, Indiana
Victorian Gothic mansion. Contents include: neo-Baroque friezes, ceilings and decorations; Victorian stained glass; cedar staircase. Outdoors: gardens, the 'lions of Harlaxton'.
◐ ££ 🗂 ⊒ ✕ ⊛ P
off A607 Melton Mowbray to Grantham

HARRINGTON HALL, Spilsby Tel: (0790) 52281
Home of Lady Maitland
17th-century manor house on earlier base. Contents include: the Maitland collection (pictures, furniture and porcelain, from Loughton Hall, Essex); display of weapons; morning room (connections with Tennyson and 'Maud'). Outdoors: gardens, garden centre.
◐ £ 𝄞 ⅏ ⊛ P ⅏
off A158 Horncastle to Skegness.

LONDON
SOUTHSIDE HOUSE, Wimbledon, London SW18
Tel: 01 947 2491
Home of Major Malcolm Munthe (The Pennington-Mellor-Munthe Trust)
17th-century house. Contents include: family portraits and other pictures (artists include Van Dyck, Hogarth, Romney, Frith, Burne-Jones, Viking Munthe); baroque hall; Prince of Wales Room (with cabinet of curiosities); Music Room, with portrait of Emma Hamilton.
◐ (Winter) ££ 𝄞
in Wimbledon, off A219 ⇌ Wimbledon

SYON HOUSE, Brentford Tel: 01 560 0881
Home of The Duke of Northumberland
16th-century battlemented mansion remodelled by Robert Adam. Contents include: furniture by Robert Adam; marble statues in Roman style; frieze panels by Casali; paintings by Lely, Huysmans, Van Dyck, Gainsborough, Zuccarelli, Reynolds, Rubens and others; 17th-century map by Moses Glover. Outdoors: gardens, garden centre; conservatory by Paxton; motor museum of British cars; art centre; butterfly house.
◐ £ 🗂 ⊒ ✕ ⅏ ⊛ 🅼 P
off A4 London to Staines ⇌ Brentford

MERSEYSIDE
MEOLS HALL, Southport Tel: (0704) 28171
Home of the Hesketh family
17th-century mansion. Contents include: Charles II Coronation chairs; paintings by Breughel, Tillemans, Poussin, van Utrecht. Outdoors: gardens.
◐ £ 𝄞 ⊒ ⊛ P
off A570 Southport to Ormskirk

NORFOLK
BEESTON HALL, Beeston St Lawrence Tel: (0692) 630771
Home of Sir Ronald Preston Bt
Georgian mansion in early Gothic Revival style. Contents include: pre-revolutionary Russia memorabilia; 18th- and 19th-century English, German, Russian and Japanese furniture; Venetian chandelier. Outdoors: gardens, wine cellars.
◐ £ 🗂 ⊒ ⊛ 🦋 P
off A1151 Wroxham to Stalham

┌───┐
│ YOU ARE ADVISED TO CHECK DETAILS BEFORE VISITING A HOUSE │
└───┘

EUSTON HALL, Thetford Tel: (0842) 66366
Home of The Duke of Grafton
17th-century hall rebuilt in the 18th century. Contents include: royal and other court portraits by Lely, Reynolds, Van Dyck and others: 'Mares and Foals' by Stubbs; doll collection; 17th-century Spanish and English furniture. Outdoors: gardens; pleasure grounds; temple designed by William Kent.

◑ £ ⌂ ▱ ☕ ❋ P

off A1088 Thetford to Ixworth

HOLKHAM HALL, Wells-next-the-Sea Tel: (0328) 710733
Home of The Viscount Coke
18th-century Palladian mansion. Contents include: ceilings from designs by Inigo Jones; ancient Greek statuary; paintings by Rubens, Van Dyck, Nicholas and Gaspard Poussin and Gainsborough, among others; furniture designed by William Kent, Brussels and Mortlake tapestries; original Genoa velvet upholstery; restored kitchen. Outdoors: gardens; pottery; 'Bygones' collection: Holkham Great Barn.

◑ £ ⌂ ▱ ☕ ❋ P ♿

off A149 Wells to Hunstanton

HOUGHTON HALL, King's Lynn Tel: (048 522) 569
Home of The Marquess of Cholmondeley
18th-century Palladian mansion. Contents include: interiors by William Kent; original mahogany Great Staircase: chiaroscuro murals; Grinling Gibbons carvings; Delft china; Sèvres porcelain; Brussels and Mortlake tapestries; 18th-century Spitalfields silk hangings; paintings by Van Loo, Kneller, Oudry, Zoffany, Reynolds, Van der Velde, Sargent and others; busts and reliefs by Rysbrack; Chinese Chippendale and other lacquer furniture; collection of miniature soldiers. Outdoors: stables with heavy horses and Shetland ponies; harness room; parkland walks.

◑ ££ ⌂ ▱ ✗ Ⓜ ▥ P ♿

off A148 King's Lynn to Fakenham

OAKLEIGH HOUSE, Swaffham Tel: (0760) 24280
Home of William Holliday
Elizabethan house with Georgian façade. Contents include: early 17th-century staircase; Georgian interiors; Nursery, with Victorian and later toys; glass paperweight collection. Outdoors: gardens.

◑ £ ▱ ❋

in Swaffham, off A47

ST FAITH'S PRIORY, Horsham St Faith Tel: (0603) 898093
Home of Mr and Mrs David Ashton
Refectory wing of medieval Benedictine priory. Contents include: 12th-century medieval wall-paintings; medieval tiles; holy water stoup. Outdoors: gardens.

◑ £ ⚑ ⌂ ▱ ❋

off A140 Norwich to Cromer

NORTHAMPTONSHIRE
BOUGHTON HOUSE, Kettering Tel: (0536) 82248
Home of The Duke of Buccleuch and Queensberry
17th-century mansion, with strong French influence. Contents include: Mortlake tapestries; Versailles writing table; paintings by Murillo, El Greco, Batoni, Carracci, Teniers, Kneller and others; wall and ceiling paintings by Chéron; furniture by Boulle and others; carpets. Outdoors: gardens, adventure playground, nature trail.

◑ ££ ⌂ ▱ AV ⚘ ❋ ✿ ▥ P ♿

off A43 Kettering to Stamford

DEENE PARK, Corby Tel: (078 085) 278
Home of Edmund Brudenell
Large Tudor country house. Contents include: Charge of the Light Brigade memorabilia; 16th-century Nonsuch chest; portraits by Reynolds and Van Dyck; 17th-century Dutch and 18th-century French furniture. Outdoors: old-fashioned rose garden; wooden bridges in the Chinese style; Victorian summerhouse.

◑ ££ ⌂ ▱ ✗ ❋ P ♿

off A43 Kettering to Stamford

ELTON HALL, Nr Peterborough Tel: (083 24) 468
Home of Mr and Mrs William Proby
17th-century house with later additions. Contents include: paintings by Gainsborough, Reynolds, Constable, Millais; Henry VIII's prayer book; Louis XVI furniture; 17th-century Japanese lacquer work. Outdoors: Victorian rose garden; Victorian state coach.

◑ ££ ⚑ ⌂ ▱ ⚘ ❋ P

off A605 Oundle to Peterborough

HINWICK HOUSE, Wellingborough Tel: (0933) 53624
Home of R.M. Orlebar
Queen Anne house. Contents include: paintings by Van Dyck, Lely, Kneller; lace; tapestries and needlework; porcelain; costume collection (1840–1940). Outdoors: gardens.

◑ £ ⚑ P

off A6 Rushden to Bedford

LAMPORT HALL, Northampton Tel: (060 128) 272
The Lamport Hall Trust
17th-century mansion, with later additions. Contents include: High (State) Room; 17th-century plasterwork; family portraits and other paintings (artists include Guido Reni, Van Dyck, Lely); Venetian and Flemish cabinets; King Charles I's Bible; England's oldest garden gnome; 18th- and 19th-century furniture. Outdoors: gardens, with Sir Charles Isham's rockery.

◑ £ ⌂ ▱ ⚘ ❋ P ♿

on A508 Northampton to Market Harborough

SOUTHWICK HALL, Oundle Tel: (0832) 74064
Home of Christopher Capron
Medieval manor house with later additions. Contents include: 18th-century and Regency chimney-pieces and fireplaces; Elizabethan barrel-roofed bedroom. Outdoors: gardens; exhibitions of Victorian and Edwardian artefacts and costume, local bygones and musical instruments.

◑ £ ⚑ ▱ ❋ P

off A605 Oundle to Peterborough

YOU ARE ADVISED TO CHECK DETAILS BEFORE VISITING A HOUSE

NORTHUMBERLAND

ALNWICK CASTLE, Alnwick Tel: (0665) 602207
Home of The Duke and Duchess of Northumberland
Medieval border fortress with 18th- and 19th-century additions. Contents include: marble grand staircase; Venetian mosaic pavement; paintings by Canaletto, Tintoretto, Titian, Sebastian del Piombo, Palma Vecchio, Van Dyck and Turner, among others; Italian sculptures; display of Napoleonic War volunteer weapons; library of 16,000 volumes. Outdoors: park landscaped by Capability Brown; bridge by Robert Adam over the River Aln; museum of antiquities; regimental museum of the Royal Northumberland Fusiliers.
◑ £ 🗂 Ⓜ P
in Alnwick, off A1

BAMBURGH CASTLE, Bamburgh Tel: (06684) 208
Home of The Lady Armstrong
Norman castle, with later additions and restorations. Contents include: Saxon well; the 'Bamburgh Beast' (mythical animal in Anglo-Saxon goldwork, found at the castle); collections of weapons and armour; paintings by Kneller and others; ornaments by Fabergé; museum of industrial archaeology; porcelain collections. Outdoors: view across Northumbrian sands to Lindisfarne.
◑ £ 🗂 ⊡ ✕ Ⓜ ら
in Bamburgh, off B1341

CHILLINGHAM CASTLE, Wooler Tel: (06685) 359
Home of Sir Humphry Wakefield Bt
Late medieval castle. Contents include: dungeons; priestholes; Elizabethan long gallery; early English oak and walnut furniture; tapestries; 16th-century documents. Outdoors: gardens, museum, antique shop, woodland walks.
◑ £ 🗂 ⊡ ✕ ✿ ⚒ Ⓜ P ら
off B6348 Wooler to Bellshill

PRESTON TOWER, Chathill Tel: (066 589) 227
Major T.H. Baker-Cresswell
14th-century pele tower. Contents include: turret rooms with reconstruction of contemporary living conditions; displays of historic and local interest.
○ £ P
off A1 Alnwick to Berwick-upon-Tweed

NORTH HUMBERSIDE

BURTON CONSTABLE HALL, Kingston-on-Hull
Tel: (0964) 562400
Home of John Chichester-Constable
Elizabethan country mansion, with later additions. Contents include: collection of 18th-century scientific instruments; 17th- and 18th-century furniture; 18th-century 'flying' (cantilevered) staircase; family portraits and other paintings; contemporary drawings and designs for the 18th-century alterations. Outdoors: gardens, carriage museum, lakes, playground.
◑ £ 🗂 ⊡ ✕ ⚘ ✿ Ⓜ P ら
off B1238 Hull to Aldbrough

CARLTON TOWERS, Goole Tel: (0405) 861662
Home of The Duke of Norfolk
Victorian country house. Contents include: Dutch, English and French furniture; Victorian stained glass; collection of bronze and marble urns; priest's hiding-hole; extensive interiors and furnishings by John Francis Bentley; linenfold panelling; collection of paintings, predominantly on Catholic themes; early Worcester and other English china. Outdoors: gardens, rose garden.
◑ £ 🗂 ⊡ ✿
off A1041 Snaith to Selby

SLEDMERE HOUSE, Driffield Tel: (0377) 86208
Home of Sir Tatton Sykes Bt
18th-century country mansion. Contents include: Cantonese enamel table; Chinese Chippendale chairs; family portraits; paintings by Gheeraerts, Romney, Lawrence and others; plasterwork to 18th-century designs by Joseph Rose; Chinese armorial dinner and tea services; 'Turkish Room'; Library. Outdoors: gardens; stables; park by Capability Brown.
◑ £ 🗂 ⊡ ✕ ✿ P ら
off B1253 Norton to Bridlington

NORTH YORKSHIRE

CASTLE HOWARD, York Tel: (065 384) 333
Home of the Hon. Simon Howard
Major country mansion; first work of the baroque architect John Vanbrugh. Contents include: Greek, Roman, Italian and other statuary (including the Delphi Altar); Meissen, Crown Derby and Chelsea china; Delft tulip vase: Chippendale furniture (including child's high chair); paintings by Holbein, Rubens, Tintoretto, Poussin, Van Dyck, Lely, Gainsborough, Reynolds and others; stained glass by Burne-Jones and William Morris; costume collection. Outdoors; park, lakes, Temple of the Four Winds, mausoleum.
① £££ 🗂 ⊡ ✕ AV ✿ Ⓜ ⚘ P ら
off A64 York to Malton

FAIRFAX HOUSE, York Tel: (0904) 655543
York Civic Trust
Restored Georgian town house. Contents include: The Noel Terry Collection of paintings, furniture and late 17th- and early 18th-century clocks, fully catalogued; Joseph Cortese stucco work; reconstructed 18th-century kitchen with utensils and plates.
◑ £ 🗂 Ⓜ
in York

KIPLIN HALL, Scorton Tel: (0748) 818178
Kiplin Hall Trust
Jacobean house. Contents include: rococo plasterwork; 18th-century portraits and furniture. Outdoors: park; medieval fishponds.
◑ £ P
off B6271 Richmond to Northallerton

YOU ARE ADVISED TO CHECK DETAILS BEFORE VISITING A HOUSE

NEWBY HALL, Ripon Tel: (0423) 322583
Home of Robin Compton
17th-century mansion. Contents include: Adam interiors (including Entrance Hall, Library, Tapestry Room, Sculpture Gallery); William Weddell's classical sculpture collection; tapestries; furniture by Chippendale and others; paintings by Romney, Carracci, Angelica Kauffmann and others; Circular Room with 'grotesque' decoration; Victorian 'Motto Bedroom' and Billiards Room; antique chamber pot collection. Outdoors: gardens (25 acres); park; statue of John Sobieski/Charles II; family church; adventure gardens; miniature railway; steam boat (Sundays); plant stall.
◔ ££ ❒ ☕ ✕ ❀ ♣ ✿ ⛺ P ♿
off B6265 Ripon to Boroughbridge

NORTON CONYERS, Ripon Tel: (076 584) 333
Home of Sir James Graham Bt
Jacobean manor house. Contents include: paintings by Lely, Romney, Batoni; Chamberlain Worcester china; Berlin porcelain; family wedding dresses; William Morris furnishings. Outdoors: walled garden; orangery; 18th-century lead statues; garden centre.
◕ £ ❒ ❀ P ♿
off A1 Wetherby to Scotch Corner

RIPLEY CASTLE, Harrogate Tel: (0423) 770152
Home of Sir Thomas Ingilby Bt
Georgian mansion added to 16th-century tower. Contents include: Chippendale, Hepplewhite and Louis XV furniture; Georgian mirrors; collection of Lalique glass; Civil War arms and armour; rare embroidered Elizabethan chalice cover; 1832 'Reform' jug; paintings by Kneller, Gainsborough, van Bergen, Frain, Jordaens and Vanmour, among others; library including 16th-century volumes; collection of majolica. Outdoors: gardens, playground.
◑ ££ 🚶 ❒ ☕ ✕ ❀ ⛺ P
off A61 Harrogate to Ripon

ST OSWALD'S HALL, Fulford Tel: (0904) 37756
Home of Roy Grant
12th-century chapel, converted to medieval hall. Contents include: early oak furniture; St Oswald's Book of Hours (15th-century illuminated manuscript); embroidery; St Oswald's Madonna (Russian icon).
◑ £ 🚶 ⛟ P
off A64 York to Leeds

STOCKELD PARK, Wetherby Tel: (0937) 62376
Home of Mrs Rosamund Gough
Small 18th-century mansion with late 19th-century additions. Contents include: 18th- and 19th-century furniture; 'crinoline' staircase. Outdoors: gardens; playground.
◕ £ 🚶 ☕ ✕ ❀ ⛺ P ♿
off A661 Wetherby to Harrogate

SUTTON PARK, Sutton-on-the-Forest Tel: (0347) 810249
Home of Mrs Nancie Sheffield
Early Georgian manor house. Contents include: needlepoint carpets; collection of Japanese (Imari), Meissen, Bow, Chelsea, Worcester, Dresden, Chinese and Dutch porcelain; furniture by Chippendale; Dutch marquetry. Outdoors: gardens; woodland walks; nature trail; Georgian icehouse.
◑ £ ❒ ☕ ❀ P
off B1363 York to Helmsley

NOTTINGHAMSHIRE
HOLME PIERREPONT HALL, Radcliffe-on-Trent
Tel: (06073) 2371
Home of Mr and Mrs Robin Brackenbury
Tudor mansion with later additions. Contents include: English furniture; William Morris bed-hangings; Minton and Davenport china; Bulgarian icon. Outdoors: gardens; rare breeds.
◕ £ ❒ ☕ ⛟ ❀ P ♿
off A52 Nottingham to Radcliffe

OXFORDSHIRE
ARDINGTON HOUSE, Wantage Tel: (0235) 833244
Home of Mr and Mrs D.C.N. Baring
18th-century brick manor house. Contents include: Imperial staircase; painted ceiling. Outdoors: gardens.
◑ £ 🚶 ❀ P
off A417 Wantage to Didcot

BLENHEIM PALACE, Woodstock Tel: (0993) 811325
Home of The Duke of Marlborough
Baroque palace designed by Sir John Vanbrugh. Contents include: the Churchill Exhibition; the Marlborough tapestries; interiors by Nicholas Hawksmoor; bronzes by Epstein and others; marble work by Grinling Gibbons; portraits by Kneller, Closterman, Reynolds, Van Dyck, Sargent and others; French furniture, including some from Versailles; Meissen and Sèvres porcelain; statues and monuments by Rysbrack. Outdoors: Capability Brown park; gardens; adventure play area; train; motor launch; nature trail; arboretum; Vanbrugh's Grand Bridge; lakeside temples; Column of Victory.
◯ £££ 🚶 ❒ ☕ ✕ ⛟ ❀ ♣ ✿ ⛺ P ♿
in Woodstock, off A34 Oxford to Stratford-upon-Avon

BROUGHTON CASTLE, Banbury Tel: (0295) 62624
Home of The Lord Saye and Sele
Elizabethan manor house with medieval origins. Contents include: medieval undercroft; early 14th-century heraldic stained glass; busts by Rysbrack; Crown Derby and Coalbrookdale porcelain; Council Chamber of Local Parliamentary Committee (Civil War). Outdoors: gardens; 15th-century gatehouse; broad moat.
◑ £ ❒ ☕ ❀ P ♿
off B4035 Banbury to Shipston-on-Stour

FAWLEY COURT, Henley-on-Thames Tel: (0491) 574917
Congregation of Marian Fathers
17th-century mansion, by Sir Christopher Wren. Contents include: Polish military collection (including armoury); Polish manuscript collection; paintings (including Giordano's 'Delivery of St Peter'); classical sculptures; Wyatt interiors; Grinling Gibbons ceiling. Outdoors: gardens.
◑ £ 🚶 ❒ ☕ ❀ M P ♿
off A4155 Henley to Marlow

KINGSTON HOUSE, Kingston Bagpuize Tel: (0865) 820259
Home of The Lord and Lady Tweedsmuir
Late 17th-century manor house. Contents include: English and French furniture; Chinese porcelain; cantilevered staircase; English watercolours; Victorian doll's house. Outdoors: woodland garden, 17th-century stable block; early 18th-century gazebo built above an Elizabethan cockpit.
◑ £ 🚶 ❒ ☕ ❀ P
off A415 Abingdon to Witney

YOU ARE ADVISED TO CHECK DETAILS BEFORE VISITING A HOUSE

KINGSTONE LISLE PARK, Wantage Tel: (036782) 223
Home of Mrs Leopold Lonsdale
17th-century mansion with later additions. Contents include: 'flying' staircase; 18th-century English furniture; glass collection; miniature furniture collection; needlework, antique and contemporary; paintings by Gheeraerts, van Goyen and others. Outdoors: gardens.
◑ ££ ⬚ ⬡ P
off B4507 Wantage to Wanborough

MILTON MANOR HOUSE, Abingdon Tel (0235) 831287
Home of Mrs Marjorie Mockler
Carolean manor house. Contents include: Strawberry Hill Gothic Library; family portraits and other paintings (including Murillo's 'Assumption' and Kneller's 'Churchill Sisters'); English porcelain; Chapel, with vestments, missal and chalice of Bishop Challoner; Admiral Benbow's telescope; Chinese bedroom with 18th-century Chinese wallpaper; pianola made for Queen Victoria's youngest daughter; teapot collection. Outdoors: gardens.
◑ £ ⚲ ⬚ ✕ P
off A34 Oxford to Newbury

ROUSHAM PARK, Steeple Aston Tel: (0869) 47110
Home of Charles Cottrell-Dormer
Jacobean country house, remodelled by William Kent and others. Contents include: interiors by Kent (Painted Parlour and Great Parlour); family portraits by Lely, Kneller, Reynolds and others; other pictures by Breughel, Dobson and others; defensive front door; General Dormer's collection of Italian bronzes. Outdoors: landscape garden by Kent; formal gardens; 17th-century pigeon house.
◑ ££ ⚲ ⬡ P
off A423 Oxford to Banbury

STANTON HARCOURT MANOR Tel: (0865) 881 928
Home of the Hon. Mrs Gascoigne
Late medieval kitchen with 15th-century tower and gatehouse. Contents include: paintings; silver. Outdoors: formal and woodland gardens; woodland walks; water-bird and fish sanctuary.
◑ £ ⬡ ⬚ ⬡ P ♿
off B4449 Eynsham to Standlake

STONOR PARK, Henley-on-Thames Tel: (049 16) 3587
Home of The Lord and Lady Camoys
Medieval house, with Tudor and Georgian additions and alterations. Contents include: Library, with large recusant book collection; St Edmund Campion Room (with exhibition); family portraits; paintings by Ludovico and Antonio Carracci, Tintoretto, Kneller and others; tapestries; 17th-century Venetian globes with stands; chapel with 18th-century Gothic interior. Outdoors: gardens; stone circle.
◑ £ ⬡ ⬚ ⬡ P ♿
off B480 Henley to Watlington

SHROPSHIRE
SHIPTON HALL, Much Wenlock Tel: (074 636) 225
Home of Mr and Mrs Nicholas Bishop
Elizabethan manor house. Contents include: fine rococo plasterwork. Outdoors: Saxon church; medieval dovecote; Georgian stable block; tithe barn; gardens; working pottery.
◑ £ ⚲ ⬡ ⬡ P
off A458 Shrewsbury to Bridgnorth

UPTON CRESSETT HALL, Bridgnorth Tel: (074 631) 307
Home of Mr and Mrs William Cash
Medieval and Elizabethan manor house and gatehouse. Contents include: Elizabethan panelling and fireplaces; Jacobean furniture; tapestry. Outdoors: gardens.
◑ £ ⚲ ⬡ P
off A458 Bridgnorth to Shrewsbury

WESTON PARK, Shifnal Tel: (095 276) 207
Home of The Earl of Bradford
Renaissance house with later extensions. Contents include: Gobelins and Aubusson tapestries; paintings by Holbein, Van Dyck, Bassano, Reynolds, Stubbs, Gainsborough and Ferneley; letters from Disraeli to the third Countess of Bradford; early English and Italian furniture; collection of Bow, Derby and Chelsea figures; Oriental porcelain; Disraeli's parrot. Outdoors: gardens; orangery; temple; woodland walks; adventure playground; pets corner and toddlers' playground; pottery; museum of 'bygones'; aquarium; nature trails; miniature railway; picnic area.
◑ £ ⬡ ⬚ ⬡ ✕ ⚲ ⬡ ⬡ ⏚ P ♿
off A5 Telford to Cannock

SOMERSET
BARFORD PARK, Bridgwater Tel: (027 867) 269
Home of Col. Michael Stancomb
18th-century country house. Contents include: family portraits; 18th-century furniture. Outdoors: gardens; Victorian pleasure ground, with archery glade; park with lake.
◑ £ ⚲ ⬡ P ♿
off A39 Bridgwater to Williton

THE BISHOP'S PALACE, Wells Tel: (0749) 78691
Home of The Bishop of Bath & Wells (The Church Commissioners)
Fortified palace. Contents include: vaulted hall. Outdoors: Jubilee Arboretum; wells; moat.
◑ £ ⬚
in Wells, off A39

BRYMPTON d'EVERCY, Yeovil Tel: (0935) 862528
Home of Mr and Mrs Charles Clive-Ponsonby-Fane
Ham-stone Tudor and Elizabethan manor house with Palladian South Front. Contents include: paintings by Pannini, Riley, Lawrence, Soldi, Kneller, Dobson, Lear and others; Parker Knoll antique chair collection; I Zingari cricket memorabilia. Outdoors: gardens; clock tower; priest house; vineyard; cider museum; distillery; picnic area.
◑ ££ ⬡ ⬚ ⬡ ⚇ ⏚ P ♿
off A30 Yeovil to Crewkerne

COMBE SYDENHAM HALL, Monksilver Tel: (0984) 56284
Home of Mr and Mrs William Theed
Elizabethan manor house. Contents include: 'Drake's cannonball'; original Sydenham arms; early English furniture. Outdoors: Elizabethan gardens; old English rose garden; woodland walks; trout farm; old corn mill.
◑ ££ ⬡ ⬚ ✕ ⏚ ⬡ ⬡ P
off B3188 Wiveliscombe to Watchet

YOU ARE ADVISED TO CHECK DETAILS BEFORE VISITING A HOUSE

FORDE ABBEY, Chard Tel: (0460) 20231
Home of Mark Roper
Medieval monastery. Contents include: Mortlake tapestries after Raphael; 16th-century panelled ceilings. Outdoors: 18th-century and Victorian gardens; arboretum; rock garden; bog garden; ponds; fruit gardens; nursery and plant centre.
❶ ££ ⌂ ⊟ ❀ P ♿
off B3167 Tytherleigh to Cricket St Thomas

GAULDEN MANOR, Tolland Tel: (09847) 213
Home of Mr and Mrs James Starkie
Sandstone manor house. Contents include: Jacobean plaster work; Turberville coats-of-arms and other relics; family collection of English furniture. Outdoors: bog and herb garden; plant sales.
❶ £ ⚲ ⌂ ⊟ ❀ P ♿
off A358 Taunton to Williton

HATCH COURT, Hatch Beauchamp Tel: (0823) 480208
Home of Cmr and Mrs Barry Nation
18th-century country house. Contents include: China Room (containing Minton, Wedgwood, Royal Worcester, Sèvres and Japanese ware); paintings by Munnings and others; museum of memorabilia connected with Princess Patricia's Canadian Light Infantry and Andrew Hamilton Gault. Outdoors: gardens; deer park.
❶ ££ ⚲ ⊟ ❀ ⌸ P
off A358 Taunton to Ilminster

MIDELNEY MANOR, Drayton, Langport Tel: (0458) 251229
Home of Major R.E.F. Cely Trevelian
16th/18th-century manor house. Contents include: unusual painted overmantel; early panelling. Outdoors: gardens; 17th-century falcon mews; heronry.
❶ £ P
off B3168 Hambridge to Curry Rivel

POUNDISFORD PARK, Taunton Tel: (082 342) 244
Home of Mr and Mrs Ralph Vivian-Neal
H-shaped Tudor house. Contents include: 16th-century moulded ceilings; 18th-century longcase clocks; collection of Chelsea, Meissen, Marcolini and Derby figures; Chelsea, Derby, Worcester, Leeds, Wedgwood and oriental china; family and other portraits. Outdoors: gardens.
❶ £ ⚲ ⊟ ✕ ❀ P ♿
off B3170 Taunton to Honiton

STAFFORDSHIRE
CHILLINGTON HALL, Wolverhampton Tel: (0902) 850236
Home of Mr and Mrs Peter Giffard
18th-century manor house. Contents include: original Georgian staircase; Giffard family portraits and busts; Saloon by Sir John Soane. Outdoors: gardens, park and lake landscaped by Capability Brown; temples in the Grecian and Italian styles; woodland walks.
❶ £ ⚲ ❀ ⌸ P
off A449 Wolverhampton to Penkridge; M54 (junction 2)

ECCLESHALL CASTLE, Stafford Tel: (0785) 850250
Home of Mr and Mrs Mark Carter
William and Mary mansion. Contents include: European and Oriental porcelain; collection of Victorian first editions; 18th-century mahogany bedroom furniture; 17th-century oak furniture; Victorian toys and books; equestrian paintings by Herring father and son; collection of paintings by other Yorkshire artists. Outdoors: moat garden; nature trail.
❶ ££ ⚲ ⌂ ⊟ ✕ ❀ ⌸ P ♿
off A519 Eccleshall to Newcastle-under-Lyme

HOAR CROSS HALL, Burton-on-Trent Tel: (028 375) 224
Home of Mrs Gwynyth Jones
19th-century Elizabethan revival mansion. Contents include: William Morris wall-coverings from original blocks; collection of Victorian costumes and textiles; period teapots; militaria. Outdoors: gardens; woodland walks.
❶ £ ⌂ ⊟ ❀ P ♿
off A515 Sudbury to Yoxall

WHITMORE HALL, Newcastle-under-Lyme Tel: (0782) 680235
Home of Rafe Cavenagh-Mainwaring
Carolean manor house. Contents include: family portraits from 17th century onwards. Outdoors: Tudor stable block.
❶ £ ⚲ P
off A53 Newcastle to Market Drayton

SUFFOLK
DITCHINGHAM HALL, Bungay Tel: (050 844) 250
Home of The Earl and Countess Ferrers
Queen Anne house. Contents include: the 'Lesser Shirley Pedigree' (17th-century heraldic document); stuffed Chartley bull; family portrait by Van der Vaart. Outdoors: park landscaped by Capability Brown; lake.
❶ ££ ⌂ ⊟ ❀ P
off A143 Beccles to Bungay

HAUGHLEY PARK, Stowmarket Tel: (0359) 40205
Home of Alfred Williams
16th-century manor house restored in 1962-4. Contents include: collection of 16th- and 17th-century Dutch paintings; period furniture and furnishings. Outdoors: gardens; oak-roofed barn; woodland walks.
❶ £ ⚲ ❀ P ♿
off A45 Stowmarket to Bury St Edmunds

KENTWELL HALL, Long Melford Tel: (0787) 310207
Home of Mr and Mrs Patrick Phillips
Elizabethan manor house. In process of restoration to original fabric; visitors can expect to see work in progress; annual 'Kentwell Re-Creations.' Outdoors: costume exhibition; rare breed farming stock.
❶ ££ ⌂ ⊟ ➶ ❀ P
off A134 Sudbury to Bury St Edmunds

LAVENHAM PRIORY, Lavenham Tel: (0787) 247417
Home of Mr and Mrs Alan Casey
13th-century hall house with Tudor additions. Contents include: paintings, drawings and stained glass by Ervin Bossanyi; abstract mural by Colin Dales. Outdoors: decorative pargetting; Lavenham woolmark; herb garden.
❶ £ ⌂ ⊟ ✕ ❀ P
in Lavenham, off A1141

YOU ARE ADVISED TO CHECK DETAILS BEFORE VISITING A HOUSE

OTLEY HALL, Ipswich Tel: (047339) 264
Home of Mr and Mrs J. G. Mosesson
15th-century moated hall. Contents include: carved oak ceilings; linenfold panelling; 16th-century wall paintings on plaster. Outdoors: gardens; canal; nutteries; 16th-century vine motif pargetting.

● ££ ⌂ ⊒ ✕ AV ✊ ⊛ P ☖
off B1078 Wickham Market to Needham Market

SOMERLEYTON HALL, Lowestoft Tel: (0502) 730224
Home of The Lord and Lady Somerleyton
Victorian Jacobethan mansion. Contents include: chimney-piece carving attributed to Grinling Gibbons; 18th-century Flemish tapestry; Venetian mirror; library of Victorian books; paintings by Reni, Clarkson Stanfield, Kneller, Landseer and others. Outdoors: Victorian gardens by William Nesfield; maze; glasshouses by Paxton; clock tower; miniature railway.

● ££ ⌂ ⊒ ⊛ P ☖
off A143 Bungay to Great Yarmouth ⇌ Somerleyton

WINGFIELD COLLEGE, Eye Tel: (037 984) 505
Home of Ian Chance
14th-century college with later alterations. Contents include: timber-framed Great Hall; Cloister Passage and first-floor Gallery; 17th- and 18th-century interiors; Press Room with working Columbian printing press, dated 1840. Outdoors: gardens, with topiary and collegiate fish pond.

● £ ⊒ AV ⊛ P
off B1118 Diss to Stradbroke

SURREY
DETILLENS, Limpsfield Tel: (088 33) 3342
Home of Donald Neville
15th-century hall house with Georgian façade. Contents include: original 15th-century timbers; collection of British and foreign Orders and Decorations; display of Mason's ironstone china; collection of Louis Wain cat paintings. Outdoors: gardens; museum.

● £ ⚹ ⊛ ⊠ P
in Limpsfield, off A25

LOSELEY PARK, Guildford Tel: (0483) 571881
Home of James More-Molyneux
Elizabethan mansion. Contents include: family and other portraits (subjects include Edward VI, James I and his wife, Charles II, and the More-Molyneux family in 1739); marble table and wooden panelling from Henry VIII's lost palace of Nonsuch; Grinling Gibbons carvings; William IV's Coronation Chair; carved chalk overmantel; tapestries; four-poster beds and bed-hangings. Outdoors: gardens; play area; farm tours (with Jersey herd established in 1916).

● ££ ⚹ ⌂ ⊒ ✕ ⊛ P ☖
off A3 Guildford to Petersfield

WARWICKSHIRE
ARBURY HALL, Nuneaton Tel: (0203) 382804
Home of The Viscount Daventry
Elizabethan house with 18th-century Strawberry Hill Gothic interior. Contents include: plasterwork ceilings and chimney-pieces; marquetry furniture; Jacobite and Georgian glass, Chelsea porcelain; portraits by Romney, Lely and others. Outdoors: informal gardens; woods including some of the original trees of the Forest of Arden; veteran cycle exhibition.

● ££ ⚹ ⌂ ⊒ ✕ ✊ ⊛ P
off B4102 Nuneaton to Fillongley

RAGLEY HALL, Alcester Tel: (0789) 762090
Home of The Marquess of Hertford
17th-century mansion with Georgian interiors. Contents include: 18th-century English furniture; 18th-century table silver; Sèvres, Spode and Minton china; 18th-century Chinese figures; paintings by Vernet, van Haarlem, Schut, Reynolds, Dahl, Wissing, Van Loo, Hoppner, Lely, Bourdon and others; 20th-century portraits by Judy Cassab; 20th-century painting by Ceri Richards and mural by Graham Rust. Outdoors: gardens; adventure playground; country trail; stable-yard with artist's studio.

● ££ ⌂ ⊒ ✕ ⊛ ✾ ⚏ P ☖
off A435 Birmingham to Evesham

STONELEIGH ABBEY, Kenilworth Tel: (0926) 52116
The Stoneleigh Abbey Preservation Trust
Part-Elizabethan, part-Georgian mansion, on medieval abbey site. Contents include: Elizabethan panelling; 18th-century plasterwork after Cipriani; family portraits; library (with Byron portrait); 'Queen's Bedroom' (also called 'Jane Austen's Room'); chapel. Outdoors: gardens; medieval abbey gatehouse; adventure playground; nature trail; miniature steam railway.

● ££ ⚹ ⌂ ⊒ ✕ ⊛ ⚏ P
off A444 Coventry to Leamington

WARWICK CASTLE Tel: (0926) 495421
Warwick Castle Ltd
Medieval castle with 17th- and 18th-century state rooms. Contents include: 1,000-piece collection of arms and armour; Beauvais and Brussels tapestries; Italian, Dutch, French and English furniture; 18th-century Chinese porcelain; 18th-century English and Irish chandeliers; state bed used by Queen Anne; portraits by Kneller, Van Dyck, Dahl and others. Outdoors: gardens; conservatory housing 'Bear and his Ragged Staff' exhibition; pageant field; Castle Mount; river island; reconstructed rose garden.

○ £££ ⌂ ⊒ ✕ ⊛ P ☖
in Warwick, off A445 ⇌ Warwick

WEST MIDLANDS
HAGLEY HALL, Stourbridge Tel: (0562) 882408
Home of The Viscount Cobham
18th-century Palladian mansion. Contents include: plasterwork by Vassalli; busts by Rysbrack and Scheemakers; busts of Roman emperors; Chippendale furniture; collection of miniatures; Soho and Mortlake tapestries; portraits by Van Dyck, Reynolds, Batoni, Van Loo and others.

● ££ ⚹ ⊒ P
off A456 Birmingham to Kidderminster

WEST SUSSEX
ARUNDEL CASTLE, Arundel Tel: (0903) 883136
Home of The Dukes of Norfolk (Arundel Castle Trustees)
19th-century castle with original Norman Keep and Barbican. Contents include: Venetian 16th-century and English, French and Dutch 18th-century furniture; gesso pageant shield attributed to Pordenone; relics of Mary Queen of Scots; 14th to 18th-century armour; Gobelins and Brussels tapestries; portraits by Van Dyck, Mytens, Kneller, Gainsborough, Reynolds, Millais and others. Outdoors: gardens; extensive grounds; Early English Gothic private chapel.

● ££ ⌂ ☖
in Arundel, off A27 ⇌ Arundel

YOU ARE ADVISED TO CHECK DETAILS BEFORE VISITING A HOUSE

GOODWOOD, Chichester Tel: (0243) 774107
Home of The Earl of March and Kinrara
Georgian mansion. Contents include: collection of Sèvres porcelain; paintings by Kneller, Reynolds, Lely, Van Dyck, Canaletto, Stubbs, Romney and others; marine paintings; Charles II marquetry cabinet; silver Peninsular War trophy; Gobelins tapestries; Japanese and Chinese lacquer and Louis XV furniture. Outdoors: park; plantation of Cedars of Lebanon; cricket pitch and pavilion; pavilion containing ice-house; stables; motor circuit; golf course; racecourse.
◑ ££ ▢ ☕ P ♿
off A27 Chichester to Arundel

HAMMERWOOD PARK, East Grinstead Tel: (034 286) 594
Home of David Pinnegar
18th-century mansion. In process of restoration. Occasional musical evenings are held.
◑ £ ✗ ☕ AV ✿ P ♿
off A264 Tunbridge Wells to Eastbourne

PARHAM PARK, Pulborough Tel: (090 66) 2021
Home of Mrs P. A. Tritton
Elizabethan manor house. Contents include: 18th-century marble relief by John Deare; 16th- and 17th-century English furniture; 18th-century lacquered longcase clock; Elizabethan and Stuart needlework; early English needlework bed and wall-hangings; Tudor and Stuart royal portraits; allegorical portrait of Prince Henry Frederick by Robert Peake; pictures by Snyders, Claude, Reynolds, Gainsborough, Romney and Stubbs; painted ceiling by Oliver Messel. Outdoors: gardens; pleasure grounds; children's playground; deer park; church with 18th-century box pews.
◑ ££ ▢ ☕ ❀ ⩚ P ♿
off A283 Pulborough to Storrington

ST MARY'S, Bramber Tel: (0903) 816205
Home of Peter Thorogood
15th-century timber-framed house on earlier foundations (Knights Templars building). Contents include: 'Painted Room' (with 16th-century *trompe l'oeil* arcades); room occupied by Charles II; unique medieval 'shutting window' in 12 sections; 16th-century gilded wall-leathers; Elizabethan panelling and carving; priest's hole; Venetian stone fireplaces. Outdoors: gardens, with topiary.
◑ £ ☕ ✕ ❀ P
in Bramber, off A283

WEST YORKSHIRE
BRAMHAM PARK, Wetherby Tel: (0937) 844265
Home of George Lane Fox
Queen Anne mansion. Contents include: paintings by Kneller, Reynolds (of the Duke of Cumberland) and others; collection of animal and sporting paintings; family portraits; House of Commons journal containing the indictment of Charles I; collection of silver gilt. Outdoors: formal gardens in the French style, inspired by le Nôtre; museum.
◑ £ ✗ ❀ ❦ M
off A1 Micklefield to Wetherby

HAREWOOD HOUSE, Harewood Tel: (0532) 886225
Home of The Earl and Countess of Harewood
Palladian mansion. Contents include: Chippendale furniture designed for the house; interiors by Robert Adam; Sèvres porcelain collection; collection of pictures by Turner, John Singer Sargent, Frank Salisbury, Sir Alfred Munnings, John Piper, El Greco, Bellini and others; Coalport and Leeds ware and Derby porcelain; collection of Meissen figures; 17th- and 18th-century Chinese porcelain; French 'organ' clock. Outdoors: gardens; rose garden; exotic bird garden; adventure playground.
⦶ £££ ▢ ☕ ✕ ✿ ❀ ⬆ ⩚ P ♿
off A61 Leeds to Harrogate

WILTSHIRE
BOWOOD, Calne Tel: (0249) 812102
Home of The Earl of Shelburne
Georgian mansion by Robert Adam. Contents include: Lansdowne collection of paintings and statuary; collections of porcelain, costumes, silver, Indiana. Outdoors: gardens; landscaped park; 'hermit's cave'; rhododendron walks; adventure playground; plant centre.
⦶ ££ ▢ ☕ ✕ ✿ ❀ ⩚ P ♿
off A4, Calne to Chippenham

CHALCOT HOUSE, Westbury Tel: (037 388) 466
Home of Mrs Ethne Rudd
Palladian manor house. Contents include: collections of Boer War and First World War memorabilia; collection of modern paintings; needlework and tapestry; Carolingian glass pictures, prints, cartoons and china. Outdoors: gardens; walks; croquet lawn.
◕ £ ✗ ❀ P
A3098 Westbury to Frome

CORSHAM COURT, Corsham Tel: (0249) 712214
Home of The Lord Methuen
Elizabethan stone manor house with 18th- and 19th-century additions. Contents include: important collection of pictures of the Italian, Spanish, French, Flemish, Dutch, English and Maltese Schools, fully catalogued; furniture by Adam, Chippendale, Sheraton and others; classical style ceilings by Thomas Stocking; mirrors by Thomas Johnson; 18th-century Chinese porcelain; Staffordshire pottery collection; Silesian, Venetian and Waterford glass; Italian and French bronzes. Outdoors: gardens; rose gardens; arboretum; Gothic bath-house; two ice-houses.
◔ ££ ❀ P ♿
in Corsham, off A4

LONGLEAT, Warminster Tel (098 53) 551
Home of The Marquess of Bath
Elizabethan mansion. Contents include: 17th-century tooled Spanish leather interior in State Dining Room; 19th-century 'Cries of London' salt-cellars; 17th- and 18th-century clocks; 17th- and 18th-century French, Flemish, Italian and Portuguese-Indian furniture; paintings by, among others, Titian, Van Dyck, Lely, Rottenhammer, Dahl, Hoppner, Jansen; Red Library of 6,000 volumes; Meissen porcelain. Outdoors: rose gardens; butterfly gardens; orangery; pet's cemetery; safari park; miniature railway; maze; 'bygones.'
○ ££ ✗ ▢ ☕ ✕ ❀ ✿ P ♿
off A362 Frome to Warminster

YOU ARE ADVISED TO CHECK DETAILS BEFORE VISITING A HOUSE

NEWHOUSE, Redlynch Tel: (0725) 20055
Home of George Jeffreys
17th-century hunting lodge in Y-formation with Georgian wings. Contents include: allegorical 'hare' picture; Nelsoniana; museum of costume 1750–1925. Outdoors: outbuildings with exhibition of agricultural and domestic 'bygones'.
◑ £ 🏛 P
off B3080 Downton to Brook

SHELDON MANOR, Chippenham Tel: (0249) 653120
Home of Major and Mrs Martin Gibbs
Ancient manor house dating from 13th century to 17th century. Contents include: English and continental porcelain; Nailsea glass; linenfold panelling; early English oak furniture; painting by Tissot among others; memorabilia from American War of Independence. Outdoors: gardens; agricultural bygones; chapel; stables; 18th-century granary on staddle-stones; water garden.
◑ ££ 🗂 ⊟ ✕ ⛄ ⛐ P ⛑
off A420 Chippenham to Bristol ⇌ Chippenham

WILTON HOUSE, Salisbury Tel: (072 274) 3115
Home of The Earl of Pembroke
17th-century mansion by Inigo Jones, with later alterations by James Wyatt. Contents include: important paintings including works by Breughel, Rubens and Rembrandt, Van Dyck and Reynolds; 55 gouaches of the Spanish Riding School in Vienna; furniture by Thomas Chippendale and William Kent; lock of Queen Elizabeth's hair; manuscript poem by Sir Philip Sidney; classical and 17th-century marbles; 17th-century Chinese porcelain; sash worn in the Crimea by Florence Nightingale. Double and single Cube Rooms under restoration (restricted viewing until 1988–90). Outdoors: gardens; display of miniature model soldiers; Edwardian dolls' house; adventure playground; model railway; garden centre.
① ££ 🗂 ⊟ ✕ ⛐ P ⛑
off A30 Salisbury to Exeter ⇌ Salisbury

SCOTLAND
BORDERS
AYTON CASTLE, Eyemouth Tel: (089 07) 81212
Home of David Liddell Grainger
19th-century Scottish Baronial castle. Contents include: 19th-century decoration schemes; Victorian plasterwork and woodwork.
◑ £ P
in Ayton, off A1

BOWHILL, Selkirk Tel: (0750) 20732
Home of The Duke of Buccleuch and Queensberry
19th-century Scottish mansion. Contents include: substantial collections of French furniture; paintings by Canaletto, Guardi, Gainsborough, Reynolds and others; the Buccleuch collection of portrait miniatures; Sir Walter Scott memorabilia. Outdoors: gardens; adventure playground.
◑ ££ 🗂 ⊟ AV ⛄ ⛐ 🎨 ⛰ P ⛑
off A708 Selkirk to Moffat

FLOORS CASTLE, Kelso Tel: (0573) 23333
Home of The Duke of Roxburghe
19th-century palace, built round Georgian mansion. Contents include: Brussels, Beauvais and Gobelins tapestries (including the medieval 'Day of Pentecost'); Chinese porcelain collections; French furniture; family portraits and other paintings (by Gainsborough, Hogarth, Reynolds and others); collection of stuffed birds (including the now-extinct Passenger Pigeon). Outdoors: gardens; children's playground.
◑ ££ 🗂 ⊟ ✕ ⛐ ⛰ P ⛑
off A6089 Kelso to Lauder

MANDERSTON, Duns Tel: (0361) 83450
Home of Mr and Mrs Adrian Palmer
Edwardian mansion. Contents include: silver staircase; collection of liveried Russian sledging seats; blue john urns, obelisks and candelabra; paintings by Lutyens and Landseer; kitchens with original Edwardian fittings. Outdoors: stables; marble model dairy; mock Border keep; woodland and formal gardens.
◑ ££ 🗂 ⊟ ⛐ P
off A6105 Duns to Berwick-upon-Tweed

MELLERSTAIN, Gordon Tel: (057 381) 225
Home of The Earl of Haddington
18th-century mansion by William and Robert Adam. Contents include: Robert Adam interiors; family portraits; paintings by Veronese, Van Dyck, Ramsay, Maes, Maria Varelst, Gainsborough, Constable, Frith and others); tapestry and needlework; statue busts by Roubiliac; 18th-century furniture; Strasbourg faience turkey tureen. Outdoors: gardens.
◑ ££ 🗂 ⊟ ⛐ P
off A6089, Lauder to Kelso

NEIDPATH CASTLE, Peebles Tel: (0721) 20333
Lady Elizabeth Benson
Medieval castle with later additions. Contents include: rock-cut well; pit prison.
① £ P
off A72 Peebles to Carluke

THIRLESTANE CASTLE, Lauder Tel: (057 82) 254
Home of Capt. the Hon. Gerald Maitland Carew (The Thirlestane Castle Trust)
Mainly 16th-century castle with 17th and 19th-century additions. Contents include: rich 17th-century plaster ceilings; pictures by Romney, Reynolds, Hoppner and others; furniture mainly 19th century; Border Country Life Museum; exhibition of historic toys. Outdoors: gardens.
◑ ££ ⚲ 🗂 ⊟ ⛐ 🏛 P
off A68 Edinburgh to Darlington

TRAQUAIR, Innerleithen Tel: (0896) 830323
Home of Peter Maxwell Stuart
'The oldest inhabited house in Scotland.' 17th-century mansion on medieval foundations. Contents include: Jacobite glass and other Jacobite memorabilia; 18th-century Scottish and Dutch paintings; 17th-century harpsichord; Mary Queen of Scots mementoes, including her rosary and crucifix; 16th-century Flemish oak carvings; 15th-century Koberger Bible and Nuremberg Chronicle; collection of Stuart miniatures. Outdoors: gardens; the Bear Gates; working brewery; craft workshops; woodland walks.
① ££ 🗇 ⌷ ✕ ⊛ ⅏ P ♿
off A72 Peebles to Galashiels

DUMFRIES & GALLOWAY
DRUMLANRIG CASTLE, Thornhill Tel: (0848) 30248
Home of The Duke of Buccleuch and Queensberry
Baroque castle on medieval base. Contents include: paintings by Rembrandt, Holbein, da Vinci, Lely, Kneller, Gainsborough, Reynolds and others; 17th- and 18th-century furniture (including cabinets made for Louis XIV); silverware; Grinling Gibbons carvings; relics of Prince Charles Edward Stuart; household portraits (including chef Joseph Florence). Outdoors: gardens; working craft centre, adventure playground, woodland walks.
◑ ££ 🗇 ⌷ ✕ AV ⌚ ⊛ ⅏ ⋔ P ♿
off A76 Thornhill to Kirkconnel

MAXWELTON HOUSE, Moniaive Tel: (084 82) 385
Home of Paul Stenhouse (The Maxwelton House Trust)
Early Renaissance house. Contents include: wheelstair; 17th-century fireplaces; secret room; Annie Laurie's Boudoir; 17th-century furniture; needlework. Outdoors: garden; chapel; museum of farm and domestic tools and implements.
◑ £ ↗ ⊛ ⋔ P
off A702 Dalry to Thornhill

FIFE
EARLSHALL CASTLE, Leuchars Tel: (033 483) 205
Home of Major and Mrs David Baxter
16th-century castle. Contents include: Long Gallery with painted ceiling; broadsword collection; antique gun collection; collection of mugs (including Coalport, Worcester, Minton, Derby); Scottish oak furniture; paintings by George Stubbs and others; museum (exhibits include Highland pipes played at Waterloo). Outdoors: gardens (with topiary 'chessmen'); picnic area.
◑ ££ ↗ 🗇 ⌷ ⊛ ⅏ ⋔ P
off A919 Leuchars to St Andrews ⇌ Leuchars

GRAMPIAN
BRAEMAR CASTLE, Braemar Tel: (033 83) 219
Home of Capt. A.A.C. Farquharson of Invercauld
Highland fortress, mainly 18th century. Contents include: furniture by Adam, Hepplewhite and Chippendale; 18th-century four-poster bed with hangings of the Farquharson tartan; display of black Wedgwood pottery. Outdoors: star-shaped defensive wall.
◑ £ ↗ 🗇 P
off A93 Blairgowrie to Ballater

FASQUE, Fettercairn Tel: (056 14) 201
Home of Sir William Gladstone
Late Georgian mansion. Contents include: Gladstone memorabilia; Victorian bathroom; library; collection of stuffed birds of prey and mammals from the estate; 18th- and 19th-century furniture; Edwardian domestic offices. Outdoors: walled garden; stable block; park with red deer and Soay sheep.
◔ £ ⌚ ⋔ P ♿
off B974 Marykirk to Banchory

HIGHLAND
CAWDOR CASTLE, near Inverness Tel: (06677) 615
Home of The Earl Cawdor
Scottish fortified home; medieval and later. Contents include: tapestries; portraits (including painting of Emma Hamilton); bottle dungeon; 17th-century kitchen; the 'Cawdor hawthorn'. Outdoors: moat; flower gardens; wild garden; putting green; nature trails.
① ££ 🗇 ⌷ ✕ ⊛ ⅏ P ♿
on B9090 Inverness to Nairn

DUNROBIN CASTLE, Golspie Tel: (04083) 3177
Home of The Countess of Sutherland (The Sutherland Trust)
19th-century château on earlier base. Contents include; family portraits by Reynolds, Lawrence and others; family regalia (court dress, uniforms etc); Grinling Gibbons carvings; gilt four-poster bed slept in by Queen Victoria; china collection; Sub-Hall collection (including fire-engine). Outdoors: gardens, family museum (Pictish stones, geology, hunting trophies, curiosities).
◑ £ 🗇 ⌷ ✕ ⊛ ⅏ ⋔ P
off A9 Bonar Bridge to Brora ⇌ Golspie/Dunrobin

DUNVEGAN CASTLE, Isle of Skye Tel: (047 022) 206
Home of John MacLeod of MacLeod
Medieval castle with later additions. Contents include: the Fairy Flag; the Dunvegan Cup; other clan relics (including Rory Mor's drinking horn); MacCrimmon pipes; family portraits by Zoffany and others: St Kilda relics; pit dungeon. Outdoors: gardens; seal colony on loch.
◑ ££ 🗇 ⌷ ✕ AV ⊛ P ♿
at Dunvegan, off A863

LOTHIAN
DALMENY HOUSE, South Queensferry Tel: (031 331) 1888
Home of The Earl and Countess of Rosebery
Gothic Revival mansion. Contents include: the Rothschild Collection (French furniture, tapestries and porcelain); the Rosebery Collection (early Scottish portraits and furniture, 18th-century portraits, Goya tapestries); the Napoleon Collection; mementoes of the Rosebery and Rothschild racing successes (including King Tom bronze). Outdoors: gardens, shore walk from Forth Bridges to Cramond.
◔ £ ↗ 🗇 ⌷ ⊛ P ♿
off B924 Edinburgh to South Queensferry ⇌ Dalmeny

GOSFORD HOUSE, Longniddry Tel: (08757) 201
Home of The Earl of Wemyss
Late Victorian Italianate wing attached to Robert Adam central block. Outdoors: water gardens.
◔ £ ⊛ ⚘ P ♿
off A198 Aberlady to Longniddry

YOU ARE ADVISED TO CHECK DETAILS BEFORE VISITING A HOUSE

HOPETOUN HOUSE, South Queensferry Tel: (031 331) 2451
Home of The Marquess of Linlithgow (The Hopetoun House Preservation Trust)
18th-century classical mansion. Contents include: ceilings and other work by Adam brothers; 18th-century furniture by James Cullen; Antwerp tapestries; paintings by Canaletto and others (including family portraits); museum (family papers, costumes, furniture, china). Outdoors: stables ('Horse and Man in Lowland Scotland' exhibition); gardens; nature trail; deer park.

① ££ 🗂 ☕ ✕ ⊛ 🐾 Ⓜ P &
off A904 Edinburgh to Bo'ness

LENNOXLOVE, Haddington Tel: (062 082) 3720
Home of The Duke of Hamilton and Brandon
Medieval castle, with 17th-century additions. Contents include: death mask of Mary Queen of Scots; the container of the 'Casket letters'; family and other portraits (including that of the Duke and Duchess of Lennox, by Lely); furniture owned by the Duchess (including cabinet given to her by Charles II). Outdoors: gardens.

◑ £ 𝔨 🗂 ☕ ⊛ P
off B6369 Haddington to Gifford

STEVENSON HOUSE, Haddington Tel: (062 082) 3376
Home of Mrs J. C. H. Dunlop (The Brown Dunlop Country Houses Trust)
Late 16th-century grange house with late Restoration and Georgian additions. Contents include: French, Chinese and English furniture, including a table owned by Dr Johnson; 16th-century Tibetan tapestry; Worcester china; portraits by the American painter C.B. King. Outdoors: gardens and pleasure grounds.

◑ £ 𝔨 ⊛ P
off A1 Edinburgh to Berwick-upon-Tweed

WINTON HOUSE, Pencaitland Tel: (0875) 340222
Home of Sir David and Lady Ogilvy
Jacobean mansion with later additions. Contents include: pictures by Van Dyck, Van Goyen, Raeburn, Alan Ramsay, Canaletto and others. Outdoors: gardens.

◑ £ ⊛ P &
off A6093 Haddington to Dalkeith

STRATHCLYDE
BLAIRQUHAN CASTLE, Maybole Tel: (06557) 239
Home of James Hunter Blair
Early 19th-century castle. Contents include: contemporary furniture and furnishings commissioned for the house; original rent table; Thai silk wallcovering; 1810 mechanical piano; collection of cartoons and watercolours by F.C.B. Cadell. Outdoors: gardens; 1820 glasshouse; pinetum.

◑ £ 🗂 ☕ ⊛ ♧ Ⓜ P &
off B7045 Kirkmichael to Straiton

FINLAYSTONE HOUSE, Langbank Tel: (047 554) 285
Home of Mr and Mrs George MacMillan
18th-century house with 19th-century additions. Contents include: collection of 600 dolls; collection of Victoriana. Outdoors: gardens; woodland; adventure playground; ranger service.

◑ £ ☕ ⊛ 🐾 Ⓜ ⋔ &
off A8 Langbank to Port Glasgow ⇌ Woodhall

INVERARAY CASTLE, Inveraray Tel: (0499) 2203
Home of The Duke and Duchess of Argyll
18th-century castle, with later additions. Contents include: 18th-century neo-classical interiors; Beauvais tapestries; 18th-century furniture; family portraits by Kneller, Gainsborough and others; weapons collection; oriental and European porcelain collection; Victorian furniture and paintings; castle kitchen; war museum. Outdoors: gardens.

◑ ££ 🗂 ☕ ✕ ⑤ ⊛ 🐾 Ⓜ P &
in Inveraray, off A83

SORN CASTLE, Ayr Tel: (0290) 51611
Home of Mr and Mrs R.G. McIntyre
14th-century castle. Contents include: Scottish school 18th-century paintings; furniture. Outdoors: gardens; motor museum

◑ £ 𝔨 Ⓜ P
off A76 Kilmarnock to Cumnock

TOROSAY CASTLE, Craignure, Isle of Mull Tel: (06802) 421
Home of Mrs David Guthrie-James
Victorian castle in 'Scottish baronial' style. Contents include: family portraits; paintings by Sargent, Landseer, Leslie and others; Devonshire House Ball Book (complete record of costumes worn at the 1897 ball given by the Duchess of Devonshire in London); Viking Room ('Last of the Windjammers' exhibition); family scrapbooks and archives (including links with Winston Churchill); nursery with Edwardian rocking-horse. Outdoors: gardens; Statue Walk with Bonazza statuary collection; miniature railway link with ferry terminal.

① £ 🗂 ☕ ✕ ⊛ P &
off A849 Craignure to Fionnphort

TAYSIDE
BLAIR CASTLE, Blair Atholl Tel: (079 681) 207
Home of The Duke of Atholl
Medieval castle with later additions. Contents include: letter from Mary Queen of Scots; Jacobite relics; original copy of the National Covenant (one of four); armour in which Viscount Dundee was fatally wounded at Killiecrankie; 18th-century furniture, carvings, plasterwork, needlework; Sèvres and other porcelain collections; portraits (including family portraits) by Lely, Zoffany and others; furniture used by Queen Victoria; pistol collection; collection of costumes and uniforms. Outdoors: deer park; nature trails; pony trekking.

① ££ 🗂 ☕ ✕ ⑤ ⊛ 🐾 P &
off A9 Pitlochry to Inverness ⇌ Blair Atholl

GLAMIS CASTLE, Glamis Tel: (030 784) 242
Home of The Earl of Strathmore and Kinghorne
Medieval castle with later additions. Contents include: paintings (including 'The Fruit Market' by Rubens and Snyders) and family portraits; tapestries; armour; the Glamis jester's motley; porcelain collection; the Royal Apartments (Queen Mother's Sitting Room and Bedroom, the King's Room); the 'Family Exhibition' (family museum; exhibits include the bullet-proof jerkin worn by Claverhouse, the Old Chevalier's watch, and the phaeton used as a girl by the Queen Mother). Outdoors: gardens; nature trail, play area.

◑ ££ 𝔨 🗂 ☕ ⊛ 🐾 ⋔ P &
off A94 Dundee to Kirriemuir

SCONE PALACE, Perth Tel: (0738) 52300
Home of The Earl of Mansfield
19th-century palace on earlier base. Contents include: French furniture; 16th-century needlework (including Mary Queen of Scots' bed-hangings); clocks; ivories; family portraits and other paintings (including Zoffany of Lady Elizabeth Murray and Dido); porcelain collection (including Meissen, Sèvres, Ludwigsburg, Chelsea, Derby and Worcester); collection of 'vernis Martin'. Outdoors: gardens; Moot Hill; pinetum; adventure playground.
① ££ ⚓ ⌂ ⊑ ✗ ⛵ ⚘ ♨ ⋒ P &
off A93 Perth to Braemar ⇌ Perth

WALES
CLWYD
BODRHYDDAN HALL, Rhuddlan Tel: (0745) 590414
Home of Col. The Lord Langford
William and Mary country house with 18th- and 19th-century additions. Contents include: pre-Civil War armour; collection of naval and regimental swords; Egyptian mummy of the 18th Dynasty (c. 1200 BC). Outdoors: French garden; woodland garden.
❶ £ ⚓ ⊑ ⚘ P
off A5151 Rhuddlan to Dyserth

TOWER, Mold Tel: (0352) 3220
Home of Charles Wynne Eyton
Fortified border house. Contents include: barrel-vaulted ceilings. Outdoors: lake; landscaped park.
❶ £ ⚓ P
off A494 Mold to Queensferry

GWENT
LLANVIHANGEL COURT, Abergavenny Tel: (087 382) 217
Home of Col. and Mrs Somerset Hopkinson
Tudor mansion on earlier base with 17th-century alterations. Contents include: paintings by Van Dyck, Carlo Dolci, Gambardella and others; Italian, French and early English furniture; Ming figures. Outdoors: gardens.
❶ £ ⚓ ⌂ ⚘
off A465 Abergavenny to Hereford

PENHOW CASTLE, Newport Tel: (0633) 400800
Home of Stephen Weeks
12th-century castle, with later additions. Contents include: Keep Room and Seymour Room (connected by 'booby trap' staircase); 14th/15th-century Great Hall and Lower Hall; Restoration house, with panelled Dining Room and Parlour; 18th-century Kitchen; house-keeper's room. Outdoors; moat with bridge; inn; banqueting barn; guest house; events field; audio guided tours.
① ££ ⌂ ⊑ ✗ AV ⛵ P
off A48 Newport to Chepstow

TREDEGAR HOUSE, Newport Tel: (0633) 62275
Newport Borough Council
17th-century mansion with twenty state rooms. Contents include: Morgan family portraits; rosewood morning room furniture; 18th-century Delft chimney tiles; domestic quarters with original fittings. Outdoors: gardens; adventure play area; craft workshops; carriage rides; orienteering; fishing; boating.
① £ ⚓ ⌂ ⊑ ✗ ⚘ ⋒ P &
off A48 Cardiff to Newport ⇌ Newport

GWYNEDD
BRYN BRAS CASTLE, Llanrug Tel: (0286) 870210
Home of Mr and Mrs Neville Gray-Parry
Victorian country house. Contents include: Louis XV furniture, art nouveau stained-glass windows; Stuart wall panelling; early Victorian Tudor revival sideboard. Outdoors: gardens, knot garden; observation tower; waterfall.
① £ ⌂ ⊑ ✗ ⚘ P
off A4086 Caernarfon to Capel Curig

PLAS GLYN-Y-WEDDW, Llanbedrog Tel: (0758) 740763
Home of Dafydd ap Tomos
Victorian Gothic mansion. Contents include: modern Welsh painting, ceramics and sculpture. Outdoors: gardens, sea views.
① £ ⌂ ⊑ ⚘ P &
off A497 Abersoch to Pwllheli

SOUTH GLAMORGAN
FONMON CASTLE, Barry Tel: (0446) 710206
Home of Sir Brooke Boothby Bt
Medieval castle with later additions. Contents include: rococo interiors; family portraits by Hogarth, Reynolds and others; the Fonmon Book of Hours (15th-century French); 17th-century great kitchen, with pewter plate collection. Outdoors: gardens.
① £ ⛵ ⚘ P
off B4265 Barry to Llantwit Major

YOU ARE ADVISED TO CHECK DETAILS BEFORE VISITING A HOUSE

INDEX

PHOTOGRAPHIC ACKNOWLEDGEMENTS

The publishers, authors and the Historic Houses Association would like to thank the owners of the houses for their kind permission to use photographs. Unless otherwise credited, the copyright is held by the house owners.

English Life Publications Ltd pp.17, 20, 22, 60, 217, 245, 261;
British Tourist Authority pp.29, 222 (below), 256;
The National Motor Museum, Beaulieu p.33;
Jeremy Whitaker pp.38, 40, 240, 244;
Eric Crichton/The Field Magazine p.45;
Pilgrim Press Ltd pp.47, 112, 185;
John Elliott p.52;
The Mountbatten Archives p.53;
George A. Hall p.63;
Royal Commission on the Historical Monuments of England p.86;
Woodmansterne p.92;
John Dewar Studios, Edinburgh p.94;
Glamorgan Archive Service p.113;
National Museum of Wales p.111;
John Miller/Homes and Gardens p.115;
Country Life pp.121, 151;
Courtauld Institute of Art pp.124, 176;
Mark Fiennes p.148;
Jarrold & Sons Ltd p.250;
A Winsor Fox p.173;
Judges of Hastings p.188;
Norwyn Photographic Ltd p.189;
Smallwood p.197;
Chris Lane p.226;
Kent Edwards Litho Ltd p.238.